More praise for
The Guts to Try

"This book speaks volumes of the call to courage that saw these magnificent men and their flying machines put their lives on the line to restore freedom to me and my fifty-two colleagues held hostage in Tehran. In that effort they failed. But they succeeded—and gloriously so—in demonstrating unbounded courage and, God yes, in showing that they did indeed have the guts to try."

— L. BRUCE LAINGEN
Former chargé d'affaires, U.S. Embassy, Tehran, and former hostage

"We all owe Jim Kyle a debt of thanks for having the guts to write *The Guts to Try*. We all have wondered: What really happened? What went wrong? Could the Iranian rescue mission have really worked? How could a nation spending $200 billion a year on defense end up in the middle of the Iranian desert one helicopter short? Kyle and Eidson answer these—and scores of other questions that have nagged every American since April of 1980—in a page-turner that makes the reader feel we're on the mission with him every step of the way. It's the most detailed, readable 'after-action report' in decades."

— BENJAMIN F. SCHEMMER
Author of *The Raid* and a soon-to-be-published Ballantine book on the USAF's Special Tactics Units

THE GUTS TO TRY

THE UNTOLD STORY OF THE IRAN HOSTAGE RESCUE MISSION BY THE ON-SCENE DESERT COMMANDER

COL. JAMES H. KYLE, USAF (Ret.)

with JOHN ROBERT EIDSON

BALLANTINE BOOKS • NEW YORK

A Ballantine Book
Published by The Ballantine Publishing Group
Copyright © 1995 by James H. Kyle

www.ballantinebooks.com

ISBN 0-345-44695-X

Manufactured in the United States of America

First Ballantine Books Edition: May 2002

10 9 8 7 6 5 4 3 2 1

To the Memory of

Captain Harold L. Lewis, Jr., USAF, aircraft commander
Captain Lyn D. McIntosh, USAF, copilot
Captain Richard L. Bakke, USAF, navigator
Captain Charles T. McMillan II, USAF, navigator
Tech Sergeant Joel C. Mayo, USAF, flight engineer
Staff Sergeant Dewey L. Johnson, USMC, helicopter crew member
Sergeant John D. Harvey, USMC, helicopter crew member
Corporal George N. Holmes, Jr., USMC, helicopter crew member

This book is dedicated to the eight brave men who died on the Iranian desert on that ill-fated April night in 1980 when our attempt to rescue the embassy hostages failed. Their names are inscribed on a prominent marble marker in the shadow of the mast of the battleship *Maine* at Arlington National Cemetery, standing in testimony to the sacrifices that our military forces are willing to make to protect this great country against tyranny and international hostage blackmail anywhere in the world. It is in their memory that this story is told in hope that they will not be forgotten and the bitter lessons of the Iran rescue mission will not have been in vain.

CONTENTS

Memorial to Jim Rhyne   x
Preface   xi
Prologue: Disaster in the Desert   1

PART ONE—PLANNING/ASSEMBLING THE FORCES

1	A Note of Urgency	13
2	The Joint Task Force	18
3	The Beginning	22
4	The Puzzle	45
5	A Plan Takes Shape	53
6	Operation Rice Bowl	63
7	The Spectres	74
8	Opening Drills	82
9	The Rotorheads	93
10	The Yuma Experience	105
11	Night-Two	114
12	The Black Paper	120

PART TWO—REHEARSAL/FINE TUNING

13	New One-Two Punch	129
14	On the Chopper Block	136
15	The Fez Insertion	141
16	The Rehearsals Begin	149
17	Getting Our Act Together	159
18	Masirah Resolve	166
19	Oman Initiative	172

20   Code Word "Ornament"   182
21   Secret Mission to Desert-I   188
22   Oman Decision   193
23   The President Bites the Bullet   198
24   Last Rehearsal   210

PART THREE—THE MISSION

25   Move 'em Out!   219
26   Smoke and Mirrors   227
27   The Shell Game   231
28   Ready and Waiting   242
29   Countdown!   250
30   Next Stop, Desert-I   266
31   Haboob!   278
32   Cue Tip/Desert Landing   288
33   Struggle in the Dust   295
34   Rendezvous in the Desert   307
35   So Close, Yet So Far   319
36   Catastrophe!   328
37   Get the Hell Out!   339
38   Taps for Eagle Claw   346

PART FOUR—RETROSPECTIVES

39   The Aftermath   353

Epilogue: Anatomy of a Failed Mission   368
Glossary   385
Acknowledgments   389
Index   391

ILLUSTRATIONS

Figure 1   The first plan   60
Figure 2   Organizational chart of the Joint Task Force   68
Figure 3   The Fulton Recovery System   178
Figure 4   Night-One routes   204

Figure 5   Helicopter refueling plan   205
Figure 6   Night-Two aircraft flow   206
Figure 7   Night-Two plan   207
Figure 8   C-130 formation   273
Figure 9   Helicopter formations   276
Figure 10   Helicopters encounter dust   286
Figure 11   Helicopters in second area of dust   289
Figure 12   Helicopters 1 and 2 relaunch   302
Figure 13   Helicopter 5 turns back   305
Figure 14   C-130s at Desert-I   308
Figure 15   Aircraft refueling positions   320
Figure 16   Helicopter collision with C-130   336
Figure 17   Desert accident scene   340

MEMORIAL TO JIM RHYNE

Jim Rhyne, a legendary pilot in the clandestine service, was killed in a civilian aircraft accident near his North Carolina hometown on April 2, 2001. Many of us in the special operations business knew Jim personally, and some flew with him in the veiled world of stealthy missions, a setting where he was accustomed to danger.

Jim's exploits date back to the early days of his flying career, when he was regarded as one of the Air Force's best fighter pilots. During the Vietnam War era, in a quest for bigger challenges, he flew shadowy missions for Air America in Laos.

My association with Jim Rhyne was as the pilot of the Otter aircraft that he flew to Desert-I. The unparalleled success of that reconnaissance mission was critically important in the decision to undertake the rescue attempt.

Jim was one of the finest pilots to ever strap into a cockpit. He was an icon among pilots and set the standards that others in this business strive to achieve. He loved his country, and no mission was too tough for this intrepid aviator with near magical skills . . . a man larger than life itself. And a life interrupted far too soon.

Jim may you always fly on the wings
of Eagles. . . . God bless.

PREFACE

In April 1980, President Jimmy Carter sent a military mission into Iran to rescue fifty-three Americans who had been held hostage in Tehran since the previous November. This mission fell apart on a desolate desert, the Dasht-e-Kavir, and eight brave men perished in the flaming wreckage that resulted from the collision of two aircraft at Desert-I, a remote area being used as a helicopter refueling site.

In the aftermath of this disaster came congressional and military investigations, several books, and numerous articles—massive volumes of information, most of it either slanted or out-and-out wrong.

Unfortunately, there was a landslide of hyperbole that rushed headlong past the story I lived through in the months that led up to the mission and endured in the aftermath. When I read the sensationalized stories written about the operation, I often wondered if it was the same rescue mission that I had participated in. The details certainly did not jibe with what I already knew and what I came to know as I unraveled more facts about what really happened on that tragic night.

The American public has been subjected to a great deal of misinformation about this operation—about the planning, training, execution, and people involved. In what seems to have become a favorite sport of so many authors, Pentagon-bashing, the Iran rescue mission is used as a starting point in a chain of arguments leading to a broad-brush conclusion of military incompetence.

So, what we have out of all of this self-styled wisdom is a hodgepodge of diatribe concluding that the Iran rescue mission was a disaster from the beginning and preordained to fail before it ever got off the ground. Whether or not that is true I will leave up to you, the reader, to decide.

For years, I watched and waited in vain for the American people to be told the truth about this mission . . . until I was forced to conclude that this just wasn't going to happen. I had participated in a mission that failed, something all military men fear, and I really wasn't sure I knew why, which only made it worse.

After I retired from the Air Force, I devoted nearly three years of research and investigation to verify my recollections and those of my compatriots on the mission, and to assemble the material for this book. It was a major challenge to compile such an abundance of information, and it couldn't have been done without the support and encouragement of many individuals who generously contributed their time and expertise to help me get the facts straight. For this I am eternally grateful. Although, for various reasons, I haven't named them, they know who they are.

Admittedly, others declined to contribute and wanted to put the past behind them. I did provide them copies of the draft manuscript for review and comment. Those who responded indicated that, in general, I had the story right.

I would hasten to add that since time dulls the memory, conversations between individuals in the story should not be taken as verbatim. They are based on best recall of what was said and are certainly very close to the words spoken at the time.

As for reconstructing the details of the flight plans of the rescue mission flown on the night of April 24, 1980, it took many of us long hours to recompute the data, insert what we heard on the radio, then add to that the activities that we were involved in at different locations as the mission progressed. We knew where the C-130 forces were at any given time, and therefore we could predict where the others were with reasonable accuracy. Again, the times and distances cannot be absolutely precise.

Thus, the story of the Iran rescue mission is as complete as I could make it. I have tried to tell not only the Air Force story, but important aspects of the Delta Force, Marine, and Navy involvement, as well. This was a joint service operation, and a complete and accurate account requires weaving together the diverse roles played by all of its participants. Obviously, the story is told with some emphasis on the Air Force, since I was responsible for those units.

So, this is not a regurgitation of old facts, but is as accurate a recapitulation of what happened as can be made from sources that participated in the mission.

In addition to my desire to set the record straight, I have another reason for telling this story. There is an old truism that those who ignore history are destined to relive it. Some lessons learned from the Iran rescue mission concerning the use of Special Operations Forces (SOF) have gone unheeded.

Front page news events change. Presidents and world leaders come and go, yet this country still finds itself embroiled in trouble spots around the world. In many cases, Special Operations Forces are among the first to be ordered into action in these areas, as they are the best trained and equipped to deal with low intensity conflicts faced by the United States.

However, I believe that SOF units have been used in some combat situations where conventional forces would have been better suited for the mission. Leadership seems all too quick to use the top of the line fighting units in routine operations.

One of the most basic lessons in the use of SOF is that they are at their best when they can capitalize on their unique night-fighting capabilities to overcome numerically superior forces. More than once, on-scene task force commanders have employed these forces in daylight combat situations where they could not fully exploit the elements of surprise and speed. Consequently, they were overcome by superior numbers and unnecessary casualties resulted.

We also learned long ago that when American forces are committed to combat, they must have the full backing of the U.S. government, and be provided the necessary war fighting equipment to get the job done.

I believe that Americans should have a better understanding of the inner workings of Special Operations. This, in my opinion, is one of the most important military capabilities of our time, especially as it relates to combating international terrorism, hostage situations, and insurgency. As one comes to appreciate the difficulties of such undertakings and understands what is entailed in putting together these controversial ventures, one will see why the forces involved must, indeed, be special.

This, then, is the story of the Iran rescue mission—from its beginnings in the planning rooms of the Pentagon to its ignominious failure in that godforsaken desert in Iran—as we lived it.

PROLOGUE

DISASTER IN THE DESERT

April 25, 1980

<u>Washington Star Service</u>

WASHINGTON—President Carter, in a somber television address to the nation, said today that he acted out of "necessity and duty" in ordering a commando-style operation to try to rescue the American hostages from Iran.

The all-volunteer mission, which was aborted because of helicopter equipment failure, cost the lives of eight American crewmen. They died when two of the rescue aircraft collided on the ground after a refueling operation in a remote desert location in Iran.

Addressing the nation from the Oval Office at 7:00 A.M., the President said the responsibility for the failed rescue mission was "fully my own" and expressed his personal sorrow over the loss of American lives.

DASHT-E-KAVIR, IRAN, APRIL 25, 1980

The desert in front of me was a boiling, exploding inferno. I was transfixed by horror. The two burning aircraft, an H-53 helicopter and a C-130 tanker, resembled prehistoric monsters locked in mortal combat.

Red-hot chunks of streaking metal painted incandescent lines across the landscape. Jet fuel, bullets, grenades, and missiles were the ingredients in this flaming caldron.

For chrissakes! How many men are trapped in there?

We had mounted a Herculean effort to come to this place we called Desert-I on a mission of mercy—to rescue fifty-three Americans being held hostage in Tehran by the Iranians. Now this!

Not only had we been forced to abandon our mission, but our withdrawal had erupted in disaster—two of our aircraft had collided—and we had casualties. Calamity heaped on despair. It was devastating.

But there wasn't time to stand around dealing with our emotions; we had to get this catastrophe sorted out and get out of here. This conflagration was bound to attract attention.

With each shuddering explosion, the very guts of the C-130 shot into the night sky, arcing upward like Roman candles.

I could see the desert landing zone clearly through my night-vision goggles (NVGs). There were five abandoned RH-53 helicopters sitting in their original refueling positions behind where the four "gas-station" C-130s had been parked earlier.

Two of the C-130s had departed, carrying part of the rescue force with them. A third was waiting to leave, and the fourth was still burning furiously at the crash site.

The three helicopters nearest the fire on the north side of the road were riddled with holes from the shell fragments and chunks of metal rocketing out of the burning, exploding wreckage that had been a C-130 tanker.

There was a growing pool of leaking fuel around these helicopters. If this ignited, the whole area could become a funeral pyre for us all.

On the south side of the road that split this improvised desert airfield were two more abandoned helicopters, but they were undamaged—a safe distance from the flying debris. However, one of them had arrived at Desert-I with what was reported as an unrepairable hydraulic problem.

I looked toward the far end of the north departure runway. I could see the Iranian fuel truck that had been intercepted and blown up by our roadblock team had almost burned itself out.

A Mercedes bus, also intercepted at the roadblock, was parked on the road separating the two landing strips, its forty-some hapless passengers still squatting along the embankment at the shoulder. I could see the bewilderment on their faces. They had witnessed quite a drama over the past four hours. I wondered what sort of tale they would tell at the gendarmerie post when they got to one. Would anyone believe their bizarre stories?

The C-130 that was our ride out of there was waiting on the

improvised sand runway, its engines running. It was waiting for Major John Carney, my chief combat controller, and myself. But first I had to be satisfied that no members of the rescue force were out in that desert. After all that had gone wrong, I was going to be damn sure that nobody was left behind.

John and I scanned the area again and again, but saw no signs of life. I kept hoping that some of our missing men would appear out of the desert darkness. Slowly, the realization was sinking in—we were finished here. Everyone who was coming was already aboard the C-130. Despite repeated attempts, we couldn't get to the trapped bodies of our comrades. We would have to leave them behind.

"John, we've got to get the hell out of here." He gave me a thumbs-up and we boarded the aircraft.

As I climbed up into the darkness of the cargo compartment, I could see the injured crew members stretched out on the deflated fuel bladder. Some Delta Force troops were tending to the burn victims, trying to ease their pain.

There was still enough fuel in the waterbed-like bladder to make walking difficult—it was sort of like stumbling around on a layer of Jell-O. Unfortunately, the wave effect created by the bladder undulations was aggravating the pain of the burn victims. They were crying out in torment as they were bounced around by the shifting beneath their hastily constructed stretchers. There were men sprawled out everywhere, and it was difficult to keep from stepping on someone as I tried to find a place to park myself for takeoff.

I looked around the cargo compartment. I could see a mixture of rescue team members settled down for the ride back to our staging area. There were Delta troopers, combat controllers, helicopter crewmen, and members of the C-130 refueling crew. All were lying on the near-empty fuel bladder, using it as a cushion against the hard floor. The C-130 bladder aircraft were an emergency means to transport the rescue force out of the Iranian desert and lacked the comforts of aircraft fitted for hauling passengers.

One of the burned helicopter pilots, Major Jim Schaefer, was being attended to by Delta soldiers. He was in shock, his face discolored with burned flesh.

Nearby, his badly burned copilot was mumbling: "I told him to pull up—I told him we weren't going to make it."

The most desperately injured was the C-130 radio operator, Tech Sergeant Joseph Beyers. He had extensive burns all over his body, arms, and hands. His cries could be heard over the roar of the engines and cut right to the core of my soul. Delta medics were administering morphine to ease his pain and comforting him as best they could until we could get him to the waiting doctors at Masirah, Oman, our forward staging base.

Those of us who weren't injured sat in stunned disbelief. The full realization of what had happened had not hit home yet. As I looked around, the faces mirrored the bitter despair I was feeling.

Fleeting across my mind were thoughts of the thousands of flying hours, hundreds of unit training exercises, numerous joint training events and rehearsals, all to prepare a complex and ingenious plan to rescue our hostages . . . and then to end like this. What a godawful shame!

When six helicopters arrived at Desert-I it had looked as if we were over the last hurdle and would soon have Delta Force on its way to Tehran. Then, in a matter of minutes, our hopes and dreams were dashed by a mechanical problem—a broken helicopter. There would be no second chance. Of this I was certain. Our hopes for a rescue mission had just gone down the drain.

I looked at my watch. It was 3:30 A.M. What had started as a forty-minute refueling rendezvous with the helicopters had become a frustrating four hours and thirty-six minutes in the Iranian desert. The whole chain of events had evolved into the most colossal episode of hope, despair, and tragedy I had experienced in almost three decades of military service, which encompassed the Vietnam War and several police actions.

We were not a bunch of stumbling, bungling apostles of violence. Most of our rescue team members were dedicated Special Operations professionals with solid reputations for being able to get the job done when others couldn't. Accomplishing the high-risk impossible mission was our stock in trade. But there was nothing more we could do now except get the survivors safely back to our launch base at Masirah.

I signaled the loadmaster, Master Sergeant Ray Doyle, to tell our pilot, Major Jerry Uttaro, to get rolling.

The powerful engines built smoothly to takeoff power and the giant propellers bit into the desert air. We began moving, slowly at first, from where we had sunk into the sand. Gradually, our speed picked up as we moved across the desert-floor landing strip on the north side of the road. Our takeoff roll seemed interminable as the big transport labored to break free of the sandy grasp of the desert surface.

These twenty-five-year-old birds had taken a severe beating over the past five months. I was hoping against hope that this aircraft was equal to one more challenge. We didn't need any more disasters.

Almost without realizing it, I found I was yelling at the top of my lungs: "Go, you son of a bitch. *Go! Go! Go!* Come on, baby. *Fly! Fly! Fly!*"

The main wheels bumped one more time and we were airborne, leaving Desert-I in our dust. What a fantastic airplane! It was straining for airspeed and altitude, but it had made it.

Man—I love this airplane!

We were headed down our exit route, and everyone was breathing a bit easier. As Desert-I became a memory, grief was setting in . . . grief for the men we had left behind in that pyre. I was painfully realizing that a sad chapter had just been indelibly imprinted in the pages of military history. It would not be listed among the epic battles—indeed, no enemy action figured in this tragedy.

I would forever see the disaster at Desert-I as a maze of missed opportunities mixed with incredibly bad luck. Fate had dealt us a hand so full of problems that it finally overwhelmed us. Everything that could go wrong, did so—and in monstrous proportions.

I made my way forward to the cockpit to use the satellite radio. I needed to inform Major General James Vaught, the Joint Task Force commander, and Lieutenant General Philip Gast, the deputy commander, at Oman, that we were en route to Masirah. I would also report our casualty status, as best we could determine. We were trying to pin down which Task Force members had been lost in the crash so that an accurate list could be relayed to the Pentagon.

Having accomplished all I could for the moment, I settled back for what seemed like the longest flight of my life, although it took only a little over four hours.

As weariness settled in, I sank into solitude and thought back over the events of the past twelve hours. It seemed like a lifetime.

How could so many things have gone wrong?

The questions kept churning around in my weary mind:

Where did all that dust come from? Before launching, we were given a two-day clear-weather forecast.

Why did the helo pilots have such a rough time getting through the dust?

Why did three helicopters fail to complete the mission?

What caused the No. 3 helicopter to crash into the C-130?

What went wrong with our command and control network?

Communications between the helicopters seemed to have been totally inadequate, and we had had difficulty following the progress of their flight to Desert-I.

We had been confident of the helicopter rendezvous and refueling stage of the operation; it had gone well in training and rehearsals. The toughest part of the mission was in the next stage—getting Delta into Tehran, assaulting the embassy, and then getting everybody out.

We were still listening for an answer to our request to have Navy tactical aircraft bomb the equipment we had left at Desert-I. This approval had to come from Washington, and I was hoping it would come soon.

Meanwhile, it was getting light and we were leaving Iranian airspace. Below, I could see numerous oil tankers and cargo ships steaming through the murky waters of the Persian Gulf. It didn't matter if they saw us now. We had nothing to hide. We were safe.

We had a smooth landing in the morning calm of Oman and parked beside the other C-130s. Military doctors from our support team had been awaiting our arrival so they could tend to the injured. Special medical evacuation aircraft were due to pick up the burn victims and get them to a hospital equipped to treat them.

The rest of us numbly piled out of the plane, still dazed by what we had been through. There was an awkward silence; words were not adequate to express our grief, and we were fighting to control our anger lest we say something we would regret. The Marine aircrews were huddled by themselves; no one was having much to do with them.

I went over to Jim Schaefer, the pilot of the helicopter involved in the crash. The doctors were tending to his burns.

"What happened out there, Jim?"

"I don't know. I thought I crashed in a left turn out in the desert. I didn't realize I'd hit the C-130 until I was crawling away from the fire—that's all I know."

I could see he was in considerable pain, so I left it at that—it was not a time for questions.

General Gast, visibly distressed, came over to where we were standing and said he had to have a precise roll call to determine who was missing.

We all grouped together by service and rechecked our rosters. There was no bitching or grousing—just the professional compliance you would expect from veteran crews and soldiers.

My worst fears were soon confirmed. We had lost five Air Force men—Captain Hal Lewis in the C-130 tanker and four other cockpit crew members. Hal's aircraft had been struck from above and behind. He had never seen what hit him. In addition, three helo crew members who had been trapped in the cargo compartment of their copter had perished.

It had all happened so fast we hadn't been able to get to them before the fire did. This made the abort at Desert-I far more costly than I could accept. I asked myself over and over, *What could I have done to prevent the crash?* But there was no simple answer. It all came down to a multitude of fateful events. It always seems to be a combination of factors that leads up to a catastrophe.

General Gast took the casualty report and headed for the communications tent, leaving us again to our own thoughts. We were starting to talk—exchanging words of encouragement. It's amazing what a little hot coffee and a smoke will do for your morale when it has sunk so low you can stand on it.

It wasn't long before Military Airlift Command C-141s landed and the injured were taken aboard, along with Delta's troops and the Marine helicopter crews. In a short time, they were on their way to Egypt.

By 8:00 A.M. on the morning of April 25, only the C-130 crews, combat controllers, and maintenance support personnel remained at Masirah.

After the initial shock had worn off and the debriefing had been completed, I decided to do some visiting to see how everyone else was doing.

I made a circuit of all the aircrews. They were scattered around the campsite in small groups. We mostly made small talk, but I wanted them to know just how proud I was of the courageous job they had done. The C-130 crews and combat controllers had not failed in any part of the operation and had a right to be proud of what they had accomplished. They had inserted Delta into Iran on schedule, set up the refueling zone, and gassed up the helicopters when they finally arrived. Then, when things went sour, they had saved the day with an emergency evacuation by some incredibly skillful flying. They had gotten the forces out of Iran to fight another day—a fact they can always look back on with pride.

As we were talking, we spotted a small lorry coming down our flight line. It seemed to have come from the other side of the airfield, where several British airmen employed by the Sultan of Oman's Air Force were billeted.

The lorry bounced to a stop in front of our maintenance crew tent. Two men got out, set two boxes down, and jumped back into the truck, which sped off in a cloud of dust.

A couple of loadmasters walked over to the boxes, looked at them, and then came hauling them to the operations tent on the double.

As they drew near, one of them yelled, "Hey, you guys, look what the Brits brought us—two cases of cold beer. And there's a note written on the outside of the case."

A knife came out and the flap was cut off the case and handed to Lieutenant Colonel Roland Guidry, commander of the Air Force Special Operations unit, which had lost the five airmen in the fire. A spokesman told the colonel, "Your unit bore the greatest loss—this should be yours to frame."

As far as we were concerned, no greater tribute had ever been paid by the military service of one country to that of another.

The handwritten note simply said: "To you all, from us all, for having the guts to try."[1]

---

[1]The "guts to try" motto is displayed proudly on the briefing-room wall of the 8th Special Operations Squadron, Hurlburt Field, Florida, along with mementos of the Son Tay, North Vietnam, raid and Grenada action.

PART ONE

PLANNING / ASSEMBLING THE FORCES

1

A NOTE OF URGENCY

Combined News Services

TEHRAN, Iran (Nov. 4, 1979)—A mob of Iranian students overran U.S. Marine guards in a three-hour struggle Sunday and invaded the U.S. Embassy in Tehran, seizing American staff members and some Iranian employees as hostages, Tehran Radio reported. They demanded that the United States send the exiled shah back to Iran for trial, the radio said.

No serious injuries were reported. Tehran Radio said as many as 100 hostages were being held, but an Iranian Foreign Ministry spokesman said he believed there were 35 Americans and seven or eight Iranians.

The spokesman, reached in Tehran by telephone from New York, said an estimated 200 or 300 students were involved.

ALBUQUERQUE, NEW MEXICO, NOVEMBER 11, 1979

It was a little after 10:00 on a bright fall night. I was turning into my driveway, returning home after dinner, when I spotted the note taped on the garage door. My heart gave a little skip. I wasn't used to having notes stuck on my garage door. It's sort of like telegrams; it has to be bad news.

I left the headlights on while I got out of the car to see what it was.

"Urgent. Contact Lee Hess . . ." And it gave a phone number that I recognized as Pentagon. The note was signed by Major Doug Brazil, an AC-130 gunship pilot who had served with me in Thailand during the Vietnam War.

I rushed into the house and gave Doug a call to let him know I'd gotten the note and find out if he knew what it was about. He said he didn't, but that Lee was serious about the urgency and wanted me to call no matter what the time was.

I couldn't suppress my excitement as I dialed the Pentagon number. This obviously wasn't a social call. Not at that time of night . . . and from the Pentagon. Something was up. A voice answered and stated the number I had just dialed, a practice I was familiar with in the Special Operations business.

"This is Colonel Kyle calling for Major Lee Hess."

"Wait one," the voice said.

Lee had been a Special Operations protégé of mine back at Pacific Air Forces (PACAF) headquarters in the mid-'70s, and I knew he was still in "the business," now on the Air Staff. I hadn't heard from him, except for Christmas cards, for several years.

Since it was after midnight in Washington, I was certain that Lee had something pretty hot to tell me.

"Kimo. Is that you?"

"Kimo" is "Jim" in Hawaiian, and Lee and his wife, Ginny, had always called me that.

"Major General Bob Taylor wants you here—like yesterday. How soon can you make it?"

"Are you shittin' me, Lee? What's he want me for?"

"This is no joke. It's urgent. I can't tell you anything more than I already have. Just get here—and fast."

Now I was really cranked up. The tone of his voice told me that this was serious business.

I told him I'd start calling airlines and would get back to him as soon as I had something, but it wouldn't be easy at that time of night.

He rogered that and we broke off so I could get moving.

As I was calling, I thought about Major General Bob Taylor. I had known him back at PACAF in the mid-'70s, when he was director of plans. I had worked a couple of projects with his staff and had come to know him as a tough taskmaster.

But the burning question was, what the hell did he want with me? I hadn't seen him in years and had no idea what his job was in the Pentagon.

I finally found a ticket office open and got a booking on a 3:30 A.M. flight, due to arrive at Washington National Airport at 10:30 Monday.

I called Lee back, and he said, "When you get to Washington, take a cab to the Pentagon River Entrance. Go to the guard post and call this number, and I'll come and get you."

His final words were: "Bring enough clothes to last you for a while . . . and don't worry, it's for real."

I was left with a dial tone and that old familiar knot in my stomach that always showed up when I was heading into the unknown. I thought, *I hope my boss buys this story.*

Meanwhile, my thoughts were racing.

I had just been assigned to the Kirtland Air Force Base resource management shop of the 1606th Air Base Wing, which provides planning, supply, transportation, finance, and accounting support to some 140 tenant organizations representing all services. Pretty tame stuff after the previous ten years in Special Operations. But then, the Air Force had a hard time finding places for us "snake eaters," especially after the end of the Vietnam War. There just weren't that many jobs for all the colonels in that career field.

So here I was . . . in Albuquerque. My wife, Eunice, had stayed in Honolulu, our permanent home, and kept her civilian job with the Air Force. I was on what the Air Force calls an unaccompanied tour, living off base, and had just gotten settled in a house I was attempting to buy.

What is this all about?

I had my suspicions. It had been just a week since radical militants in Iran had taken over our embassy in Tehran, and they were holding a lot of Americans hostage. The country was in an uproar, and I knew there had to be extensive activity in the Pentagon planning rooms over this one. Something had to be done. These people were telling us to take international law and stick it in our ear. I suspected that Special Operations considerations would be high on our list and that somehow this late-night summons was connected.

But I won't know until I get there.

I packed a garment bag and a shoulder bag with mostly summer wear, since that was about all I had. The New Mexico weather had been just right for my Hawaii garb.

Now I was dialing Jack Sheppard, the wing commander, with a wild story and very little detail. And, to make matters worse, it was almost midnight and I was probably waking him up.

A sleepy voice answered, "Colonel Sheppard."

"Sir, this is Jim Kyle. Sorry to bother you at this hour, but I have just been directed by a general officer in the Pentagon to report there immediately for special duty."

I assured him that I knew the officer who had relayed the message and that it was for real.

I told him I was sorry I couldn't tell him more, but he knew everything I did.

He didn't hesitate. "Get going and let me know more when you get there—if you can."

Before I rang off, I said, "Boss, don't tell anybody where I've gone. Just say I'm on a special project—nothing else."

Meanwhile, I had one more tough phone call to make. What in God's name was I going to tell Eunice?

As I was dialing Honolulu, I was thinking that no way would she be fooled by some cock-and-bull story. So I made up my mind to tell her all I knew. After all, she had worked for the Air Force for twenty-five years, had a top secret clearance, and knew full well how to deal with sensitive information.

It was still early Sunday evening in Hawaii when she picked up the phone.

"Hi. It's me. Your long-distance roommate. This is going to sound crazy. . . ."

I told her about the phone conversation with Lee Hess, whom she knew well, and of General Taylor's request for my presence first thing Monday morning. Eunice also knew the general from his time at PACAF, where she worked. When all was said and done, she knew what I knew. Better plans would have to wait until I could get settled in Washington.

We also talked about the financial arrangements on the house, now in limbo. At the moment, there was nothing we could do about it. My mail would be sent to her, so she could keep my bills paid.

It was like abandoning ship, dumping all my affairs in her lap, but I had no choice. She had always been very supportive and had learned to live with the uncertainties of being married to a career military officer.

By now, my engines were so revved up that I decided to skip sleep and head for the airport.

When I walked into the near-empty terminal building it was 1:30. As I paid for the ticket I was thinking what a strain this was going to be on the bank account. I was hoping that someday I would be reimbursed for the travel, lodging, and meal costs.

I then went to the boarding gate to spend what seemed to me to be an endless wait accompanied only by thoughts of the night's mysterious events and what it all meant.

As the jetliner lifted off and began its climb out, I took one last look down at Albuquerque, little knowing what lay ahead or how long it would be before I saw that city again.

2

THE JOINT TASK FORCE

November 12—Hostage Day 9
<u>Associated Press</u>
WASHINGTON—President Carter today ordered an end to U.S. purchases of oil from Iran in reaction to the eight-day seizure of the American Embassy in Tehran where some 60 hostages are held captive.

He urged Americans to increase their efforts to conserve oil, saying his action poses a "real challenge" to the nation and will test American strength and determination.

Carter said he took the action to eliminate any suggestion that economic pressures could be used to force what he called "unacceptable demands on our country."

It was a gloomy, overcast morning when my cab pulled up to the Pentagon's river entrance. I had never been to the "Puzzle Palace" and had mixed feelings of excitement and apprehension.

I went through the identification drill with the guard at the door and then was directed to a phone. I called Lee Hess.

"Come rescue me. I'm at the River Entrance."

In less than five minutes, I spotted a familiar figure coming down the corridor—medium height, slight build, receding hairline. As he drew near, I could see it was Lee, all right, but the characteristic bushy black mustache was missing . . . an obvious casualty of Pentagon standards of decorum. He had the typical pallor of a staff officer long buried in the planning rooms of the five-sided monolith, and his butt was dragging. I could tell by the rumpled uniform that he hadn't been home for a few days.

This is something big, all right. Lee looks like he's been rode hard and put up wet.

Still, he managed a broad smile as we shook hands.

"Hey, Kimo, howzit? Welcome to Chaos Control."

As he took me in tow, I chuckled at his analogy, glad to see he hadn't lost his sense of humor. We moved down a wide corridor labeled "E-Ring," past the office of General David C. Jones, Chairman of the Joint Chiefs of Staff. We passed a couple more VIP offices before heading down a dimmer corridor that contained imposing portraits of former chairmen of the Joint Chiefs, an impressive lineup.

About halfway down the hall, Lee made a hard right into a curtained-off doorway that I hadn't noticed. The sign at the door read "JCS/SOD" (Joint Chiefs of Staff/Special Operations Division). Lee entered the combination in the cipher lockbox, a buzzer sounded, the door opened, and we entered a carpeted hallway that had several offices along the left side, each a beehive of activity.

We emerged into the administrative area. There were two doors, one leading to the division chief's office and the other to a small anteroom. This one led to another secure door that opened into the Unconventional Warfare Branch. You had to have a special badge to get in there.

My mind was racing.

So this is the inner sanctum—where it's all been happening.

From what I was seeing and bits of overheard conversation, I now had no doubts that we were planning for some kind of military options in Iran.

But what do they want me to do? Who will I be working for? What have they come up with so far?

I went through the check-in routine with the Special Operations Division administrative chief, Yeoman Bill Collins. He validated my security clearance, assigned me a special entry badge, and had me sign the access roster for special intelligence information.

Lee then led me through the special security door into the UW Branch working area.

There was no doubt what was going on in here—there were pictures of the hostages, maps of Iran and surrounding areas, reconnaissance photos, and classified documents posted on wall boards all over the place.

When we walked in, the swirl of activity slowed while everybody looked us over. Since all were dressed in civvies, my first impression was that there was no military rank system in this group. I found this was not the case after I was introduced to the chief of the office, Army Colonel Jerry King, a strapping Vietnam vet with piercing blue eyes and a clenched set to his jaw.

As I listened to the colonel, I quickly became aware that a week of wrestling with the hostage crisis with no apparent answers was a source of growing frustration. Although he had the face of a poker player, the carefully controlled exterior couldn't hide the agitation that was just below the surface. I would soon learn that Jerry King had an immense capacity for work and a well-earned reputation for bluntly speaking his mind.

He led me around and introduced me to the members of his staff, which was surprisingly small. Jerry had been ramrodding most of the rescue planning for the Joint Chiefs. He had been a Special Forces battalion commander, and before that a Ranger, and he had extensive combat knowledge of joint Special Operations forces and how they functioned.

Lieutenant Colonel Bob Horton was Jerry's Air Force expert. This lean, soft-spoken pilot had a solid background in Special Operations C-130s and some knowledge of heavy-lift helicopter operations. Bob was involved in making up the charts depicting routes to and from Tehran, a tedious but necessary task.

The Navy specialist, Commander Maynard Weyers, was a short, wiry guy, tough as nails. He had extensive combat experience from a Vietnam tour with Navy SEAL (Sea, Air, Land) teams. Jerry said the commander ran to and from work every day, some five miles each way, rain or shine. Weyers had been doing some of the planning and was helping Bob Horton build charts and briefing books toward developing a rescue plan.

Handling intelligence chores for the group was Nick Kilgore (not his real name), a studious, bespectacled Air Force lieutenant colonel with extensive experience in military deception and operational security.[1] Nick had been intelligence officer for the Readiness Command Counterterrorism Task Force, which had participated in hostage rescue scenarios on numerous occasions.

Kilgore, who was almost buried under a pile of recon photos, stuck his head out for a quick hello, and I quickly learned that he

---

[1] When pseudonyms are used, it's because the individuals (for various reasons) have asked that I not use their real names.

was extremely frustrated at the shortage of information he was receiving from the various intelligence agencies.

I heard comments floating around that we were on a short fuse (ten days) to launch, but this was ludicrous. I could now see we had a long way to go just to get organized.

Meanwhile, I was beginning to get a picture of what type of task force was to be formed. Usually, when a mission requires more assets and skills than any single branch of the service has, a combined organization is formed. The Chairman of the Joint Chiefs selects one branch to provide a joint task force commander—usually based on the type of mission to be performed. In this case Army Special Forces had been handed the ball.

An Army two-star general named James B. Vaught, now in Europe, had been appointed commander of the Joint Task Force (COMJTF). Vaught was booked on a Concorde SST and was scheduled for a briefing in Washington that afternoon. I was to be his deputy commander.

I hadn't expected that. I had assumed I'd be primarily involved with the Air Force component. Also, I was certain General Vaught didn't know me from Adam, and most commanders insist on choosing their own deputies.

Jerry was already handling the operational planning, and an Army Special Forces colonel, Charlie A. Beckwith, was in charge of the ground assault forces.

One of General Vaught's first tasks would be to determine what forces he would need for the job. I would be his deputy for planning, training, rehearsing, and directing the JTF in conducting a hostage rescue mission.

I was surprised to hear from King that the Special Operations Division didn't have a counterterrorism branch. He told me that on two occasions he had tried to have such a branch formed and assigned to Special Ops, but somehow the responsibility for counterterrorism wound up in the Current Operations Division—and this division was not involved in planning the rescue mission.

When the hostages were taken, the Chairman of the Joint Chiefs grabbed the Unconventional Warfare Branch to work the problem—bureaucracy struck again. It took a crisis to sort out an organizational issue that should have been resolved long ago with a functioning staff attending to such matters. The Unconventional Warfare Branch was rightfully assigned the job for now, but without the benefit of added staff personnel.

I asked Jerry where the rest of the JTF staff was, and he told me that none had been selected outside of his own people, a few Pentagon Special Operations staff officers, and two Special Forces Detachment Delta liaison officers. I didn't know what Delta was (few people did), but would soon find out.

Thus, I expected to see the standard Joint Unconventional Warfare Task Force (JUWTF) organization formed.[2] General Vaught would be the commander, with each service providing a commander to manage its people. This may sound like a lot of commanders, but there is no doubt about the command line—General Vaught would be calling the shots and would report directly to the Chairman of the JCS. And, of course, the Chairman would answer to the President through the Secretary of Defense.

This is very touchy ground, because none of the services likes to give up operational control of any of its forces. I have personally felt the wrath of general officers unhappy at funding and equipping forces they can't use to support their missions.

Cooperation of all the services in a combined effort to support the JTF commander is essential if the effort is to succeed. Yet all too often, interservice bickering hampers the effectiveness of the task force and endangers the outcome of the mission. This has been a major problem since World War II. However, for want of a better way, we would again use this type of organizational structure for the Iran Task Force.

Before I left, I asked Jerry, "When can I get briefed on the current status in planning?"

"It would be better if you came back this afternoon so we could brief you at the same time as we do General Vaught. But I'll be briefing General Meyer, Army Chief of Staff, in about thirty minutes. If you'd like, you can slip into the back of the room and listen."

As I was leaving, Jerry told me not to nose around the rooms

[2]In such a task force the commander has operational control of all Special Operations field units to achieve his objectives, but exercises command through subordinate service component commanders. This means that in addition to his personal staff, there are Special Operations commanders for Army, Navy, Air Force, and Marine forces who report directly to him.

adjacent to the entrance corridor, since there were other compartmented planning cells at work in these rooms. I did not have a need to know what these activities were. He also warned me that visits from generals, admirals, Department of Defense officials, and other staff types were commonplace and to check everyone's clearance before giving any briefings. There were many people snooping around who had no need to know what we were up to, and they had to be considered potential leaks.

Lee and I then adjourned to a cubbyhole at the back end of the entry hallway, grabbing coffee and doughnuts as we passed the galley. Lee called these stark, sterile surroundings the Back Room, and it would be my home for the next several months.

Waiting for the Meyer briefing, we talked over what I had learned in this whirlwind morning. I asked Lee when it might be appropriate to meet with General Taylor. He said the general knew I was there but was tied up in the Operations Planning Group (OPG) and would probably be down for the Vaught briefing.

Lee was called away, and I was wondering just how far in over my head I was getting. I was uncomfortable with what I'd seen, and I felt this wouldn't change until there were more people around to form the task force staff—especially unconventional warfare experts.

There was a large cast of staff officers coming and going throughout the day, and I was thinking that all the new faces and heightened activity at the Special Ops Division's main entrance might attract the attention of those familiar with the routine of that office. It wouldn't take a rocket scientist to figure out that something was in the wind.

As I watched the thrashing around, one of the doors opened and a familiar face popped out. It was Air Force Colonel Dick Dunwoody, commander of the 1st Special Operations Wing (SOW) at Hurlburt Field, Florida. He spotted me and sauntered over. "Kyle, what are you doing here?"

"All I know so far is that I'm here to meet with an Army general named Vaught and get briefed on what I'm to do. What are you up to?"

He gave me a vague answer about being there on a special project for General Bob Taylor. I told him that I had also been summoned by General Taylor. We both left it at that.

I figured Dunwoody had been selected as the JTF Air Force component commander, since we all seemed to be there for the same reason. As I saw it, he was the logical man to run the Air Force show, which would probably involve his Hurlburt wing. Time would prove me wrong.

I had maintained a close working relationship with various members of the 1st SOW staff since entering the AC-130 gunship program in 1970, and these relationships had continued as I served in the Pacific in various Special Operations positions.

Dick managed the Special Operations aircraft and crews assigned to the Continental United States (CONUS), and his wing was the central point from which overseas commanders obtained augmentation of airplanes, helicopters, and staff assistance. The 1st SOW inventory had a few MC-130 Combat Talon transports, the only fixed-wing AC-130H gunships, and two models of Special Operations helicopters. 1st SOW was now a pathetically small force of some 3,000 people and 28 aircraft as compared with the nearly 10,000 personnel and 550 aircraft in the program at the peak of the Vietnam conflict. Unfortunately, most of those assets had either been given to countries in Southeast Asia or reassigned to CONUS units and the Reserves.

The front-door buzzer jarred me out of my thoughts. In came a tall, distinguished-looking four-star general, followed by a shorter, youthful-looking three-star. Yeoman Collins jumped up and escorted the generals through the secure door into the briefing area. He seated them at the conference table, facing a myriad of charts. I slipped into a seat at the back.

Collins told me that they were General Edward Meyer, the Army Chief of Staff, and his deputy for operations, Lieutenant General Glenn Otis. Their faces were serious, and there were no amenities, so Jerry King started the briefing.

The primary recommendation involved a direct assault on the embassy by Delta Force. This required using Army CH-47 Chinook helicopters to carry Delta from eastern Turkey into Iran. A refueling stop somewhere in Iran was required to make that scenario feasible. A remote site to pull that off clandestinely had as yet not been determined.

Other proposals had the rescue force being launched from Bahrain, Kuwait, or Saudi Arabia, but General Meyer ruled these out for various reasons, not the least of which were unacceptable geopolitical sensitivities. They were telling the planners to find other ways to insert the rescue team.

It seemed to me that the Army chief was laying on a lot of real estate restrictions, which was bound to make a tough job much tougher. If this rescue mission was so critical to our national interest, why were roadblocks being thrown up before we had even gotten started?

It was obvious from the rapid-fire questions coming from the generals that they wanted answers that simply were not available.

Another thing was obvious: the generals were not buying what they were being told. There was too much of Delta doing this and Delta doing that, *ad nauseam*. Parachute Delta into Tehran . . . truck Delta overland . . . infiltrate Delta by sea.

One off-the-wall idea was to assault a military airfield near the embassy, seize Iranian helicopters, and attack the compound. However, there was no logical plan for getting everybody out after that. It was unclear how Delta was to evade detection, capture, or an all-out firefight while in the city. The intelligence data just weren't available to answer the generals' questions. If an attempt was launched at this time, it would be suicidal.

Meanwhile, I noticed two observers off to the side. Both wore civilian clothing. One, who I would learn was an Army major called Bucky and the Delta Force spokesman, was a stringy-muscled guy of average height. He had thick, unruly blond hair that hung down over his forehead, blending into his ruddy complexion. The hair, coupled with sharp features, gave him sort of an ornery Dennis the Menace look.

Bucky's rumpled clothes were in sharp contrast to those of his companion, named Wade (not his real name), also an Army major. Wade looked as if he had just stepped out of a bandbox, well groomed with standard military haircut. He was chewing tobacco and using a Styrofoam cup for a spittoon—a practice I soon came to think of as a Delta Force trademark.

Although I had not met these two, I was certain they were the Delta liaison officers Jerry had told me about.

I watched them as various options were being discussed. There was a lot of head shaking, squirming, and feet shuffling.

They obviously didn't like what they were hearing. The tobacco-chewing Wade muttered repeatedly, "That ain't a very slick idea."

Just as suddenly as it started, it was over. The generals got up and General Meyer left us with a parting thought: "Your team should quit trying to plan what Delta is going to do; that's Charlie Beckwith's job. Your job is to figure out how to get Delta in, then get them out when the job is done and the hostages are in tow."

There were too many generals stirring the pot to suit me, and I didn't know the command relationship between these heavy-weights and the Joint Task Force. General Meyer acted as if he was in charge, and he had made it clear who was running Delta.

It didn't make sense—briefing the Army chief of staff on a nonexistent rescue plan. We hadn't even gotten organized yet. (I must say, however, that in the weeks and months that followed, General Meyer was very supportive of the task force. On numerous occasions he rolled up his sleeves and worked elbow-to-elbow with us. Although his nickname was Shy, from what I saw, there was nothing shy about him.)

It was now afternoon, and I was surprised at how fast the time had passed. We were definitely on a fast track, and high-ranking general officers seemed to be calling the shots.

Everyone was on a short fuse to come up with workable options for the President, and we needed all the expertise we could summon. I appreciated the general's concerns about hasty actions that would accomplish nothing and end up getting a lot of people killed—but at the same time the pressure was immense for us to come up with some sort of fast-action plan to get our hostages back.

The biggest question I had was, why didn't we already have a counterterrorism force ready to go?

The irony of the situation struck me. Special Operations is the outfit needed to counter this and other types of terrorism, and yet is fighting for its existence each budget cycle as the bucks go up for grabs. The emphasis—and most of the funds—is lavished on new-generation fighters, bombers, missiles, or transports.

At this time, the Special Ops fleet—battle-scarred and weary from Vietnam—was twenty-five years old. Yet, anyone who thought the bozos who make plans, programs, and budgets would consider buying us some new airplanes was sadly mistaken. Special Ops hardware usually ends up at the bottom of the priority list, with the idea that Congress will fund it if it wants it. In fact, the program was suffering from such blatant neglect that it was on the verge of being disbanded and turned over to the Reserves.

I had it on good authority that the top brass at Tactical Air Command (TAC), to which Special Operations was assigned, considered the program an albatross and wanted to dump it. They resented—even despised—missions involving counterterrorism, counterinsurgency, and guerrilla warfare because of the volatile political overtones and cost in manpower and funds.[3]

Special Ops had recently taken another blow to the solar plexus when some myopic planner gave all of our heavy-lift choppers to a tactical communications unit. This left us without the means to deliver assault forces deep into hostile territory— short-sightedness that would come back to haunt us.

As I sat there sipping my coffee and contemplating the situation amid the hurricane of activity around me, my thoughts turned to the C-130, the bird I'd spent most of my career flying, and a vital part of unconventional warfare. Special Ops had only fourteen MC-130s distributed worldwide. There were four in Europe, and four in the Pacific, and the remaining six were in Florida. And typically, three or four of these would be out of commission for maintenance at any given time. This shortfall wreaks havoc with a task force commander's ability to support Special Operations mission requirements.

By comparison, a standard TAC airlift squadron has sixteen C-130s and there are usually three squadrons in a wing, with almost fifty aircraft total.

Despite the shortage of MC-130s, the Air Force did have an excellent capability to deliver personnel deep inside hostile territory with its Combat Talon fleet. But this was only because of the foresight of a few maverick officers who in the mid-'70s had

---

[3]Responsibility for Air Force Special Operations was transferred to the Military Airlift Command in March 1983. However, to improve operational efficiency, the Air Force Special Operations Command (AFSOC) was established in May 1990 at Hurlburt Field, Florida, to assume full responsibility.

crusaded for a Special Operations C-130 in-flight refueling capability.

But the *coup de grâce* to the dying program was the lack of career opportunity. Few career Special Ops officers were being assigned to key headquarters management positions—in effect blocking their career progression to the command level. Naturally, this was killing the incentive of those interested in remaining in Special Ops. This is an atrocious management policy that still exists.[4]

For the Iran mission, it was too late to rectify the poor planning of the past. It would make more sense to have this force well equipped, well manned, and well trained to tackle this type of mission quickly as it arose. Unfortunately, we were stuck with scraping together meager assets in our efforts to assemble a suitable air capability.

Despite this gloomy scenario, the good news was that at the time of the hostage crisis there was an abundance of Special Operations personnel still around, just itching for a chance to show what they could do.

It was midafternoon Monday when the Joint Task Force commander, Major General James Vaught, arrived at the Pentagon. He was rushed through a preliminary situation update with the Army Chief of Staff, General Meyer. He went from there to the office of the Chairman of the Joint Chiefs, where General Jones gave him verbal mission orders and basic operating guidelines.

Next, it was on to the Special Operations Division for his briefing on the status of the hostage situation and what options were being considered. Jerry King gave the briefing, with Nick Kilgore providing the intelligence update. It was similar to the Jerry-and-Nick show that had played earlier for General Meyer.

The new commander looked tired, but this didn't dull the intense concentration of this man with the deep-set eyes and chiseled-granite features.

The general spoke very little and listened intently to the

---

[4]Arthur T. Hadley's book *The Straw Giant* describes the situation aptly as keeping the able from contributing to the action (KAFCA). I have watched Special Operations organizations being purged of experienced career staff officers specially trained in unconventional warfare and replaced by command clones who march to the headquarters' conventional-force drumbeat.

briefing, making notes from time to time. As I watched the tightly controlled exterior, I wondered what the inner man was like. Who was this man who had been chosen to pull this task force together and accomplish this "mission impossible"?

He pressed Kilgore hard for some meaningful intelligence but soon discovered what the rest of us had—there was very little. Nick told him that the nightly television broadcasts from Tehran were one of the better sources. It was better than nothing, but Nick had no idea what was going on inside the embassy and the other buildings in the twenty-seven-acre compound.

Equally troublesome to the general were the frenzied, screaming crowds in the streets around the embassy. His query for ideas on how to avoid a head-on encounter with these mobs was met with silence.

I think it was Colonel King who finally spoke: "The element of surprise may get you up to the wall and over, but when the first shot is fired, you can expect the mobs to mass quickly, and Delta could be hopelessly trapped in a sea of rabid humanity."

Right then General Bob Taylor slipped into the briefing area. He caught my eye, nodded, and smiled.

General Vaught's frustration at the lack of solid planning information was obvious. It was also obvious that he wasn't too crazy about the rescue options being presented.

After the briefing, he made it clear that we were starting from square one and that he was in the driver's seat. I mentally applauded. It was a pleasure to see him take charge.

I was further heartened by his astute response to the briefing:

"First and foremost, total surprise is the only hope we have for success. The Iranians have to be convinced we are not going to use military force so they'll relax their security around the embassy. Then, and only then, we might be able to insert Delta and get them into the compound undetected for a surprise takedown."

He then gave us a pep talk, stressing the urgency to develop a workable rescue plan as soon as possible. He admonished us to concentrate on sound, logical tactics and to steer away from blind alleys. "Every option proposed must have a means to recover if things go wrong."

His next point was what I had been waiting to hear. "You will not be pressured by anybody to go off half-cocked on a rescue attempt not properly planned. When we go, it will be with the people fully trained and rehearsed in a plan that we all sincerely believe has the best possible chance of success. If anybody tries to put the pressure on you to do otherwise, I want to know about it."

He ordered that all questions from senior officers outside the task force that concerned what we were doing were to be directed to him. He was obviously trying to free us from being intimidated by flag officers (generals and admirals) from our respective services who might want a say in what we were doing. "You only have to satisfy one general—me," he said.

He told us he wanted recommendations any of us might have for highly qualified people who could be brought into the JTF to assist, but made it clear that he would make the decisions. This was to control the size of the JTF and to maintain secrecy. He believed, as many do, that the more people who know about an operation, the greater the chances of a security leak.

His parting shot was, "Work starts at 0700 each morning and goes until I say we quit each night. I want to know where you are at all times, so keep the admin chief's locator up to date."

He then went into a closed-door session with General Meyer and a burly man in civvies whom I would later recognize as the Delta Force commander, Colonel Charlie Beckwith.

I then had a chance to reminisce with General Taylor about the good old days back in PACAF. He also confirmed that I would be working for General Vaught but was to channel my activities through him so he could keep track of what was going on.

General Taylor told me that he had selected me for this job because of my Special Operations work and because they wanted a colonel with Pacific Theater experience. That was a puzzler. I couldn't connect the Pacific comment with a Persian Gulf operation. But no matter. I was damned proud to be part of this operation.

As General Taylor left, I was feeling more comfortable in my role on the team. I had met the JTF commander and had an Air Force point of contact to help make things happen.

What a day! It seemed impossible that it had started for me in Albuquerque.

One thing I knew for sure—this was going to be a monumental task. The hostages were being held in the center of a major city nearly halfway around the world, and at that time I hadn't the foggiest notion of how we could sneak a force into the embassy and get them out of there.

3

THE BEGINNING

November 13—Hostage Day 10

<u>Combined News Services</u>

U.S. officials said today that they have established telephone contact with the U.S. Embassy in Tehran, but refused to say whether there have been any significant negotiations with the Iranians who are holding 63 Americans hostage there.

State Department spokesman Hodding Carter said communication with the Iranian students who control the embassy was established several days ago. The students "have taken verbal messages, taken them down very carefully, and said they would transmit them to the hostages," he said. "It's been going on for a while."

I was up, shaved, dressed, and ready to go to work when the wake-up call came at 6:00 A.M. I had spent a restless night, my mind overflowing with the events of the day before and the problems of the future.

After yesterday's revelations, my hopes for a diplomatic solution were even more fervent. Anything we could do would take time . . . and with Khomeini's unpredictability, nobody could even guess at how much time we had.

I arrived at the Special Operations Division well ahead of General Vaught's 7:00 starting time. I had entered the Pentagon through a different entrance and was patting myself on the back for not getting lost.

The general was already there, poring over the notes he had made at yesterday's briefings.

There was a noticeable drop-off of activity in the rooms to the left of the entrance corridor. Dick Dunwoody was nowhere in sight. Only a couple of his men were around, and they looked as if they were wrapping things up for a move. I didn't know it then, but it would be months before I would see Dick again. His outfit was already moving into position for possible action.

I headed over to say good morning to the general, and he motioned for me to enter and have a seat.

He leaned back and looked at me intently. "Kyle, I have a long-standing policy when I first meet people: in God we trust, all the rest I check." (I would learn in the coming months that the general was noted for this type of homespun philosophy.)

"Tell me about yourself. What is your background and experience in the Special Operations business?"

I gave him the rundown:

In 1970, night armed-reconnaissance missions along the Ho Chi Minh Trail over Laos in AC-130 gunships from a base in Thailand . . . close air support missions for special ground units in northern and central Laos, South Vietnam, and, on occasion, Cambodia;

1971, moved to the Special Operations Division at 7th Air Force Headquarters in Saigon at Tan Son Nhut Air Base . . . scheduling all types of USAF gunship combat missions throughout Southeast Asia, as well as Special Operations helicopters . . . coordinating MC-130 Combat Talon movements in support of U.S. and South Vietnamese Special Forces . . . coordinating Allied Special Operations air activity with ongoing American operations . . . close affiliation with the Military Assistance Command Vietnam Studies and Observation Group (MACV-SOG) in Saigon, working a number of Special Forces insertion and extraction missions when Air Force support was required;

Christmas of 1971, back to Thailand for a second shooting season with the AC-130 gunship unit, this time as operations officer;

May of '72, at Headquarters Pacific Air Forces (PACAF) in Hawaii as branch chief for all Pacific-based Special Operations units. It was then that I established contacts worldwide in the Special Operations community. By the time I left PACAF, I'd had about ten years in the Special Ops business.

I also told the general about experience I gained with a photo-mapping wing (MAC), which had operated in a number of countries. This outfit, now disbanded, flew C-130 reconnaissance aircraft, used primarily to take aerial photographs and compile geodetic data for making precise maps and targeting missiles. We'd utilized unprepared airstrips of all descriptions.

Throughout all of this, I had gotten pretty good at operating C-130s into and out of sand, mud, and dirt strips throughout South America, Southeast Asia, and Ethiopia, including a couple of spots not on any maps.

Plus, I had airdropped about anything you could get into the airplane—trucks, paratroopers, fuel bladders, and, on occasion, mail to Air Force people manning remote mountaintop communications sites.

Up to this point, I had logged over 9,000 flying hours—6,000 in the C-130 and 1,000 of those in Vietnam combat. There was not much that could be done with the airplane that I hadn't done.

"Fine," the general said. "Right now I need you to take charge of the Air Force part of this mission, and we'll worry about the deputy commander duties when we get a few things sorted out."

Obviously, my guess that Dick Dunwoody would be the air component commander was wrong—he had totally disappeared.

"Okay, good. Now, what do you know about Delta Force?"

"Nothing, really. I've heard the name being tossed around a lot as the only outfit capable of pulling off a rescue mission like the Iran situation, but that's it."

So he filled me in. "Delta is a select Special Forces unit of about seventy men, specifically organized, trained, and equipped to take down hostage situations. They have just recently been certified for this type of mission in a specially designed exercise to test their capabilities."

He told me that the main obstacle to their use at this point was that they relied on operating in a relatively permissive environment. Combating an armed mob in the streets between them and the hostages was not a situation they had expected, so one of our major planning objectives was to neutralize the area around the embassy. Delta had to be given a reasonable chance to pull off an assault, rescue the hostages, and escape with them.

"Until we find a way to get Delta into and out of the embassy without a massacre occurring in the streets, there will be no rescue attempt."

I didn't doubt the wisdom of that statement, but how would

we ever be able to control the street crowds, short of raining concentrated firepower into the area to discourage their presence?

I went to my Back Room office, pulled out my charts, and began studying the Persian Gulf area. I wanted to be as well prepared as possible for the morning review session, familiar with potential routes into Iran and times and distances from possible jumping-off points. The Chairman of the Joint Chiefs would sit in on these first sessions until he was satisfied that we had established a sound course of planning.

My first meeting with General Vaught had made an impression on me—he was going to be a tough commander.

I knew little about the man except what Jerry King had told me. The general had been working in the Pentagon as assistant to the Director of Army Operations. It was Jerry's understanding that he had been recommended by General Meyer to head up the Joint Task Force.

A man could hardly be put in a tougher position. But he had a reputation for getting the tough jobs done. During the siege of the Citadel of Hue in Vietnam, he had commanded the forces that had driven the North Vietnamese from the city. It was a bloody fight, but he had had the courage to sustain the battle through its darkest moments and, as the saying goes, had snatched victory from the jaws of defeat.

Although his background was primarily Army Rangers, Special Operations was not totally foreign to his experience. In recent years, he had performed well as Joint Task Force commander on several counterterrorism field training exercises involving hostage situations. He had also been present at Delta's recent validation exercise as a hostage rescue force.

Jerry told me that one other general had been considered for the COMJTF job—Army Major General Bob Kingston, who had a distinguished career in Army Special Forces and had had a share in building Delta Force. Although he was the more experienced of the two, he was commanding the 2nd Infantry Division in Korea at the time and his absence from that position for any extended period could not have been plausibly explained.

On the other hand, General Vaught was already in the Pentagon with a supporting staff and needed no special cover for his activities. He was the logical man for the job and certainly didn't have to justify himself as qualified to command the JTF.

As I pored over the maps and charts, I thought of what General Vaught had said about not attempting the rescue until we could find a way to circumvent the mobs in the streets. They were still being shown nightly on TV, milling around the embassy and chanting their hate-America slogans. Catching the Iranians by surprise didn't seem possible.

I was trying to think of a tactical air asset that would scatter the mobs—something with pinpoint accuracy that could do the job without blowing the embassy away as well. My thoughts began to focus on the AC-130 gunship. It had certainly proved its value in supporting ground forces in Southeast Asia.

Turning back to the maps, I located points from which an operation could be launched into Iran, but all had one common drawback: distance. If we used helicopters, they would have to be refueled somewhere inside Iran's borders in order to get back out. Where in God's name would we find a place to do that? Ideally, in-flight, I thought. That way we wouldn't have to go through the difficulties of positioning fuel inside Iran, either by paradropping it or landing and pumping it off.

We weren't far enough along to have identified an airdrop zone or a landing area. In-flight refueling looked like the best bet to me. That way, the C-130 tankers could lead the choppers partway to the target, similar to the way they had on the North Vietnam Son Tay POW rescue attempt in 1970. Also, in-flight refueling was a standard procedure for Air Force search and rescue forces in Vietnam.[1]

As I pondered the options, Lee Hess walked in. He apologized for his absence, saying he'd been stuck over in Operations Planning Group (OPG) working with another planning cell. This was the first time I realized Lee had other irons in the fire. But there were a lot of compartmented operations in this area. You learn not to ask questions about any weird goings-on you might see.

OPG was a new term to me, so I asked Lee about it. He said it was a crisis action group that worked in the National Military Command Center and handled unique support problems asso-

---

[1] Contrary to Richard A. Gabriel's allegations in his book *Military Incompetence*, in-flight refueling of the helicopters was one of the early options considered. Without an airfield near the Iranian border for a launch base, this tactic was not feasible, because of the tankers' range limitations.

ciated with the Iran situation. General Taylor was running the show, which explained why I hadn't seen much of him in the Special Operations Division.

Using the map, I showed Lee what I had been thinking about—pairing tankers with the choppers hauling Delta into Iran. He had been in on some earlier discussions of this concept and offered Turkey as the ideal country to launch from, since the Turks were NATO allies and were accustomed to seeing our C-130s and choppers flying around their country.

It was nearing 8:00 A.M., so I headed for the morning meeting of the JTF, armed with three or four options that could be used to launch a rescue mission. At the time, I didn't know how complex the problem really was—there would be no quick, easy solutions.

General Vaught's office was already crowded when I walked in for this first meeting of the Joint Task Force. I saw a lot of stars, few familiar faces.

The general introduced me to Lieutenant General Philip Shutler, USMC, JCS director for operations; Rear Admiral "Dutch" Schoultz, USN, liaison for the Chief of Naval Operations; and Vice Admiral Thor Hansen, USN, director of the Joint Staff. General Taylor was there, as were Jerry King and Nick Kilgore, and Delta's liaison officers, Majors "Slick" Wade and Bucky Burruss.

I was introduced to Dick Meadows, also in civvies, and told that he worked for Delta Force. I was to learn that this soft-spoken, steely-eyed former military man had participated in the Son Tay raid and had, over the years, logged more time behind enemy lines in Korea and Vietnam than he had in friendly territory. I would also learn that Dick was a man of few words, rarely speaking up in our ensuing daily meetings, saving his comments for the closed-door sessions.

Rounding out the cast for this first get-together was a CIA representative. He was introduced as having been stationed in Iran and being an intelligence expert on that country.

I had thought I might meet Charlie Beckwith at this meeting, but once again this was not to be. I found out later that he and part of his force were in the Piedmont country of North Carolina at a place Beckwith called Camp Smokey. They were already working on the ground tactical plan to assault the embassy. In the meantime, his liaison officers would inform him of the Pentagon planning.

The cast was assembled and waiting for the Chairman, General Jones. As I looked around at the star-studded group, I was hoping that more Indians would appear on the scene soon. We were top-heavy with chiefs.

When General Jones walked in and General Vaught introduced him around the table, I never dreamed I would ever be in the same room with the Chairman of the Joint Chiefs, let alone working with him.

The Chairman was tall and trim. He looked very tired. The circles under his eyes seemed out of place with his otherwise impeccable appearance. It was obvious that he had put in many long days on this problem already.

For the second time in as many days, I heard a general officer come down hard on security as *the* top priority. The Chairman told us in no uncertain terms that no one outside of this team could be allowed to find out what we were doing.

In our working groups, we had to be careful what we said and who we said it to.

The telephone was our worst enemy—we were to use only the secure phones and dedicated teletype systems that would be installed.

And we were to be especially cautious with our working papers—they could not fall into unauthorized hands.

Once we finished with our planning notes, charts, maps, and other papers, they were to be given to the security section for destruction in "burn bags."

He further told us that we would not be writing a formal plan for whatever option we finally chose (a departure from usual procedures). He did not want anything in writing that had even the remotest chance of falling into the hands of someone who could blow the cover on our mission. (The only thing resembling an official record of our meetings that I ever saw was a thick blue book containing notes taken by Jerry King or one of his assistants. This notebook was tightly controlled by King.)

General Jones made it clear that whatever plan we might

come up with would require the President's approval. He told us that Dr. Zbigniew Brzezinski was passing President Carter's guidance down the line and that we would be told what we needed to know for our planning.

On the other hand, since the State Department was opposed to any military option, we were not to deal with any of that agency's personnel on this matter. (Tragic, because we needed the State Department's special capabilities to help us solve this complicated puzzle.)

Throughout this briefing, the Chairman stressed time and again that we were not planning a raid on Iran. President Carter wanted to free the hostages and if possible get everyone out alive.

General Jones described it as a surgical operation, with a small team assaulting the embassy and getting our hostages out. In his words, we had to develop "the capability for a rapid clandestine insertion into Tehran, with a surprise entry into the embassy and as little violence and loss of life on either side as possible. Then a rapid exfiltration of the rescue force and former hostages."

It was President Carter who was attributed with that part of the mission statement that read, ". . . with as little violence and loss of life to either side as possible." He feared that unnecessary bloodshed against the Iranians would spur retaliation against Americans still in Iran after the mission.

The Chairman then summarized our task, double-underlining secrecy. He told us that it was essential to organize the JTF, develop the plans, select the force, conduct the necessary training, deploy the force and its equipment, and execute the mission all in an environment of airtight security.

The general was asked if we would be allowed to use existing Special Operations points of contact throughout our worldwide networks.[2]

"Absolutely not! These people are in highly visible positions

[2]At the time, we had good people in place to provide support for exactly this type of mission. A good example was the Joint Special Operations Support Element at MacDill Air Force Base, Florida. This unit provided unconventional warfare expertise to unified commanders for staff augmentation in support of regional contingencies or a major conflict. Some of these people should have been utilized for our mission.

and their involvement would draw attention to what we are doing, making it doubly difficult to conceal our operation."

This answer took me by surprise. Not being able to use our covered contacts at various levels of command was going to make it that much tougher.

It would be difficult to deceive our Special Ops people throughout the various commands, and what's more, they would have been able to help us make things happen without drawing undue attention—that was their sole purpose for being where they were. These were some of the best minds in the business, and it was going to hamper us to be denied their expertise.

Some of the permanent staff in the Pentagon (old heads in Special Ops) had told me General Jones preferred to assemble select groups of fifteen to twenty officers to deal with sensitive problems. He reasoned that this way he could get solutions more quickly and keep the situations more closely controlled.

Along these same lines, we were not to use our contacts in foreign Special Operations units—the British SAS, the German GSG-9, or the Israeli commandos. Again, I felt this was an unfortunate restriction. These groups had far more experience in dealing with terrorism than we did and their expertise would have been very helpful to our planning.

In the meantime, it was obvious that we would be putting this JTF together on an alphabet-soup basis—a man from here, another from there.[3]

It became apparent early on that a helicopter-supported operation offered the best prospects for getting Delta out of Tehran after the rescue. But it was also apparent that we had much work to do on figuring out the best way to get them into the city. The distance involved made it obvious that we were going to have to come up with some kind of refueling plan.

Using Jerry's charts, we went down the list of countries bor-

---

[3] The Holloway Commission and Paul Ryan, author of *The Iran Rescue Mission*, refer to an existing JCS Contingency Plan that they claim contained an organizational and planning framework for Special Operations missions (which the JTF chose not to implement). Most of us on the JTF staff were familiar with this document but viewed it as not being useful in the context of our organization and planning problems. Other than providing a list of forces based on escalating levels of conflict it had little value for our purposes. The JTF was certainly aware of what Special Operations units were available to us.

dering Iran that offered a likely jumping-off point—looking for those that would be supportive of, or at least neutral to, our presence.

General Jones ruled out Oman, the United Arab Emirates, Qatar, Bahrain, Kuwait, Pakistan, Saudi Arabia, Yemen, Israel, and Turkey, for either political or operational security reasons.

To explain his reasons, he told of an attempt in mid-February to move Air Force helicopters into Iran through Turkey. This was when the embassy had first been stormed, along with the Military Assistance Advisory Group headquarters, and Khomeini's mobs had taken a hundred Americans hostage. Fortunately, these captives were released. That time, we were lucky.

But the experience made the general's point. He said some Turkish official had blown the cover of the chopper force's presence and we were forced to abandon the effort. It was easy to see why the Chairman was touchy about security. However, he had no problem with using Turkey as an escape route, after secrecy would no longer be so critical.

The potential jumping-off points he could accept were Diego Garcia and Egypt, where we already had established bases, with possible use of Saudi Arabian airspace and bases in Somalia and Kenya.

It doesn't take a genius to see that the distances involved in operating from these countries would not be possible for the helicopters—the transports, perhaps, but not the helos. We had to get closer!

The Chairman turned to Admiral Schoultz. "How about a helicopter launch from some type of ship operating in the Indian Ocean?"

The admiral admitted that might be possible, but "what kind of ship and what type of helicopters?" He wasn't wild about using an aircraft carrier and disrupting its fighter operations. And there were no amphibious assault ships, with their specially developed helicopter capabilities, in the area.

"Well, we'll have to study the particulars some more, but let's look at that closely as one of our better launch options for the helos," the Chairman concluded.

It seemed to me that this option made the most sense. We would have more control aboard a carrier than we would staging helicopters in a foreign country where it would be tough to hide our intentions. We were really going to have to finesse this part of the mission. Also, we would need to figure out how and where to refuel the helos.

We then focused on another option—some type of surface transportation from Turkey. This idea was made credible by the success Texas businessman Ross Perot had in getting two of his Electronic Data Systems (EDS) employees out of Iran. Perot had employed former Son Tay raider Colonel Arthur D. "Bull" Simons to lead a small team into Tehran to get the two out of prison and spirit them out of the country.

Simons had considered any attempt to penetrate Tehran airport security too risky, so they escaped over land to the northwest. They exited at the Turkish border on February 15, 1979. One of the keys to Simons's success was an Iranian guide, loyal to EDS, who bribed guards and fast-talked the group through numerous revolutionary force roadblocks.

However, Delta Force would be much larger than this group and obviously much more difficult to move in this manner. It was too risky. If Delta was discovered, it would be disastrous.

Another option, parachuting Delta into the outskirts of Tehran with infiltration by foot, went over poorly with the Delta reps. They said Colonel Beckwith felt an air insertion would scatter the forces too much and there was too great a potential for disabling injuries. "What would we do with a man who broke his leg? We need a healthy force on the ground, intact and ready to fight."

I could see their point. I had seen too many parachute accidents myself to downplay their concerns, yet I still thought this was a good option. On the other hand, I also knew that to parachute a small force into a place you couldn't get them out of would be foolhardy. However, I felt that problem could have been solved eventually.

This brought us to what was perhaps our major problem at this point—lack of intelligence data. We certainly wouldn't be able to pull this off without more information than television and news reports, which was about all we had at the time.

We were going to need cooperation from the CIA, the Defense Intelligence Agency (DIA), the FBI, the National Security

Agency, the Defense Communications Agency, and the Defense Mapping Agency. In particular, we needed input from the CIA's in-country Iran assets—the people who had their eyes on the embassy and could provide detailed answers to our questions.

The Chairman acknowledged the necessity of intelligence information and said he would get the Department of Defense intelligence community moving to support us. On the other hand, he knew well the difficulty of tapping into the CIA network. Admiral Stansfield Turner, the CIA director, had not seemed very cooperative in responding to Joint Task Force requests for crucial information about what was going on in Tehran and at the embassy. Scuttlebutt had it that the admiral didn't believe we were serious about a rescue mission; CIA priorities were focused elsewhere.

I found this hard to believe, because our mission had been ordered by the President. We all had the same Commander in Chief, didn't we?

We learned the real reason for the dearth of intelligence information when our CIA liaison informed us that the CIA had no agents in Iran. They had had to get out when Khomeini's revolutionaries seized the city. There were no sources in Tehran to feed us the information we needed—a disappointing revelation. This would be a major problem throughout the project. It would be months before we would begin receiving reliable information from Tehran.[4]

By now, we'd been at it about four hours and had plenty to work on. General Jones told us he'd meet with us each day until we came up with a feasible rescue option. He ended this keynote session after directing us to focus on finding the best combination of locations, tactics, and equipment to make the mission workable.

After returning to my cubbyhole, with all that had transpired ricocheting around in my brain, one thought crystallized: the

---

[4]In a conversation years later with the former CIA director, Admiral Turner said he devoted most of his time to supporting the rescue mission from the outset. It was his position that the military expected too much too soon from the Agency and that it took time to reestablish their human intelligence resources in Iran after the fall of the shah. Another Agency source made a similar statement.

capability to accomplish this mission, as defined by the Chairman, simply did not exist in the U.S. military forces. Unfortunately, it took the seizure of an American embassy in a far-off land to ram that fact home.

4

THE PUZZLE

November 14—Hostage Day 11
<u>Knight-Ridder News Service</u>
WASHINGTON—Like a grim international chess contest with lives at stake, the increasingly tense struggle between the United States and Iran remained at an apparent stalemate today following President Carter's quick action to block about $5 billion in Iranian assets in this country. . . .

A State Department spokesman said today that "things are very much unchanged." Diplomatic sources said the daily anti-U.S. demonstrations continued outside the occupied embassy.

It was Wednesday morning, after another restless night.
Those distances—the Chairman really hung one on us.

It was like a bad dream that you wake from only to find the nightmare is real. Right now, there seemed to be no way we could pull this thing off in less than two nights—one to get Delta in and a second to pull them and the hostages out. There just wasn't enough darkness to do it in one night, and we had to have darkness.

I was back in my Pentagon cubbyhole with my head in the charts, searching for some way to launch from countries adjoining Iran.

With the choices we'd been given—Egypt, Diego Garcia—we were looking at between 5,000 and 6,000 nautical miles round trip. This translated into twenty hours of flying time for C-130s with at least two, maybe three, in-flight refuelings. Too long, dammit. Too long. And too much vulnerability. It would take a miracle to escape detection.

Somalia and Kenya were a little closer, but we had no ongoing flight operations from either, thus no cover for our movements.

How about a different aircraft?

The C-141? No in-flight refueling capability and not enough range without it. At least not with the payloads we needed.

The gigantic C-5? It could be refueled in flight, but lacked the low-level radar systems to penetrate Iran's coast and stay on the deck to escape detection. Those "big mothers" were just too much airplane for what we had to do. The C-130 was it.

Wait a minute, I thought. *The Chairman did leave the door open to overfly Saudi territory. This would cut the round trip to about twelve hours. How about the long route on night one and the shorter one on night two? That makes sense. Vary the routes, cut the chances of detection. We'll still have to refuel going in and on the way out, but we won't need as many KC-135 tankers.*

This idea would need a thorough scrubbing down, but definitely showed promise. I decided it was time to bring some navigator/flight planner types aboard to crunch numbers. Before the day was over, I would ask General Vaught for permission to add three people to my planning group.

Even though we didn't know where we would be linking up with the helos, there was no doubt that it would be about 600 miles inside Iran. So we could at least draw up the basic C-130 routing and compute a ballpark estimate of the fuel required.

Right now, the helicopter piece to the puzzle was missing, and we needed it soon. We needed to know how many, how much fuel they would need, where they would launch from, and what route they would fly.

Having to depart from Egypt or Diego Garcia ruled out using Air Force or Marine C-130 tankers to refuel the helos in flight—the C-130s would need refueling as well and they didn't have the plumbing to take on gas.

This capability—an air-refuelable tanker—just didn't exist, and the Strategic Air Command's long-range KC-135 tankers couldn't fly slowly enough to refuel helicopters.

It was becoming apparent that we were going to have to use the Air Force Special Operations MC-130s—the only tactical transports capable of in-flight refueling.

PACAF had four of these Combat Talon aircraft and Hurlburt had three. Seven MC-130s worldwide—a pitifully small force and widely dispersed. We might find some way to use the Talon aircraft based in Europe, but they didn't have the refueling modification.

I knew we could possibly use the Tactical Airborne Command and Control Squadron aircraft at Keesler AFB, Mississippi, which had refuelable EC-130s, but they weren't normally used to transport personnel and equipment.

Also, five AC-130 gunships were equipped for refueling and their crews were trained for extended over-water deployment, but there was no role for them in the scenario. Still, it was too early to be ruling anything out; time would tell.

I was still hoping we could convince the Chairman to give us a launch base closer to Iran—Turkey, Oman, or even Saudi Arabia. Then we could put the helos behind HC-130 tankers (which wouldn't require refueling over these shorter distances) and air-refuel them on the way in and coming back from Tehran.

The restrictions were beginning to be overwhelming. A sense of frustration was coming over me. You can't solve a puzzle if some pieces are missing (or, as in this case, removed from the board).

How had we managed to get into this mess in the first place?

I'd had it with this brain drain and needed a break to sort out my thoughts. Near the galley, Nick Kilgore's intelligence team was busily preparing to tape the nightly 5:00 news broadcast.

My frustrations boiled out as I joined them. "Here we sit in a barren room at the Pentagon, trying to figure out how to move a meager bunch of airplanes, helicopters, and a rescue team into position some six thousand miles away to free sixty-three of our fellow citizens unlawfully held hostage in our own embassy. Once we get to a country that will accept us, we still have two thousand miles to travel to get to Iran, then eight hundred miles of hostile territory to negotiate before arriving in Tehran.

"When you think back over the years, we have spent billions on foreign aid to these countries surrounding Iran and yet *not one* of them has offered to help us get our hostages back. America is sorely lacking for friends."

There had not been one concrete offer to help us militarily, other than from President Anwar Sadat of Egypt. A few countries had extended words of support, but no action.

Then I turned to another disturbing question:

"Why did we leave this small embassy staff behind when we

pulled out most of our people after the first takeover attempt in February?

"Were our diplomats fooled by Iran's shaky leadership? Did they really believe that our embassy would or could be protected by the Iranian government?

"And where was the CIA? Were they blind to what was happening? Couldn't they see that Iran was totally controlled by Khomeini and his religious zealots?"

The Ayatollah couldn't have cared less about international law or world opinion. The hostages were being used as pawns to focus world attention on his revolution and to apply leverage to get his hands on the shah.

Reza Pahlavi was in a New York hospital being treated for cancer he had been suffering from for at least six years, unbeknownst to our government. It was this move to New York that had precipitated the hostage crisis, and it hadn't really made much sense. This was playing right into Khomeini's hands.

Surely somebody in the administration, State Department or CIA, had realized the risks involved in this well-intentioned decision.

Nick Kilgore pitched in, "Speaking of puzzlers . . ." He dug through the video tapes and pulled out a segment of the nightly news he had recorded on November 9, just five days after the takeover. "Check this out."

He put the cassette into the recorder and the screen came to life. The militants were holding several documents up to the camera that they had found in the files or pieced together from shredded classified waste. One was a secret memo to the State Department from chargé d'affaires Bruce Laingen: "The shah should not be admitted into America until we have obtained a new and substantially more effective guard for the U.S. Embassy in Tehran."

I was dumbfounded. "For God's sake, why did Washington go against the warning of their senior diplomat on the scene about such a decision?"

We all just sat there shrugging our shoulders and blinking like frogs in a hailstorm. No one in the room had an answer.

Hadn't our State Department gotten Laingen's warning? If it had, why had it ignored it?

We were facing an international crisis over the Iranian hostage situation, not having fully recovered the confidence we had lost in the jungles and tangled politics of Vietnam. We seemed unable to protect our citizens or embassy on foreign soil, and vital strategic and economic interests were at stake as well.

We had our marching orders: limited-size force . . . as little violence as possible . . . numerous political limitations on operating areas. As one of the Vietnam veterans in our group pointed out, these were some of the same stumbling blocks that had gotten us into trouble in the Southeast Asia war.

Another old head pointed out that there was legitimate concern among White House advisers that stronger measures, such as invasion or bombing, could threaten the lives of the hostages and invite Soviet intervention.

Conceivably, the oil supply to the West could be cut off, triggering an escalation of hostilities. So, maybe our leaders were right in ordering development of a small surgical rescue operation.

As we sat there kicking the possibilities around, there wasn't one of us who believed that a small rescue force had any more than a snowball's chance in hell. We didn't have the means to get Delta clandestinely into Iran and into position for a surprise assault on the embassy.

There were outside military analysts recommending a larger-scale airborne-type raid, an option we felt had bloodbath written all over it.

Obviously, the purpose of any rescue mission was to get the hostages out alive, and the Rambo approach—shoot 'em all and sort 'em out later—works only in the movies.

While we were talking, the TV news being recorded focused on the chanting mobs. They were burning the shah in effigy and chanting "hate America" slogans. The newscasters were continuing the nightly drumbeat of events in Iran portraying the United States as a helpless giant and inflaming the emotions of Americans to urge the President and Congress to do something about the crisis.

Jerry King came up with an idea that I hadn't considered: "The President is facing reelection next year, and he'll have to do something before then. He can't let this drag on. He's going to have to decide which way to go, diplomacy or military force."

We all knew that the diplomatic route had to be followed as far as it would take us, if possible all the way to a negotiated release.

This was our country's first direct confrontation with international terrorism, and it was a worst-case scenario. It certainly couldn't be compared to Entebbe or Mogadishu, both of which had been raids on remote airports.[1] Our people were being held in a bastion at the center of a major city, thousands of miles away and surrounded by their captors and hordes of screaming mobs that were armed to the teeth.

It was at this point, I think, that we nevertheless resolved to by God find a way to rescue our hostages that would work.

I busted out of there and headed for General Vaught's office to get his okay on the three flight planners I needed. He readily concurred.

While I was in the boss's office, a face out of the past appeared. Chuck Gilbert (not his real name) from the CIA air section walked in. Chuck looked like a college professor—large-framed, shiny black hair with a touch of gray at the temples, glasses riding low on his nose and accentuating his bushy eyebrows, deepset eyes. Looking at him, no one would ever suspect his legendary deeds in covert and clandestine flight operations.

Chuck warmly shook hands and spoke softly in his New England accent. "General, I'm here to offer my services in whatever capacity they can best be used."

General Vaught welcomed this offer, cursing the fact that we had more problems than answers, and told Chuck, "We can use all the help you can give us."

Chuck and I had first crossed paths at Hurlburt Field back in 1975 at a USAF School of Special Operations course titled "Dynamics of International Terrorism." I was a student and he was one of the lecturers. I thought it fitting that our paths had crossed

---

[1]On July 3 and 4, 1976, Israeli commandos conducted Operation Jonathan, a raid on Entebbe International Airport in Kampala, Uganda, to rescue 105 Israelis taken hostage on an Air France jetliner by hijackers sympathetic to the Palestine Liberation Organization. Six terrorists were killed, and the Israelis also lost six (two military and four civilians). On October 18, 1977, the West German GSG-9 successfully stormed a hijacked Lufthansa airliner at the airport in Mogadishu, Somalia, killing four Arab terrorists and rescuing eighty-six hostages.

again in this place and time. He had a wealth of experience and knowledge we could draw upon.

As much as I enjoyed seeing Chuck again, I had to get moving. I found Lee Hess and gave him the news we had the okay to bring in three flight planners. He recommended Lieutenant Colonel Les Smith from Hurlburt—a highly experienced Combat Talon navigator. Smith was operations officer for his unit and could return to Hurlburt after the planning phase to initiate the training program to prepare the aircrews for the mission.

The second name Lee came up with was Major Doug Ulery, another old-head navigator with whom both Lee and I had worked in Korea. He could come up with original ideas—we needed those more than ever now.

Rounding out the threesome was Major Paul Gorsky from TAC headquarters at Langley AFB, Virginia, another top-notch Talon navigator. Paul would act as our liaison with TAC headquarters and handle command matters that might conflict with what we were trying to do.

These decisions were possible because Special Operations is a small community when compared to fighter, bomber, or airlift commands; therefore those who excel in this trade are well known. This is a major advantage in selecting individuals to perform a given task.

As the time for the late-evening news approached, I headed for the videotaping area. I found Kilgore and his crew had their machines in action while the Delta liaison officers were watching intently. I recalled Nick's words about how valuable these TV newscasts from Tehran were and compared that with the negative impact of the mass media attention and the psychosis the newscasters unwittingly spawned with their reports; we had to take the bad with the good.

I could see that the mobs were still ominously present, and some of the hostages were being paraded blindfolded before the delighted masses. Damn! It was infuriating! We strained to identify each hostage as he passed fleetingly before the camera. There was no way to tell where they were being held within the embassy compound or what condition they were in. We desperately needed our own intelligence sources there.

Several watchers commented that it was hard to believe these militants were simply run-of-the-mill students. We had seen too many signs of terroristic techniques to believe that they were all amateurs. How many college students can handle automatic weapons and know the tactics of taking over buildings; can piece together shredded documents; can use blindfolds, isolation, interrogations, intimidation, mock trials, and other insidious methods of creating fear?

If not students, who were they? How were they organized? Who gave their orders?

One CIA report linked the militants to the Palestine Liberation Organization, saying that some were terrorists trained by that group. Some were alleged to have Marxist leanings and to be using the Islamic revolution for political gain. Perhaps they were former members of the armed forces or Iran's revolutionary guards (Pasdaran). We plain didn't know who they were—there were no international police files on any of them.

Whether the so-called students were terrorists or not was not the real issue. Delta was trained to eliminate them swiftly and silently whoever they might be. But to do that, we had to have time to prepare a plan and get the forces ready.

Every man on the Joint Task Force fervently hoped that the negotiators could buy us that time . . . and that the hostages would bear up physically and mentally until we could get them out should the negotiations fail.

5

A PLAN TAKES SHAPE

November 15—Hostage Day 12

<u>Associated Press</u>

The Moslem militants holding the U.S. Embassy in Tehran today angrily rejected suggestions by a top Iranian official that some of their 98 hostages, including all women, be freed. They declared that only Ayatollah Ruhollah Khomeini and the Iranian people can tell them what to do.

In Tunisia, meanwhile, Arab League ministers rejected a Libyan demand for joint Arab diplomatic and economic reprisals against the United States for freezing Iranian assets in American banks.

In the days following those first briefings, we all fell into a routine of early-morning arrivals and planning sessions that ran on late into the night. Seldom conscious of time, we didn't break for chow until our growling stomachs forced us to.

In our round-table sessions with the Chairman, we continued to pursue the idea of forward-basing the rescue force close to Iran (as in Turkey) but were persistently rebuffed.

Although we weren't about to give up on this point, we didn't have time to worry about it. Right now, we had to find out who and what we were up against. We put the computers to work compiling lists of former military advisers to Iran, along with others who might know about the Iranian defense systems.

We ended up with a parade of those on the lists, closeting them in a nondescript back room we set up and probing them for every fact they could give us on Iran. We did not tell them why they were being questioned and told them to forget it ever happened.

Gradually, we came up with a picture. We pinpointed the weaknesses in the Iranian radar defenses and learned they were not prepared to fire their surface-to-air missiles (SAMs). This was confirmed by reconnaissance photography—they had no missiles on the platforms ready to launch.

We determined their night fighter interceptors were impotent and the radar systems used to vector the fighters toward intruders were marginal at best. We also knew what radars to knock out to ensure that the fighters would get no assistance from their ground control centers.

Intelligence photos established that most of their antiaircraft guns were not a threat. In fact, many were still stored harmlessly in weapons caches where they had been when Khomeini's forces took over the country.

Yet, while this information increased our confidence that we could penetrate Iran undetected, we knew that we had to maintain the secrecy of this mission. Our cover could not be blown before Charlie Beckwith's Delta Force was over the wall and the fight started. At that point, we could surgically apply whatever firepower was necessary.

With these launch-point restrictions, we focused our planning on a remote location in Egypt we called Wadi Kena (the Egyptians call it Wadi abu Shihat). It seemed to fill the bill as our hub of operations. From there we could move the JTF aircraft into position for the rescue mission and the KC-135 tanker operation and other support aircraft, as well.

Wadi Kena was a fighter/bomber base built for Egypt by Russian engineers during the Nasser era for use in his wars against Israel. It was crudely constructed and poorly maintained, and sand, dust, flies, and searing heat put it near zero on the comfort scale. But we would be there at most for a week. More important, we could sequester our support equipment and other peculiar operations gear there with little fear of discovery.

This is not to say that we weren't concerned about the constant vigilance of Soviet spy satellites. We would plan our aircraft dispersal carefully to confuse the Soviet "eye in the sky."

The fact that our Air Force was constantly operating tankers, transports, and fighters in that area made it ideal for us. When the time came, we could run our own version of the old shell game, slipping our JTF aircraft into the shuffle with no one the wiser.

The Chairman's idea for a main operating base was fine, but I still wanted to get at least a small portion of the insertion force in closer. I continued a quiet search for such a location.

Meanwhile, Navy planners were concentrating on finding the best launch platform for the helicopters. They considered using amphibious assault ships designated LPH and LHA, ships specially designed to carry helos. However, these were ruled out because it was felt they would attract too much attention—they were not normally a part of Carrier Task Force 70, which was sailing in the Indian Ocean at that time. LHAs and LPHs, which resemble small aircraft carriers, are usually associated with a Marine Amphibious Ready Group.[1] The helos lift the Marine assault forces ashore and provide support. These ships also carry amphibious landing craft.

The Navy planners finally opted for the aircraft carrier as the best launch platform for the helicopters. The whirlybirds could be hidden below deck during the day and then brought up on the elevators and flown at night. And, of course, we already had Carrier Task Force 70 in the Indian Ocean. The carrier could steam around with the helos below deck and then maneuver into position for launch at the right time. Far better than operating the helos from a base on foreign soil for an extended period of time and risking detection.

This decision, which General Jones supported, drove us to consider using some type of long-range, heavy-lift, ship-borne helicopter that was common to Navy operations. We needed a bird that would not draw suspicion from the Soviets or from the ship's crew. A helicopter mine-clearing force aboard the carrier would make a plausible cover story, since rumor had it that the Strait of Hormuz might be seeded with mines.

Throughout our planning, the Soviet intelligence network was always a primary consideration. Their extensive trawler activity near our fleet operations and their reconnaissance coverage of U.S. bases, along with communications monitoring and their eyeball sources, would be a constant threat once we started to move. We were concerned that if they figured out what we were

---

[1]At the time, Marine Amphibious Forces were not deployed in the Indian Ocean. In mid-February 1980, President Carter dispatched the Marines to the area to beef up security in the region—a decision ostensibly linked to the Soviet invasion of Afghanistan.

doing they would tip the Iranians to set a trap. In an operation like this one, either you have strict security or you have none.

Now that we had decided on a launch platform for the helos, we had to find the right bird. Days were spent interviewing every rotary-wing expert in the Pentagon, and after scrutinizing every type of helicopter in the inventory, we came up with the Navy's RH-53D Sea Stallion.

The RH-53D could carry removable internal auxiliary fuel tanks in addition to its external tanks, boosting its range to about 750 miles. It had foldable rotor blades and tail boom so it could be stored below deck on a carrier. And it had a cargo compartment big enough to carry twenty fully equipped Delta Force commandos, as well as extra fuel.[2]

This would allow us to get everybody out of Tehran in one trip with five or more helos (with internal tanks removed). We felt we had to have this capability—we didn't want to give the Iranians a second shot at our rescuers by shuttling back and forth between the embassy and the extraction site.

The clincher for the Sea Stallion was that we could make up a good cover story (mine clearing) to explain their presence in the Indian Ocean.

It was determined that the Navy would supply the pilots and crew chiefs, augmented by Marine copilots and door gunners.

A Navy captain named Jerry Hatcher was assigned to put together the helicopter operation with a Marine colonel, Chuck Pitman, looking after the interests of the Marines involved. I was anxious to get together with them, because my flight planners were due to arrive and we were going to need information on the helicopter plans before we could fit the airlift-support role into the picture.

Captain Hatcher, a Pentagon staff officer assigned to Naval Operations, had the background for employment of shipborne helos and would, with Colonel Pitman's help, obtain the helicopters and spare parts for our mission. He would also assist in setting up a training program to prepare the Navy crews for the mission.

---

[2]Each man, fully equipped, weighed nearly 270 pounds. At the time, the maximum gross weight at which an Air Force HH-53 Pave Low helicopter could operate was 42,000 pounds, 6,000 less than the RH-53D. With the fuel load required for this mission, the Pave Low could not carry passengers or cargo.

Colonel Pitman was working for Air Force Lieutenant General John S. Pustay on the Chairman's Joint Service Support Staff. He would assist in organizing the training of Marine crews and advise both General Jones and General Vaught on the helicopter program.

Pitman was regarded by the Marine Corps as one of its foremost helicopter experts. This Vietnam veteran with a distinguished combat record also had extensive experience in planning contingency evacuations of American noncombatants from hostile foreign hotspots.

I knew little about the capabilities of Navy and Marine aircrews to fly Special Operations missions, but assumed they had been selected because of some type of previous experience.

At this point, our plan was to airdrop the fuel for the choppers, because we thought it would be too risky to assault and capture an Iranian airfield to use as a gas station. Besides, for this scheme we would need additional forces to take and hold a field for about twenty-four hours. This also had the potential for blowing the lid off of our secrecy. So we put such notions aside, at least for the moment.

Meanwhile, the Defense Intelligence Agency had been painstakingly going over hundreds of aerial photos of the Dasht-e-Kavir, looking the barren landscape over for a location to set down our C-130s. So far they hadn't found anything remote enough or with a crust that appeared solid enough to support a C-130. I was adamant that we would not land in the desert unless somebody actually went to the proposed landing site and made sure it was usable. I wasn't going to have any airplanes bogging down in that desert and screwing up the mission.

General Vaught was pursuing a plan to airdrop fuel bladders into a remote area some 300 to 400 miles southeast of Tehran, along with a small security force to assemble the bladders and pumping equipment. After setting up and camouflaging at this forward refueling point, they would notify the helicopters that they were ready for the rendezvous.

To meet our objective of total surprise, the rescue force would train to operate at night without lights—total blackout. General Vaught had driven this point home, and I was pondering how to get the C-130 aircrews started on this training.

The helicopters, with Delta on board, would launch at night in clear weather from an aircraft carrier in the northern Indian Ocean. They would refuel at the bladder gas station in the desert, then drop Delta off at a hide site near Tehran. The helos would fly to their hideout to wait through the next day until nightfall. Then Delta would secretly move into Tehran on Night-Two, assault the embassy, overpower the defenses, rescue the hostages, and link up for extraction by the same helicopters. The entire group would head out to a nearby airfield south of Tehran which would be secured by a Ranger force. Then everyone would jump on MC-130s and get the hell out.

This called for a two-night operation, with a layover for Delta and the helos near Tehran during daylight. Because of the over-800-mile distance from the carrier to Tehran and the refueling stop for the choppers, there wasn't enough darkness to permit a takedown of the embassy on the first night.

We could see early on that the desert refueling operation was going to be crucial—and tricky. We would have to find a large, flat area firm enough for the fuel bladders and the helicopters and remote enough to prevent discovery. The bladders would have to survive the airdrop intact, be rolled into groups, and be hooked up with hoses and pumps.

It would be a formidable task for the security team, but until the fueling stations were set up, the helos with Delta aboard would not launch from the carrier. Obviously, anyone stumbling onto the operation would be captured and held. Should someone spot the security team from a distance, we would have to wait and see what the Iranian reaction would be, assuming the word ever reached Tehran. With the internal chaos of Khomeini's government, we felt there was a good chance any such encounter would go unreported. But we would have to be certain before continuing.

So here we were, in mid-November (twelve days since the embassy takeover), and we had a plan. It was only for an emergency and needed a lot of fine tuning . . . but if circumstances dictated fast action, at least we had one.

The three C-130 navigator/route planners—Les Smith, Doug Ulery, and Paul Gorsky—arrived on November 16.

Lee and I lost no time in briefing them and putting them to work. We gave them all the details we had on the MC-130 fuel-bladder operation for refueling the helos and got them started on planning specific routes from two widely divergent launch bases.

For the first night, we would plan a route from Wadi Kena down the Red Sea and through the Bab el Mandeb (the strait between the Red Sea and the Gulf of Aden); avoiding Saudi Arabian airspace (Figure 1). The route then would go eastward over the Arabian Gulf, paralleling the shoreline of Southern Yemen and Oman, followed by a swing northeast into the Gulf of Oman. Then we'd cross near the Strait of Hormuz at low level and penetrate the Iranian coast between the radar sites at Jask and Chah Bahar.

Route planning would be hazy beyond this, because we needed to know the exact coordinates of a refueling rendezvous with the helicopters to determine a precise path into Iran.

The Night-Two course would be across Saudi Arabia. We decided to use this routing only once, because I didn't want to tempt fate with the obvious possibilities of detection by crossing Saudi airspace two nights in a row.

After getting the plan up to the Iranian coast, all we could do was study the radar network of that country's interior to determine low-level routes that would skirt detection en route to the area south of Tehran—a nearly impossible task with no more intelligence information than we had.

For an alternate route, we needed a launch plan from the British-owned island of Diego Garcia, located in the Indian Ocean some 2,200 nautical miles southeast of Iran. This flight would be plotted entirely over water, with coastal penetration at roughly the same point as in the Egypt launch option.

We told the navigators to work out en route refueling points based on when the MC-130s would need gas and to compute the quantities for each. These calculations would have to take into account the overall time to an airdrop zone within 300 to 400 miles south of Tehran and the time required for the C-130s to return to their launch bases.

Once the planners could determine the generalized flow plan, we would ask the KC-135 planner, Major Dave Reckermer from the Operations Planning Group, to figure out how many aircraft he would need to meet the MC-130 fuel requirements. We also had to come up with a base for the KC-135s to operate from.

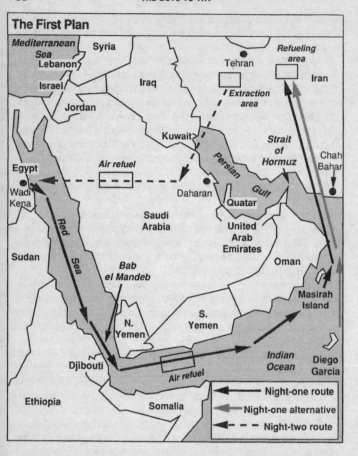

The First Plan

Mediterranean Sea — Lebanon — Syria — Israel — Jordan — Iraq — Tehran — Refueling area — Iran

Extraction area

Kuwait — Persian Gulf — Strait of Hormuz — Chah Bahar

Air refuel — Daharan — Quatar — United Arab Emirates

Egypt — Wadi Kena — Red Sea — Saudi Arabia

Sudan — Bab el Mandeb — Oman — Masirah Island

Djibouti — N. Yemen — S. Yemen — Indian Ocean — Diego Garcia

Air refuel

Ethiopia — Somalia

Night-one route
Night-one alternative
Night-two route

As if they didn't have enough to keep them busy, I further directed them to plan a route for the C-130 squadron at Kadena Air Force Base, Japan, to move into position via Diego Garcia. The Hurlburt Field Combat Talons were to deploy to Wadi Kena via the Atlantic Ocean. In keeping with our low profile, we would approach Iran from two staging bases, not concentrating the force in any one place. These two widely separated launch bases highlighted the fact that we would be facing one hellacious training problem when we began to rehearse the rescue scenario.

As for the second night's extraction operation, we would overfly Saudi airspace from Egypt and refuel in-flight. This route would have to be immune from detection by radar sites in the area. We would drop down to low level at the Saudi eastern coast and cross the Persian Gulf on the deck, penetrating the Iranian radar net through a gap we had spotted.

Getting up to Tehran was still an open-ended plan on Night-Two, since the location to land and extract the rescue force and hostages had not as yet been determined. However, the navigators were to come up with the best in-country route to avoid radar nets, fighters, surface-to-air missiles, and antiaircraft artillery threats.

We stressed the urgency of finding these data because we had been told we might have to deploy overseas at any moment.

We had dumped some serious navigation planning problems on the "number crunchers," as they were affectionately called, but they took it in stride and got right down to the task.

In the following days, the pieces started to fall into place. During this time, the navigators were hit with frustrating changes that made for frayed nerves, and plenty of bitching—but they hung in there and did an outstanding job of producing the data we needed.

Even so, we still had two major holdups to piecing together the air operations picture: a desert refueling site and an extraction airfield in the Tehran area hadn't been chosen. I was certain that the planners for Delta Force, the Navy helicopter contingent, and the Army Rangers were facing far more difficult problems.

Les Smith, senior officer in the navigator plans group, hit me with a mind-blower:

"By the way, Colonel, did you know some of the 1st SOW AC-130 gunships were deployed to Guam on November 13 along with our 1st SOW commander, Colonel Dunwoody?"

I'm sure the look on my face must have answered his question. It took me a minute to recover. "No, I didn't. But why Guam?"

His shrug was enough of an answer. He had no idea.

Since Dick Dunwoody and his planners had been missing

from the Special Operations Division for a week, I wasn't that surprised at the deployment news. But Guam?

This defied an answer. For AC-130s, Guam was an impossible distance from Iran for any strike missions . . . unless it was just a staging location on the way to a forward base. If so, I wondered where that base might be and, more important, what the target was.

Dammit! Too many unanswered questions.

It didn't make sense for them to be deploying for a strike mission while we were sitting here planning a rescue. Why would the Chairman plan an action that could cause the militants to increase security around the hostages? I was seeing too many things that just didn't make sense.

I needed coffee, so I headed for the galley area, and lo and behold who should appear but the 1st SOW operations officer, Tom Wicker. I knew him from my visits to Hurlburt. After just hearing the disturbing news about the 1st SOW, it was quite a coincidence to run into its ops officer here.

We exchanged greetings and dodged each other's questions about what each of us was doing at the Pentagon. I learned that he was going overseas, along with Lieutenant Colonel Dick Gadd, USAF, one of Lee Hess's associates in the Air Staff Special Operations shop.

It would be months after this chance encounter before I would see either Tom or Dick. I later found out they deployed to the Indian Ocean to go aboard an aircraft carrier to provide liaison for the Dick Dunwoody mission that was then at Guam . . .

. . . and it would be Thanksgiving Day before I found out what that AC-130 mission was. The problems it would cause would turn out to be humongous.

6

OPERATION RICE BOWL

November 20—Hostage Day 17
<u>Combined News Services</u>
Ten more American hostages were freed from the U.S. Embassy
in Tehran early today and left by an Iranian airliner for Paris,
from which they were to fly to West Germany to join the three
hostages (one woman and two blacks) released Monday. . . .

Ayatollah Ruhollah Khomeini had ordered that all blacks and
women among the 63 hostages "whose spying was not proven"
should be released.

But two women and one black man remain among the 50 still
held hostage at the embassy, apparently considered by the students to be "spies." . . . The ayatollah threatened Sunday that if
the United States did not return the deposed shah for trial, the
hostages suspected of being spies would be put on trial.

More threats! Dammit, if the ayatollah thought he could split
American public opinion by releasing women and blacks, he
was mistaken. It was becoming obvious that the Iranians didn't
understand us any better than we understood them. Our entire
country was polarized against Iran.

The President had started getting tougher with the Khomeini
government on November 12 with the cutoff of Iranian oil
imports.

The next day, the Justice Department began a crackdown
on Iranian students in the United States. Many of them were
demonstrating in the streets of our major cities against our government. It seemed incredible that we were treating these people
(and their diplomats) as welcome guests while they were trying
to justify taking Americans hostage.

Then, on the 14th, we hit 'em in the pocketbook—the President froze all Iranian assets in American banks after the Khomeini government tried to make withdrawals. Perhaps this would create some movement on the diplomatic front.

By this time, General Vaught had decided that we would call the operation "Rice Bowl" to confuse anyone who found out we were in session. This name might point the thinking of the overly curious toward Southeast Asia—thinking reinforced by the fact that there really were plans to airdrop rice to the beleaguered Khmer guerrilla forces in Cambodia.

This misnomer was an example of a Special Operations tactic known as cover and deception (C&D). C&D is an essential element of tactical strategy in clandestine operations.

Our Task Force's C&D objective was to make the Iranians believe there was no reason to be alert to hostile action and then, when we did strike, to create confusion in the minds of the revolutionary military commanders. The end result of a successful C&D operation for our small rescue force would be the critically essential advantage of surprise at the point of the embassy assault.

We had already received a boost to our cover and deception objectives in the November 19 issue of *Time* magazine:

> . . . *would it thus not be natural, if the Americans continued to be held hostage, for Washington to dispatch commandos to rescue them?* Time *put this question to nearly two dozen experts in and out of government. Their near-unanimous negative conclusion was summed up by Elmo Zumwalt, Jr., the former chief of naval operations: "I think it's pretty much out of the question." . . . Surprise is so difficult to achieve because U.S. planes would be detected as they neared Iran. . . . So enormous would be the problems of using force, therefore, that the Carter administration could never seriously consider the military option. . . .*

We were hoping for more such articles. We had to buy time while the hostage situation was sorting itself out.

As we filed in for our Tuesday-morning meeting, it was obvious that things were starting to move. In the past week, the size of our ad hoc team had rapidly expanded as the concept of operations began to take shape.

A dynamic new personality was assigned to the team in the person of Major General (later promoted to Lieutenant General) Philip C. Gast, former chief of the U.S. Military Advisory Group (MAAG) in Iran. General Gast had gone through the first embassy takeover (in February) and had been forced to exit Iran during the November revolution. His background made him especially valuable to our team. He not only knew the Iranian military capabilities but was savvy to the politics of the Iranian government, although this was fast becoming ancient history, since the military had failed to bring order to the revolution and Khomeini had seized control.[1] General Gast had been heavily involved in assisting President Carter's emissary Air Force General "Dutch" Huyser, who had been sent to Tehran in January to persuade the Iranian military to transfer its loyalties from the Shah to a replacement civilian government. Although his background was basically in fighter aircraft, the general had a respectable grasp of Special Operations techniques and an appreciation for the unique methods and marginal safety criteria we usually trained and operated under.

Within days of joining us, General Gast brought aboard other staff officers, Lieutenant Colonel Bob Dutton and Major "Pappy" Stoles, who had served under him in Iran.

Bob had worked with General Gast in the MAAG as an adviser to the Iranian Air Force and knew Iran's air defense capabilities, in addition to having extensive knowledge of airfields, military bases, and disposition of forces. Bob also had air commando experience flying B-26s in Laos during the early stages of the Vietnam War.

Pappy was an electronics warfare officer, expert in countering the Iranian radar system. He had been an adviser to the Iranian Military Aircraft Control and Warning Systems program. He could tell us how to detect and defeat the Iranian radar network, which unfortunately was an American system and pretty good. However, on the positive side, the Iranians lacked the technical knowledge to keep the electronic gear operating at all of their radar sites.

---

[1] Ambassador William Sullivan predicted that the Khomeini government would eventually prevail in the struggle to control Iran. It is puzzling that Washington seemingly ignored their senior on-scene diplomat at the time.

Two more important newcomers to the team were Army Lieutenant Colonels Pete Dieck and Sherman Williford.

Pete was assigned as our communications officer, with access to the best equipment in the Joint Communications Support Element (JCSE) inventory.[2] He had just arrived when the Unconventional Warfare Branch anteroom began to fill with numerous dedicated Teletype systems. We completely circumvented normal circuits and set up special equipment to communicate directly with our field units, which minimized exposure of our sensitive message traffic.

Sherm, a Vietnam veteran, was the commander of a select Ranger battalion. He was to provide forces for securing the refueling site and the extraction airfield. With his spit-and-polish attire and white sidewall haircut, he made the rest of us look disreputable. All of Sherm's troops that I met were hardcore warriors.[3]

And it was at this meeting that I finally met Colonel Charlie Beckwith—my first encounter with the controversial Special Forces combat veteran I had heard so much about. When we were introduced, I realized that this was the guy I had seen going into General Vaught's office that first day.

It's hard to sort out my first impression of Charlie, because his reputation preceded him. He was husky, about six feet tall, with ample muscle on his rawboned frame. I remember thinking he looked like a man you wouldn't want to tangle with, meaner than a junkyard dog, strong-jawed, a glint of fire in his eyes. Charlie's a rough, gruff, shoot-from-the-hip, abrasive guy who just happened to put together a first-class commando unit against tremendous bureaucratic resistance. He exuded pride in Delta Force and its unique capabilities, the likes of which the average American could not begin to comprehend, but should be comforted in knowing exists.

---

[2]A JCSE is a communications support element that augments joint operations with qualified technicians and the latest state-of-the-art equipment for command and control purposes.

[3]Unfortunately, with all of the new people on board, orderly planning did get sidetracked on occasion. In fact, for a short time it seemed we had two separate staffs functioning independently of each other until Jerry King restored centralized management. To keep everybody working from the same sheet of music, all planning initiatives were subsequently routed through him.

If you had a responsibility to support Delta, he was going to make damn sure you could deliver. He would test you time and again until he was confident of your reliability. That propelled him smack dab into the middle of everybody's business, and often the sparks would fly—oh, how they'd fly!

The Army was light-years ahead of the other services in having a certified combat unit capable of dealing with hostage situations. I was told by people who should know that Delta was second only to the British Special Air Service (SAS), which has had decades of experience in counterterrorism. American proficiency was considered more on a level with that of the German GSG-9 Border Guards (an elite unit born out of the Black September terrorist action at the 1972 Munich Olympics).

So, as we went into this meeting, about the only element lacking was a logistics officer to tend to our requests for support equipment and supplies to sustain field operations. With these mounting requirements, we would need one soon. For now, it was up to each component commander to see that his forces were properly equipped. (See Figure 2, page 68.)

I envied Beckwith in this regard. He already had an established supply system, responsive to his needs and with funds available to obtain special gear required.[4] The rest of us were left with beg, borrow, or steal procurement methods the likes of which I hadn't seen since Vietnam.

As the meeting got under way, the Chairman confirmed that the Navy RH-53D was the chosen helicopter and laid out the details. The helos were to come from a Navy minesweeping unit at Naval Air Station, Norfolk, Virginia. The Navy had gotten thirty of these specially configured aircraft in the early '70s and had been using them worldwide in a mine countermeasures role. They were to be manned by Navy and Marine aircrews.

The unit tapped to provide the Rice Bowl helos had just returned from extensive exercises in Canada and was in the process of reassembling the machines to resume local training. When the skipper of this unit, Commander Van Goodloe, was alerted to prepare for a secret mission, he was not given any details and therefore assumed it was to be an Indian Ocean mine

---

[4]The JTF never did develop an effective system to manage finances, which was a continual source of problems, as we had no way to pay for needed equipment.

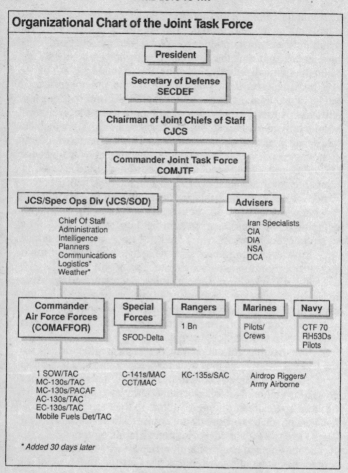

Organizational Chart of the Joint Task Force

President

Secretary of Defense SECDEF

Chairman of Joint Chiefs of Staff CJCS

Commander Joint Task Force COMJTF

JCS/Spec Ops Div (JCS/SOD)

Chief Of Staff
Administration
Intelligence
Planners
Communications
Logistics*
Weather*

Advisers

Iran Specialists
CIA
DIA
NSA
DCA

Commander Air Force Forces (COMAFFOR)	**Special Forces**	**Rangers**	**Marines**	**Navy**
	SFOD-Delta	1 Bn	Pilots/ Crews	CTF 70 RH53Ds Pilots
1 SOW/TAC MC-130s/TAC MC-130s/PACAF AC-130s/TAC EC-130s/TAC Mobile Fuels Det/TAC	C-141s/MAC CCT/MAC	KC-135s/SAC	Airdrop Riggers/ Army Airborne	

* Added 30 days later

countermeasure mission. It was on this assumption that he chose his aircrews. Marine Lieutenant General Shutler in conjunction with Chuck Pitman selected the Marine aircrews. These fliers also were not told the true nature of the mission.

There were seven five-man helicopter crews selected. The Navy provided the squadron commander, and Navy pilots were in command of the helos because of their familiarity with the RH-53D.[5] The Marines would fly as copilots to utilize their experience in operating over land at extended ranges and from unprepared landing zones. The Marines also knew how to handle the .50-caliber machine guns to be mounted in the doorways of the choppers.

Jerry Hatcher and Chuck Pitman were assigned to figure out the helicopter fuel needs and where best to establish a rendezvous point for the airdrop of fuel bladders. Additionally, they would coordinate with Colonel Beckwith to determine how many RH-53s would be required to insert Delta into Iran and then get the rescue force and hostages to an extraction airfield.

As I listened, I was thinking that I knew Air Force helicopter pilots who had operated aboard carriers (even some smaller ships) and were experienced in most of the tactics that would be required, including the use of night-vision goggles.

However, these pilots were spread throughout various Air Force squadrons, and rounding them up would certainly raise a few eyebrows. From the standpoint of security, perhaps the Navy/Marine selection was more practical. My concern was that we select the best people for the job, and I suspected that the Navy pilots had little, if any, experience operating in the desert, or on night low-level, long-range, deep-penetration missions into hostile territory.

Carrier operations had little resemblance to the tactics required for this mission. Could the Navy pilots master all of these things in the time we had available? That's where the rubber meets the road—we'd soon find out.

"Seventy shooters!"

A heated debate had developed between General Vaught and Charlie Beckwith over the size of the commando force needed to do the job. The agitated Special Forces colonel insisted that he would have to have seventy men, while General Vaught was just as adamant that any number over forty would be too many. The

[5] I do not view the Navy and Marine helicopter crew selection as a matter of each service having to play a role in the rescue mission (service bureaucratic parochialism, as some have called it). At that point, it was more a matter of those owning the equipment flying their own aircraft. Right or wrong, that seemed to drive the initial selection of aircrews. If anything, the fault was in a failure to perceive the training problems this decision would later produce.

general also expressed concern that the helicopter force needed to airlift seventy commandos could reach unmanageable size.

Underlying this exchange was the fact that the Delta commander and the Joint Task Force commander didn't get along. This was the first time I had seen Charlie in action, and he lived up to his reputation as a tough infighter—obviously he wasn't awed by rank.

Charlie launched into a staccato explanation of what his forces had to do, and why the number had to be seventy.[6] He and his "combat-savvy" staff officers had given the subject more than casual attention. He rattled off almost to the man what each would be required to do once through the embassy wall and inside the compound.

Beckwith didn't budge . . . and the number of shooters officially became seventy.

With seventy commandos, they concluded that four helicopters, plus two spares, would be needed to carry Delta and the required special support equipment.[7]

The Chairman picked up the secure phone and put in a call to the Commander in Chief Atlantic. Holy smoke! He was directing CINCLANT, Admiral Harry Train, to prepare six RH-53D helicopters for shipment to Diego Garcia—details to be worked out later.

If anyone there had had any doubts about the decisiveness of

---

[6]Gayle Rivers, British author of *The War Against the Terrorists*, speaks out strongly against America's use of an "armada-sized" force to attempt the hostage rescue. He favors instead a small, highly skilled group of expert counterterrorists similar to that used by the British SAS to neutralize the terrorists at the Iranian Embassy in London (1980). This comparison is ridiculous. If the hostages had been in downtown Washington, D.C., it would have been relatively easy for Delta Force, as well. It also should be noted that Rivers's credibility has been called into doubt by the London *Times* and his claim to being a former member of the SAS has been proved false.

[7]In *The War Against the Terrorists*, author Rivers relates sketchy details of a get-together at which he and a small group of multinational counterterrorism operatives formulated a plan to assault the embassy and free the hostages. He claims this plan was put forward to Washington but vetoed on grounds that it wouldn't be an all-American operation. I don't know if President Carter (or his advisers) ever received such a plan.

General Jones, those doubts were laid to rest then and there. I'm sure Admiral Train wondered if he'd ever see his helicopters again.

The Chairman also notified the Commander in Chief Pacific, Admiral Robert Long, that his carrier task force in the Indian Ocean would accommodate these helicopters, emphasizing that this was a most sensitive matter and was to be treated as close-hold information.

Here it was, November 20, and the wheels were now set in motion to move the helicopters aboard the aircraft carrier *Kitty Hawk* steaming toward the Indian Ocean. On the other hand, we didn't have much of a plan yet on how we would use the chopper force.

The Chairman was concerned that if the ayatollah carried out his threats against the hostages, we wouldn't have forces in position to do anything about it. He wanted those six RH-53s aboard the carrier and ready for emergency use in case the President was forced to order action that would require moving American forces into Iran.

The Special Operations MC-130s were selected to carry Rangers and their equipment for the airfield assault and to air-drop fuel bladders to set up a rendezvous point for the helicopter force. Strategic Air Command KC-135 tankers would be used for in-flight refueling of the MC-130s.

The Ranger company would go into action on the second night, riding in on the MC-130s and securing an extraction airfield (we had yet to identify such a field). The helicopters would carry Delta and the hostages from Tehran to this airfield, then the C-130s would haul everyone out of Iran.

Charlie Beckwith wanted Special Operations combat controllers to train Delta for the fuel airdrop and asked for the team commanded by Air Force Major John Carney (at that time based at Charleston AFB, South Carolina).[8] Charlie had worked with Carney on numerous occasions and trusted him—but that didn't

---

[8]Special Operations combat controllers are an offshoot of the World War II Pathfinder teams that were parachuted into combat zones to set up clandestine airstrips or airdrop zones for commando raiders. They are a tough breed of cat and have come a long way since those early days, with much new hardware and greatly broadened skills tailored to working in hostile territory.

mean he wanted John and his team to go into Iran with Delta. He was dead set against taking any personnel into Iran who were not part of his commando force, figuring they could be a burden to him in a combat situation. He figured anything that needed doing could be learned by Delta's troops.

Charlie won this point . . . and he wasn't done yet. The next item on his agenda was air support over the embassy while Delta was taking it down and getting the hostages out. Like everyone else, he was worried about those screaming mobs. He didn't want them swarming into the area and engulfing his force in a mass of humanity from which escape would be impossible.

Of course, given the circumstances of how the rescue was going to have to be performed, any air support would have to be closely controlled. We weren't going to go that far just to have Delta and the hostages shot up by our own aircraft. Also, the President had made it clear there was to be no carnage in the streets. This would require an aircraft that could unleash firepower with surgical accuracy at night.

I had already thought about it, and the only aircraft I knew of that could do this was the Air Force's AC-130 Spectre gunship. The Spectre, with an in-flight refueling capability, also had the range we needed. Fighters or bombers were definitely not suitable, with ordnance that could easily obliterate the embassy and surrounding areas. I had flown the AC-130 in night close-support missions and was intimate with its capabilities. With this aircraft, I knew we could pinpoint targets with the required firepower.

Some of Charlie's soldiers had worked with AC-130s in Vietnam, and he knew the accuracy of their fire-control systems with 20mm, 40mm, and 105mm cannon. He wanted the AC-130.

Dammit, that's just great. We need these birds and they're on Guam.

I didn't have an idea how to get my hands on them, because I didn't even know why they were there. But we would have to have them soon for training with Delta and the Rangers.

The decision would be up to the Chairman. At least we'd planted the seed in his mind. He would have to decide the priorities for the AC-130s—there weren't enough in-flight-refuelable

Spectres in the Air Force inventory to handle more than one long-range mission at a time.

As the meeting ended, my juices were really flowing. We had gotten more done in this one meeting than in all the others combined. It was a red-letter day! Sure, we still had much to decide and much, much more to do, but we were finally on track and building up a head of steam.

7

THE SPECTRES

November 22—Hostage Day 19
<u>Associated Press</u>
WASHINGTON—A buildup of U.S. Navy aircraft carrier striking power in the Indian Ocean-Arabian Sea area is a visible warning that President Carter may order retaliatory strikes against Iran if American hostages are harmed or killed.

On orders of Carter, the 81,000-ton carrier *Kitty Hawk*, with its 85 bombers, fighters and other warplanes, left the U.S. naval base at Subic Bay in the Philippines on Wednesday. The *Kitty Hawk* was escorted by two destroyers, a cruiser, a frigate and a tanker.

The ultimate destination of the *Kitty Hawk* is being kept secret, but the powerful force is expected to move toward the Arabian Sea.

By my third week in Washington, I could have negotiated the rutted path across the grounds between the Pentagon and my Crystal City hotel blindfolded. I welcomed the exercise and relief from the mental strain of the marathon planning sessions that these walks afforded.

The constant diet of sandwiches and irregular restaurant meals had taken a toll on my weight—I had dropped about twenty pounds. But I could afford it, since I had arrived in Washington with over 200 pounds hanging on my six-foot-one frame.

My sparse wardrobe was beginning to show the ravages of time and continuous use. The liner of my blue blazer was becoming tattered and was hanging below the coat line in places. Beckwith never bypassed an opportunity to needle me about who my tailor was. No sweat—a pair of scissors took care of that in short order. I wasn't there for a fashion show.

I was beginning to resemble some of the Delta liaison officers coming and going from JCS/SOD. Bucky, Slick, Country, and I made quite a natty quartet when we hung out together. But I was missing the Smith Brothers face hair—no mustache or beard. I didn't chew tobacco either, but I continually puffed on fat stogies, which made up for it. We were noted for our puffin' and spittin'.

The funding for Rice Bowl was taking a long time to sort out. I guess JCS was short of contingency funds, so for the time being, each unit would have to continue funding its own personnel.

It was Thanksgiving Day . . . just another work day.

I ambled into the Special Operations Division at the usual early hour. General Taylor was waiting for me. "Jim, I've got General Vaught's permission for you to work on a short-suspense special project today involving the AC-130s. With Dunwoody's people on Guam, you're the resident expert. I need you to determine the feasibility of an AC-130 strike on an airfield deep in Iranian territory . . . and I need the answer by early tomorrow morning."

He told me this would be one of several projects to punish the Iranians if they did anything stupid to our hostages. Apparently, during an earlier planning session with the President's National Security Adviser, discussions had centered on various airstrike options against Iran should Khomeini start killing our people.

I started working on computing the geometry and firing orbits and reviewing ordnance-effects charts. The Chairman wanted to be briefed on the study, which I labeled the "Golden BB Option," early the following morning, so I wasn't going to have much of a Thanksgiving.

But Yeoman Collins and his wife had other ideas. It was about noon and my nose was in firm contact with the grindstone when "the Yeo" placed a magnificent feast in front of me—turkey, dressing, ham, mashed potatoes and gravy, candied yams, and pumpkin pie. This couple outdid themselves in cooking up a Thanksgiving dinner for us working slobs, and they endeared themselves to us forever. This thoughtfulness provided some semblance of a Thanksgiving for those of us confined to the

Back Room. At least the thirteen hostages that had just been released were now home having Thanksgiving with their families.

As the day wore on, I knew that to complete the Golden BB concept I would need the plans for the AC-130s now on Guam. I needed to know if I could piggyback Golden BB onto whatever plan they had and at least have the benefit of what they had already learned. When I informed General Taylor of this, he had Lee Hess escort me to the Operations Planning Group, where they were working on numerous offensive options against Iran. Great! Now I was going to learn why the Spectres were on Guam, and this might help me figure out ways to incorporate them into the rescue mission as well.

Lee led me through a maze of passageways into the bowels of the National Military Command Center and to a special room set aside for General Taylor's OPG.

Air Force Colonel Dave Forgan was running the show here, and he had Major Jim Quinn brief me on the Guam mission. The plan was, if the go-ahead was given, for Dick Dunwoody's force to move forward to Diego Garcia to launch a night strike mission against a coastal target in Iran.

The strike force would have Navy fighter cover from the Indian Ocean carrier task force. SAC KC-135 air-refuelable tankers (ARTs) were in place at Diego Garcia to refuel the gunships on both prestrike and poststrike legs of their mission.

The round-trip distance for the Spectres was 5,000 nautical miles, but the crews at Guam were certainly not strangers to long-range missions. I found out that when Dunwoody deployed the four AC-130s, they flew the 7,200 nautical miles from Hurlburt Field to Guam nonstop in twenty-nine and a half hours with four aerial refuelings per aircraft. Compared to that, the twenty-one-hour mission I was planning for them would be a piece of cake. Well . . . they might get shot at more on this one, but that was nothing new to these combat veterans.

After the briefing, I asked if they could get me a secure phone hookup with Lieutenant Colonel Floren White or Lieutenant Colonel John Gallagher, the commander and ops officer of the AC-130 outfit on Guam. I needed to review my Golden BB plan with them to see if they agreed with my ballistics and feasibility assessment.

In minutes, the call was through to the SAC command post on

Guam and I was giving White and Gallagher the basics of Golden BB. I told them to mull it over and get back to me in about four hours. They liked the idea of the attack on the airfield and eagerly accepted the challenge.

I returned to the Back Room to arrange my planning documents. I was to accompany General Taylor to the Chairman's office at 6:30 A.M. to lay out the Golden BB plan.

It was about 4:00 A.M. when John Gallagher called from Guam. The message was what I was hoping for: "Yes, the strike mission is possible. We'll make a junkyard out of the place."

Golden BB was feasible! Of course, total surprise was the key. We would have to catch the Iranians napping and knock out their air defense radar system. No small task, but knowing the havoc a Spectre can produce, I had little doubt about the outcome if this plan was put into action.

Why tactical fighters or bombers were not chosen for this job was never explained to me, but I assumed that they had been considered and ruled out. We seemed to be obsessed with less provocative surgical-type missions at that time.

At 6:30 A.M., I was firmly ensconced in the Chairman's outer office, having a helluva time staying awake, while General Taylor was in laying out the plan for him. I was only there in case some question came up that wasn't answered in the folder, which was just fine with me.

In about twenty minutes, General Taylor came out with a broad smile on his face. "Good show. The Chairman bought it. Now, keep it under wraps and updated in case it is ever called for."

General Taylor also wanted target studies on various locations in Tehran. The Chairman wanted a list of targets and supporting data compiled for his review. As best I could determine, these would be considered for punitive strikes after the hostages were rescued.

What an enlightening day this Thanksgiving had been! With all this gunship business, I now had solid information on what had been going on all around our rescue effort . . . and I could see serious conflicts. While I was in the Operations Planning Group I met people working on other options that ranged from fighter-bomber strikes to the seizure of Kharg Island. Even naval blockades of the Persian Gulf were being planned.

Judas priest! If any of these plans were put into action, we could kiss any rescue mission goodbye. Any punitive attack would surely put the Iranians at a level of alert that would make a rescue mission impossible. On the other hand, if Khomeini and his thugs started killing hostages, rescue would become a moot point. Retaliation attacks would be the only game in town, militarily.

That morning, I asked General Vaught if he knew about all of these strike packages. Man, did that hit a nerve!

He growled: "I may not be aware of all of their plans, but I have the Chairman's assurance he will not employ any of those avenging schemes without first consulting me."

I suggested that we bring in the key gunship planners from Guam and read them in on our mission. Perhaps it would clear the air if they could see both sides of the coin. Even though compartmented in their group, it could keep things on track if they knew what was going on in Rice Bowl.

He considered this for a moment, then said, "Okay, go ahead. But only the primary planners. I'll tell the Chairman."

I immediately called Floren White on Guam and told him to get to the Pentagon as soon as possible, and to bring his ops officer and a flight planner with him.

They were to be briefed for a totally different mission from the one they had deployed for . . . and it wasn't Golden BB.

When the planners from Guam arrived four days later, we already had the go-ahead to use the AC-130s for close air support to cover Delta.

Meanwhile, I gave them their briefing and could sense their mounting excitement. John Gallagher's grin got wider and wider as the briefing progressed, and I thought his eyes were going to pop out as I went over the rescue plans and how the gunships would fit in. I'd worked with John on a special mission in Korea and knew him to be a tiger in the cockpit.

In a whirlwind of activity over the next couple of days, we went over all aspects of the mission.

For target study, I had selected aerial photographs showing the embassy buildings and grounds and Tehran's Mehrabad Airport. Also, other key targets in Tehran were reviewed for potential strikes to help Delta to withdraw after the embassy assault.

For inside the embassy grounds we worked out a grid system for directing fire into specific areas. It was an alphanumeric system similar to automobile maps of cities and could be used by Delta's ground controllers to provide a quick reference to a target for the gunships. This system would hold radio jabber to a minimum while directing fire. Delta's spotters would tell the gunship sensor operators the letter and number on the map corresponding to the desired target. The gunshippers would then locate this point on their TV-like screens and provide steering guidance to the pilot, who would maneuver the aircraft into position and commence firing when cleared by Delta.

We also spent considerable time going over the rules of engagement for preventing unnecessary killings. If Delta felt that mobs were about to form or that the revolutionary militia was attacking their flanks, the AC-130s would be called in to fire ordnance into the streets to discourage them. But there was to be no firing on the mobs or anyone else unless directed by Delta to save American lives.

Targets at the airport were Iranian F-4s as well as transports and tankers. If aircraft movement was detected, the Spectres were to prevent the fighters from taking off. We definitely did not want F-4s attacking the C-130s or the helicopters as they were getting out of Iran. There was also a plan in the works to have Navy fighters provide cover for the departing forces.

The ground-control radar site north of the airport was also on the target list. Without radar for vectoring, even if any fighters were to get airborne they would find it almost impossible to locate us in the darkness with our lights off.

We confirmed our earlier estimate that there was also a marginal capability for the Iranians to employ their American-made surface-to-air missiles against us. But because they still didn't have any of these on the launch platforms, we gave this a low probability as a threat.

Our intelligence team had also verified that there was little threat from antiaircraft artillery, since most of the Iranian big guns remained stored in holding areas.

Their heavy-caliber machine guns could present problems for our helicopters, but our RH-53 crews would have .50-caliber guns to defend themselves, and the AC-130s could help suppress that threat also.

However, the gunships' mission was to keep the mobs off the streets around the embassy. They would be carrying a special type of munitions, developed for use against trucks in Vietnam, that produces a spectacular sparkling effect. This ordnance was an excellent fire starter, and I felt confident that it would hold even the most fanatical of mobs at bay.

When we got to the training aspects of the Spectre role, it was clear that this would have to be carried out from Guam, where the gunships would remain for the time being. I told the AC-130 planners that current commitments wouldn't permit any of the gunships to return to CONUS. Some of the Kadena-based C-130 low-level experts were to be sent to Guam to instruct the crews in the special tactics required.

To approximate the gunship profile for the rescue mission, a training scenario was laid out in that part of the world. The AC-130s would depart Guam, and rendezvous with KC-135 tankers en route to a country in the western Pacific. After refueling, they would drop down on the deck to enter that country's coast, continue on to a simulated embassy location, then pop up to firing orbit and fire their weapons. Finally, they would drop back down to low level, exit the country, link up with the KC-135s for refueling on the return leg, and land on Guam some seventeen hours later. This was identical to the Night-Two Egypt-to-Iran-and-back scenario of the actual mission.

The Guam crews would need night-vision goggles for their low-level night training, and we rounded up enough to get them started; more would come later.

Secure radios for command and control presented a problem we hadn't solved. All of the Joint Task Force elements were experiencing the same difficulty, and our communications officer, Pete Dieck, was thrashing around for a solution. Pete and Delta's communications people were trying desperately to get their hands on state-of-the-art satellite radios. We were going to have to have reliable and secure command and control communications.

Another problem we would have to solve was increasing the AC-130 fuel reserve with external tanks to add range and loiter time over Tehran. There were still some of the engineering experts around who had built the gunship for use in Vietnam, and we were confident they could solve the problem. With this part of the mission now on track, two of the gunship planners headed back to Guam to put together a training program and further develop their tactics. I didn't know at the time when we would be able to get the Spectre force back to Hurlburt for incorporation into our CONUS training and rehearsals, so we would just have to plow ahead. In the meantime, we'd use a surrogate crew that knew nothing about the Iran mission and move forward with the training program. John Gallagher would stay around for a few weeks to work with this crew and set up demonstration exercises with Delta Force.

Although they would be training halfway around the world from the rest of the rescue team, I was confident that if President Carter called our number, the Spectre crews would be ready.

8

OPENING DRILLS

November 27—Hostage Day 24
<u>Associated Press</u>
TEHRAN, Iran—Islamic militants said today they have rigged the U.S. Embassy to blow up on command, and the Iranian armed forces went on alert as Tehran seethed with rumors of an impending U.S. attack and warnings that American agents were plotting to infiltrate the embassy.

The UN Security Council was gathering in New York to discuss the Iran crisis. But Ayatollah Ruhollah Khomeini, convinced the United States had the council on its side, rejected in advance any decision it might make as "dictated by Washington."

It had been three weeks since Lee Hess escorted me through the corridors of the Pentagon and into that inner sanctum where the Iran rescue mission was being planned. Three weeks of full-throttle effort and now we were ready to concentrate on training.

We had known from the beginning that the rescue was not going to be easy. But we had solved many difficult problems and were still working on others. We had the basics of a reasonable plan, and the latest Iranian threats heightened our anxiety and fired up our determination to get it into the field, where we could continue to fine-tune it until we had a winner.

With various political, geographical, and logistical restrictions, it was going to be tough to put this baby together and still maintain super-tight security. The book hadn't been written on this one yet.

In 1970, Major General LeRoy J. Manor, USAF, the Joint Task Force commander of the Son Tay Raiders, sequestered his entire force at a remote location where he had them all under his thumb. He developed his training plan in mid-August of that year and started training in early September. They were kept together rehearsing at one location as a unit in total isolation.

From this secluded area, they rehearsed their North Vietnam POW camp assault over a hundred times before departing to the war zone in Southeast Asia. They launched from an American air base, conducted a hit-and-run raid over relatively short distances, and recovered to the same country they had launched from on the same night.

By comparison, Operation Rice Bowl was a much more complex two-night arrangement with a much larger force, operating over much greater distances. Our units would have to launch from widely diverse geographical areas, join at a rendezvous somewhere in Iran, refuel, and proceed to the objective area to insert the assault force. Then, on the second night, we'd do the same thing to pick up the commandos and the rescued hostages.

It was a "dicey" command control problem from the outset. Getting all of the JTF assets into position at the proper time and place was going to require masterful coordination. Each commander would lead his unit through the entire operation from start to finish. We who were planning the rescue would also direct the training, supervise the rehearsals, and eventually participate in the actual mission. Separate staffs did not perform these functions; we were one and the same—doing it all.[1]

There was no formal training plan; each commander was responsible for preparing his forces for the combined Joint Task Force rehearsals we would soon be conducting.

We all had significant training tasks ahead of us:

- Initially, Beckwith was to train his Delta Force at Camp Smokey, develop his embassy assault tactics, and determine the weaponry he would need.
- Air Force combat controllers would provide Delta training assistance in setting up a drop zone for aerial delivery of the fuel bladders.

[1]In his book *Military Incompetence*, author Gabriel is again wrong in stating that none of the men who planned the Iran rescue mission were directly involved in the execution phase as in the Son Tay raid. He further states that none of the mission commanders were involved in the planning process. Wrong again! In fact, I found very little in this book that was right.

- Navy and Marine helicopter crews from Naval Air Station, Norfolk, would fly to Camp Smokey and train with Delta in night formation flying and special insertion procedures. They would also test the bladder refueling system.

- The composite helicopter unit and Delta would eventually move to the airfield at Yuma Proving Ground in Arizona and set up operations at a nearby location that the Marines selected. From there, they would train for desert operations.[2]

- General Vaught directed that I be responsible for the Air Force training program and act as his air component commander for fixed-wing assets.

- The 8th Special Operations Squadron's MC-130 night blacked-out landing training would take place at Hurlburt Field and nearby auxiliary landing strips. The C-130s would practice procedures for airdropping fuel bladders at Pope AFB, North Carolina.

- The 1st Special Operations Squadron, the MC-130 unit at Kadena Air Base, Japan, would be working on their night-landing techniques at Pacific bases so they would be as proficient as the CONUS units.

- Sherm Williford's Rangers would develop airfield seizure skills at Wright Army Air Field, Georgia, and we would bring in the MC-130s for practice when they were ready for them.

- KC-135 tankers were to be positioned to provide in-flight-refueling training with the MC-130s, and these aircrews were to develop special techniques in night blacked-out, no-communications join-ups. (I was to oversee this training also, but was provided an officer from the Strategic Air Command to manage the tanker forces. Other KC-135s were needed to practice with the Pacific-based C-130s, and I had to keep an eye on what they were doing, too.)

- Jerry King, assisted by Bob Horton and Maynard Weyers, was to act as coordinator for all CONUS training to pull the

---

[2]The helicopter unit had been formed on an ad hoc basis and was the only JTF element not having a parent unit. Providing support for a hodgepodge setup such as this constantly created management problems that would have been handled routinely by a parent headquarters. It would have been far better to assign a single unit from one service for this part of the mission.

Joint Task Force program together. They would be receiving the training requests on secure phone and Teletype circuits and passing them to the component commanders for implementation. (Colonel King's small Unconventional Warfare Branch would quickly become overtaxed by all the staff actions requiring attention, a serious manpower problem that was never resolved.)

- General Vaught would visit the various task force units in the United States to monitor their training and to provide guidance and continuity. He would make sure that the units were developing the required levels of proficiency and training for the proper events to support a common scenario.

- General Vaught and General Gast, accompanied by CIA liaison officers, would make frequent visits to Camp Smokey to touch base with Beckwith and the Delta planners and, when necessary, brainstorm solutions.

- Beckwith and the helicopter experts were given the added problem of finding a plan to get chargé d'affaires Bruce Laingen and his two associates out of the Ministry of Foreign Affairs, which was about a mile from the embassy.[3]

It was obvious from the way we were forced to train that operational security was going to be a continual problem. Most of the units were going to have to fit practice for their rescue mission specialties in with their normal schedules to keep their local headquarters from focusing undue attention on them (we were authorized only to brief key supervisory people at each base).

This was to become one of the more difficult aspects of the training program, especially for the Air Force units. You can't just go flying airplanes willy-nilly anyplace you want to without attracting attention. We would be forced to use trusted key personnel to stop interference from outsiders.

[3]We had known Laingen and two others had been detained November 5 and placed under armed guard at the ministry. Had we been able to exchange information with State Department counterparts, other information we needed could have been more readily available as well. It was a mistake not to have this channel open.

As in the case of the Son Tay raiders, it would have been ideal to isolate the task force where we could pursue our training program under cover.

There was one site we wanted to use that would have supported our entire force, but we were refused permission to use it.[4] We were told national security priorities would preclude our use of that location. The remaining installations that we examined could not accommodate this large a force without compromising security.

Another problem with this large-scale isolation criterion was that we had no idea how long we would have before we might be called on to swing into action. This depended on the President's decision based on an assessment of the diplomatic situation.

It would have been a nightmare to keep several hundred people sequestered for months on end. As desirable as this security precaution is, it was designed for short periods of time. After that, all sorts of unmanageable problems could surface.

For these reasons, we became locked into the practice of bringing the forces together for training and then returning them to their normal duties at their home bases. Only Delta Force and the helicopter crews at Yuma were able to maintain any semblance of isolation. Eventually, even Delta gave up on the idea.

So, any comparison of the logistics of Operation Rice Bowl and the Son Tay raid would have to be relegated to the apples-and-oranges category. The neatly packaged Son Tay operation was a far cry from the much larger, more diverse Rice Bowl.

Rice Bowl training and other preparations were greatly hampered by distance, communications, and time-zone problems created by the physical separation of the forces.

We were up against an entirely different type of target from Son Tay, with very different defenses and geography. The Son Tay group knew when they wanted to attack the POW camp and could back their training program off from that point. We operated in a vacuum, not knowing when, or if, we would be called

---

[4]Some published reports and various authors have been critical of the JTF for failing to locate the entire force at one site and training together for the mission. Be assured that a concerted effort was made to accomplish this, but unnamed persons or agencies thwarted these attempts. This may have been due in part to a belief at the time that a military rescue mission was not a serious consideration.

upon. And, of course, the Son Tay operation was conducted in wartime, when it's much easier to move forces undetected because of the high level of military activity throughout the war zone.

Our orders were to develop a military rescue plan that had a reasonable chance to succeed and then wait for National Command Authority to determine if it would be used. Not knowing if and when we would launch was difficult to handle emotionally—it was tough to keep the forces mentally up for the mission. However, there was a plus to this timing—the longer we waited, the more time we had to improve our tactics.

Ours was a tenuous amalgamation of forces held together by an intense common desire to succeed—but we were slow in coming together as a team.

As we set forth on the training phase, each component commander was going to have to exercise strong, innovative leadership to make this mission gel.

Since General Vaught had directed that all rescue operations conducted in Iran would be accomplished without lights, the helicopter and C-130 crews would be flying, landing, taxiing, and taking off with their birds blacked-out. If anyone happened to hear us, we'd make it damn tough for them to see us or identify us as American.

Because our plan centered on a desert refueling operation, a major part of our training effort would be directed at the helicopter crews using night-vision goggles for blacked-out operations in areas of heavy dust. Commander Van Goodloe likened it to flying a visual flight rules mission (in the clear) under partial instrument conditions.

The Chairman had given us the go-ahead to commence a concentrated flying program to develop night-vision-goggle tactics. We were going to have to teach ourselves, and time was at a premium.

I was concerned that the C-130 crews would be biting off more than they could chew in these early operations, since their flying hours for proficiency training had been reduced by budgetary constraints. Special Operations crews had been maintaining only a minimum qualification level in night blacked-out tactics. I wanted to ease into this operation with the best-qualified people.

I had directed Les Smith, my lead number cruncher on the navigation problems, to set up a contact point in our Special Ops unit at Hurlburt to get this program going. He tapped Lieutenant Colonel Bob Brenci, the squadron chief pilot, and they handpicked the crews. The criteria were to select fliers who could best handle the demanding skills that had to be mastered and who had the know-how to experiment with the gadgetry available.

At the outset, none of our C-130 units had any night-vision goggles, nor were there procedures for their use. Most of the Special Ops crews had seen these awkward devices and were not excited about using them.[5] So we were starting the C-130 training at the same point as the helicopters were—square one.

The helicopter unit at Hurlburt had a limited quantity of the scarce goggles that they had been training with. Since their birds were of the short-range variety and they had no possible role in the rescue, our needs for the devices took precedence. They were told only that the MC-130s were to have priority in developing procedures for using the contrivances.

We had to develop our own tactics to land in the dark on a blacked-out runway and do it with the same proficiency as daylight landings. This was key to our operational concept and would have to be mastered before we could hope to put a combined training scenario together.

Brenci was told to take it one step at a time and to allow the crews to build confidence in these new techniques. Again, I was struck by the excitement of professionals eager for the opportunity to plow new ground—they were champing at the bit. Experience standards that fliers are required to meet to become Special Operations crew members are among the highest in the

---

[5]These devices had been around since the early '70s, and it was a mystery to me why there had not been a more aggressive effort to perfect blacked-out flying utilizing them. Pilots told me the biggest reason was that the goggles were cumbersome and a flying safety risk. The field of vision is restricted to about 40 degrees, with a loss of visual acuity and depth perception. At low altitude (200–300 feet), the pilot can see ground definition well, but image distortion makes the aircraft seem lower than it actually is. Despite this, with concentrated training it is possible to discipline the perception and become proficient in this type of operation.

Air Force. These men know up front that they are flying war machines and are not members of a joy-riding aero club.

On the other side of the world, the MC-130 crews at Kadena Air Base, Japan, were handcuffed by the realities of the NVG shortage. They had no goggles and we couldn't find any for them. I told the unit's commander, Lieutenant Colonel Ray Turczynski, that he had to do the best he could with the old eyeball tactics while we tried to scrounge some up.

One of the tougher jobs these C-130 unit commanders had was selecting crews. Everybody wanted in on the operation, and only about half of the available personnel were needed. The commanders had to go with experience and consistent performance. This put many of the younger troops on the sidelines for this once-in-a-lifetime mission opportunity.

The search for the night-vision optical devices once again pointed out the need for a logistics officer to keep on top of the constantly surfacing needs for hardware. It was going to be tough enough keeping these widely scattered units on track in their training without having to worry about equipping them with special gear that was difficult to find. This had been taking up too much of my time and energy, so I was delighted when General Vaught announced he was recruiting an expert in this field to handle these chores. Jerry King had been pushing for this almost from the beginning.

In the meantime, Lee and I had used up a lot of hours and cashed a lot of green stamps with old friends in the Special Operations community worldwide in our quest for the NVGs. We would eventually need to equip every crew member with the device.

I had also been thinking hard about aircraft modifications and hardware additions we would need to better equip the birds for the mission. I told Lee about these concerns and asked, "Who in the Air Force MC-130 business can we go to in confidence and have them do these 'spook-works' type of engineering plans for us?"

His answer was to pick up the phone and dial an office on the West Coast. He told whoever was at the other end who I was and then put me on the line. I found I was talking with the commander of an Air Force Logistics Command special projects office in California, Lieutenant Colonel Ken Oliver. After I explained the situation, he said, "I'll do what I can, but without any funding authority to pay for what you want, I don't know how far I can go. I'll get moving on your requests and go as far as I can."

All of these problems notwithstanding, we now had our C-130 training program moving. The aircraft's name, Hercules, was certainly appropriate, because we had a Herculean task for it.

Safely operating the airplane was my foremost concern, but we realized that there was a risk factor involved in such experimental training. I would accept full responsibility for any accident, since these crews were taking on this precarious training based on General Vaught's orders to me. All of our butts were on the line.

Meanwhile, an MC-130 had flown to Pope AFB, North Carolina, and made the first practice airdrop of 500-gallon fuel bladders, pumps, and hoses like those that were to be used at the helo refueling point in the Iranian desert.

General Vaught called in one of his longtime Army Airborne associates, Colonel Bill Foley, from Fort Lee, Virginia, to take charge of the aerial delivery loading and rigging. Foley and his assistant, Chief Warrant Officer John Lamonica, developed the container delivery procedures to be used by the MC-130 loadmasters. The system they came up with, which relied on gravity to extract the load through the rear of the aircraft, required special rollers to accommodate the bladder pallets.

This was the first time 500-gallon blivets (a slang term for the bladders) had ever been dropped by Special Operations crews using the container delivery system. Unfortunately, the testing at Pope was limited to the drop of a single bladder, while mission requirements called for dropping five at a time.

Nevertheless, we felt we were ready for a large-scale training event with the choppers, Delta, Rangers, and combat controllers. A small group of Rangers would parachute in with the bladders and set up the helicopter refueling point. Our main concern was to drop the blivets in clusters close enough to the refueling point to minimize the work required to get them into position.

*   *   *

While the blivet operation was proceeding, I also had to consider the other side of the refueling coin—providing the C-130s the range for their long haul.

General Taylor pointed me to USAF Colonel Billy Batson for the air refueling support we would need from KC-135 tankers (we called them gas-passers). Batson, the Strategic Air Command's tanker manager at Offutt AFB, Nebraska, hastily organized a headquarters staff group to oversee support to the various KC-135 detachments that would be working with the JTF.

Unbeknownst to me, they already had detachments at Guam and Diego Garcia supporting Dunwoody's AC-130 group and were working on procedures for blacked-out night refueling training. These procedures would later prove readily adaptable to the MC-130 operation.

I asked Batson to support our CONUS MC-130 training and handpick crews to work with us as permanent members of our Rice Bowl team. We needed select tanker crews trained and assigned to support the MC-130s and AC-130s throughout the rescue mission.

For this, Billy would require operating locations at Guam, Diego Garcia, Wadi Kena, and in the CONUS. The tanker crews would be performing on a "need-to-know" basis—they would know what to do and who to do it with, but wouldn't be told the purpose of the mission.

The Hurlburt MC-130 crews worked on developing procedures for refueling from the KC-135s without lights or radio communication, but were running into problems. We needed the benefit of what the AC-130 crews on Guam had already found out. They had refined their techniques and had effective tactics in accomplishing this challenging task. We would have to learn their procedures and employ them in our CONUS training.

At the same time, I instructed Ray Turczynski to begin similar training with his unit at Kadena. He sent two of his pilots to Guam to learn the AC-130 tactics.

Having ridden through this refueling operation numerous times, I can say with certainty that this procedure is truly an "immaculate reception." Without a doubt, it separates the skilled pilots from the average airplane drivers. Some make it look easy, while for others it can be akin to a size-18 woman trying to struggle into a size-12 dress—painful to behold.

It is also critical that the navigators become experts in using their radar sets for the air-to-air rendezvous and join-up.

What makes this operation so difficult is the performance characteristics of the two airplanes involved. For the aircraft to travel at the same speed, the jet tanker is approaching stall, using its wing flaps to virtually hang in the air, while the turboprop C-130s have to be pushed to near full throttle to stay in position to take on fuel.

But this air refueling was vital to this mission, and the aircrews were going to have to master these techniques if we were to succeed.

9

THE ROTORHEADS

November 28—Hostage Day 25

<u>Associated Press</u>

WASHINGTON—President Carter says he cannot set a deadline for the release of 50 hostages by Iran and he's asking the American people to be determined but patient.

"Excessive threats" of military action could cause the death of the hostages, a calm, deliberate Carter said in a nationally broadcast news conference today.

Carter refused to discuss the military options he is considering. "I'm determined to do the best I can, through diplomatic means and through peaceful means, to insure the safety of our hostages and their release."

Even as the President was speaking to the American people, six RH-53D Sea Stallion helicopters were slipped aboard the aircraft carrier *Kitty Hawk* as it passed near the island of Diego Garcia en route to the Indian Ocean.

Commander Van Goodloe had sent his squadron executive officer to head up this deployment of aircraft, aircrews, and maintenance people. However, this detached unit was not told of the rescue mission and its personnel believed they were there for a minesweeping operation.

Not only that, the carrier task force commander aboard the *Kitty Hawk* was not fully aware of the helicopters' mission. He had been briefed that the helos were there for several contingencies, one being a possible hostage rescue mission.

There was an impression that the naval task force commander did not consider the rescue option likely and therefore the helos were held in reserve for a minesweeping operation. Flying time and spare parts were conserved for that eventuality.

The *Kitty Hawk* was headed to join the aircraft carrier *Midway* in the Indian Ocean. The Joint Chiefs wanted to flex America's muscles in that area and add clout to the carrier strike force should the Iran situation escalate.

The timely *Kitty Hawk* transit of Diego Garcia was not just coincidence. It was a well-orchestrated event to, among other things, slip the JTF helicopters aboard ship and move them within launch range of Tehran.

It was during this move that we had a near-miss on operational security that could have compromised the mission. As the copters were being loaded onto giant C-5 Galaxy transports at Norfolk NAS, Virginia, the local newspaper tumbled to the activity. The next day's edition carried an article, complete with photos, speculating that the helicopters might be heading for a carrier sailing near Iran to be used in a rescue mission.

This on-target guess kept our cover-and-deception troops hopping as they manufactured a smokescreen that had the helos going to the West Coast for training. Fortunately, there was no follow-up to the story and it died a quick death.

Meanwhile, Goodloe moved his composite group of Navy and Marine aircrews to Yuma. There they would train in an environment similar to the Iranian desert. Chuck Pitman and Jerry Hatcher had made all arrangements to get the force settled in at Yuma and training resumed.

Marine Major Jim Schaefer was assigned to assist Van Goodloe in training the Navy/Marine crews. Jim had been working at Yuma Marine Corps Air Station in a weapons-and-tactics squadron developing procedures for ship-to-shore helo-lift of Marine assault forces. He was the Marine Corps' expert at night low-level tactics and a logical man to direct the training of the Navy minesweeper crews trying to learn these procedures. Chuck Pitman had selected Jim for this job and assigned him to the Joint Task Force as an adviser.

Yuma was ideal from our standpoint—remote, with good cover because there were always mysterious activities taking place there.

The helicopter crews would train secretly from this field until the rescue mission was given the go signal. Now we would see if they could hack the program.

Naturally, since Delta Force would be riding on the copters,

Charlie Beckwith had more than a passing interest in the aviation abilities of these crews. Reports back from Camp Smokey had it that Charlie was coming down on them pretty hard. The word was that he was openly critical of their abilities. He had participated in several local training flights and did not consider the pilots to be aggressive enough. He preferred pilots with a "barn-storming" attitude who weren't afraid to stick their necks out to get the job done.

Not only did these crews have no one with a Special Operations background and experience in night low-level tactics, but there was only one pilot with any in-flight refueling experience. They had their work cut out for them.

I had been trying to think positively about the helicopter pilots, telling myself that they would learn what they had to do. After all, they were the best mine countermeasure chopper pilots the Navy had; surely they could adapt to this mission.

My optimism was short-lived. Not long after the move to Yuma, I was cornered in the Back Room by Jerry Hatcher, who was troubled about the night training under blacked-out conditions. He told me his pilots felt they were violating Navy regulations "each time they fly these sorties," and wanted to know what authority or regulations the Air Force pilots were operating under.

"Jerry, the Air Force has no manuals or operating instructions on this. My guidance to the crews has been 'Keep it safe and use good judgment and common sense.'"

Jerry said he felt that if the helicopter crews were going to take the risks associated with NVGs and low-visibility flying in the dust, someone should give them a waiver to the Navy operating restrictions that forbade what they were doing. Furthermore, he said that these tactics would eventually result in an accident.

I countered, "We all have our necks stuck out on training for this mission, Jerry, but we've found no other way of getting the job done to meet General Vaught's requirements for blacked-out flying. We're getting better at NVG procedures each time we train, and our confidence is building in using the goggles in all sorts of situations. If I thought the crews were doing anything unsafe, I'd stop them. That is your responsibility, too. But be damn sure you recognize the difference between taking an acceptable risk and an outright unsafe situation. That is where common sense and judgment are critical and experience must be your guide."

I reminded him that our Special Operations crews are more accustomed to working with Rube Goldberg devices, because that is the nature of our business. "Developing unconventional warfare tactics and techniques is our stock in trade," I told him.

General Taylor had made it clear to me what my responsibility was: "Do what you have to, but don't have an accident."

I could tell Jerry was still not satisfied. In all fairness, I knew the Navy pilots' concerns stemmed from the fact that this was a totally unfamiliar ball game to them. On the other hand, they were going to have to hunker down and sink their teeth into this mission or step aside for somebody that would. As the senior Navy helicopter expert involved, Jerry had few choices: "Lead, follow, or get the hell out of the way"—an attitude of combat veterans for centuries.

As Jerry headed off to see Admiral Schoultz about this problem, I was thinking that he had only one course to follow—bite the bullet and get on with the program.

Hatcher wasn't the only one who felt this way. Sometime earlier, Van Goodloe, the helicopter flight leader, had voiced similar concerns to me. If their commanders felt this way about it, what was running through the minds of the aircrews?

The "troops" must have confidence in their abilities and their leaders in order to undertake a mission of this magnitude and complexity. I found Charlie Beckwith's words about barnstorming pilots kept running through my mind. If they failed, it would be a real showstopper.

Meanwhile, General Vaught and General Gast were busy laying the groundwork for a test of the Night-One scenario. This would take place at the Yuma Arizona Proving Ground Range. It would be the first joint training effort.

This event would show us where we were and bring out any weak spots that would need more concentrated effort. Also, it would let us see how workable our plans for Night-One were.

To keep sufficient aircraft available, we would need to do a lot of

MC-130 shuffling in and out of depot repair, rescheduling maintenance and accelerating the in-flight-refueling modifications.

We would have to marry the capabilities of the Pacific and CONUS units to meet the mission requirement for five MC-130s with at least one or two spares. And, as rapidly as the situation changed, I was not overly confident that we wouldn't need more of these birds by launch time.

It was coming together slowly, but we were making progress each day. When there was a setback, we would come up with a better way to accomplish the troublesome task. This was one of the main purposes for the individual unit training before putting the joint force together.

Each unit was developing new techniques and tactics that were not to be found in any operating manuals. We were learning the special jobs that General Vaught had defined for us to support the Rice Bowl rescue plan.

As we moved steadily toward the Yuma training exercise, we pinned down many of our requirements, but it became clear that we were going to need considerable airlift support from now on to get the job done.

When we turned our attention to this pressing need, *voilà!*— in walked Lieutenant Colonel John Godowski, who introduced himself as the Military Airlift Command Special Plans Group representative and trusted agent for Joint Task Force support.

Godowski was there to receive our airlift requests and to assign the necessary aircraft to fill the bill.

John set up a channel within the Joint Task Force through which airlift requests were passed. This was efficient and eliminated the duplication of effort we had experienced before.

He was no newcomer to this type of project. He had programmed airlift for Delta on many occasions and was highly regarded for his ability to employ deception to cloak the movement of aircraft carrying sensitive cargo.

John's first job for us would be to set up C-141 airlift to support the Yuma training exercise. He would orchestrate Delta's move to Yuma and the transfer of the fuel bladders from Pope AFB to Davis-Monthan AFB, Tucson, Arizona, where the C-130s would deploy.

* * *

After Godowski tended to the Yuma details, we briefed him on the actual Rice Bowl scenario so he could begin assessing the airlift requirements for both Egypt and Diego Garcia to cover either contingency when we finally selected our forward base of operations.

There were numerous pallets of materials programmed for movement to the forward base if we were given the go-ahead. Wisely, we had begun building our list of supplies early on.

Jerry King's troops were just putting the finishing touches on a flow plan that charted the selective movement of some of our special equipment overseas. It portrayed graphically what day a particular load would have to depart the CONUS to be in place at the forward staging base at the right time. In this plan, the first load would be made up of the least-sensitive materials, such as cots, mosquito netting and housekeeping items, which would not cause speculation. Later loads would be increasingly sensitive until all of the equipment—fuel bladders, gunship ammunition, aircraft ground support equipment, etc.—was in place.

All we needed to activate this plan was the announcement of D-Day for the mission. We would then work backward on the chart to start the loads moving on the correct dates. These moves were spread out over several days so as not to attract attention by bunching up the airlift aircraft at any one field.

Jerry's people constantly revised this chart as more equipment was pressed into use to accommodate changing plans and priorities.

Another officer, Lieutenant Colonel Ron Michaels, joined Jerry's staff to work out a storage plan for equipment and a parking plan for aircraft at the forward bases.

Ron made scale drawings of Wadi Kena and Diego Garcia and used miniature paper airplanes to devise parking plans. It became obvious from Ron's "Ouija board" that Diego Garcia had limited ramp space and would be crowded. We looked again at Egypt as offering a better airfield for our main operating base.

Old Ron took a lot of kidding about his "paper dolls," but these simulations played a valuable role in our decision process.

Two new faces also showed up at this stage of the game—Army Colonel Pete Andre, from the Special Operations Division of Pacific Command (PACOM) Headquarters in Hawaii, and Air

Force Colonel Jim Keating, from the PACOM Contingency Plans shop. Both were here as representatives of their admiral, to work with the Joint Task Force and keep their boss apprised of what was going on.

We gave Pete and Jim the Rice Bowl briefing and then engaged in a rap session. Pete told us about alternative bladder refueling methods that might be useful to us. Although our present training scenario was established, I was interested in anything that would improve our techniques.

Jim was to work with Bob Dutton in reviewing our Rice Bowl helicopter operations. New ideas and constructive criticism are essential to the vitality of any planning group.

With the Rice Bowl plan becoming more manageable and the first joint training exercise set, tensions around Special Ops were beginning to ease. I was looking forward to escaping the Pentagon catacombs and getting back to the flight line and the smell of jet fuel being converted to noise.

As I was wrapping things up in my cubbyhole that evening, "Slick" Wade along with a new Delta liaison officer named "Bumpkin" (pseudonym) sauntered in with an offer I couldn't refuse:

"Hey, Colonel, how about joining us for dinner?"

They were heading out into the suburbs to one of their favorite prime rib restaurants to devour some beef. Colonel Jim Keating, our CINCPAC liaison, was also going along. Jim had bested Slick in a spirited one-arm pushup contest, and was still celebrating his victory.

After putting our names on the waiting list, we found a spot near the bar to have a beer. As we were sipping our brew, Slick cracked open his briefcase just far enough for us to get a glimpse of a rod he was packing. Crissakes! Keating and I nearly stained our Fruit of the Looms.

I made a point of not looking at him and in a low voice said, "Hey Slick, are you planning to blast the horns off a steer and cut your own prime rib?"

He smiled coolly, and, with an innocent but full-of-mischief look, replied, "I've got Delta's operational funds in the briefcase—several thousand bucks."

I chuckled, "Holy Toledo! What have we gotten ourselves into with you guys?"

The Delta troops just sat there, grinning like Cheshire cats, barely containing their laughter.

Oh well, what the hell. At least jail will get us out of the Pentagon for a while. We were beginning to feel like hostages ourselves.

Fortunately, nobody else saw the briefcase episode, and we managed to relax and enjoy delicious dinners. I was learning that Delta had some damn colorful troops in its ranks, and most of them were just as full of surprises as old Wade. But then, they wouldn't be where they were if they were just plain everyday folks like the rest of us.

I relished every moment with them and was proud that they included me in their fun and games during those rare moments away from the job.

These sojourns may have been on the lighthearted side, but the hostage situation and what we were doing continued to weigh heavily on our minds.

With December approaching, the hostages' ordeal was stretching toward a month.

General Vaught called me into his office to discuss plans for the December 3 joint training, which was to be a partial run-through of the Night-One events. He said our planning staff would be flying to Camp Smokey to go over the details with Beckwith.

The general wanted me to take the navigator flight planners with us so we could go through a complete scrubdown of the Rice Bowl rescue scenario, as well as the upcoming practice session.

Back in my planning room, I briefed Lee Hess and the navigators. I told the planners to draw up the maps for the Yuma airdrop to include a night low-level navigation route for the MC-130s to fly en route to the drop zone.

We would only use two MC-130s and one gunship for the exercise, as it was only a limited run-through of the Night-One scenario.

Objectives of the Yuma exercise were to see where we were in our helicopter training; to practice setting up a drop zone; to deliver the fuel blivets in a cluster close to the helicopters; to refuel the helos; and to demonstrate the gunship's accuracy to Delta.

When we arrived at Camp Smokey, Charlie Beckwith was waiting to drive us to his headquarters building. As the car made its way along the road that wound through the forest engulfing the camp, I could hear the staccato sounds of weapons firing. The occasional "whumph" of a larger explosion would rattle the windows of the car.

As we drove along to the chorus of weaponry, we passed several cottages, but there were no signs of life. It was sort of eerie.

What a super place to isolate forces preparing for this kind of a mission. It was not quite large enough for the entire Task Force, but it would have been great to have such a place for all of us.

Shortly, we pulled up in front of a modern brick bungalow about fifty yards off the road. Inside, the place had all the comforts of home.

As was usual with these meetings, the generals went behind closed doors with Charlie for about an hour before we all sat down together. They would be going over the embassy assault, and we didn't need to know those details.

The rest of us gathered around a scaled model of the embassy compound that had been put together by a team that knew what it was doing. It depicted the entire twenty-seven acres and fourteen buildings. Delta's planners had spent countless hours studying the model and detailed floor plans, trying to come up with the best way to break through the twelve-foot-high wall that surrounded the compound and then find and free the hostages and get everyone out to the helicopter pickup point. The sand table was a fantastic planning aid, but Delta still needed a heap more intelligence information on the goings-on in that compound. Until some better sources turned up, the planners would have to do a lot of guessing.

The heavyweights emerged from their closed-door session and we got down to brass tacks, starting with the Yuma training event.

We went over where each of the force components would be based, how they would get there, and in what numbers.

I was surprised to hear that Delta's number was now up to

ninety. This would mean more helos and more fuel. The four helos we had planned for wouldn't be able to carry ninety—we would have to use the two spares, as well.

This turned the discussion to the possibility of adding two more helicopters to the six we had aboard the *Kitty Hawk* for the mission. Jerry Hatcher and Chuck Pitman were to verify the added lift requirements to determine how many more choppers would be needed.

General Vaught said that General Gast and Chuck Gilbert of the CIA would go to Yuma as advisers for the helicopter training.[1]

Although General Gast was not a helicopter expert, he could sure see if the crews could fly the choppers the way General Vaught wanted. And if there were problems, he could get to the bottom of them fast.

The only obvious equipment at Yuma would be seven RH/CH-53 helicopters (allegedly tied to operations at the nearby Marine Air Station). The Navy and Marine helicopter crews were living in quarters on the Army post that supports the Yuma Proving Ground facility. The local Army cadre paid little attention to them.

Delta would arrive at Yuma in a C-141 late at night so as not to attract attention as they moved into the large hangar complex where they would be billeted.

General Vaught then turned to the current version of the actual rescue scenario, outlining the plan we would be testing. He had decided to revise the tactic of airdropping fuel into the desert to establish a fuel cache; there were too many uncertainties involved. The tactic now was for the helos to fly to a preselected remote rendezvous point, and land—and then the C-130s would drop the bladders. This idea would cut the ground time and reduce the risk of something going wrong.

The time needed for bladder assembly, hose hookups, and

---

[1]Author Richard A. Gabriel states in his book that an Air Force officer was put in charge of helicopter training and continuous tension developed between the helo pilots and this officer over how to train. He wrote that bureaucratic infighting was resolved when a Marine colonel (Pitman) was placed in charge of training and the Air Force officer (Kyle) was reassigned as the on-site commander at Desert-I. Absolutely untrue. At no time was I in charge of helicopter training—that job belonged to Hatcher and Pitman.

refueling had to be determined. After establishing an average time for these steps, we could tell when each component would have to launch to allow us to complete this activity and still make it to Tehran under cover of darkness.

So far, so good. This part of the plan appeared workable. But from that point, things got muddier.

The plan was still for two nights, so where would we offload Delta and hide the choppers overnight?

How would we get Delta into the city and up to the wall undetected?

When Delta called for the helicopter extraction, could the choppers land in the vacant athletic field inside the compound? If not, where? The embassy area appeared too small to handle any more than one helo at a time.

How many helos would we need for the extractions at the embassy and the Ministry of Foreign Affairs?

What airfield would we use for the extraction from Iran?

General Vaught told us that our intelligence team was checking out an airfield fifty miles south of Tehran that showed promise. However, we needed a lot more information about the physical layout and security force at the field.

An airfield this close to Tehran? I thought. *Maybe we can go with a one-night operation.*

There might be helicopters in the DOD inventory that could be partially disassembled and hauled into Iran aboard C-130s, then reassembled for the flight to Tehran. If this could be done with enough choppers big enough to haul Delta and the hostages, we might be able to discard the carrier-launch idea.

I made a note to jump right on this idea with the helo experts when I returned to the Pentagon. Anything to avoid that damnable ground-refueling drill en route.

We then turned to some of our earlier ideas for inserting Delta into Tehran—using trucks, or possibly parachuting the commandos in. These hadn't gotten any more attractive, but in this racket you never want to wholly discard any idea. It might just fit into the scheme later on.

So be it. Charlie's planners felt trucks might be the ideal way to move Delta into position for the assault and catch the Iranians by surprise.

We still lacked agents inside Tehran to set up such an arrangement, but Beckwith said he would like to try working that out with his own people. He wanted General Vaught to get the Chairman to put pressure on Director of Central Intelligence Stansfield Turner to support the idea.

The general agreed, but expressed his disenchantment with Turner's assistance—"nonsupportive." About all we had gotten from the Agency so far was jumbled intelligence reports that bore little relevance to our rescue mission.

Discussions continued late in the day on a weighty list of topics. As the meeting ended, we all felt the frustrations of beating a dead horse. We had flapped our gums a lot but hadn't solved many of our problems.

General Vaught perceived the dejection in the room and laid some more of his homespun philosophy on us.

"One could get the impression from our efforts to date that we have nothing but problems and very few answers. In fact, we have been blamed for acting confused while carrying out conflicting instructions."

This drew chuckles.

As the mood lightened, he finished up with another of his patented pep talks, closing by saying, "We've got to remember the magnitude of the problem we face and keep things in perspective.

"As with everything, practice makes perfect, and that's what we need most . . . to get on with our training program and make something happen."

The boss rose abruptly and headed for the door with the rest of us hot on his heels. We all were antsy to get moving. Next stop, Arizona.

10

THE YUMA EXPERIENCE

December 4—Hostage Day 31

<u>Associated Press</u>

TEHRAN, Iran—Acting Foreign Minister Sadegh Ghotbzadeh says the U.S. Embassy hostages will be put on trial "for sure," Iran's state television reported today.

The reported remark was the first time a top official had made such a definite statement of Iran's intent to try the hostages. . . .

It was a crisp, clear Arizona morning at Davis-Monthan Air Force Base. It felt good to escape the stale Pentagon atmosphere and breathe the clean desert air.

We had come in the day before with two MC-130s and an AC-130 gunship and immediately set up a command post at Base Operations. The word was that we were involved in an Army Operational Readiness Inspection, and our comings and goings were little noticed.

About midmorning, we were flown to Yuma Army Air Field for a planning session. We were whisked by car to a large hangar complex that was already buzzing with activity. Most of the people from the Smokey summit were there, along with the helicopter crews, John Carney, our combat controller, and John Gallagher, the AC-130 operations officer. General Gast, Chuck Gilbert, and a Sikorsky helicopter technical representative were on the scene as advisers.

During our ride to the hangar area we had seen seven Navy and Marine helicopters lined up adjacent to an unused runway in a remote section of the airfield. I remembered these birds from Vietnam, where they were used by Air Force Special Operations as well as rescue units. They were "good, bad, and ugly," with a combat reputation as tough war machines.

As I walked into the expansive hangar (dubbed the Taj Mahal), I saw ragtag groups of what appeared to be civilian workmen camped all around the outside of the buildings. Before I could ask what they were doing here, someone said, "That's Delta Force."

Delta Force? Man, some of their faces resembled mug shots I'd seen on WANTED posters. They sure didn't look like any Army field units I'd ever seen. Nobody in this bunch of alien-appearing rogues could have passed a white-glove inspection—or any kind of inspection, for that matter. But then, Delta troops didn't fit any mold. They certainly weren't normal Special Forces types by any stretch of the imagination.

Our first order of business was to survey the desert for a suitable area to hold the exercise. After a short powwow, General Vaught led us outside and we boarded a waiting chopper. As it lifted off, we were suddenly engulfed in one monstrous cloud of swirling dust. The downwash of the helicopter's rotor blades had created its own dust devil. Damn! This was about as much fun as a broken leg. I couldn't see a thing, and talk about vertigo! It felt as if we were going several directions at once.

I had the less-than-comforting thought that the helo driver couldn't see any better than I could.

This interminable seat-grabbing experience actually only lasted about ten seconds and then we "popped out" on top of the dust cyclone. Once in the clear, it was situation no-sweat. The trick for the pilot is to prevent the chopper from turning or drifting in the dust cyclone, because there is no way to know if you are about to run into something or somebody.

Jeez! This was in broad daylight. I imagined what it would be like to pull this off at night with no lights, relying on night-vision goggles. The difficulty factor would take a quantum leap. The vertigo had to be a lot worse.

Then, what about landing? It would be as hard, and probably harder. Flying . . . landing blind. It would take skilled, experienced pilots to master these tactics.

I looked back at our takeoff area and saw that the Delta troops were battling to keep from being blown away by the dust hurricane we had spawned. That ragtag bunch was now a dust-covered ragtag bunch. I could almost hear the choice words about our family backgrounds.

We had been vibrating along in our airborne Mixmaster for about an hour when General Vaught sighted a promising spot and directed the pilot to land.

Once on the ground, it didn't take John Carney long to scope out the area and come up with a game plan that made sense to everybody. Carney was all over the place and in short order had an area laid out to park the choppers a safe distance from the zone where the fuel bladders would be dropped. An adjacent location was designated for Delta's soldiers to watch the live-fire demo. John Gallagher took the lead in setting up targets and double-checking the safety factors.

Beckwith's men marked off the live-fire area with reflective tape to simulate the embassy grounds. They would closely watch how Gallagher would be directing the gunships' munitions on areas designated as streets around the compound.

Soon everything was set up and we were ready for the first practice. We piled back into the helicopter and headed back to the large prefab hangar.

Our arrival was a replay of the earlier dust maelstrom, only this time the Delta troops were chowing down on C-rations. The savagely blowing dust and sand did terrible things to their cook fires, rations, and dispositions.

After landing, we had to make our way through this "hostile" encampment. As we threaded through this instant battleground, I could see the "combatants" were caked with sand and red dust . . . and I didn't want to know what their chow looked like. If looks could kill, we'd all have been dead.

After we were out of earshot, I told Les Smith, "Man, there are some bad-lookin' dudes in that bunch. I'm bloody well glad they're on our side. I pity the unfortunate Iranians they meet up with in Tehran."

Inside the hangar, General Vaught took us into a briefing room and commented on this being our first try at combined training operations and told us not to press safety factors. "If it doesn't look good, back off. We've got time to get aggressive as we gain more experience." Sage advice!

Well, everything looked good. We had a reasonable training scenario, duplicating conditions in Iran to a large extent. The Arizona desert amid mountains was ideal. There was plenty of sand, grit, and dust to create the stress conditions under which the helo crews would have to master the night blacked-out operations with the night-vision goggles.

In the process, they were experiencing degraded weather conditions, including rain, fog, limited moonlight, and the ever-present dust.

When we got back to Davis-Monthan late that afternoon, the C-141 transport had arrived with Bill Foley's 500-gallon fuel bladders and the loadmasters were busy configuring the two MC-130s for the airdrop of five blivets from each aircraft.

Sergeants Duke Wiley and Taco Sanchez were studying the container delivery system (CDS) rigging that Foley's men were using to lash up the bladders for airdrop.

Wiley and his loadmasters were concerned that after the heavy-duty strap holding the bladders was cut, the entire load would roll out too fast. They believed that as the parachute on the first blivet opened, the remaining bladders might fall on top of the billowing chute, collapsing the air cushion underneath and splattering fuel all over the desert. If this happened, the blivets would hit the ground like a ton of bricks.

This sparked a spirited debate over the rigging setup, but Wiley finally yielded to Foley's purported extensive experience in such matters and both MC-130s were configured to Army specifications.

It was shortly after dark on a magnificent moonlit night when our two MC-130s broke ground and winged along the planned low-level route toward the drop site. The flight path simulated the actual low-level route the MC-130s would be following in Iran. Longer practice routes would come later, when KC-135s would enter the training picture.

Meanwhile, six H-53s, loaded with Delta troopers, were lifting off from Yuma Army Air Field to fly their own low-level route simulating the flight from the aircraft carrier to the desert refueling site in Iran.

As the choppers headed for the refueling site, the situation began to deteriorate. The crews were having problems staying in formation and some nearly collided.

As they approached the target area, small fires were lit to mark the landing zone. Then things really got hairy. Some of the pilots, setting down in the dust, nearly lost control of their aircraft. Others gyrated in the dust as if performing some kind of ritualistic dance.

One chopper almost landed on top of combat controllers John Carney and Sergeant Bud Gonzales, who were using hand signals to help the pilot set down. They dove for the ground at the last moment as the helo swooped over, inches above their heads. Shave and a haircut, two bits.

Finally, things settled down and all of the choppers got on the ground and in position for the airdrop. Carney was heading over to talk with the helo crews to find out what the problem had been when he heard a voice coming from the aft compartment of one of the choppers: "I'll be damned if I'm riding back on this thing—I'll walk home first!"

Delta's operations officer, Bucky Burruss, combat-hardened veteran as he was, remembered the evening's ride as one of the more harrowing experiences of his career, which at times he thought would end that night.

Meanwhile, the Combat Talons were right on schedule in one-minute trail formation. The moon lit up their route as if it were daylight. Bob Brenci in the lead aircraft would make his airdrop in radio silence. John Carney would use one of the helicopter radios to warn Brenci of any safety problems.

John had been having problems with Charlie Beckwith since shortly after the arrival of the helicopters. First of all, Charlie was sure the choppers were lined up wrong. They were supposed to be sitting parallel to the C-130s' flight path, and he was positive they were perpendicular. If true, this would have the Talons flying over the helicopters to drop the blivets. John broke radio silence to reconfirm with Brenci that the C-130s' heading would keep the blivets clear of the choppers.

Then John saw that Charlie's people were setting up the airdrop beacon and ground panel markers in the wrong positions. He finally got them to position the panel properly, but the beacon ended up pointed in the wrong direction—the C-130s never received its signal.

Even though John's sole purpose there was to teach Delta how to set up the drop zone, Charlie seemed to be questioning his advice at every turn.

At one point during this exchange, Charlie retorted, "What

are you telling me—I've got some dummies out there?" Wisely, John didn't reply.

With things not going well, the worst was yet to come.

As the C-130s came roaring into the drop zone and the navigator gave the green light to release the load, all five blivets left the first aircraft in less than five seconds. The Army rigging that Duke Wiley and Taco Sanchez had questioned did just what they feared it would—it was a bomb.

The first load went out the ramp, and before the chute could deploy fully, the other four blivets fell on top of the canopy, collapsing the fluttering silk. The whole load Roman-candled into the drop zone like overripe watermelons falling off a garbage truck. Before word could be gotten to the second Talon, its load was on its way to the same fate as the first. Ten blivets were dropped—three survived. We were off to one bad-as-bad-can-be start.

Both aircraft sustained minor damage to their cargo compartments, but luckily nobody was injured. Other than generating some severe cases of "tight jaws" and inflicting a little sheet-metal damage, the incident left the aircrews no worse for wear.

The gunship mission for that night was canceled, and Delta and the helicopter people cleaned up the drop zone and, discouraged, returned to their hangar.

We repaired our MC-130s when we got them back to Davis-Monthan and discussed how to revise the rigging to solve the problem.

Meantime, General Vaught called Bill Foley down to Yuma and chewed about five pounds of prime beef off his south end. He told him to be ready to try it again the following night and "by God, get it right this time, or else!"

When Foley got back to Davis-Monthan he immediately arranged with John Godowski, our MAC airlift scheduler, to have another load of blivets flown in from Fort Bragg.

At the same time, loadmasters Duke Wiley, Ray Doyle and Taco Sanchez spent several hours with Foley's Army riggers in coming up with a new method to rig the bladders.

The blivets arrived the following day, and Wiley's loadmasters worked with Foley's people in preparing the loads. Everyone seemed happy with the rigging this time.

We again took off at dark and flew a repeat of the previous night's low-level scenario, arriving at the drop zone at the appointed time.

The helos, with Delta aboard, again went through their NVG operations in the dust, flew their low-level route, and landed at the drop zone—but not without problems. Again, pilots battled the controls in the dust, and some became disoriented and got lost during the map-reading navigation phase. It was still a hairy operation.

The second night's airdrop went off without a hitch. Delta had the drop zone marker panels set up right, and the two Talons airdropped ten bladders intact, along with pumps and hoses. The dispersion pattern was wider than hoped for, causing the ground teams quite a struggle in rounding up the doughnuts and getting them positioned near the helicopters for the refueling. They did it, but it took a lot of time and effort.

Beckwith was becoming convinced that he had neither the time nor the patience to fool around with such an unreliable and cumbersome system. This and the calamity of the previous night had built up a distinct lack of confidence in the aerial delivery option. The consensus was that we needed to find a better way. But at least for now we had a proven means to deliver the fuel if we were given the go.

The final segment of that night's training came through with flying colors. The Spectre gunship crew put on a spectacular demonstration of sustained and accurate firepower that royally impressed Delta Force. A few of the soldiers had never seen the Spectre work its magic, and it "watered their eyes." The old heads who had seen the gunship perform in Vietnam were convinced that it was essential to have the AC-130 overhead when the embassy takedown occurred. From that night on we'd have the Spectres firmly written into the plans and would train with them every time we rehearsed.

When it was all over, General Vaught held an impromptu meeting in the big hangar at Yuma. Something had to be done about the helicopter operation, and soon.

Delta troops were getting skittish about riding in the choppers the way they were being flown, and some felt they were downright unsafe. Charlie would no longer have any part in his troops being exposed to the dangers of riding with these pilots. We had to face the facts—this bunch couldn't cut the mustard.

General Gast, Chuck Pitman, and Jim Schaefer put their heads together and agreed the helicopter crews had to be replaced. General Vaught accepted their recommendation that more experienced crews were required and told Pitman and Schaefer to call in the best people available.

The general had witnessed the performances on both nights and realized that these particular pilots were not progressing fast enough.

The general also wanted a third pilot added to each copter crew to assist in navigation and flying, but was later talked out of this idea by someone in the Joint Chiefs of Staff hierarchy.

Out of the clear blue sky, another C-141 landed on Friday, the day before we were to return to Hurlburt, and off-loaded a 3,000-gallon palletized fuel bladder. This gargantuan thing made the 500-gallon doughnuts we'd been playing with look like inner tubes.

The only problem was, I didn't know why it was there or what we were supposed to do with it. So I called JCS/SOD to see if anybody there could shed some light on this new wrinkle.

Bob Dutton, one of the new planners, came on the line to explain: "Pete Andre used the system on an exercise and we sent it out to you in hopes you might find a way to fit it into your plans."

It took a second for me to react. "Bob, do you realize we need a whole new concept of operations to use this bladder arrangement? We'll need a place to land and then pump gas off the airplane to the choppers. It can't be air-dropped. Do you have a place for us to land yet?"

Dutton said they were working on it and that Nick Kilgore had a couple of spots in mind.

I told him we'd play with the system and try to figure out how best to use it.

After I rang off, I rounded up Duke Wiley and his experts and we headed for the flight line to examine this new hardware and see what we might be able to do with it.

When it was all laid out on a flatbed truck, we recognized that what we had was a customized C-130 bulk fuel delivery system from the Vietnam era. It was designed to fit in the back of a specially fitted C-130 called a Bladder Bird, which was used to haul fuel to remote airfields.

The system was fairly easy to use, but we had none of the hoses, filters, and pumps. All we could do for now was fill it with jet fuel and fly it around the flagpole to see how it handled. Then we would try a couple of night short-field landings and make sure it would ride okay.

So we slid the large aluminum pallet aboard one of our C-130s. A fuel truck was brought alongside to gas the mammoth pillow tank, which was now flat as a pancake.

As fueling started, gasoline began leaking from numerous connectors. We stopped gassing and tightened all the nuts, bolts, and seals. The system obviously had not been used for a long time.

Finally, we were able to get fuel pumped into this thing that looked like an overfilled waterbed. The fuel odor was strong, so we kept tightening fittings. By the time we were ready to fly, the pungent smell had pretty well dissipated.

As expected, the test flight was uneventful. Now we needed the hardware so we could develop procedures for pumping fuel from Bladder Birds to whirlybirds. But that would have to be done at home base.

We returned to Hurlburt, while Delta Force remained at the Yuma Proving Grounds to continue training with their weapons, practicing assaults on a simulated embassy compound, and working with the helicopters on ground blivet refuelings.

General Gast, Chuck Pitman, and Jim Schaefer remained at Yuma as well. They would organize the new helicopter crews (already en route) and start their night training.

Our first practice session had not been overly successful—we seemed to come away with more problems than we started with. But worst of all, our helicopter force was in total disarray.

11

NIGHT-TWO

December 9—Hostage Day 36

Associated Press

PALM SPRINGS, Calif.—The United States should warn Iran it will declare war on that nation if 50 Americans held hostage in Tehran are not quickly released, the former director of the Defense Intelligence Agency said in an interview published Saturday.

Retired Lt. Gen. Daniel O. Graham, in charge of the DIA in 1974–76, lashed out at the Carter administration for "inept handling of this international disgrace."

Graham called on Carter to "make it clear to the Ayatollah (Khomeini) we are willing to go to war on this issue."

From Hurlburt, we cranked up full-bore operations in an old hangar loft area that Colonel Bob Pinard set up for us. He was the maintenance honcho who would keep us supplied with aircraft for the duration of this operation. The hangar wasn't much to look at, but it was off the beaten path and nobody bothered us. I would oversee the Air Force part of the mission from here.

Pete Dieck, the JTF communications officer, equipped our loft with secure telephone and Teletype systems and we were assigned a communications team. They became our "ears," manning the phones twenty-four hours a day and ensuring that we had a secure means to communicate with JTF headquarters.

At this time, I met Lieutenant Colonel Roland Guidry, the commander of the Combat Talon squadron at Hurlburt. Because Guidry was a newcomer to Special Ops, I had been working with his ops officer, Les Smith. But end-running the squadron commander was a poor way to do business, so I briefed him on the mission and put him in charge of the Hurlburt MC-130 operations.

As I went over the nuts and bolts of what we were doing, this six-foot-two lantern-jawed Cajun was all ears.

I told him to work closely with Ray Turczynski on Okinawa. Coordination between the two units was essential to putting this thing together.

So it was in these austere surroundings that we began preparations for the next training session—the Night-Two scenario, getting out of Iran with the hostages.

The plan was to seize an Iranian airfield with Rangers, receive the helicopters with the hostages and Delta aboard, transload everybody onto the MC-130s, and get out. The Spectre gunships would be providing air cover. Since many of the Ranger Fire Direction Coordinators had never seen a gunship in action, they would have to be trained in how to employ the firepower.

Meantime, the four MC-130 crews had resumed training with the night-vision goggles. Some of the pilots were still struggling. We continued experimenting, trying to come up with a standard technique. It was hair-raising at this point, and I was seriously considering going to the research and development (R&D) people for technical help. Unfortunately, security considerations put the kibosh on that idea, so I decided to let the crews keep working on new techniques.

We took three MC-130s to Wright Field, Georgia, to hook up with Sherm Williford's Rangers to work on the next phase of training—airfield seizure.

For the next three days we tried every way we could to get the Rangers off the airplanes quickly and then get the birds into the best positions to pick up the group coming from the embassy. It was more complex than we had realized.

After the airfield seizure, the Rangers had to be in position to receive the helicopters arriving from the embassy, then get Delta and the hostages aboard the C-130s. A strict accounting procedure was necessary to make sure no one was left behind. This took some time to devise. This sorting-out had to include planning for any injured or wounded to be loaded aboard the aircraft we would have specially equipped for medical evacuation.

We also had to develop an airport traffic control system and radio procedures to keep the aircraft sorted out and to move the choppers to the right C-130s.

Sergeant Rex Wollmann, a combat controller from Hurlburt, worked with the Rangers assigned to defend the perimeter against any attacking forces, trying to teach them tactics of the AC-130.

When we got it all worked out, it went like this:

We would land the first C-130 and lower the ramp, and the first load of Rangers would come roaring out the back of the aircraft in a jeep with a machine gun mounted on it. For obvious reasons, we called them the "Rat Patrol." Four motorbike riders would be hot on their tails and this "Wild Bunch" would barrel for the surrounding buildings and neutralize any resistance.

Right behind them would come fifty-some foot soldiers in camouflage garb, armed to the teeth, to mop up and secure the field. There were about twenty-five more Rangers aboard the second and third MC-130s, and their job was to secure the more remote points on the airfield.

After three days of steady work and a few wrecked motorbikes here and there, we had the Rangers off and running in ten seconds—not bad! Using the NVGs, they were doing well in the darkness, and we felt ready to head west for a joint training session with Delta.

We also tried to train the Rangers on live-fire tactics with the Spectre, but they had difficulty learning the tricks of the trade, and we didn't have time to teach them.

General Vaught had a saying for this type of situation: "It's sorta like trying to teach a pig to sing . . . it's a waste of time and annoys the pig."

There was a message waiting when I got back to Hurlburt. The exercise coordinators in the Special Operations Division advised us to be ready to head back west. We were to test a new concept they had been working on, and this task would take about a week.

It seems General Vaught's lack of confidence in the blivet drop had spurred him to contrive a better method of delivering fuel to the helicopters.

The general had been intrigued by our rudimentary test of the C-130 bulk fuel delivery system at Davis-Monthan, and he had prodded his intelligence team to find us an airfield in Iran where we could land and use this system to refuel the choppers. He wanted Nick Kilgore to find him a reasonably remote location that was on caretaker status. We didn't want to get in a fire-fight while slipping into Iran—our initial goals of surprise still held fast.

In the meantime, while the intelligence people were searching for that location, the general wanted to get on with developing tactics for this type of operation. Thus, he directed that both concepts of inserting and extracting the rescue force be tested during a mid-December training event.

Since we had been training with the Rangers to assault the extraction airfield near Tehran, which we were now calling Manzariyeh, the JTF planners concluded that the same tactics could be employed to seize and secure an insertion airfield. Obviously, the Rangers would need a complete engineering diagram of this new target, but that would have to wait for more intelligence data.

The plan was to insert the Rangers on the first MC-130 to land and have them seize the airfield and control the surrounding area. The C-130 tankers would land and get into position to refuel the helos upon their arrival. Delta Force would come in with the choppers and assist the Rangers until the helos were gassed. Then Delta would reboard the choppers and continue on toward Tehran while the rest of the force would withdraw to Egypt. We would then recycle preparations for the C-130s and Rangers to assault Manzariyeh on Night-Two to extract the rescue force and, if we were successful, all of the hostages.

I called Jerry King at the Pentagon to inform him that we would be ready for the next shindig, but there was a problem: we'd have to jury-rig the 3,000-gallon bladder, since we lacked the proper pumps and hoses.

Jerry said that would do, as the idea was to walk through the new insertion concept and none of the field commanders had been exposed to the idea. For now, the planners were just looking to establish feasibility.

"On the other hand," he said, "General Vaught expects the extraction event to go fairly well because those procedures have been practiced." He said that the intelligence data on Manzariyeh were "looking real good" and it was almost certain that this air-field would be the linchpin for the extraction.

We were on to something good with the new insertion option. It was obvious that the planning and intelligence staffs had made progress since the last time I was in D.C. The pieces seemed to be falling into place.

I called the Special Ops Division and announced that we had a workable system, but "get us the equipment and people to do the job right!"

They said that they would pass the requirement along to a Lieutenant Colonel John Barkett, who had been brought in by General Vaught as our task force logistics officer.[1]

Now that was good news! A logistics officer . . . finally! A central point to support our supply needs. But poor old Barkett was going to need a magic lantern.

"Oh, and one other thing," Jerry said. "The old man is coming down to take a gander at your bladder refueling operation to-morrow and ride through a blacked-out landing with you guys. He wants to check out the proficiency before Saturday's event out West."

I rogered that and told him we'd have it set up for the boss.

General Vaught arrived as advertised and went straight to the bladder-system demonstration, where fuel was pumped to a lo-cally based helicopter. This satisfied him for the time being, but he was anxious to get the correct parts and bladders to enable us to refuel all six choppers with this technique.

Next on the boss's agenda was the blacked-out ride on a Talon. It was a pitch-black night—no moonlight to enhance the effi-ciency of the night-vision goggles. The general boarded and chose to stand behind the copilot's seat for a ringside view of the proceedings.

---

[1] A logistics officer is critical to a Special Operation such as this rescue mission, and one should have been assigned from the start. Barkett had to devise his own system and succeeded only through determination and perseverance. It amazed me that he was as successful as he was. He was forced to use renegade tactics to procure what we needed. This points up the need for an established classified lo-gistics support system that can effectively supply a Special Ops task force's needs and still maintain the necessary secrecy.

On the first landing, the aircraft made positive contact with the runway—very positive contact, a strut-bender. The general was speechless, mainly because he was pitched forward into the copilot's seat and his voice box took a solid whack from the headrest. He couldn't say a word for about ten minutes.

After a couple more pretty rough landings, he regained his voice and told me he'd seen enough—terminate! He wasn't happy with what he'd seen . . . and felt.

After we landed and got off the aircraft, he let me know in no uncertain terms that the landings had to get smoother. On top of this, he told me there were still too many lights on inside the plane—blacked-out meant just that! Was he mad!

He said he wanted more work on this at Yuma when we deployed out West. "I want to see far more proficiency in these tactics."

I told him that, realistically, we were getting about all we could out of the night-vision goggles. We needed some means to generate artificial light when there was no moonlight. He said he'd see what he could find for us and try to get something out to Yuma in time for the exercise.

After the general left, I had Roland Guidry assemble the pilots for a little fish-or-cut-bait session. I came down hard on them.

"Dammit! We're going to standardize our NVG procedures. You guys put your heads together and come up with the best techniques, then put 'em on paper. Each crew *will* master these procedures or be replaced. It's as simple as that. We've screwed around too long with individual preferences. We're all going to do it the same way—and that will be the right way. Now get with the program!"

12

THE BLACK PAPER

December 15—Hostage Day 42

<u>Combined News Services</u>

BRUSSELS, Belgium—The United States has cleared the way for the use of European military bases as staging points if it is forced to take military action against Iran, it was learned Friday.

The clearances, which came from a number of America's 14 allies in NATO, were conveyed to Secretary of State Cyrus Vance in two days of meetings here.

Meanwhile in Washington, President Carter was reported Friday to be "moderately encouraged" by developments in the Iranian crisis and some administration officials said they were expecting release of at least some of the 50 American hostages before Christmas.

We positioned the aircraft at Norton AFB in California for the next training session. No matter where we went, the first order of business was to establish a direct communications link to the Special Operations Division in the Pentagon. We had to be ready to respond rapidly to any orders we received.

When it got good and dark, I sent the Talon aircrews out to work on their blacked-out landing tactics.

Roland Guidry took Sergeant Wollmann, our combat controller, to a nearby Navy base, where they had the tower operator turn off the runway and taxiway lights. Each crew then flew a series of traffic patterns and practiced the now-standardized procedures for blacked-out landings.

By the time they were ready to return to Norton, their confidence had risen considerably with the obvious improvement in skill. Roland reported that most of the landings were grease jobs—the procedures were working. We'd show General Vaught we could fly 'em the way he wanted. We were eager to redeem ourselves and to patch up our damaged pride.

The next day, as the sun cleared the horizon, the three Talon aircraft lifted off from Norton for the short flight to Yuma, where a joint planning session and briefings on the coming events were scheduled.

This was the first chance I'd had to find out what had happened to the helicopter contingent since the full-scale house-cleaning in early December. The new guys were mostly Marines.

When Pitman took charge (Captain Hatcher was no longer involved), he got on the phone to General Shutler and tapped the resources of Marine helicopter pilots worldwide. Those selected were fliers whom he and Jim Schaefer personally knew as the best "stick and rudder" men. Nine pilots, including Commander Van Goodloe, had been replaced. Only four crew members from the original Navy group were still around.

Replacing Van Goodloe as flight commander was Lieutenant Colonel Ed Seiffert, a Vietnam veteran with "beaucoup" helo experience. He had arrived on the 9th and also had a hand in choosing the others.

Schaefer, who had been acting as an adviser, was assigned crew duties and became Seiffert's deputy and operations officer. Jim had a leg up on everyone else, as he had been involved in the helo training program from the beginning. Seiffert and Schaefer were now responsible for the helicopter training agenda.

With this big joint training venture staring them in the face, the new chopper crews had been practicing for only about a week and were just getting organized. It was asking a lot for them to take part in this exercise, but the pressure was on to make up for lost time. The rest of us couldn't wait—they'd have to learn as we exercised.

While this was going on, General Gast had been working with Chuck Gilbert of the CIA to get Palletized Inertial Navigation System (PINS) equipment installed in the helos. These precision systems were expected to aid the Marine pilots immensely in finding their way from the carrier across the desolate terrain of Iran. In addition, one RH-53D was fitted with an Omega navigation system,[1] which would provide a cross-check for the PINS.

With everyone assembled, General Vaught ran us through the game plan. We would practice the separate activities for the next three days and then put it all together on the last two.

These were going to be five busy days.

It was during that first night at Yuma that I had the solution to one of our bigger problems handed to me on a silver platter. We'd finished practicing the airfield seizure and refueling training and were performing blacked-out landings. The tower operator had turned off the runway lights and all of the other airfield lights and was in a mild state of shock. Our "I can hear you, but I can't see you" operations were blowing his mind.

I was overseeing the operation from the control tower when Major Keith Nightengale came up the ladder carrying a roll of black paper (Keith was another one of Vaught's special-assignment guys that kept popping up in the strangest places).

Examining the roll of paper, I said, "Okay, Dick Tracy, what's this?"

"General Vaught says to cover your landing lights with this stuff and see if it helps. It's supposed to screen out the white light and give you infrared illumination that can be seen with the night-vision goggles. The 'black light' that shines through can't be seen with the naked eye, so nobody will know your landing lights are on."

"Jeez, Keith. If it works, it solves one of our big problems. Where did it come from?"

"When he got back from Hurlburt, General Vaught was telling Chuck Gilbert"——our resourceful CIA jack-of-all-trades——"about the night landing problems and Chuck got this stuff from the Company's lab. So if it works, you can thank Gilbert. Chuck told the general that this type of paper was used back in World War II——it's been around for a while."

That's a kick in the head! I thought. *If this stuff is any good, why in heaven's name haven't our Special Ops aircraft been fitted out with it long before now?*

---

[1]This system was also installed in the mission helicopters aboard the *Kitty Hawk*.

At any rate, it was sure worth a try. And I knew Chuck wouldn't have foisted scrap paper off on us.

However, I could see one problem right away: we would have to find a way to get it over the lights so that the in-flight wind blast wouldn't strip it off. I would get right on that as soon as I got back to Norton.

We seldom saw the light of day during these joint training sessions. Normally, we finished up just before sunrise. But, of course, that was the objective—"doing it in the dark" was becoming second nature to us.

After the first two days of training, General Vaught wanted us to conduct a blivet drop at the Yuma Proving Grounds, just to prove the reliability of that tactic. So, on Monday night, Bill Foley's riggers loaded an MC-130 with five blivets and a mule tractor and the aircrew took the load out and made a perfect drop to the helicopters. Delta helped the chopper crews assemble the fat doughnuts, pumps, and hoses, and the refueling went off without a hitch. Still, it was time-consuming, even with the tractor, to round up the blivets in the dark and get them assembled.

Charlie Beckwith flat didn't like it. He reasoned that there was always a risk that one or more of the chutes wouldn't open or that one of the blivets could get stuck in a ravine and we'd end up deep in hostile territory without enough fuel to complete the mission.

I think everybody understood the risks involved in an airdrop, but the plan was workable and good to have on the shelf in case we needed it. The bulk bladder delivery system was being developed, and there were many problems. Airdropping the fuel was our best option if we were given launch orders anytime soon.

Bill Foley was ecstatic over the airdrop success and more than a little relieved to be out from under the dark cloud of the earlier failure.

A group of us took the mysterious black paper out to one of the C-130s on the flight line. First, Roland Guidry and Sergeant Tom Daigenault, one of the flight engineers, climbed up on an engine stand and taped the paper to a landing light. When we started the engines, it took the wind blast about half a second to strip the paper off.

As the man said, "If at first, you don't succeed . . ." And we tried again, and again, and again. But nothing worked. Foiled by the light's heat and wind blast, we were totally frustrated by midday. It was time to call in the experts. I rang up Ken Oliver at the Lockheed project office across town, explained the problem, and asked if he could give us a hand.

It wasn't long before Ken came rolling in, and he had his chief flight engineer, Sergeant Buie Kindle, with him. About two hours later, we had a rig that we felt confident would survive at least a couple of landings. Now we had to wait for darkness. Then we would fly down to Yuma and give it a try.

When we got out to the aircraft that night, our hopes were high, but we really didn't know what to expect.

The first thing we did was stand in front of the aircraft and have the pilot briefly turn on the landing and taxi lights. As the lights were activated, we spotted a small leak at one of the clamps holding the paper in place. A couple of twists on the screws took care of that.

Next, we all donned NVGs and had the landing lights turned on again. The instantaneous excitement was electric. "Incredible!" "Fantastic!" "I don't believe it!" The air was filled with superlatives—and *light!* We were bathed in, by God, *light!*

When the infrared taxi lights were added to the pattern, it was like standing on a stage under spotlights. I took off the goggles—pitch-black. Goggles on—light. Wow! My thoughts were racing. The elation I was feeling was indescribable.

"Enough," I yelled at the pilot. "Turn 'em off, quick, before we burn 'em out." Then, to everybody in general, "Let's head for Yuma. I'm busting at the seams to see how they work on blacked-out landings."

Needless to say, when we went through our landings at Yuma, the black paper worked beautifully. This was, indeed, a major breakthrough. From that night on, the ability to land almost anywhere in the world blacked-out at night was reality. General Vaught put the word out to all JTF component commanders: "See where the IR lighting fits into each of your tactical plans and get it installed." I was hoping the Agency had enough of the paper to go around until we could get a more permanent device available. We would be burning up a lot of it in training and rehearsals.

One other very positive thing came out of this new development—the C-130 crews were exhibiting intense pride. We could do things with our C-130s that no other air force in the world could do. Special Operations tactics were more than just words of mystical bullshit. It's just a damn shame it took so long for us to get this help.

After stumbling around in the dark for a month, the JTF had just come up with a tactical capability that vaulted us into a new era of night operations.

PART TWO

REHEARSAL / FINE TUNING

13

, NEW ONE-TWO PUNCH

December 18—Hostage Day 45

<u>Associated Press</u>

TEHRAN, Iran—Hopes for an end to the U.S.-Iran crisis received two major setbacks today as Ayatollah Ruhollah Khomeini called for the extradition of the deposed shah from Panama and government officials blamed the United States for the assassination of a high Iranian official.

Khomeini backed the hard line of students who issued a statement from the occupied U.S. Embassy compound accusing Foreign Minister Sadegh Ghotbzadeh of "excessive talking" that encouraged the United States to think Iran had changed its position on the extradition of the shah. . . .

Rehearsal night arrived, and it was almost as if Mother Nature had decided to throw in her own test of our new capability—an inky-black night. The moon had taken a powder.

Full of enthusiasm provided by the new infrared-lighting techniques, we had steadily improved our success at bladder-refueling the helos and completing the Rat Patrol insertion and seizure operations. We had also been successful in our extraction tactics.

The scenario for the rehearsal was as realistic as we could make it. The Night-One insertion would take place at the Marine Corps airfield at Twenty-nine Palms, California.

I had only three MC-130s and one AC-130 for the mission. One Talon would carry the Ranger team and the second would carry the 3,000-gallon bladder. The third MC-130 would act as a tanker but wouldn't have the bladder. We would be able to pump gas to only two or three choppers, but we could learn the techniques required for operating the system to make it a first-class gas station. With the three Talons, we would learn more about the parking and marshaling aspects required.

Bob Brenci, our MC-130 chief pilot, had been selected early on to fly the lead Talon and make the initial landing. He and his crew were particularly adept under blacked-out conditions. Bob became the "Godfather" of the Rat Patrol Rangers.

The rehearsal got under way with Brenci loading the Rangers at Yuma. Bob saw six H-53s depart for Twenty-nine Palms with Delta aboard. They would fly a night low-level navigation route and rendezvous with the Bladder Bird some three hours later.

Back at Norton, Major Jerry Uttaro was readying his bladder-laden C-130 for takeoff. Captain Bob Meller, who would be piloting the empty Talon, was also getting ready to go. They timed their launch to tag in behind Brenci's bird, which was now en route to Twenty-nine Palms. They would sequence themselves en route so that they would land fifteen minutes behind the lead with a three-minute separation.

After a two-hour modified low-level route, Brenci's aircraft set up on final approach for landing. It was incredibly dark; it was sort of like flying inside an underground cavern. The approach to the runway, barely discernible on the desert floor, was set up with radar. The navigators got the "Herky Bird" lined up perfectly, and Bob turned on the infrared landing lights and brought the plane down smoothly on the metal-planking surface. From the ground, where I was observing, I didn't see the Talon coming and I didn't hear it until Bob landed. To the observer, there was a sinister air about the whole operation.

The Rangers came boiling out of the C-130 and had the field secured within minutes. They also had five portable lights set up for the tankers, which were now approaching.

The second and third Talons slipped in like ghostly illusions just as the lead had and were positioned for helo refueling. With the naked eye it was impossible to determine what was occurring. Just watching this show gave me goose bumps.

By now, a half hour had gone by and the helicopters should have been arriving, but there was no sign of them. About fifteen minutes later, along they came, but there were only four of them.

As the choppers approached, pressure was applied to the bladder fuel system and the fittings began leaking badly. The week-long exercise had taken its toll on our makeshift system. There was a scramble to tighten everything up.

The four helos that made it to Twenty-nine Palms were positioned to take on gas, but it was an awkward maneuver at best. Even then, we had to back the C-130s partway for the hoses to reach. It was obvious that we needed better marshaling procedures, and we were also going to need longer hoses to maintain safe distances between the whirling chopper blades and the C-130s. (All aircraft kept their engines running at reduced power during the refueling.)[1]

After the four helicopters landed, I found out that the other two had aborted due to mechanical problems. Ed Seiffert's chopper had flashed Blade Inspection Method (BIM) warning lights, and the second had had an oil-pump malfunction.

This was the first encounter with an RH-53D (Navy) BIM situation. The Blade Inspection Method includes two warning lights in the cockpit to alert the aircrew to a potential problem and a second warning system, on each rotor blade, called a barber pole. The blades are basically hollow and are filled with nitrogen gas under pressure. If nitrogen pressure is lost because of some malfunction or impairment, such as a crack in the blade, the warning systems are activated. However, these indications do not necessarily mean that the pressure loss is due to a crack in the blade. A faulty filler valve has been known to be the culprit in some cases.

If the BIM lights illuminate, procedures call for a precautionary landing, engine shutdown, and visual inspection of the rotor blades to find the activated barber pole indicating which one of the five blades caused the problem. The faulty blade is then inspected to see if the source of the leak can be determined. If there is a large crack, it is unsafe to resume flying the aircraft, but if no crack is located or if it is very small, flight may be

[1]There seems to be a consensus among the Holloway Commission and authors Gabriel, Hadley, and Ryan that leaving the engines running during refueling was deafening and confusing and made command and control impossible. Believe me, if there had been a better way, we would have used it. However, early in our ground-refueling experiences with the helicopters we had determined that it was best not to shut down any of the aircraft. The C-130 engines have always been balky in restarting situations, and the helicopters had similar problems. We preferred the noise to facing stalled aircraft.

continued for up to fifteen hours. The danger in exceeding this limitation is that the crack may expand, with catastrophic results.

In this particular training situation, Ed Seiffert confirmed that both warning conditions existed, and properly grounded the aircraft for repairs. Marine CH-53s had only the mechanical warning system. It was the Marines' experience that this helicopter with such a BIM warning, should not continue to be flown for the fifteen hours; in the past some CH-53s had been and had crashed as a result. As near as I can determine, the Marines were unaware of the difference between RH-53D BIM procedures and those of their own CH-53s.[2]

As the refueling proceeded, the leaking got so bad that we had to shut down. Despite this, it was obvious that the system would work with the proper parts installed.

Once refueled, the choppers flew Delta Force to the drop-off point, where they went into hiding for the night. The helos then proceeded on to a separate location, where they were sequestered until the following night.

Meanwhile, the C-130s returned the Rangers to Yuma and then flew back to Norton, thus completing Night-One.

For the second night's assault, at the Holtville, California, airport, we wanted to try a new loading plan for the Rangers. We had found throughout our practice sessions that the airplane was congested and the troopers became disorganized in the dark. We needed to speed up their exit from the aircraft and keep them intact as assault units.

Our solution was to remove the center-aisle stanchions that form the framework for the webbed seats where passengers usually sit and line the floor with mattresses (we nicknamed it the "Sealy Configuration"). This allowed us a better loading arrangement for the jeeps and motorbikes, as well as providing the troops with a more organized seating arrangement relative to the assault sequence.

The Night-Two scenario got under way on schedule Wednesday with the three MC-130s picking up the Rangers at Yuma.

[2]Sikorsky test data available at the time indicated the RH-53D could continue flight if the situation dictated (combat conditions) after experiencing a BIM situation. If aircraft gross weight and airspeed were restricted, structural integrity could be retained up to seventy-nine hours.

They were all smiles at seeing the mattresses (first-class accommodations) and were soon settled in for the low-level flight to Holtville.

At midnight or thereabouts, Delta Force took down the simulated embassy and called for the helicopters to come and get them and the hostage stand-ins.

Simultaneously, we got the Rangers on the ground at Holtville and they had the deserted airfield secured in under fifteen minutes, using blacked-out procedures. The Rangers were getting good at prowling around in the dark. However, they still had some inadvertent encounters with objects and needed a means to provide better illumination for the night-vision goggles. (We would install infrared lens covers on their jeep and motorbike lights as soon as more black paper became available.)

When the helos arrived at Holtville with Delta and the "hostages," the Rangers were a little slow with their marshaling procedures and had difficulty with the personnel accounting.

In the confusion, the choppers departed Holtville and mistakenly left General Vaught behind. The boss jumped aboard the last C-130, grabbed Sergeant Taco Sanchez by the arm, and yelled, "Tell that damn helo pilot to get back here and pick me up—fast!" He was obviously hot under the collar. Taco passed the message on, and the chopper arrived shortly and picked the general up, to everyone's relief.

General Vaught was still disgruntled when we met for the critique in the prefab hangar at Yuma. Our two joint training sessions had not come up to expectations, even though we had made progress in some areas, particularly night blacked-out landings and the bladder-refueling tactics.

Helicopter operations were pretty shaky. The new Marine crews were having difficulty learning to fly this mission. I felt they were doing as well as could be expected considering they were dealing with unfamiliar tactics on a compressed schedule.

Ed Seiffert was in the process of replacing nine of his pilots because they lacked the flying skills for the job. He had to get better-qualified stick-and-rudder men and stabilize his force. We were still on a ten-day go status.

The boss got down to brass tacks.

We would make a concerted effort to get our second refueling option, pumping from the C-130s to the choppers, up to snuff. But the blivet drop would be it for the time being.

He then directed that all commanders utilize the black paper and said he wanted "no more alibis about not being able to see in the dark."

He laid out the training events each commander was to concentrate on before the next joint practice session, which he told us would be our first full-blown joint rehearsal of the Night-One and Night-Two options. He said this would occur in mid-January.

He hammered hard on the helicopter force to work on their night proficiency and to improve maintenance reliability. "Get more helicopters, if necessary, but make damn sure that six make it all the way through the exercise!"[3]

His next announcement knocked me off my pins. "We're going to take a break over Christmas and New Year's. Be ready to start back to work on January 2. You commanders keep a tight rein on your people and have them ready to return to duty fast, if recalled."

I couldn't believe what I'd just heard. How could we possibly put our training on hold at this time? We had barely gotten started and were certainly nowhere near ready to attempt a rescue. After we'd been busting our butts night and day to get this program rolling, it was to be shelved for two weeks. It just didn't make sense to me. The be-ready-to-go-in-ten-days stance was obviously just a motivation factor. Now, *poof,* it was gone.

Apparently it had been concluded that a Christmas stand-down was in order since the Joint Task Force had been in training since early November. I had also heard concerns that if the troops weren't with their families for Christmas it might draw attention and become a security problem.

My impression was that General Vaught didn't like this decision any better than I did, but was just passing the orders along. I had heard him say that both the Chairman and General Shutler (JCS director of operations) were obstructive and, at times,

---

[3]Colonel Jim Keating, CINCPAC liaison, had been at Yuma observing the helicopter training for his boss, Admiral Long. He reported to the admiral that the crews were not flying good formation—they were too loosely organized and sloppy.

made matters difficult for him. Maybe this was one of those times.

When we got back to Hurlburt that night, my adrenaline was still surging. I knew it was going to be tough to walk away from the concentrated training we had been undergoing, with many events yet to be perfected.

None of the JTF commanders liked the idea of losing control of their people for two weeks—we all were worried that we would spring a security leak. Also, when everyone returned, it would be almost like starting over.[4]

It was a full plate to leave untouched for the next twelve days—but orders are orders. So be it!

---

[4] Charlie Beckwith and I had similar concerns that letting the forces go home over Christmas was a far greater risk to security than keeping them locked into the training program. Someone was bound to make a slip—it was a risky decision. I later heard that there was at least one unauthorized disclosure of our secret mission, but to the credit of the wife involved, she kept the information under wraps.

14

ON THE CHOPPER BLOCK

December 22—Hostage Day 49
<u>Associated Press</u>
TEHRAN, Iran—Ayatollah Ruhollah Khomeini, saying he wants
the 50 hostages to have a "Christmas in peace," has cleared the
way for holiday visits by Christian clergymen to the hostages in
the occupied U.S. Embassy. He said black clerics would be given
priority.

Some of the hostages have not been seen by outsiders since
Moslem militants demanding extradition of the deposed shah of
Iran seized the embassy Nov. 4.

On my return to Washington that Saturday, it was freezing
cold, and since I had been charging around in Florida, Arizona,
and California, I hadn't done anything to winterize my
wardrobe, but I found out during the day that the weatherman
wasn't the only one who had a chilly reception in store for me.

As soon as I arrived at the Pentagon, I went looking for Lee
Hess to get an update on what had been going on there. I
couldn't believe the hustle and bustle in the Special Operations
Division. There were many new faces.

I headed for the Back Room to find Lee.

"Lee, who the devil are all these people running around the
hallowed halls of SOD?"

He smiled. "Most of them are communications types that
work for Colonel King. They operate the Teletype systems in the
alcove between admin and the colonel's Unconventional Warfare shop.

"Also, we finally have a full-time logistics officer, an Army
lieutenant colonel named John Barkett."

"Yeah, I already heard about him. He's supposed to be

working on getting hardware for the bulk bladder system. I want to get together with him as soon as I can."

Another newcomer who had come aboard while I was out in the field was Air Force Captain Don Buchanan, our weather expert. Naturally, he was tagged with the handle "Stormy." He had joined the team to begin working on climatological surveys of Iran and round up resources (weather reporting stations and satellite coverage) he could rely on for usable forecast data.

Unfortunately, after Khomeini's revolution, there were large gaps in weather reporting data on Iran. Stormy was going to have to come up with forecasts covering our planned routes based on what little information he could obtain from the Air Force Global Weather Center at Offutt AFB, Nebraska, and any other sources he could develop.

We were rehearsing the rescue mission to occur under clear weather conditions, and it was imperative that we develop a reliable means to verify that condition before launch.

General Vaught established a daily routine in which Stormy would brief him on the Iran weather for that day and then the following day this would be compared with the actual weather recorded in Iran for that period.[1]

After Lee had brought me up to date on the happenings at JCS/SOD, I turned the conversation to a topic that was really bugging me—the unsettled status of our helicopter component. They were already replacing some of the helo pilots from the newest bunch, and I was thinking it was high time they looked in the direction of the Air Force.

"Lee, if we're serious about replacing some of the new helicopter pilots, then we should bring in some Air Force people with Vietnam Special Ops or search and rescue experience. They do this kind of work for a living. It wouldn't take them long to pick up on this mission.

"The new aircrews have only been at it a couple of weeks and now they're standing down. If we could get the Air Force

---

[1]He missed a few times at first, but his accuracy improved through the following days and weeks. By the time we launched the rescue mission, confidence in Stormy's forecasting seemed very high. However, I'm not sure there was a valid method to verify the accuracy.

helicopter pilots into training by January 2 they wouldn't have that much to catch up on."[2]

I was so certain this would solve a lot of problems that I felt it was my duty to pursue it. I decided the best route to take would be to get General Taylor's support as soon as I could break in on his schedule. Besides, he would want a firsthand report on what had been going on out in the field.

Later that morning I got to brief him on the Yuma training. While doing that, I put in my pitch for bringing in some Air Force crews as helicopter replacements. I urged him to talk with the Chairman.

He said, "I'll look into the matter and get back to you with an answer."

Now that I had General Taylor interested, I was so confident that Air Force chopper pilots would soon show up that I headed back to my office and called Lieutenant Colonel Bill Takacs, in my opinion the "main man" in Air Force heavy-lift tactical helicopter operations. I wanted to give him a heads-up that his talents might soon be needed for a special mission.

After Bill got on the horn, I told him that I was calling just to make sure of his availability—a special mission was involved. "Nothing's official yet, but start thinking about picking five of the best H-53 pilots the Air Force has . . . and stay near a phone for the next few days. But forget this phone call; this conversation did not take place!"

By the time we stopped talking, Bill had probably chomped clear through his cigar. He was rarin' to go if the call came.

Now we're getting somewhere!

I knew that Bill Takacs, with the help of Lieutenant Colonel Woody Kimsey of the rescue service, could pull in some top-drawer "rotorheads" to augment the JTF crews. The Air Force had these kinds of people sitting around on their cans out there

[2]There was a rumor (unsubstantiated) making the rounds of the Marine helicopter crews that the Air Force Rescue Service had been offered the opportunity to assume responsibility for the helicopter portion of the rescue mission but had declined. The rumor had it that the Rescue Service was concerned that becoming involved in an assault operation might jeopardize its ability to operate freely in its international mercy-mission role. I have been unable to verify this, but if it was true, it was an unfortunate decision that denied the JTF access to highly qualified crews.

in operational units and in staff jobs doing menial tasks, and we needed their expertise badly.

A handful of them could be pulled out of various units without jeopardizing operational security. After all, some twenty people for the Marine aircrews at Yuma came from the Marine Corps Air Station at New River, North Carolina, and any security problems caused by the vacant slots in that unit didn't seem to concern the general staff. The old argument rejecting Air Force pilots because their absence might cause a few raised eyebrows would no longer hold water.

It wasn't that Air Force helicopter pilots were necessarily any better than those from other branches, but that they had flown these types of sorties in Vietnam and were still maintaining proficiency in them. Some had limited experience with night-vision goggles, and most, if not all, had flown in dust at low level.[3]

It was clear to me that Air Force crews could have been trained and ready to go much sooner than any others. I thought this was a primary consideration, and therefore I couldn't understand why these crews were being overlooked, especially now that some of the second group of Marines were also on the chopping block.

The Army had many fine rotorheads around who had experience in similar missions, but none of them were qualified in the H-53; anyway, we didn't have time to train them.

I didn't care what type of uniforms were in the cockpits of the Joint Task Force helicopters, it was the minds and skills in the uniforms that I was interested in. Considering the team we had put together—Delta, the Rangers, and the C-130 crews, all top-of-the-line—we couldn't settle for less in the helicopters. A chain is only as strong as its weakest link.

I spent most of that day hanging around the Special Ops Division with only one thing on my mind: how General Taylor had fared with the Chairman on the helicopter issue. I was having a hard time concentrating on anything else and didn't accomplish much.

---

[3]This was confirmed later by Colonel John Roberts, former commander of the 20th Special Operations Squadron (helicopter) at Hurlburt. He said he had six crews NVG-qualified who had been training in night low-level tactics under combat conditions in the desert. Equally important, nine of his people were former CH-53 pilots and could have been requalified in short order.

Finally, in midafternoon I got to chat with the general, and what he had to say floored me.

"We are going with all Marine replacements to the helicopter crew force. They have already been selected and will soon be in place at Yuma."

I couldn't believe it. "Sir, did the Chairman make that decision?"[4]

"Jim, how the decision was arrived at is a moot point. It's been made and General Jones has approved it. It's a closed matter! Get behind the Marine crews and support them."

I could see the door slam on the subject, but felt compelled to say what was on my mind.

"General, I want to say this now so there will be no 'I told you so' recriminations later. I hope we don't live to regret this decision."

I left it there with General Taylor, but was not yet ready to let it drop completely. I talked with both General Vaught and General Gast and urged them to rethink the issue.

I'm not sure whether General Vaught pursued the matter further, but the decision was apparently set in concrete. It was a delicate subject and we were told to stop talking about it—the die was cast.

There comes a time when a staff officer has to shut up and get on to the next thing. Case closed, court adjourned; I'd been heard and lost my case.

I certainly didn't want interservice bickering to become an issue—this mission was too important.

---

[4]An assistant close to the Chairman at the time revealed that General Jones felt he could not take the helicopter mission away from the Marines. The Chairman was embroiled in a heated argument with the Marine hierarchy over their tactical aircraft (fighters) coming under wartime operational control of a joint service theater air commander. Also, General Jones placed complete confidence in the advice of his director of operations, General Shutler, and in Colonel Chuck Pitman, his highly regarded helicopter expert.

15

THE FEZ INSERTION

December 24—Hostage Day 51
<u>Associated Press</u>

TEHRAN, Iran—Foreign Minister Sadegh Ghotbzadeh said today that explosives had been found in mail going to the 50 American hostages at the U.S. Embassy in Tehran, Tehran radio reported.

While quoting Ghotbzadeh as saying explosives had been discovered in mail sent to the Americans, Tehran radio made no mention of how or where the bombs were found.

It was afternoon before I had a chance to ask Lee how the AC-130 overseas training at Guam was getting along. He told me that they had been flying seventeen-hour low-level training missions in Korea every two or three days and were getting in some live-fire training on a bombing range near Saipan, in the Marianas.

The Okinawa-based C-130 squadron had been concentrating on blacked-out landings, but had only recently obtained night-vision goggles. An Army source in Hawaii had been identified and our Special Operations "moles" had gotten their hands on twenty-five of the devices. Turczynski now had enough NVGs to equip at least four crews and start training with them in Korea over the holidays.

They needed to catch up with the Hurlburt crews. The Christmas training schedule wasn't going to win Ray any popularity contests with the wives, I thought, but it couldn't be helped. What was worse, he couldn't give the families any reasons for disrupting their holiday plans.

I was surprised and a bit nonplussed when Lee informed me that the AC-130 crews at Guam were taking a holiday and being transported back to Hurlburt, leaving their aircraft behind. In fact, they were due to arrive en masse at any time now. This seemed crazy to me. Why return these AC-130 people and leave their aircraft behind?

Again I wondered whether we were really serious about doing anything in this hostage situation.

One plus factor: this could be an excellent opportunity to have our MC-130 and AC-130 aircrews exchange information on training techniques.

I turned to other matters. "Lee, I need to get with Bob Dutton and Jim Keating to see where we are on these two airfields in the latest plan change."

"You mean Manzariyeh and Fez?"[1]

"Manzariyeh, I know. Fez, I assume, is the airfield selected for insertion. Do we have any aerial photos yet, or layouts of the runways?"

"Yep, Nick Kilgore has photos and Jerry King's troops have drafted runway schematics to scale, using small paper aircraft to shuffle around to work out a parking plan."

Lee and I continued on to the Unconventional Warfare office. We stopped at Kilgore's shop to look over the aerial photos of these Iranian airfields. The detail and clarity were amazing. I could even see thirty or forty people playing volleyball near the operations building; this stuff was good.

Neither Bob Dutton nor Jim Keating was around, so I cornered Jerry King and Bob Horton. I asked to see the schematics they had made up to test the marshaling plans. As Jerry explained it, this airfield southeast of Tehran and near the small city of Fez was to be seized by the Rangers on Night-One and used to refuel the helicopters. We had to have this type of airfield to support the bulk bladder option.

I told Jerry, "It makes sense to me to add two more MC-130s to the flow of aircraft from Egypt so we can keep Beckwith's forces together for the insertion part of the mission. The aircraft carrying the Rangers would land first and secure the Fez airfield. Next would come the two C-130s with Delta aboard, followed by the bladder birds.

"Upon completing the refueling, the choppers would head on

---

[1] Fez is a pseudonym, used for security reasons.

to the drop-off site with Delta aboard and the C-130s could be withdrawn to Egypt with the Rangers aboard."

When this idea was presented to General Vaught, he was quick to approve, and Beckwith was ecstatic. He hadn't relished the idea of dispersing his forces among six helicopters for the ride in from the carrier. And, for that matter, he wasn't that keen about putting Delta aboard the carrier at all—it would be a security risk getting his gang out to the ship posing as a bunch of sailors returning from liberty.

My initial reaction to Fez was that it looked pretty risky. There were military personnel stationed on the premises, and it was only about ten or fifteen miles from a town. There was also a dirt road that passed the end of the runway, running south to another city. The intelligence people told me this route was lightly traveled in the daytime, but they weren't sure about night traffic. They were trying to determine that.

As I looked at the schematic of the Fez runway and parking ramp areas, I could see it would be a tight squeeze for our MC-130 marshaling plan. This was a small-town airport.

The runway was long enough, but very narrow. It would be tricky turning the C-130s around on this confining concrete slab. We would have to use reverse propeller thrust to back up and jockey the big birds around, but it was do-able.

Also the parking area, where we would position three C-130 tankers to refuel the choppers, was extremely small. Using Bob Horton's paper airplanes, we finally came up with a workable plan for the C-130s and six helicopters.

Other than not knowing what size military force we faced at Fez or the traffic count on the road near the airport, it seemed we had an insertion airfield.

Initially, there was a plan for the Rangers to seize and hold Fez until the rescue mission was completed (more than twenty-four hours), then withdraw. The idea was to capture any Iranians who strayed into our operation at the airport and detain them until the hostages had been freed, then release them when we departed. However, the prolonged vulnerability of the Rangers holding Fez ruled against this option, and we decided to fly any captives who might be taken out to Egypt with us on Night-One—a better way to preserve the secrecy of the insertion phase.

As we only had recce photos to go on, it would be up to the intelligence experts to determine exactly what we could expect. Most of us felt the Rat Patrol would be able to handle the small group of Iranians we'd seen so far. Our main concern was capturing everybody at the site before any could get away to warn the authorities in the nearby town. If we could do that, then it looked like a feasible option (Plan B). After all, this was a fairly remote area at the edge of the Dasht-e-Kavir, not Chicago's O'Hare Airport.

Kilgore told me that they were looking at a couple of other airfields, just in case Fez didn't work out, but for now, Fez was it.

Although the airfield seizure option was far better than dropping blivets in the desert, most of us were hoping the intelligence team could find a remote desert location (Plan C) where we could land and accomplish the refueling. There were a lot of risks in the Fez option.

Although I favored Plan C, any support I gave would be contingent on someone going to the site and conclusively determining that the sand crust and subsurface were hard enough to support a 165,000-pound C-130 tanker.

A rock-hard surface in a totally secluded area was what I wanted—where only the camels would know we'd been there. But I wasn't holding my breath waiting for the recce mission to happen.

I had another motive for wanting a reconnaissance flight: I wanted to see if it could get through the coastal defenses undetected. Our chart studies and analyses to date indicated we could make it, but I'd feel a lot more confident if we had the answer to both of these questions before the actual mission.

So much for the Fez airfield. Bob Horton handed me his schematic and aerials of the extraction airfield at Manzariyeh.

"Holy smoke! This is fantastic! It's a perfect setup. I don't see any signs of activity—just a beautiful piece of concrete. What is it used for?"

Bob said it was a special runway the shah had constructed where he could watch his air force conduct bombing and strafing exhibitions. The only buildings were a semicircular domed grandstand, used by visiting dignitaries to observe the firepower demonstrations, and a small caretaker shack.

The airfield was some fifty miles south of Tehran, and the

main highway to Khomeini's holy city of Qum ran southward past the east end of the runway. The layout of the runway and taxiways was identical to those of our major Air Force bases in the United States. The runway was two miles long and 140 feet wide, with high-speed turnoffs 2,500 feet from each end. A taxiway used for parking looped behind the shah's grandstand.

It was made to order, with ample room to maneuver aircraft. The Rat Patrol scenario we had been practicing fit Manzariyeh to a T.

I turned to Kilgore, who was standing nearby observing my reactions. "It's all too perfect, Nick. What's wrong with the place?"

"We haven't found much of anything to complain about. The runway setup is right, and there doesn't seem to be any caretaker force around."

I was still skeptical. "It just looks too easy. There must be a fly in the ointment somewhere. Is there any evidence of obstructions, such as barrels or vehicles, being placed on the runway at night?"

"No, no sign, but we're not one hundred percent sure yet."

"Well, you know, we're going to have to have that pinned down."

I decided right then to equip one of the MC-130s with a forward-looking infrared (FLIR) system to scan the runway and ensure it was clear of obstacles. The FLIR would have to come from Ray Turczynski's outfit on Okinawa, because it was the only unit that had them installed. We decided that one of Ray's aircraft would have to be moved to the United States to participate in training and test the idea.

Of course, the FLIR was only part of the solution. What would we do if we found one or both of the runways blocked? We had two choices: have some troops parachute onto the field and remove the garbage, or abort and return to Egypt.

(General Vaught settled that when I discussed it with him later: "The Rangers and combat controllers will be prepared to parachute into Fez and Manzariyeh and clear the runways, if necessary.")

Next, I asked Nick if there was any chance of reinforcements coming down the road from Tehran.

"They shouldn't even know we're there if we make the assault clandestinely," he replied, and others nodded agreement.

The only danger that Nick could see would be a chance encounter with passing Iranian forces stumbling onto our operation. We'd have to plan for that eventuality.

I thought about that for a minute, then said, "We can help the Rangers control the ground situation by putting a gunship over Manzariyeh in addition to the two over Tehran. That will help the Rangers keep peace in the valley, won't it?"

Everyone nodded assent, and I continued, "Remember also that once the two AC-130s finish at the embassy, they will escort the choppers to Manzariyeh, giving us three gunships to cover the extraction. How about that?"

Everyone agreed that between the Rangers, the helos' .50-caliber guns, Delta's weapons, and the AC-130 firepower there should be enough muscle to hold off a sizable Iranian force should a firefight develop.

General Vaught had told us that we shouldn't have to hold the extraction airfield over an hour or an hour and a half at most, if we maintained the element of surprise. That should be time enough for Delta to breach the embassy walls, rescue the hostages, get to the helicopters, and make it back to Manzariyeh. With a little luck we could secure and hold the extraction airfield without a shot being fired.

Nick showed me some pictures of the embassy grounds disclosing that the militants had implanted metal fence posts in the area marked off as the athletic field, making it impossible for a helicopter to land inside the embassy walls. Unless the posts could be removed by Delta, the soccer stadium just across Roosevelt Avenue seemed the only logical pickup point.

Kilgore seemed happy with the flow of recon photos he was getting, but he was still troubled by the lack of eyewitness reports from inside Iran. Nick still lacked information that only covert agents in the city could provide.[2]

The helo planners were still looking for a good place to land at

---

[2]General Vaught told the Chairman, in so many words, "I can't do this mission without help from the CIA." The frustrations over the lack of human intelligence were about to be resolved. The Agency had already inserted an agent into Tehran, and critical intelligence for detailed planning would soon be available.

the Ministry of Foreign Affairs to get Laingen and the other two officials.

It should take the helos only about thirty minutes to fly from the soccer stadium to Manzariyeh. Once they were clear of the city, the threat would be greatly reduced.

I really liked what I'd seen in the photos and schematics used to formulate an assault and marshaling plan. Our intelligence team and the experts on Iran had done a bang-up job putting this together.

My enthusiasm grew, and I detected a growing consensus in the Joint Task Force staff that we were fast approaching a secondary plan that offered a better chance of success than air-dropping the fuel.

Seeing the Manzariyeh layout reminded me of an idea that had been flitting around in my brain since that visit to Camp Smokey.

"Jerry, has anybody thought about revamping the rescue scenario to a one-night operation? Now that we have this airfield and it's only fifty miles south of Tehran, why not airlift some type of small helicopters in aboard C-130s, land, roll 'em out, onload Delta, and assault the embassy?"

Everyone agreed that it was an idea that needed to be explored, but Jerry said, "We haven't really had time to study what model helicopters could do the job. Most helos that the various services own will not fit into a C-130 without extensive disassembly of their rotor blades and gearbox components."

More important than the mechanical aspects of inserting the helos and Delta for a hit-and-run assault were Charlie Beckwith's feelings about a one-night operation to rescue the hostages. It would be up to him to weigh the pros and cons and let us know whether to pursue this concept.

Before we could start toying with that idea, we needed to flight-plan precise navigation routes for the Fez and Manzariyeh options, to include KC-135 tanker refueling requirements for both MC-130s and AC-130 gunships. I told Lee Hess to get Les Smith, Doug Ulery, and Paul Gorsky back on it after the holiday break.

As I was getting ready to leave the operations and plans area, I noticed Lieutenant Colonel Ron Michaels over in the corner still playing with his "paper dolls." He had schematics of Wadi Kena,

Egypt, and Diego Garcia laid out and was reviewing parking plans for all the aircraft planned for employment in the rescue mission.

"Ron, have you pinned down where the overseas main operating base will be yet?"

"Wadi Kena," was his confident reply. "Diego Garcia can't handle all the aircraft, and it's too far from Iran anyway. Wadi Kena has better facilities to store all our support gear, as well."

Ron held up Bob Horton's matrix showing deployment of our key support materials to Egypt. "We've got this chart finished, and we're ready to start moving our support materials forward as soon as we get the word." He told me that Dave Forgan's Operations Planning Group staffers were really exercising Wadi Kena vigorously now, with all sorts of aircraft deployments into and out of the area. Our planners wanted that operational footprint well established so we could hide our Rice Bowl aircraft among the ongoing operations.

16

THE REHEARSALS BEGIN

January 10—Hostage Day 68
  <u>Associated Press</u>
  TEHRAN, Iran—A top Iranian official offered hope Wednesday
  for release of the Americans held hostage in the U.S. Embassy,
  but cautioned against optimism.

  Ayatollah Mohammed Beheshti, first secretary of the ruling
  Revolutionary Council, told reporters there was not yet any
  reason for optimism about the release of the hostages . . . but
  added:

  "There is some movement. I am not sure if this movement will
  be seen in a few days. Maybe [it will be in] a few weeks."

  . . . And the Carter administration, frustrated by its inability to
  negotiate the release of the hostages, began preparing the
  American public for a protracted crisis that might last for weeks
  or months more.

The hiatus was behind us and we were back to full throttle.
There was much to be done, and, of course, we had no idea how
much time we had.

With the new insertion option and the growing size of the
Delta contingent, we had to bring in more equipment and
personnel and revise the flight planning . . . and get it all on
track fast.

It was during this period, with the helicopter numbers ratchet-
ing upward, that I set my sights on the in-flight-refuelable
EC-130 Airborne Battlefield Command, Control, and Communications (ABCCC) aircraft based at Keesler AFB, Mississippi.
These birds were equipped with a railroad-car-sized communications capsule that slid in and out of the cargo compartment.

With the capsule removed, two of the 3,000-gallon bulk bladders in tandem on large metal pallets could be inserted in the cargo compartment. This setup would allow refueling of ten choppers (if necessary) with three C-130s. Pumps, filters, and hoses would be strapped to the cargo-loading ramp so that when lowered the system could be ready for action in five minutes. Pretty slick.

However, there was still security to consider. We couldn't commandeer these planes and keep them for long before somebody would come looking for them. I decided it was better to wait and see how many helos we would end up using. We knew the bulk bladder system worked because of our own tests and its record in Vietnam. So it was just a matter of timing—when could we take the Keesler birds and not blow our cover?

Another positive development to come out of changing the refueling operation was the addition of Tech Sergeant Bill Jerome from the Mobile Fuels Detachment at MacDill AFB, Florida. Jerome became top kick of the JTF ground refueling.

Although we headed into our first joint rehearsal short of everything imaginable, we were hoping that all of the individual unit training would come together to produce a smooth run-through of the forty-eight-hour rescue scenario.

Bob Brenci's bird with the Rat Patrol aboard would be leading the flow of MC-130s, followed by Bob Meller and Captain Marty Jubelt carrying ninety Delta Force troopers in the next two "Sealy-configured" aircraft. Jerry Uttaro would bring up the rear with his Bladder Bird (Guidry had nicknamed this flying filling station the "EXXON Configuration"). We had managed to bring in one of Ray Turczynski's PACAF aircraft (equipped with FLIR), and I was anxious to test our runway-clearing tactics.

Unfortunately, we didn't get to test anything that night because the KC-135s that were to refuel us over Texas failed to show up. The lead tanker had aborted because of a landing-gear malfunction and his partner had played follow the leader. (This was a one-time problem that never should have happened and was resolved that night.)

*　　*　　*

The Night-Two rehearsal featured some outstanding flying by the MC-130 pilots as they landed and picked up the Rangers in a driving rainstorm.

The KC-135 refueling went smoothly and things were looking good as the 130s approached Indian Springs, Nevada, flying in trail three minutes apart. The FLIR aircraft made the runway pass and flashed an all-clear to Brenci, who was hot on their tail. But Brenci's bird was too low and he had to take it around and the other three landed, throwing everything out of sequence and putting the Rat Patrol on the ground last.

This taught us another painful lesson—the pressure altimeters on the C-130s were not accurate enough for NVG operations. The radar altimeter, with its precision readings, would have to be the primary instrument in gauging height on these landings.

Also, traffic control and marshaling at the extraction field still caused too much confusion, and at General Gast's insistence, the Air Force combat controllers were assigned these duties.

In the Indian Ocean, the aircraft carrier *Nimitz* had arrived on station to replace the *Kitty Hawk* and our six JTF RH-53D Sea Stallions had been flown aboard. The *Nimitz* had picked up two additional birds en route, so we now had eight choppers in position to support the rescue operation. All were equipped with Omega navigation systems (the PINS being used in training would be taken to the carrier by the Marines).

After leaving Yuma, Van Goodloe and his Navy pilots had been sent to the *Kitty Hawk* to take charge of the mission choppers. They found a sorry state of affairs. The RH-53Ds had been kept below deck most of the time ("hidden from Soviet trawlers"). Spare parts had also become a problem, because of the extended supply pipeline, and the birds were not being flown much. They were trying to turn this situation around, but General Vaught was getting increasingly antsy over this key element of the JTF not being where he could keep a close eye on it.

General Vaught's discontent with the CIA eased a bit as he finally saw some results. The agency brought an agent named Bob, an Anthony Quinn look-alike, out of retirement and inserted him into Iran. He was to collect information on the location of the hostages, embassy defenses, a helicopter laager, a Delta hide site, and the best routes into and out of the city.

In spite of this, Delta's intelligence section was screening its own people in a search for agents to send into Tehran. However, General Vaught was not ready to tread on the CIA's sacred ground.

With the reservations about the Fez insertion option, our intelligence section had spotted a place they called Desert-I as perhaps having better potential to fulfill our needs. It was a large, flat area ideally located about 530 nautical miles inland from the south coast and about 220 miles from the area that had been selected for Delta to hide in overnight. These distances were well within acceptable fuel ranges and flying times for the helicopters—close enough to Tehran to enable them to make it to Delta's hide site, then fly twenty-five minutes to their laager location under cover of darkness. They would still have enough fuel for the Night-Two exfiltration mission.

However, there was a drawback: an unpaved road ran smack dab through the middle of what would be the landing zone. The sand-encrusted, compacted road appeared to be used and maintained like a country road in the United States.[1] It connected the small towns of Yazd, 135 miles to the northwest, and Tabas, some 58 miles to the east. The location was certainly remote enough, but any possibility that Iranian vehicles might be driving through the middle of our refueling operation made me skeptical.

A preferable second desert location, more remote, had been ruled out because the surface appeared too soft to meet our landing criteria—and as far as I was concerned, Desert-I would be on the back burner until we could send someone out there for an on-site survey of the conditions. I remained steadfast in my proviso:

"We will not land our C-130s on any desert floor without a solid determination that the subsurface will support their weight."

The use of Desert-I had obvious risks, but just how big those

---

[1] In *Military Incompetence*, author Gabriel is totally off base in his statement that the road passing through Desert-I was a well-traveled, paved highway.

were was anybody's guess—and believe me, there were lots of guesses. Much more information was needed about the place before we could even begin to get serious about using it. And more important, we would need the President's approval before we could send someone to look it over.

With the burgeoning size of the rescue force, I began giving serious thought to a topic General Vaught and I had discussed, that we might be better able to perform the extraction with the larger C-141 Starlifter transports. In addition to the 53 hostages, we now had 120 in the Delta contingent, about 100 Rangers, and as many as 56 helicopter crew members to airlift out of Manzariyeh—some 330 in all.

The Military Airlift Command operates these big jets in Saudi Arabia regularly, and I figured we could slip a couple of birds into the country and accomplish what we had to do without attracting too much attention.

I decided to explore the idea of using C-141s for the job, with at least one set up in a medical evacuation configuration to handle any hostages that might need medical attention, or to tend to any wounded members of the assault force. The speed and range of the C-141s would provide a big advantage in getting all of these people out of Iran rapidly.

The Rangers would still come in on C-130s to seize and hold the airfield, and they could leave on the same birds after everyone else was out.

I had our MAC man, John Godowski, set up a task force to select MAC aircrews and send them to Hurlburt for blacked-out landing training with the night-vision goggles.

Our communications system was worrying me considerably. All we had to work with was an unreliable high frequency (HF) system with "homemade" code instructions for piecing together messages—minimally acceptable. I felt that hostile listeners could easily detect these transmissions and get a fix on our position.

Pete Dieck was trying to get as many of the new satellite (SATCOM) systems as possible, but these devices were as scarce as hens' teeth.

Delta now had a portable SATCOM, with secure voice capability, to experiment with, but that was about it. I told Pete that we needed something like this on the C-130s and choppers, and we needed it bad.

True, we were training to do the job in radio silence. But, if something went wrong, we would need to sort things out fast with a reliable and secure radio system.

"What if, for some reason, we had to haul ass out of Iran and everybody wasn't aboard?"

This had been bothering me.

I put Lee Hess on it and he called in Captain Wayne Purser, a search and rescue (SAR) specialist working in the Air Force Special Ops office.

I asked Captain Purser to come up with a plan that would provide a means of finding and extracting downed aviators or assault force members stuck in Iran after the completion of a secret mission.[2] I didn't give him any more information than he needed to know for this plan.

We theorized that SAR helicopters, probably the new Air Force Pave Low HH-53s, could be flown into Saudi Arabia aboard C-5s at about the time the embassy assault was taking place. This would put them into position for a search and rescue effort twenty-four to forty-eight hours after the assault.

January 30 . . . good news!

Six U.S. Embassy staff members had been in hiding since the takeover and were slipped out of Iran by the Canadians over the weekend (with an assist from the CIA).

God bless those magnificent Canadians! We needed that!

First, the bad news:

A freak ice storm hit North Carolina, grounding our C-130s at Pope Air Force Base and forcing us to postpone our next rehearsal for several days. Incredible what we had to go through just to rehearse this cotton-picking mission—endure weather that didn't even exist in Egypt or the Persian Gulf!

[2]Ironically, I didn't hear much from Wayne Purser from that time on. The SAR option was placed in compartmented status in the Operations Planning Group, and I didn't have access to any details of the plan. I only knew that Purser continued to be involved and that I would be told what I needed to know if and when I needed to know anything about it.

Then, the good news:

We roared into February with two of our best days since the whole thing had started.

The Night-One assault on a remote Nevada airfield (simulating Fez) was nearly perfect—the refueling over Texas, the blacked-out landings, the Rat Patrol takedown of the field, the arrival of the choppers, the refueling, and getting Delta and the helos into place while the C-130s withdrew. Safety observers on the scene were flabbergasted by the effectiveness of the blacked-out operation, and enthusiasm among the aircrews was sky-high. We had by God proved that we could run this complex set of events and make the plan work.

Night-Two was another success—the surveillance and take-down of the embassy, the coordination of the AC-130 gunships, and the withdrawal and exfiltration from Indian Springs, Nevada (Manzariyeh). "We did it!" We all savored those forty-eight-and-some hours, our first real success in this demanding mission. We now had a workable plan and the means to carry it out!

A buoyant General Vaught rushed the news to the Chairman and his staff: "We have a workable plan." But he came away from this private session deflated. He would later describe it as feeling "like I was in a state of limbo."

News reports coming out of Tehran and Washington were having a profound effect on high-level attitudes toward the Joint Task Force. As in the past, with the improvement of the diplomatic climate, our mission seemed to be moving toward the back burner.

Also, there seemed to be a nameless, faceless (but formidable) body of criticism building behind some of those closed doors in the Pentagon. Apparently our critics felt our plans relied excessively on bold initiative and that we lacked sufficient forces and firepower as stipulated in the Principles of War.

General Vaught, concerned at the effect this whole negative situation might have on morale, was planning to order another rehearsal for the near future to keep the force busy and polishing proficiency. But the Chairman put the kibosh on that idea. He said it was unnecessary in view of the rapidly improving diplomatic situation.

So, with things back to a crawl and nothing much we could

do about it, I headed to Hawaii for the break I had missed in December, and Chuck Pitman and his RH-53 maintenance specialist, Captain Larry Sherwood, made a beeline for the *Nimitz* to check on the choppers.

The diplomatic euphoria didn't last long, however, and I soon found myself highballing it back to Yuma for a hurry-up joint rehearsal. The Iranians were turning the screws again and the big boys were getting nervous.

In this exercise, Twenty-nine Palms would again be used to simulate Fez and Yuma Army Airfield would be Manzariyeh for Night-Two. However, it was not shaping up as an ideal rehearsal—we had only three C-130s available and the weather was looking pretty iffy.

Of course, the rescue mission was planned to go only under visual flight conditions, and we wouldn't launch with a bad forecast. The Marines were still relying heavily on map reading, using the PINS as a backup to navigation, so good visibility was essential.

The weather that night taxed everyone's skills to the limit. After being treated to a hairy helicopter ride through the Little San Bernardino Mountains to Twenty-nine Palms, I was ringside at a beautiful demonstration of flying skills as the C-130 crews brought their big birds in with picture-perfect landings.

General Vaught, a man who utters precious few compliments, said, "They really showed me something."

The choppers couldn't make it through the storm, but we were able to salvage the night by shifting the exercise to Yuma.

Again, we proved we could accomplish all the tactics and maneuvers required, including adjusting to an abort situation.

All was not roses, however. The news Chuck Pitman brought back from the *Nimitz* was worse than terrible and had General Vaught highly agitated.

When Chuck and Larry Sherwood arrived aboard the carrier, they found the worst possible mess, from our standpoint.

Van Goodloe told them the RH-53Ds had been flown about five or six hours each over the past two and a half months, because of a critical shortage of parts. Actually, Nos. 7 and 8 hadn't been flown at all—they had been cannibalized for parts to keep the others flying. Nobody had told Goodloe about the latest requirement (for eight choppers), so he had been concentrating on keeping six birds flying.

Also, because a Soviet trawler had been trailing the task force, the RH-53D flying had been restricted so as not to attract undue attention. Despite Goodloe's efforts to keep the helos maintained and on a short fuse for the rescue mission, the carrier task force commander had other ideas. The flying time was being conserved *to support future mining operations*! Can you believe it? Dammit, the mining operation was our cover story!

I have doubts that the *Nimitz* could have gotten six Sea Stallions airborne for a rescue mission during that early two-to-three-month period.

Chuck went behind closed doors with the task force admiral and the skipper of the *Nimitz* and stressed the urgency of recognizing the true mission of the RH-53Ds. He asked that a system be established to increase the level of spare parts and specified that each helicopter had to be flown twenty-five to thirty hours a month on sorties equal in duration to those planned for the rescue mission (eight hours).

At the same time, Larry Sherwood was going over requirements and establishing procedures with the maintenance crews aboard ship.

Before Pitman left the *Nimitz*, he asked the skipper to establish a system of daily reports to the Special Operations Division on the maintenance status, parts problems, and flying time of the helicopter force. That way, the Marines and the JTF staff could monitor the "get-well" program.[3]

The helicopters were not the only problem. Time was starting to work against us.

With March almost upon us, we were down to about eleven hours of darkness in which to perform the Night-One insertion, and it would take the chopper crews eight and a half hours of this (with no delays) to get everything done and get into hiding for

---

[3]Van Goodloe recalls that a meeting held aboard the *Nimitz* after Pitman's visit was devoted to upgrading the priority of support for the helicopters. He says that the spare-parts situation and flying operations improved over the following three weeks but then regressed into lethargy generated by doubts the rescue mission would ever be launched.

Night-Two. And the last C-130 tanker had to be clear of Iranian airspace nine hours into darkness. In essence, about nine and a half hours of darkness was the minimum we could live with— and May 1 would be the last day we would have that.

Also, the temperature factor was turning against us. Aircraft do not perform well in extreme heat. The 90-plus temperatures forecast for Iran in March–April would put us at our limit. We would have to launch within the next sixty days or wait for the cooler temperatures of November.

There had been talk of putting two more RH-53s aboard the carrier (bringing the total to ten), to increase the helicopter lift-carrying capability. After May 1, 1980, there would be insufficient darkness to complete the insertion phase of the mission regardless of how many choppers we had.

17

GETTING OUR ACT TOGETHER

February 28—Hostage Day 117

<u>Associated Press</u>

A former Iranian official said a meeting had been arranged today between an international commission and the American hostages being held by militants in Tehran, but the captors said they had not decided whether to permit it. The hostages, in their 117th day of captivity, are threatened with at least 10 more weeks of confinement.

The official news agency Pars reported that Akbar Hashemi Rafsanjani, former Iranian interior minister, said members of the UN commission studying allegations against the deposed shah would meet with the hostages.

We were back in Delta's stockade when General Vaught gave us the word: "This task force is ready to go to Iran."

And we were all convinced of that after our recent successes.

He told us to keep hitting the training hard and have our units ready for another joint rehearsal in late March.

"This is no time to let down," he said. "And keep looking for better ways to do things. We are not locked into any concept."

The general confirmed that he had been having second thoughts about Fez and said that he had persuaded General Jones to request a ground reconnaissance mission to Desert-I. "If this concept proves feasible, we'll go with it." This was met with enthusiasm throughout the room.

There was good news in Nick Kilgore's intelligence update. We now had solid intelligence through his sources that the Delta drop-off point (Desert-II, as some called it), hide site, and helicopter laager were confirmed as usable locations and should be incorporated into our plans.

What Nick didn't tell us was that Charlie had actually had a face-to-face session with the CIA agent, Bob, who had been to each of these locations, including the extraction airfield at Manzariyeh. He had driven to each site, surveyed the areas, and evaluated them as to suitability for their intended use.

However, Charlie was still concerned that the CIA agent did not have the operational background to make such critical judgments, and he remained steadfast in his position that personnel with Special Forces backgrounds be inserted to look these areas over. In Charlie's words, "I'm not about to risk the lives of my soldiers on the evaluation of an individual who doesn't have the operational experience to make such a judgment. I want people who I personally know and have total confidence in to look at these areas."

There was another piece of the puzzle fitting into place at this time that most of us were not told about. Another CIA operative, a wealthy Iranian who was working with Bob, had acquired a warehouse near the outskirts of Tehran and procured six Mercedes trucks and two vans to support some semblance of a construction operation. The trucks were to be kept in a rented warehouse and moved about on occasion to ensure their mechanical reliability.

When the time came, they would be driven to the Delta hide site, some fifty miles southeast of Tehran. The Delta soldiers would be hidden in the trucks among construction materials and smuggled into the city to a point near the embassy wall. The agents had driven along the road and gone through one or two gendarmerie roadblocks just to be sure Delta wouldn't run into anything that couldn't be handled.

There was something else bothering Charlie.

"If we arrive at the wall and I see a problem, I want to be able to slip the attack thirty minutes to an hour. And I don't want AC-130s overhead and the Manzariyeh assault to occur before we go over the wall."

I told him we could hold the AC-130s and MC-130s at the KC-135 tanker orbit over Saudi Arabia for about forty to fifty minutes, but at that point fuel would become critical and they would have to resume course. This would also require that he make the decision to hold off the assault at about two and a half hours before the planned over-the-wall time. The flying time from the tanker orbit would necessitate an early hold decision.

Charlie felt he needed more flexibility than that.

I suggested that we set up a second holding point behind a 3,000-foot mountain near Manzariyeh. This would screen us from the radar site near Tehran's Mehrabad Airport, where the nearest Iranian Air Defense fighters were based. If Charlie gave the word to hold, the AC-130s would be only about twenty minutes from the embassy. Our fuel reserves would allow us to orbit about forty minutes. This would enable him to put the assault on hold as late as twenty minutes prior to scheduled takedown.

Operational security could not be totally guaranteed under this situation, and I speculated that the Iranian coastal radar net could possibly detect the AC-130s as they penetrated the north end of the Persian Gulf landmass east of the city of Abadan. If detected, we planned to send out deceptive radio messages in Farsi, hoping to confuse the Iranians long enough for the Spectres to get to the embassy before anyone figured out who they were.

Charlie was to orchestrate this holding maneuver by sending out code words on the SATCOM radio. The lead AC-130, MC-130, and heló would all be monitoring the command net for his call. If no message was received, we could assume that the takedown would be on schedule. I asked Charlie to send his radio operators and key controllers to Hurlburt to work out the procedures and practice with the gunshippers.

General Vaught had another surprise for us. "I'm establishing a 'murder board' to examine every detail of our operational plans."[1]

This was one announcement that was greeted with a major

---

[1]The Holloway Commission criticized the Joint Task Force "for not having a small group of individuals with credible experience in Special Operations to act as consultants and review the plan," perhaps detecting flaws in planning that ultimately affected the mission accomplishment. The JTF did form a "murder board," but this group's members came from the JTF staff, which is probably not a good idea inasmuch as a murder board should be composed of independent thinkers, protected from the repercussions that occur when one criticizes his compatriots.

lack of enthusiasm. Murder boards are not popular among military planners, and some regard them as unnecessarily meddlesome.

The general continued, "This board will be used to conduct 'what-if' drills on each segment of our plans to determine if our tactics and procedures are sound and what alternative options are open to us should scheduled events not go as planned."

General Gast was to be in charge of the board, and Lieutenant Colonel Bob Dutton and Colonel Jim Keating would work with him in the process of dissecting and examining our brains.[2]

Later in the day, I learned we had made some progress in working satellite communications into our mission. Ken Oliver's Special Projects Office was devising hatch-mounted antennas that could easily be installed on any of the C-130s. At least this would give us the capability to link the lead Talon into a satellite command and control net.

This was a good start, but we would need to expand the capability considerably to have the flexibility needed. One of the major drawbacks was that the C-130 SATCOM system was being installed separately from the radio operator's panel. This would require an additional radio operator to monitor the SATCOM system. The aircrew couldn't listen in on this system and would have to rely on the radio operator to relay the messages.[3]

The SATCOM radio operators were to come from Pete Dieck's Joint Communications Support Element. They were to keep the flight crew advised of any SATCOM traffic. Delta Force would provide combat-experienced radio operators for the choppers, since these people were going to Tehran, where the shooting would start.

---

[2]General Vaught was fully aware of the intense rivalries this type of arrangement could spawn, but was also convinced of the necessity of making absolutely sure each detail of the plan could undergo microscopic examination and emerge as a sound course of action. These murder-board sessions made for some hostile face-offs for the component commanders, seemingly to the devilish delight of the boss. These became the forums on which he relied to determine the strengths and weaknesses of our plans. Actions to overcome "soft spots" were largely based on the outcomes of these unpopular, but necessary, debating battles.

[3]The EC-130 ABCCC aircraft was set up with the SATCOM panel on the flight deck, but the aircrew still could not listen in on this system, a marginally satisfactory arrangement.

There still weren't enough SATCOMs, but we were working on it. If the contraption worked as advertised, it would be another major hurdle that technology had helped us over.[4]

I told Roland Guidry about a program I had discussed with the Marines to get in some in-flight-refueling training with Rescue C-130 tanker crews.

"It seems to me that our MC-130s could somehow be equipped to in-flight-refuel the helos. I want you to run some tests with the Special Ops helos at Hurlburt and see if you can come up with a system we can modify to meet our needs. I'm hoping we can find some way around this ground rendezvous."

With General Vaught's words about Desert-I in mind, I huddled with Guidry and John Carney for a close look at Desert-I with an eye to what operational adjustments this option would dictate.

From the photos, it appeared that the south side of the road offered the most compact landing area. It seemed to have less loose sand and paralleled a straight stretch of road about 4,000 feet long—enough to land and take off.

The key to landing would be touching down at precisely the right spot and rolling to a stop parallel to the road. It would be tough for the landing aircraft to spot this point because of the lack of visual references (the desert surface would all look the same through night goggles). We'd have to come up with some way to readily spot this critical point.

From the photos, it looked as though the north side of the road might also be usable for landing. You could see tracks where vehicles were taking a shortcut across that area to avoid a prominent bend in the road. We would have to wait for the recce mission before we could determine if a dual runway operation could be set up using both sides of the road.

We would need 800-foot swaths about 4,000 feet long on each side of the road to handle six C-130s and eight helicopters. A

---

[4]I was anxious to exercise this capability but was told it couldn't be used until we were on the actual mission for fear of compromising our newly acquired system. Delta would have their ground SATCOMs to play with, but no others would be placed in service until the mission.

survey party would have to thoroughly examine the proposed landing area to make sure there were no soft spots. We had to be absolutely certain that none of the aircraft would bog down.

It was academic that we would have to practice landing on dirt- or sand-crusted surfaces for this option. There were airfields in the Hurlburt area that would support this type of training, but many voiced concern about what this might do to the antennas on the belly area of the Talons. These fragile systems could not endure sustained beatings, so operating in the dirt would have to be accomplished with caution.

We decided that the FLIR system would play a vital role if we used Desert-I. The lead aircraft, with this TV-like sensor on board, would make a pass over the area so we could make sure no vehicles, people, or anything else was in the landing zone.

The first aircraft on the ground would have a roadblock team on board that would rapidly off-load and secure the area in a manner similar to the Fez Rat Patrol operation. Obviously, we would have to be prepared for the eventuality that someone might wander into our operation. We would have to plan on detaining any Iranians who stumbled into the landing zone—and would definitely have to fly them out with us. We would leave the details of this to Delta and the Rangers.

Meanwhile, I was still thinking about how we could mark a desert landing zone when I overheard a discussion about blowing a hole in the embassy wall. This set me to thinking about the radio transmitters that remotely trigger explosive devices and how this might be adapted to turning on lights.

I turned for help to Bucky, Delta's brain trust for tactics. We set up some demonstrations by triggering explosives from one of our C-130s flying in the area and caught Chuck Gilbert's attention. He offered to throw the ball to the CIA lab and see what it could come up with. "I'll get back to you in a few weeks," he said.

There was a sense of urgency to this. If the President should happen to okay the recon mission, the lights would have to be taken to Desert-I and planted. We estimated the batteries for the lights would have to survive thirty to sixty days. This would have to be a durable system, not some hastily thrown-together junk.

Chuck had come through for us with the black paper, and we had no doubts he'd do it again.

The issue of conducting a one-night rescue operation using small helicopters carried aboard transports was also resolved at this meeting. We'd been looking at carrying Army UH-1 (Huey) helicopters in C-130 or C-141 transports and landing at Manzariyeh, rapidly off-loading them, and reassembling the rotor systems. Then with Delta aboard, we could assault the embassy.

Beckwith didn't like the idea for several reasons, not the least of which was standing around waiting while mechanics got the helicopters ready, a couple of hours at least. He also thought the choppers were too noisy and he would lose the element of surprise.

Then he made the key point: "Look here! I have damn little intelligence on the location of the hostages, how heavily defended the embassy is, and what the situation is like in the streets around the place. I need time to slip into the city and reconnoiter the area before we take it down. The best way to do that is by the truck idea we are working on now. A two-night operation gives me the time I need to be sure we're not walking into a bloody massacre!"

That closed the issue as far as I was concerned. It was the ground commander's call and my job to support his plan as he saw it. But it seemed like a good capability that we should not ignore, one that might come in handy some day.

18

MASIRAH RESOLVE

March 4—Hostage Day 122

<u>Associated Press</u>

The militants holding the U.S. Embassy in Tehran today refused to allow the UN investigative commission to visit all their hostages until after the panel reports to the world on the alleged crimes of the shah and America.

The new conditions imposed by the militants seemed to rule out a meeting between the American hostages and the commission during the five commissioners' current visit to Tehran, expected to end by this weekend. The new stand also set the militants on another collision course with President Abolhassan Bani-Sadr.

I was back in the Pentagon. The situation was getting murkier in Iran, and the President had so far rejected the Desert-I recon mission. As March got under way, we would keep scrubbing down the Fez option and work on a Desert-I concept, just in case. It looked like it was going to be business as usual.

General Vaught would keep pressing General Jones to nudge the President toward approving the recon mission. If we were serious about this thing, we had to have that mission.

It had been over a month since I had had an update from Lee Hess, and we needed to get our heads together. I was very fortunate to have Lee as my right-hand man. He knew Special Operations inside out and had an uncanny ability to know what I wanted done before I knew it myself. He kept the ball rolling during my increasingly frequent trips to the field for training and rehearsals. He was indispensable to the Joint Task Force staff.

We sat down for a powwow in the Back Room. Lee had a list

of significant items to cover with me, so he took out his notebook and started from the top:

- General Taylor had been transferred to MacDill AFB, where he would act as deputy commander of the newly formed Rapid Deployment Joint Task Force (RDJTF).[1]
- Rumors had it that General Gast was ticketed for his third star and would become vice commander of the Tactical Air Command.
- Les Smith, our chief Combat Talon planner, was being transferred to Kadena Air Base to become operations officer of the 1st Special Operations Squadron, Ray Turczynski's outfit.
- The AC-130 gunships were back from Guam and all aircraft and crews were at Hurlburt. The crews had been given update briefings and would participate in the next rehearsal. Colonel Tom Wicker (1st SOW/Deputy for operations) also returned with this group and took command of C-130 operations.

As I was forming a question, Lee read my mind: "The Chairman still wants us to keep AC-130 target folders handy to use on the rescue mission should we want to strike a few select targets after we have the hostages safely out of town." He showed me that the target folders were still posted adjacent to the wall charts associated with their particular reconnaissance photos—ready for immediate use.

He continued with his list:

- The MAC C-141 crews at Charleston AFB, South Carolina, had been conducting concentrated night blacked-out training with night-vision goggles and had satisfactorily demonstrated their tactics at a remote Nevada field in mid-

[1]The RDJTF, commanded by Lieutenant General P. X. Kelly, USMC, came about as a result of congressional histrionics following the Soviet invasion of Afghanistan while the United States had to stand by and helplessly watch. General Taylor's transfer would leave us without an Air Force general officer on the JCS/SOD staff. Another Air Force major general, Richard Secord, was involved, but not operationally. He seemed to be working on Middle East assistance issues for General Jones and General Vaught.

February. The crews were confident and considered themselves ready for our next rehearsal. The C-141s would now be used for the Night-Two extraction of the hostages, Delta, and the helo crews—a big plus in terms of speed and emergency medical capability.

Lee then put down his notebook and got out the radar coverage study for over Saudi Arabia, saying, "I think you should see this."

As I looked over the charts, it was obvious that our planned KC-135 refueling tracks over the uninhabited central desert region were well clear of Saudi air defense radar. But—and this was a big but—the point where we planned to exit Saudi territory and fly low-level across the Persian Gulf was practically touching the outer limits of the radar sites at Bahrain and Daharan. We could probably make it through undetected on Night-One, but trying it again on Night-Two would be pushing our luck. We'd stick with the current plan to take the long route south across the Arabian Gulf and then up to Iran.

To cut across Saudi territory on Night-Two, our plan called for five KC-135s to refuel four MC-130s and four gunships en route from Wadi Kena, Egypt, to Manzariyeh, and then refueling them again on their return to Egypt.

In all, twelve aerial refuelings would take place over Saudi Arabia. These operations would have to be coordinated with them if a decision was made to attempt the rescue.

An even larger tanker package (fourteen KC-135s) would be required to support the much longer insertion route to the south. A better solution would be to find a Night-One launch base closer to Iran.

While we discussed these options, Marine Major Bob Mattingly, who had been working over in the corner of the Back Room (we were now sharing our cubbyhole with the Marine helo planners), perked up his ears. I had noticed that he seemed to constantly have a pipe in his mouth that belched smoke like one of those old coal-burning locomotives. He got up and came over to where we were talking and asked, "Have you Air Force types considered operating your C-130s out of the Oman-owned island of Masirah?"

"Yes, we have. But we were told early on that we couldn't use

Oman, Bahrain, Saudi Arabia, Kuwait, the Arab Emirates, Iraq, or Turkey. We've tried constantly to get a piece of real estate closer to Iran, but without much luck.

"We were told these countries were all too risky from a standpoint of political sensitivity and operational security. The only crack in this stone wall has been being allowed to use Saudi airspace for refueling . . . if we can avoid detection.

"We'd like to do it two nights in a row, but with some twenty-nine aircraft in the picture, it looks too risky. As unattractive as it is, it looks like we're stuck with using the southern route across the Indian Ocean on Night-One."

He frowned and said, "Well, Colonel, that's unfortunate. As I see it, Masirah is the place you should use. It's remote, and with the Brits there on contract to the sultan. I'm sure they'd help out, if in no other way, by ignoring your presence. Yep, that's the place you need for launching your C-130s on Night-One."

"Bob, I couldn't agree with you more, but the brass shut that door a long time ago."

He shrugged and expelled a cloud of smoke. I could feel my frustration building into resolve.

I turned to Lee. "Dammit! Mattingly's right! We've known this from the start. The time is ripe to run this up the flagpole again!

"We need to convince the powers-that-be that a two-night operation over Saudi Arabia is excessively risky and the insufferably long route south is pure nonsense. Let's work out a concept for operating from Masirah and bounce it off General Vaught.

"How about asking Nick Kilgore for the aerial photos and schematics of Masirah . . . and we'll need an intelligence update. Then we'll see what we can come up with."

I told Lee to alert the Kadena MC-130 crews to be at Hurlburt for our late-March runthrough. Because Lee and I were both on leave when the last rehearsal was being set up, the Pacific crews were left out. That didn't sit well with me, and I told Lee we would have to ensure that all crews were getting equal training from then on.

"No sweat, Kimo. We'll have them there."

With Lee's update completed, I told him about my project to

get the helo pilots and Talon crews on track to develop an in-flight-refueling capability for the JTF choppers. I asked him to put me in contact with the Air Staff's resident expert on rescue operations to see if he'd pull some strings and get a quickie training program for us.

Meanwhile, Roland Guidry would be trying out various ideas on modifying the MC-130s to see if a refueling system could be developed. I was expecting his preliminary report in about a week.

Wayne Purser's name surfaced again (the same guy who was working the JTF search and rescue plan) as the man to set up the training. Lee picked up the phone, and by the time he put it down everything was under way.

I rang up Ken Oliver, my man at the Lockheed Special Projects Office, and asked him if he knew of any modifications to convert an MC-130 into a tanker. He said he'd do a quick engineering study and get back to me. He wasn't overly optimistic, even if there was a way, that they could have six aircraft modified in the next thirty to sixty days.

After hanging up, I filled Lee in on our little fireworks display at Bragg. "Chuck Gilbert has the CIA lab people working overtime to come up with a first-class system for us. If the recon trip to the desert gets an okay, I hope we'll have these pop-on lights ready in time."

We had a lot of irons in the fire. It was just a matter of which one got red-hot first.

"May 1 is about as late as we can wait. Someone had better start making some decisions in this town pretty soon. We really need that recon to Desert-I. General Vaught is just not that crazy about Fez, and I'm not sure that the in-flight refueling will be a viable option within the next thirty days unless we get an okay on Masirah. It really limits our chances of success if we have to run this mission from Egypt."

Lee knew it; I was preaching to the choir.

This talk about Hurlburt reminded me to tell Lee to get a Talon crew over to Keesler AFB to check out the ABCCC EC-130s we planned to use as Bladder Birds. We'd need a report on what had to be done to them so we could use them on the rescue mission. General Vaught had okayed the visit, but it was just to look the situation over. The boss had also agreed that we should borrow one of these aircraft by midmonth for some training at Hurlburt. We would need a week or two to learn about any peculiarities the bird might have, especially during night blacked-out landing, low-level trail formation, and in-flight refueling.

We would use our own crews to fly them. These Airborne Battlefield Command, Control, and Communications aircraft weren't equipped with the sophisticated radar and navigation systems that were in the Talons, so the crews were to take a few flights to get the feel of them. We'd need to develop tactics for the MC-130s to lead the ABCCC birds into Iran at low level.

"Okay Lee, while you're at it, tell the Hurlburt troops that when they get their hands on an EC-130, load it up with two 3,000-gallon fuel bladders and actually pump gas. We want to check that bladder configuration out completely. Also, remember that the Keesler people are not to know why we have their plane. Answer no questions."

He said, "I don't think we have to worry about that. If you'll recall, we have a trusted agent there in Colonel Robbie Robertson. He can manipulate the aircraft movements without any problems."

Of course! Robbie had been Bob Pinard's maintenance deputy at Hurlburt until his recent transfer to Keesler.

Despite all of the frustrations we had encountered on this long journey, some of the chips were starting to fall into place. Now if we could just get an approval on Masirah and the President would okay the reconnaissance mission to Desert-I, the goose just might lay two golden eggs.

19

OMAN INITIATIVE

March 10—Hostage Day 128

Associated Press

A member of Iran's governing Revolutionary Council said the council would not take custody of the American hostages in Tehran and that it was "unlikely" that the UN investigating commission would meet the American captives, the official Pars news agency said today.

Tehran radio said the five commission members would probably leave the Iranian capital Tuesday.

With March well under way, we were all hard at work sorting out new angles to improve our operational concepts. I didn't feel as much as if I were in a pressure cooker as before, and it seemed to me that everyone else was experiencing the same relief. We were all working steadily and taking things in stride. Before, there had been a tendency to charge around like wild bulls. I think we were all more settled because we had a couple of viable solutions to our mission and were devoting our energies to fine tuning these plans.

There was a lot of closed-door activity in General Vaught's office now. All sorts of people were coming and going, including the Chairman and other high-level types.

Other government agencies seemed to be showing a renewed interest in our activities, and with this came a greatly increased spirit of cooperation. Now when we requested support, we were getting it. The bureaucratic roadblocks we had been running into over the past few months seemed to be coming down.

As I saw this change taking place, I noticed a growing consensus throughout Washington officialdom (the State Department excepted) that diplomacy was not going to resolve this matter and hence our rescue mission was growing in stature and status. You might say we were being pushed toward the front burner. The JTF effort was still intense and the working hours long, for the most part.

It was during that second week in March that Bucky Burruss and Major Pancho Rodriguez showed up to talk to General Vaught. Although they didn't tell me what they were seeing the general about, I was quite sure it had something to do with Charlie's insistence on slipping his own people into Tehran to look things over and check Bob's CIA information. A casual comment I heard Jerry King make one day in the Back Room led me to believe this would happen soon.

I joined the Delta troops for dinner that night and afterward brought up what Lee Hess and I had been up to with the Masirah thing. They jumped on the idea with enthusiasm. They wanted to see what Lee and I had come up with, and if it looked right to them they would join me in a frontal assault on General Vaught with the idea.

The next morning, we pored over the flight planning maps and charts. I showed them the radar coverage of Saudi Arabian airspace, our planned routes, and the narrow gap we had to squeeze through at the Persian Gulf. Their reaction to clandestinely crossing these routes twice was "No way, José." The Delta troops hated the thought of that long flight to Iran as much as we did—especially if we got caught trying to get them inserted.

Then I laid out the chart showing the short distance from Masirah to Iran, which allowed penetration of the southern flank of that country through a wide gap in the radar coverage. One of the coastal search radars had been out of commission for some time, which would make coastal penetration a cakewalk. Once past the coast and the first mountain ridge we wouldn't have to contend with radar until the Tehran area. We would be able to fly as high as 5,000 feet along the ridges of the Zagros Mountains.

The C-130s could make it from Masirah to Fez in about four hours, as compared with twelve from Egypt. According to my preliminary computations, the C-130s could be on the ground at the helicopter refueling rendezvous for around two hours at the maximum and still make it back to the Arabian Sea to refuel from KC-135s for the flight back to Masirah. This would allow for any delays at the helo rendezvous.

The Delta planners liked the logic in this concept immediately and were quick to point out the advantages to their troops also. It would mean less flying time for them and result in much fresher troops making the chopper flight on to their hide site near Tehran. Not having to operate for a prolonged period at low levels would be a godsend for them. All too often the bumping and tossing along a high-speed low-level course starts stomachs to churning. As soon as the first man starts flipping up his C-rations, it sets off a chain reaction and the entire back of the airplane becomes a panorama of airsickness—not a pretty sight.

Bucky was eager to push this plan to General Vaught immediately, so we packed up the maps and charts and headed to the boss's office. When we got there we had to wait because some high-powered type was with the general.

When the door finally opened and the visitor emerged, Bucky nudged me and whispered, "That's Mr. Frank Carlucci, deputy director of the CIA."

To me, this augured well. If the CIA's top guns were coming here instead of sending messengers, the top-level cooperation must be coming together. I hoped so.

General Vaught came out to refill his coffee cup and spotted us. With a sly grin, he said, "What are you hoodlums up to? When you get your heads together, I know I'm in for a session of enlightenment."

We laughed and scrambled to get his coffee cup filled so we could get to the task at hand.

I spread the maps out on his large conference table and when he was seated, began the pitch. "Boss, you asked us all to think back through our concept of operations for this mission and see if we could come up with better ways. Well, I think we have a proposal that would greatly improve our ability to accomplish the Night-One insertion." Then I delivered the punch line: "This requires being able to use the airfield on the island of Masirah in Oman."

I knew he'd heard this idea before, but not with any details to go with it. Since he hadn't thrown me out yet, I continued with a rapid-fire summation of how we could conduct operations, pointing out the greatly reduced time and distances and the ease with which we could penetrate the coastal radar network. Bucky chimed in every once in a while with comments on the advantages to Delta and the helicopter operation.

The whole thing took us about twenty minutes, and when we'd finished the general sat there for a few minutes—no words, no change in expression. Then he looked up and said, "Leave your charts and supporting notes with me. I'll present our case to the Chairman and argue as forcefully as I can. This is a darn good plan, and I think the timing might be just right for some cooperation from our friends in the Persian Gulf region."

As we were filing out, he said, "I'll let you know the Chairman's reaction, but don't expect an answer soon. Diplomatically, this is still sensitive and will take a while to arrange—assuming the idea is acceptable."

Out in the hallway, I had to restrain myself to keep from doing cartwheels all the way to the Back Room. Man, if the Chairman bought it and was able to get the necessary approvals, the odds of a successful Night-One would go up considerably. I thanked Bob Mattingly profusely for pushing this idea and helping us resurrect a valuable concept from the cutting-room floor.

We spent the rest of the day briefing the other JTF staffers on the Masirah concept and going over the various ramifications of using this remote island to launch from.

The Special Operations Division suddenly became the scene of heightened activity as:

- Nick Kilgore pulled out aerial photos and airfield schematics of Masirah so we could start planning marshaling and parking procedures. He had already requested an updated Defense Intelligence Agency analysis on security aspects such as vulnerability to detection by satellite and Soviet trawlers.
- Bob Dutton planned to crank the Oman concept into the murder board "what-if " drills and would be ready to scrutinize the plan thoroughly should it be approved.
- The psychological operations people geared up to start building a cover story and developing deception operations that would veil our presence at Masirah.
- Jerry King's people made plans to examine the support

requirements and would coordinate this activity with our trusted agents responsible for the Oman area.

I felt that we should operate with a "bare-base" posture and not haul a lot of support gear that could arouse suspicions. By taking in a few tents, cots, and C-rations we could subsist for the few days it would take to set up and carry out Night-One. Then we could pull back to Wadi Kena for the Night-Two operation. If we finessed our movements, we thought, no one would pay any attention to us. C-130s and C-141s had been seen before at this remote island in the Indian Ocean, so we wouldn't be creating a new operational signature.

Our lengthy discussions on Masirah ended late in the evening, and everyone was charged up and ready to sort out the particular actions he would need to take to support this concept.

All of the JTF planners had good feelings about using Masirah. Now if we could just get Desert-I.

Early the next morning, I received a summons from an agitated general—the boss.

When I got to his office, he was fuming. I swear, fire was coming from his nostrils. He was as hot under the collar as I'd ever seen him. I conducted a rapid mental inventory of my recent activities to see if I might be the object of his hostility.

"I wanted to make an on-site inspection of the helicopters aboard the *Nimitz* and my request has been denied!" He ground up the words and spit them out. I confess that relief swept over me—I wasn't the object of his fury.

It was the general's style to see to the readiness of his forces personally, and he had repeatedly visited the operational units to make sure they were ready. Now he was being denied access to an element that was key to the outcome of the mission that was his responsibility. He was really torqued—he was a bomb looking for a place to explode.

"Someone has the cockeyed idea that it would be an insurmountable operational security problem if I went aboard the carrier to visit the helos. My God! If we can't come up with a cover story to handle something that simple, then we shouldn't be in this business."

Of special concern were the two RH-53s that had been put

aboard the *Nimitz* in late January. They still weren't flyable because of a shortage of critical parts. This the general just couldn't buy, not when the Navy supply system was supposedly committed to giving Rice Bowl top-priority handling. There was supposed to be a highest-level effort aimed at keeping these birds fully mission-ready. The results weren't matching up with the promises, and General Vaught wanted to know the reason why.

Jim Schaefer and Larry Sherwood were being sent to the *Nimitz* toward the end of the month, and for now, it seemed, the boss was going to have to settle for their report. He also shared Chuck Pitman's earlier concerns that the mission helos were not being flown enough to keep them tuned up for the eight-hour flight they'd have to make on Night-One. The helo maintenance and flight operations were the total responsibility of the Navy, and the daily reports he was receiving had him justifiably worried.

As is usually the case, having someone to bounce his frustrations off of had had a calming effect on the general. With the edge now gone from his anger, the general turned to me and asked, "Are you familiar with the Fulton Recovery System?"

I told him what little I knew about it. Basically, a balloon is raised on a tether line and tied to a man in a harness on the ground; then a C-130 maneuvers to hook the tether line and snatches one or two people off the ground (Figure 3). They are then reeled into the plane with the use of a high-powered hydraulic winch. I said that I'd heard the system was used early in the Vietnam War to extract personnel from deep in hostile territory and out of helicopter range. Its use was discontinued after the war because of a fatal accident.

I told the boss that Combat Talon units were now restricted to picking up dummy loads, and I continued, "I question the sanity of anybody who volunteers to be snatched off the ground and dragged behind an airplane on a skinny little line. Any mistakes and it's *adios, amigo*. But I guess whatever happened would be better than being captured."

He then told me the reason for his interest in this recovery system. The President had again turned down the Desert-I recon mission, and one of the chief concerns seemed to be what would happen to the three men programmed for the chore if their plane

The Fulton Recovery System

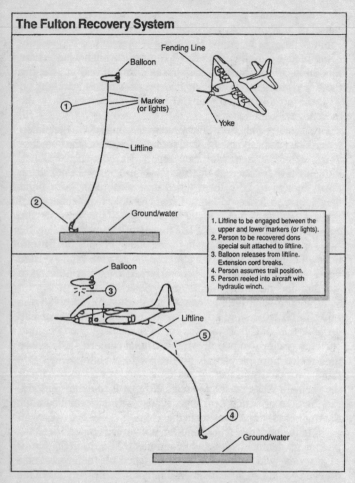

1. Liftline to be engaged between the upper and lower markers (or lights).
2. Person to be recovered dons special suit attached to liftline.
3. Balloon releases from liftline. Extension cord breaks.
4. Person assumes trail position.
5. Person reeled into aircraft with hydraulic winch.

became disabled. We needed a surefire way to get them out if they were stuck in hostile territory.

"Assuming a helicopter can't do the job, there's no doubt the Fulton Recovery System can," I told him. "The Combat Talon outfits in Europe and at Hurlburt have the equipment and train for just such eventualities."

"Can you set up a demonstration at Hurlburt for me in the next few days?"

"No problem, sir."

"While you're at it, set up some MC-130 night blacked-out landings on a dirt strip. I want to see a few of them to be sure there are no special training problems I need to be aware of."

"You got it, sir."

While we were talking training, it seemed a good time to fill the general in on the in-flight-refueling training for our helo pilots that we had set up with Air Rescue. This was to commence in the next few days at a base on the West Coast.

Coincident with this, I told him, the MC-130 people at Hurlburt were trying to rig one of their aircraft with an in-flight-refueling system so we could develop a low-level method of passing fuel to the helos.

"If we can pull this whole program together, we might be able to take the helos into Tehran nonstop behind the C-130s," I said.

I added that the MC-130s would probably have to be refueled on the return trip by KC-135s over the Arabian Sea because of the long distances now involved.

"There are many problems yet to be solved, General. If you can just get us Desert-I and Masirah, that's about all we can realistically hope for."

"Kyle, you keep working on that in-flight-refueling idea and let me know how it's progressing—that's what we really need."

Three days later, I accompanied General Vaught to Hurlburt, where we boarded an MC-130 for the demonstration of the Fulton Recovery System. The snatch-and-grab operation went off without a hitch, and I could tell the boss was impressed.

Later that night, we helicoptered out to a dirt strip north of Hurlburt and watched the night landings. They definitely rated 10 on the performance scale. General Vaught boarded one of the aircraft and observed as he rode through a landing. We'd come a long way since the landing that left the general speechless.

The boss didn't get his voice box violently massaged that night, but on the helicopter heading back to Hurlburt, he—and I too—got a liberal dose of another brand of discomfort: *fear*. We were blissfully cruising along when suddenly the rotor gearbox right above our heads began making sounds like a screaming banshee.

The pilot yelled out, "Hang on, we're going down!"

I looked out. It was pitch-black below us.

Damn! What a crummy way to end the day. The old pucker string was stretched tight.

Then, just above the trees, the grinding stopped and everything smoothed out. The pilot made a beeline for the nearest airport and set the ailing bird down in a precautionary landing.

The general and I had had enough of riding in the Sikorsky vibrator for one day and ordered up a staff car for a quiet, uneventful ride back to Hurlburt.

I spent the rest of the evening briefing Tom Wicker and Roland Guidry on the Masirah concept, telling them to start making a list of support items they needed to operate at this "bare-base" location. They were to coordinate this effort with Ray Turczynski at Kadena so we wouldn't end up with excess equipment. I told them that since the Kadena contingent would be arriving at Hurlburt in the next few days for the March 24 rehearsal, they could settle it with Ray then.

Tom said that Ray wouldn't be coming with them—he'd been put in command of another special mission. Compartmentalization had reared its ugly head again.

There are just too damn many competing requirements for our too few airplanes and crews, I thought. *I wish someone would tell me who has priority. I sure as hell don't know.*

Then Roland told me that their experiments with refueling helicopters hadn't worked out. We'd need something similar to the systems on the rescue HC-130 tankers, which have wing pods from which the hoses are unreeled, making it relatively easy.

If we were going to get a breakthrough it would have to come from Ken Oliver's engineering team at the Special Projects Office. We would spend no more time on tests at Hurlburt. We had other fish to fry.

Wicker said that the gunship live-fire training with Delta had gone well. The crews back from Guam were more confident of their procedures after the training and a follow-up rap session with Bucky and his troops.

They had also ironed out the procedures to allow Delta to adjust the assault time at the embassy by delaying the gunships at a holding point until Charlie was ready to go over the wall. These would be incorporated in the next rehearsal.

I asked them if they were having any problems with the Keesler EC-130 now in their possession. They said they hadn't had a chance to fly it that much but there hadn't been any surprises to date. They were planning on setting up a bulk refueling system and testing it within the next few days by pumping JP-4 (jet fuel) to one of their unit helicopters. They foresaw no problems with this. They emphasized that if the decision to deploy was made, they would need as much advance notice as possible so they could get the three ABCCC birds to Hurlburt. They had a considerable number of things to do to each aircraft to make them ready.

"There is one other sensitive tidbit you should be aware of," Roland said. "We have an aircraft going to an East Coast airfield tomorrow to meet some Agency types who have been working on the remote landing light system. They want to run tests, and John Carney and some of his people will be there to see how it operates. We hope to bring the whole shebang back to Hurlburt and practice with it on our dirt strip."

I was impressed. "God bless Chuck Gilbert, he's done it again. The man's a magician."

As I was leaving, I said, "I'll inform the boss of the lights. That oughtta make his day."

The next morning, as the general was about to board his plane for the trip back to Washington, he had a surprise for us. He walked up to Tom Wicker and said, "General Jones will be coming down to Hurlburt around the first week in April for a demonstration of the same events I observed yesterday. Get everything in top shape for him. The Chairman needs to see what we can do and leave with a comfortable feeling concerning our Special Operations capabilities. Meanwhile, I'll see you people out West in a few days at the rehearsal site. I'm pleased with the tremendous improvements that I've seen here since my last visit."

20

CODE WORD "ORNAMENT"

March 20—Hostage Day 138

Associated Press

THE HAGUE, Netherlands—The United States called on the World Court today for an urgent judgment against Iran for the U.S. Embassy hostage-holding, saying the American captives may face "indefinite" detention in Tehran.

State Department legal adviser Robert B. Owen said tenuous U.S. hopes for release of the hostages were shattered early this month when the UN investigating commission left Iran without seeing the 50 captives.

"The signals which are now coming out of Iran suggest that the detention of the hostages may continue indefinitely. No one in this courtroom has any way of knowing whether the Ayatollah Khomeini will continue to hold the hostages in captivity for a month or for a year or for a decade," he declared.

Amid the rapidly deteriorating situation in Iran, the administration was desperately trying to chart a diplomatic course toward a solution of the crisis . . . and the Joint Task Force was gearing up for its fourth rehearsal.

The mood in this country was growing more strident, both in the halls of Congress and in the arena of public opinion. The pressures on the President were approaching the breaking point. Add to this an upcoming election and it was clear that he was going to have to do something soon.

And with each passing day, the hours of darkness were shrinking. The administration had about three more weeks to explore diplomatic avenues before losing the rescue option to the lack of darkness.

In the Joint Chiefs of Staff/Special Operations Division the atmosphere was charged with electricity. It was like sitting on a keg of dynamite knowing the fuse was lit but not knowing how long it was. We were all scrambling to complete the intelligence picture, to perfect tactics, and to acquire the hardware to make the mission work.

Oliver's engineers had come up with the answer to the in-flight-refueling modification of the MC-130s, but performing this work would take more than a month.

I received word that the Marine helo crews were impressed with their in-flight-refueling training with the Air Rescue unit out West. They apparently had caught on to these tactics with little difficulty.

I was still reluctant to give up on the idea of air-refueling the choppers, but the distances from Egypt were just too far. We would have to have approval to use Masirah, Oman, right away in order to revise the scenario and get the people and equipment necessary to support this option. Lacking this decision, there was no other course than to focus on the air-land refueling tactics and tie this mission up in a tight package right away. We were running out of time!

CIA technicians and our combat controllers had the remote runway lighting device ready for operational use. This simple and reliable system had performed flawlessly from the start of testing. Whether we would get to use it now hinged on the President's approving the recon of Desert-I. The Chairman, CIA director, and National Security Adviser were in the process of appealing to Carter for a third time to approve the mission.

As it stood, the upcoming rehearsal would follow the Fez option. Without approval to use Masirah or recce Desert-I there was no point in factoring those options into this rehearsal.

All we could justify was to continue practice landings on sand and dirt airstrips. The chopper crews were already trained at working in the sand and dust, so if we ever did get Desert-I it wouldn't be a major transition. We had already determined that most of our Fez tactics would, with minor adjustment, work well at Desert-I.

It was the predominant feeling among the field commanders that this fourth rehearsal should be a test of the desert plan instead of the Fez option. But realistically, we could ill afford the time to rehearse a plan that had not been approved—we would have to go with the "bird in the hand."

As the Iranians were busy making threats, half a world away the Joint Task Force was positioning for the assault on Twenty-nine Palms. I was to be the safety observer at Twenty-nine Palms on Night-One and Indian Springs on Night-Two, so I joined the Marines at Yuma and would ride in with them.

Ed Seiffert seemed confident his crews could handle their part of the mission. They were comfortable performing night low-level operations and navigating over long distances under visual flight conditions, and they seemed to have mastered ground maneuvers in the dust.

However, in going over the secure radio procedures with Pitman and Seiffert, I encountered a mind-set that baffled me. They regarded the secure interaircraft radios as excess baggage and wanted to dump them. They felt that this equipment was extra weight and provided a temptation for somebody to break radio silence unnecessarily. Also, they said it took too long for the cipher function to synchronize and thus communication would be too slow to be of any use in an emergency.

I argued that problems, serious but not requiring immediacy, could arise that might be solved through use of the secure radios without compromising the mission.

I pressed my point. "How do you plan to coordinate any in-flight messages you might receive over the command net?"

"By hand signals and flashlight Morse code," Ed answered.

I blinked at that. "What if we have to talk to you from the C-130s?"

"Over the satellite radio," was his reply. "Then I can relay the information to the rest of my formation by hand or light signals."

I could see that I hadn't convinced them, even though they yielded to my arguments at that time.

When the sun went down, the task force took center stage and put on an impressive show. It was perfect—everything went like clockwork.

After the last of the helicopters disappeared over the horizon and the C-130 tankers took off for their eight-hour flight to Hurlburt, I looked over at Chuck Pitman and gave him an emphatic thumbs-up. We both knew that had this been for real, Delta would have been over the first hurdle and headed toward Tehran.

As the sun was rising the next morning, all was in readiness for Night-Two.

We had a new wrinkle in tonight's scenario. MAC C-141 transport jets would be participating in the extraction for the first time. As Air Force component commander, I was hoping they would make a good showing. I hadn't seen any of the MAC crews since their blacked-out-landing training at Hurlburt. John Godowski had kept us up to date on the progress of these big transports from Charleston AFB, South Carolina.

Shortly after dark, the task force was swinging into action again. Delta's specially trained vehicle drivers were being dropped off at a prearranged storage site to prepare the trucks that would move Delta into position for the assault, which was to occur between 1:00 and 1:30 A.M.[1]

Four MC-130s (loaded with Rangers) and an AC-130 Spectre took off again from Hurlburt Field and set out on a westerly course.

Not long after the C-130s passed the halfway point along their desolate route, the MAC C-141 was roaring off the runway at Norton AFB, California, for a two-hour modified low-level flight that would bring it into Indian Springs about fifteen minutes behind the last MC-130.

As the clock swept toward the appointed hour, everything was on schedule—the forces were poised. Delta was in position for the assault; John Gallagher had his Spectre orbiting some twenty miles away, awaiting Beckwith's radio call; the four MC-130s were in position near Indian Springs; and the chopper crews were in their H-53s waiting for their call.

At precisely 1:30 A.M., the code word, Ornament, was transmitted over the control net. The fight was on!

Beckwith's commandos went over the wall; the Spectre gunship moved overhead; the helicopters were airborne and on their

---

[1]The Iranian drivers and their American monitors had trucks to train with at a secret location. These were identical to those stored in the Tehran warehouse and, for obvious reasons, were not used in our rehearsals.

way; and the Rat Patrol aircraft was slipping into Indian Springs in total blackout to capture the field.

I was in the control tower at Indian Springs to coordinate with the Air Force traffic controllers on duty there. When I told them to take a gander at the runway through their binoculars, they couldn't believe their eyes when they spotted the lead MC-130 just as the Rat Patrol warriors came speeding out of its back end. As the other three Combat Talons came zooming onto the runway in the pitch-black, the traffic control guys couldn't get their jaws off of their chests. It was a sight to behold . . . and to the uninitiated, it must have seemed like something out of science fiction.

As the Rangers secured the airfield, the combat controllers were busy setting up the portable lights and TACAN to help the C-141 and the helicopters locate the field.

While I was enjoying my ringside view of unfolding events, Chuck Pitman was in the Huey, headed for the simulated soccer stadium some thirty-five to forty miles to the west to observe the action there. In the meantime, one of the choppers had gotten lost and screwed up the timing of the helo operation—late again! The SFers were damned peeved, to put it mildly.

Back at Indian Springs, it was time for the C-141 to land and get the medical evacuation capability in position to receive any Delta or hostage casualties.

As I watched through my goggles, I could see the big transport approaching . . . then I could hear the pilot throw the power to it. The aircraft passed over the runway at about 500 feet—a missed approach. It must have been too high on the glide slope. Then the C-141 came around again . . . and the same thing happened . . . and again . . . and again.

Damn! They're not gonna make it, and here come the choppers.

The helicopters were landing, Delta and the hostages were off-loading, and the bewildered Rangers were trying to figure out what to do with them when General Vaught called "Kings-X." The general directed that the field lights be turned on so we could get the big aircraft down. Dawn was fast approaching, and we wanted to get out of there by daylight.

I boarded the C-141 with the general, Delta, and the combat controllers for the ride back to Fort Bragg. We slept all the way, so we would be mentally fresh for the meeting the boss wanted to hold soon after our arrival. The C-141's performance had him worried, and he wanted to explore ways to fix the problem. Although we could have done the job with the MC-130s, the C-141s were much faster and had far better medical facilities. We needed to devise a reliable means to get those big birds on the ground to augment the extraction.

We landed at Pope AFB at noon and drove immediately to the Delta stockade. The answer to the C-141 landing problem had been staring us in the face—we had just been too tired to recognize it. John Carney turned the key and unlocked the solution. "Once we've used the element of surprise to capture the airfield, we can light it up like a Christmas tree. This will help not only the C-141s but the helicopters as well." This was agreed, and a satisfied General Vaught left us to work out the details.

After we had hashed this around for a while and had it pretty well figured out, an unexpected visitor dropped in—the Chairman. He was at Fort Bragg observing an exercise of the newly organized Rapid Deployment Joint Task Force and had decided to drop by to find out how the rehearsal had gone.

He went over the current plan with each of us. His questioning was aimed primarily at learning how we felt about the readiness of our units to launch on the rescue mission. It was my impression that before he left he believed that we had a workable plan and that the forces were ready to go.

The Chairman spent a good bit of time talking to Charlie Beckwith about his perceptions of the plan and training, and I believe he became convinced that Delta Force was as ready as it would ever be and a presidential decision was called for, and soon. Delta's finely honed edge of readiness could not be maintained indefinitely—it was decision time.

As he was leaving, the Chairman told General Vaught to get back to Washington as soon as possible. He wanted him to brief the Joint Chiefs on the latest plan and the readiness of the Joint Task Force.

21

SECRET MISSION TO DESERT-I

March 31—Hostage Day 149
<u>Associated Press</u>
Iranian President Abolhassan Bani-Sadr met today with representatives of the Moslem militants holding the U.S. Embassy hostages after an official Iranian spokesman said the government was considering taking over custody of the 50 Americans. . . .

President Carter, meanwhile, postponed a scheduled speech and set up a conference with national security advisers. It was learned in Washington that a message Carter sent to Iranian officials warned that the United States would order further retaliation against Iran if there is no break in the hostage situation. . . .

In Cairo, a doctor said the deposed shah of Iran's cancer had spread to his liver. . . .

It was the last day of March when things started happening.

It had been almost five months since I had my first anxious moments, trudging through the hallways of the Pentagon and into the inner sanctum of the Special Operations Division. Four months and twenty days, to be exact. It seemed more like four years.

I was in the Back Room working on another crash project for General Jones. A close-hold message had been sent to MAC, TAC, PACOM, and EUCOM commanders on March 24 advising them that the Joint Task Force would commence moving equipment to Wadi Kena, Egypt. We had been busting our butts since I had arrived back in the Pentagon from the last rehearsal, putting this all together.

With Ron Michaels's logistics deployment charts as the centerpiece and John Godowski, our MAC flight scheduler, back in JCS/SOD, we were hard at it, arranging C-141 airlift of fuel filters, hoses, bladders, tents, cots, C-rations, ground support equipment, and related gear to Wadi Kena. This was the stuff that could easily be moved into Egypt without attracting undue attention. Some ammunition for the Spectres was also being moved forward to be hidden in bunker areas at Wadi Kena.

We had been pressuring the Chairman for over a month to let us move these items forward, reasoning they could always be returned to the CONUS if the mission didn't materialize. So approval for this didn't cause much of a ripple in the speculation mill. We had become somewhat inured to the on-again, off-again nature of this mission.

However, a more provocative situation had taken place during the previous week that had me wondering. John Carney had wandered into the Back Room and casually announced, "I'm headed over to Langley to meet with the CIA operations people for some special training in preparation for the recce mission to Desert-I."

I couldn't believe it. "Don't give me that malarkey, John. Desert-I is a dead issue . . . isn't it?"

"Not at all. I'm serious. For weeks I've been working with the CIA people on the remote lighting system. Now we're going to Desert-I, to conduct the survey and install the lights."

Without another word, he wheeled and left the room. Lee and I and a handful of others just sat there looking at each other, bug-eyed, our mouths hanging open. Then we speculated about what had changed the President's mind. Was he getting serious about this mission?[1]

General Vaught had already briefed the Joint Chiefs and joined in a question-and-answer session. Although I wasn't there, I was told that the Chief of Naval Operations, Admiral Thomas Hayward, asked the general what his chief concern

---

[1]Zbigniew Brzezinski, in his *New York Times* magazine article "The Failed Mission," recalled the crucial March 22, 1980, meeting at Camp David which led to the President's decision to approve the Desert-I reconnaissance. It was at this meeting that the President was given his first full briefing on the details of the rescue mission by General Jones. Dr. Brzezinski says the turnaround in the President's thinking was, in part, due to a belief that our allies would become more supportive of economic sanctions if they thought we were planning some type of military action. And this support was forthcoming in early April. However, the President withheld a decision on launching the rescue mission at that point because diplomacy was still ongoing.

was in conducting the rescue mission. Vaught, without blinking an eye, said, "Your helicopters aboard the *Nimitz*, Admiral." He vented his frustrations about the maintenance status of the mission helicopters and his resentment at not being allowed to see personally what was going on.

The CNO was unaware of the denial of a visit to the carrier. The Navy had not been the culprit; that decision had been up to the Chairman.

Although that previous week's events had got me thinking there might be a chance we would be going into Iran after all, it wasn't until that Monday night (which, incidentally, was April Fools' Day in Iran) that I realized things were getting serious.

As I labored in the Back Room, I ran into a problem and needed some information from Jerry King. I figured that Jerry, like most everyone else in the Joint Task Force, would still be on the job. So I headed back to his office.

As I walked in, Jerry and the rest of his staff were plotting a route across the Persian Gulf into Iran, and I could tell from what was being said that this wasn't some future plan—it was in progress, happening right then.

"Jerry, is that the mission I think it is?"

"Right. They'll be landing at Desert-I in about an hour," he answered.

Talk about a shot of adrenaline! I was immediately fired up. "John Carney—that son of a gun! No wonder I haven't seen him around for the past week. Hot damn! You can bet your sweet bippie that old John's buns are puckered tight enough to chew chunks out of his seat cushion. I know mine would be."

There were nods to this as Jerry and his crew continued their plotting. Obviously, there were no radio reports—they were just using dead reckoning (speed, time, and distance estimates) to track the CIA Twin Otter across Iran. Jerry's staff was just baby-sitting this one—the CIA was running the show. (As it turned out, the dead reckoning by Jerry and his crew turned out to be amazingly accurate.)

I was anchored to that room. I sure wouldn't be able to get anything done in the Back Room while this was going on.

When it came time for the Otter to land, tensions were as tight as piano wire. It was hard for me to grasp that I had been talking to John in this building just three or four days ago and now he was halfway across the globe, digging holes and planting lights in a strange desert.

I was praying that all would go well for John—that he would return safely with a good report on Desert-I. One thing, however, that I was sure of—if anybody could do it, John could.

I found myself hanging around that night until it was time for the survey team to depart from Iranian territory. I would see John in a few days and get a full report on Desert-I.

As I was leaving Jerry's office, he was right behind me, heading for the coffeepot with his mug in one hand and a gizmo that looked like an oversized pistol in the other. He saw me looking at it and asked, "Know what this is?"

"Hey . . . I'm a pilot, not a trigger man."

"Well, you remember that Charlie wanted Special Forces agents inserted into Iran to check out the CIA intelligence?"

"Yes, I remember. But what's that got to do with the Buck Rogers ray gun?"

"Well, you see, two Special Forces guys got into Iran and reconnoitered the embassy, the Ministry of Foreign Affairs, the soccer stadium, the warehouse, and truck routes in the city. In their debriefing with Charlie and the boss, they confirmed that the plans were based on solid intelligence—everything looked workable."

"That's great news, Jerry, but what's it got to do with the cannon?"

"Well, these two saw that the Iranians have a formidable locking mechanism on the door to the ballroom in the Ministry of Foreign Affairs, where Laingen and two others are being held. So when they got back, they fashioned this baby to get 'em through that door."

"Did the DOD agents find out what buildings the hostages are located in?" I asked.

"No. We still don't know that, but it's been narrowed down to four buildings, which Beckwith's people now know more about than the construction workers that built them."

Everything that Jerry told me that night was music to my ears. Delta knew where the guards were and how to take them out, and they knew how to get inside the buildings, get the doors open, and get everyone out of the compound, all in an estimated forty-five minutes. The pieces in the intelligence puzzle were almost fitted into place.

And, he told me, Beckwith planned to go one step further by inserting one of his agents into Tehran ahead of the assault force to keep an eye on everything while the commandos moved into position. This agent, who Charlie had decided would be Dick Meadows, was to be accompanied by a former Iranian citizen named Fred, now a sergeant in the U.S. Air Force. These two would set up a reception committee at the drop-off point near Tehran and assist the assault force in getting into hiding and later on into the city. Fred knew his way around the city and would help Dick maintain his cover as a foreign businessman.

To me, it was a masterfully contrived setup, but would take nerves of steel. From my observations, Dick Meadows filled this bill.

"Damn, Jerry, we're getting serious about launching this mission?"

He shrugged, and said, "The signs are pointing in that direction."

"When General Vaught gets called in to brief the President, then we'd better have our bags packed."

22

OMAN DECISION

April 3—Hostage Day 152

<u>Associated Press</u>

Iran's ruling Revolutionary Council has delayed a decision on taking custody of the American hostages until President Carter clarifies his response to Iranian demands, Foreign Minister Sadegh Ghotbzadeh said today.

President Abolhassan Bani-Sadr, in American television interviews this morning, said he was satisfied with Carter's position and would propose the council vote to request custody of the 50 Americans, now in their 152nd day as captives inside the occupied U.S. Embassy.

Bani-Sadr was also quoted by Tehran radio as saying in an ABC News interview that Ayatollah Ruhollah Khomeini will make the final decision on a proposal to transfer custody of the American hostages.

Early the following morning, I had a call to get to General Vaught's office right away.

When I walked in, the boss was wearing a big grin. "We got Masirah approved for the C-130 operations. Get the crews studying the plans and learning their jobs. We'll also need a small-scale rehearsal at a desert site to test our tactics and go through the Desert-I procedures of refueling the helicopters."

I was in shock. The good news was coming in waves these days.

"Holy cow, boss. That's the best news we've had in five months of planning for this ballbuster."

"Yes, I think they're finally getting serious across the Potomac," he beamed, adding, "Carney will be back this afternoon, so pick his brain clean on Desert-I. I'll want to hear your plans as soon as possible.

"Oh, one more thing," the general said as I was on my way out. "I want you to go down to Langley Air Force Base and bring General Gast up to date. Since his reassignment, he's been out of touch, but he'll be going with us, if we deploy, so bring him up to speed on the latest plans."[1]

I headed for the Back Room, my mind racing with all the things I had to accomplish. Now I was worried that we'd get the order to deploy before we could get the Masirah and Desert-I scenarios sorted out. In just seven days we had gone from cruise to supersonic speed.

I immediately found Jerry King and gave him the word. He had already heard the news and was rounding up all of the planners to go over the new options and assigned areas of responsibility to expedite work.

Word was sent to Hurlburt alerting them to the changes and telling them to get Doug Ulery to the Pentagon immediately to revise the C-130 plans. Paul Gorsky from TAC was called in to work with Doug. Also, Dave Reckermer, the KC-135 planner, would work with Doug and Paul on the refueling changes.

Stormy Buchanan was fed the new aircraft routings for his weather synopsis planning.

The planners, communicators, logistics experts, and operations and intelligence staffs would have to maintain close coordination to get everything done and still not let anything important fall through the cracks.

Now, after months of trials and tribulations, we were finally closing in on our objective—the final plan.

*   *   *

[1]Even though General Gast had been promoted and reassigned to Langley AFB, Virginia, he was still considered a key adviser and would deploy with the Joint Task Force should the order be given. The fact that General Gast outranked General Vaught seems to have bothered some authors, who were critical of the command structure of the Joint Task Force. But it certainly didn't bother the two generals involved. Rank was not an issue. It would have been foolish to cast aside General Gast's knowledge and experience, since he was deeply involved in the JTF. In fact, for quite some time I had considered General Gast to be the deputy commander of the Joint Task Force, and this became official when the deployment order did come.

The author is introduced to President Carter by Major General James B. Vaught, commander of the Joint Task Force.

The Chairman of the Joint Chiefs of Staff: General David C. Jones, USAF.

Above: Special Operations MC-130s are equipped for night low-level, long-range deep penetration into hostile territory under adverse weather conditions. They are refuelable in flight.

KC-135 refueling EC-130. Due to the shortage of in-flight refuelable C-130s in Special Operations, three EC-130 aircraft were acquired from another unit to haul fuel to Desert-I for the helicopters.

AC-130 Gunship with side-firing 20-, 40-, and 105mm cannons. Unique sensor systems enable very accurate employment of weapons on hostile targets during night- or daytime operations.

Above: Aircraft lined up on the ramp at Masirah Oman, ready to launch on the rescue mission. A fourth MC-130 was held in reserve.

C-141B in-flight refuelable jet transports were to be used to speed to safety the hostages and assault forces after completion of the rescue.

Daily "buzz job" by pilots of the Sultan of Oman's Air Force (SOAF) kept things from getting dull at Masirah. Flying near sonic speed, the Jaguar pilots literally stirred up the dust as they went smoking down our line of C-130s.

Giant C-5 jet transport swallows an MH-53 helicopter in preparation for deployment to a distant location. Special Operations personnel and equipment can be rapidly moved throughout the world by this means.

Air Force Special Operations helicopters currently in use. *Front to rear:* MH-60G Pave Hawk, MH-53J enhanced Pave Low, and the MH-53H Pave Low III. Helicopters of this type were not available in sufficient numbers for use on the Iran rescue mission.

V-22 Osprey is possibly the aircraft of the future for Special Operations. Tilt-rotor technology enables the aircraft to perform both as a helicopter and a fixed-wing transport. Cuts in defense spending may kill the production program.

Above: RH-53D helicopters being lifted to the flight deck on one of the ship's elevators. Notice how rotor blades and tail assemblies fold so that airframes will fit into a confined space.

RH-53D helicopters stowed in one of the below-deck hangar bays of the *Nimitz*.

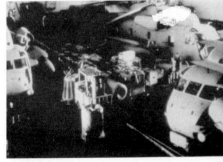

Lead elements of the Ranger "rar patrol" airfield-seizure team are shown here sporting their night-vision equipment.

Above and bottom: What remained of the crashed EC-130 tanker and RH-53D helicopter after the fire burned out.

RH-53Ds aboard the carrier *Nimitz* lined up for takeoff, April 24, 1980.

Crew of the ill-fated EC-130 tanker later involved in the accident at Desert-I. Those Air Force personnel who perished in the fire were: Back row *(from left)* Capt. Rick Bakke; *(3rd from left)* T. Sgt. Joel Mayo; *(4th from left)* Capt. Lyn McIntosh; *(5th from left)* Capt. Hal Lewis; *(6th from left)* Capt. Charles T. McMillan. Those who were burned but survived were: Back row *(from right)* Lt. Jeff Harrison; *(2nd from right)* S. Sgt. Joe Beyers.

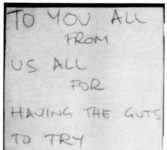

"Guts to Try" motto written on the beer-case top by British mercenaries serving in the Omani Air Force.

At Arlington National Cemetery, May 9, 1980, President Carter delivers the eulogy for the eight airmen killed during the Iran hostage rescue attempt.

President Carter addressing the Joint Task Force staff and members of the Air Force Component in the weeks that followed the aborted rescue attempt.

It was about 3:00 that afternoon when I heard that John Carney was in the Pentagon, and I went to find him only to learn that he and General Vaught were in with the Chairman.

About an hour later, I rescued him from the heavyweights and got to hear his story, a spellbinder. Men like Carney are worth a hundred planes or ships.

It seems that after a relatively uneventful flight into Iran, the Otter was landed in darkness "so black you couldn't have found warts on a toad."

The pilots were old hands in the business and had flown many such missions for the Agency. In fact, the plane captain was a former Air America Nam flier whose plane had been hit by anti-aircraft fire on one hairy combat mission and he had been badly wounded, losing part of a leg from the knee down. John said that this certainly hadn't handicapped him in any way, and because of his courage and proven ability, he was still flying missions for the Company.

When Carney got out of the Otter he assumed they had landed south of the road that ran through the site. After he unloaded the small motorbike he had shared the Otter's backseat with, he cranked it up and headed north to intercept the shoulder of the graded roadway.

John knew something was wrong when he began bouncing across vehicle tracks, apparently where truck drivers had detoured across the open area north of the road to shortcut a large elbow curve at the west end of the area we were calling Desert-I. Realizing, from the photographs he had seen, that this didn't compute, he turned his bike around and retraced his route to the aircraft.

When he got back to the Otter, he found the pilots napping. "I couldn't believe it," John said. "These guys had ice water in their veins—they were absolutely fearless."

John tapped the captain on the shoulder and asked him where they had landed. He said the CIA man opened one eye and stayed awake only long enough to say, "We landed north of the road. Look to the south," then yawned and fell asleep again.

John grumbled, "No wonder. The plan was to land on the south side." But these words fell on deaf ears, and John is not one to sweat the small stuff, so he picked up his shovel and bag of lights and steered his bike south by compass. He soon intercepted the soft shoulder of the roadbed.

Just as he was starting to check out the area and measure the landing strip, he saw lights, then heard an engine as a vehicle went by. Cloaked in darkness, John was only momentarily distracted from his chores.

For the next hour, he checked out the surface conditions, took soil samples, and buried the landing lights. During that time, three more civilian-type vehicles passed by, en route to the distant city of Tabas to the east.

By this time, John was satisfied he had taken care of all the details and his survey was complete.

He returned to the Otter and aroused the still-napping pilots, who then casually fired up the engines, and they departed Desert-I just as matter-of-factly as they had arrived.

This had all seemed so routine to John that he felt as if he must have forgotten to do something—but he hadn't. He had performed splendidly, and his analysis of the site would enable the Joint Task Force to come up with detailed plans for its use.[2]

Even his little side trip to the north provided valuable information. "The sand is a little deeper, two inches, on the north side," he reported, "but I'm sure we can set up a second landing strip there."

This would give us a strip on either side of the road and provide room for us to spread the C-130s, making it much easier to refuel the choppers and transload Delta.

The desert crust to the south was covered with less loose sand, one inch, and would be easier to move about on. It would be a little more difficult maneuvering the helos than the C-130s, but Desert-I was a usable area.

It all sounded fantastic to me, and I slapped John on the back and said, "Man, that's one hell of a job you did for us!"

Armed with John's report, we drew the flow plan for C-130s

---

[2]There was one significant sidebar to this recce trip that would later have a significant impact on the mission. When the Otter crossed the Persian Gulf, north of the Strait of Hormuz, the radar homing and warning gear aboard picked up spurious radar signals. Upon conclusion of the recce mission, these signals were determined to have come from U.S. Navy radar in the gulf area, not Iranian air defenses.

and RH-53s to come and go from a dual-strip arrangement. This was a much better operation for the six aircraft and six to eight choppers than Fez and it simplified considerably our rendezvous tactics for Night-One.

John Carney had more than done his job of collecting the information. Now he set to work and had a big hand in developing the fundamental tactics we needed to make the Desert-I plan work.

When we had it together, we ran it past General Vaught and he approved it without change.[3] He then directed Carney to proceed out West and find a desert landing strip where we could conduct a modified rehearsal of these events. The week of April 10–16 was established as the time frame for the exercise.

---

[3]Richard Gabriel's book refers to a *Time* magazine article that claims the Iranians had learned of the desert landing site through interrogation of a pro-shah counterinsurgency specialist. The article claimed the CIA had built the site for possible evacuation of the shah. If so, one wonders why the CIA agreed to send a special recon mission to determine if the site was usable. It also seems strange, if the Iranians knew about the site, that they wouldn't have had someone watching it. From what I saw of the place, only God had any hand in its creation, and He wasted little effort in the process—there was nothing there but a road graded through the desert.

23

THE PRESIDENT BITES THE BULLET

April 7—Hostage Day 156
Associated Press

Ayatollah Ruhollah Khomeini ruled today that the 50 American hostages must remain in the hands of the militants occupying the U.S. Embassy in Tehran until the new Iranian Parliament decides their fate. President Carter was reliably reported to have decided to order all Iranian diplomats out of the United States in retaliation.

. . . A well-placed administration official in Washington said President Carter reached his expulsion decision at a 2½-hour morning meeting with his top policy advisers, including Secretary of State Cyrus R. Vance. . . .

Going into the meeting, a grim-faced Carter remarked that the hostages' captors—he called them "terrorists"—had agreed to release their prisoners to the Iranian government "but the government refused."

The President was being pushed to the end of his patience. That second-rate tyrant in Iran was still playing his diabolical games with the lives of fifty-three Americans.

While Mr. Carter was at Camp David over the weekend agonizing over the stalemate in Iran, I was at Langley AFB, Virginia, briefing General Gast on our new options. The general asked a lot of tough questions, and when we were through with our discussions he was very supportive of what we had come up with. He was convinced that our chances of succeeding were greatly improved.

After about an hour of going over the mission as it now stood, I told General Gast that we would soon be needing to get control of the three EC-130 ABCCC aircraft from Keesler AFB and that he could be a big help as TAC vice commander in making this as painless for everybody as possible. I gave the general a short list of actions that needed to be accomplished when the transfer order came so that it could be done on a close-hold basis, preserving operational security.

As I drove back to Washington, I was wondering what had been going on in the Pentagon in my absence. The way things had been going, for all I knew we might have gotten the order to deploy. My speculation wasn't that far off the mark. A very distraught President was, at that very moment, edging closer and closer to that decision.[1]

During the next few days, while all of us continued going over and over our plans in the fine-tuning process, General Vaught and selected advisers were involved in a flurry of meetings with the Chairman behind closed doors.

There was a concerted effort aboard the *Nimitz* to prepare eight helicopters for launch to Desert-I in hopes that six would be able to make it through the long, grueling flight and be able to go on to Tehran. More than six would be a bonus, allowing us to spread the equipment and lighten the loads on the choppers— but everyone agreed that six was the absolute minimum needed to accomplish the mission.

The factors of shrinking daylight, rising temperatures, and the underhanded double-dealing of Iran's self-proclaimed messiah were bringing things to a boil—the eleventh hour had arrived. The JTF staff concluded that April 24–25 (a weekend in Iran) was the last possible opportunity for a rescue attempt. If we let that date slip by, it would be November before conditions were right again.

Meanwhile, the staff was busy, preparing for the next rehearsal out West.

And on April 11, President Carter was again meeting with his key advisers. General Jones had made his recommendation of April 24 and was finished walking the President through the various factors which made that date the deadline for a rescue attempt when the President announced his decision:

---

[1] According to Dr. Brzezinski's article "The Failed Mission," in the *New York Times Magazine*, it was during the Monday meeting that the President decided to break diplomatic relations and also indicated the time had come for military action.

Rescue operations should proceed without delay.[2]

The same day the President was making his fateful decision, I was on an aircraft heading for Fort Bragg. General Vaught had called a meeting of all Joint Task Force commanders and supporting staff. He wanted to review the entire rescue plan thoroughly and be sure that each leader clearly understood the roles of his personnel in the revised scenarios.

We didn't know it at the time, but this would be our last such meeting before deploying on the rescue mission. The President's decision to go with this military option was a closely held secret that none of us on the Joint Task Force staff were told. The Chairman probably told General Vaught, but I don't even know that for sure.

On the flight down to Bragg, I was sitting across the aisle from Chuck Pitman, which gave me a chance to hear about Jim Schaefer's visit to the *Nimitz* in late March.

Chuck told me that Jim had found definite improvement in the operational readiness of six of the RH-53Ds. But No. 7 had made only a few flights before breaking down and was now unflyable because of the ongoing parts shortage. And No. 8 was still grounded and waiting for parts. Although some spare parts had been obtained from the Marine Amphibious Ready Group now in the Indian Ocean, the long Navy supply lines were still falling short of their needs.

The choppers were being flown more, to exercise their systems and establish the mining mission cover, but Chuck was concerned because these were only four-hour sorties. He wanted them flown on sorties about double that to expose the helos to conditions similar to what they would be facing in the insertion scenario. He said he was sending instructions to the crews aboard the *Nimitz* to fly more long-duration sorties.

Pitman was well aware of General Vaught's disenchantment with the helicopter situation, and anger and frustration at not being allowed to look things over personally. Chuck said that after receiving Schaefer's report, the general had again voiced his concerns to the Navy at not having eight choppers ready for

---

[2]Although we didn't know of the President's decision at that time, this meeting was described in Dr. Brzezinski's "The Failed Mission."

the mission. The general knew that six were not enough and he was very suspicious of the lip service he was getting from the Navy. The facts simply did not bear out what he was being told about a "gold-plated" supply effort to get these birds in top condition. It was a worrisome condition.

I'd never seen so many people in Delta's conference room—there were over fifty. Every field unit and staff specialty associated with the Joint Task Force was represented. There was an air of intense excitement.

As usual, Nick Kilgore started things off. He gave us a run-down on the intelligence situation from all sources. Other than not including the precise location of the hostages, the intelligence picture was pretty complete.[3]

Next up was Don "Stormy" Buchanan, who went over what weather we could expect in Iran.[4] The temperatures would still be in the desired range, and other than a few scattered rain showers and thunderstorms, the April forecast for Iran seemed perfect for our mission.

John Carney then took the floor and captivated the group with his description of his mission to Desert-I. Attention was riveted on his every word.

We recognized that the road running through the site kept it from being perfect, but our photo intelligence experts had expended hundreds of hours going over thousands of aerial shots and couldn't come up with anything better. Desert-I was our choice! It was the only suitable desert site!

Then the general got down to the nitty-gritty. Working with detailed schematics, the first depicting the flow of aircraft, he went over the details of the plan. (See Figure 4.)

---

[3]For obvious security reasons, Kilgore didn't mention that Dick Meadows and Fred were being slipped into Tehran to further validate the information we had and act as a reception committee for Delta.

[4]I believe Buchanan talked briefly about localized areas of suspended dust that could be expected in the vicinity of any storms, a phenomenon the Iranians called haboobs. I seem to recall that this didn't cause much concern, since our plans included delaying the launch if the forecast indicated conditions that would prevent a visual flight situation. Unfortunately, flight crews were not briefed that this situation could be encountered.

- Three MC-130s depart Masirah carrying Delta, drivers for trucks hidden in the Tehran warehouse, a roadblock team with Farsi-speaking translators, a special assault team to take down the Ministry of Foreign Affairs, and a team of combat controllers—for a total of 139 to arrive at Desert-I under cover of darkness.
- The first MC-130 departs at dusk, one hour ahead of the remaining two, to arrive well ahead of the rest of the force and in order to make sure the area is clear for landing (using the FLIR).
- Three EC-130s follow, carrying 18,000 gallons of jet fuel for the helicopters.
- Concurrently, eight RH-53 helicopters depart from the *Nimitz* (sailing in the Gulf of Oman approximately fifty nautical miles south of the Iranian coast), heading for the refueling rendezvous.
- Once on the ground, the advance party positions the roadblock teams (Rangers and some Delta troopers) and the combat controllers set up the dual landing zone on the north and south sides of the road and start the TACAN operating.
- The second and third MC-130s, landing an hour later, bring the remainder of Delta Force.
- Two of the EC-130s land three to six minutes behind the Delta MC-130s, at which time the first two MC-130s launch for return to Masirah to reduce congestion in the landing zone.
- The third EC-130 tanker then lands, making four aircraft now on the ground: two EC-130s on the north side of the road and one on the south side along with an MC-130. The MC-130 carries three 500-gallon blivets aboard as a backup fuel supply (making enough fuel for ten helicopters).
- The helicopters arrive at Desert-I about fifteen minutes after the last EC-130 tanker is in place to allow for immediate refueling and loading of Delta. Each helo receives 1,750 gallons of fuel. If eight make it to the landing zone (LZ), three will be marshaled behind each of the two tankers north of the road and two behind the tanker on the

south side. If only six make it, two each will be positioned behind each tanker (Figure 5).

- Once refueled and loaded (planned for forty minutes after arrival), the helos proceed on some two hours and ten minutes to the drop-off point fifty miles southeast of Tehran, where Dick Meadows' reception committee will be waiting.

- The four C-130s depart Desert-I, join up with KC-135s waiting to refuel them some 120 miles south of the Gulf of Oman, and then return to Masirah.

- From the Delta drop-off point, the helos proceed approximately fifty miles northeast to a remote hideout (laager) near the town of Garmsar, where they land, set up defensive positions, and camouflage the aircraft prior to sunrise. Then they wait for Delta's call on Night-Two.

- While the helos are flying to their laager, the Delta troops are moving on foot about five miles east to a remote hilly area. They bivouac in this area, which is honeycombed with abandoned salt mines, and make final preparations for the reconnaissance of and assault on the embassy. All forces are to be concealed in their respective hide sites by dawn.

- For the rest of that day, JTF headquarters in Wadi Kena, Egypt, monitors communications circuits to determine if our insertion activity has been detected and to obtain updates on the embassy situation from Dick Meadows. Any increase in security or unusual movement of vehicles to or from the embassy could mean they are on to us, in which case we will have to consider abandoning the rescue attempt, depending on evaluation of the situation.

NIGHT-TWO

- If we haven't been detected during insertion, the hundred-man Ranger force launches from Wadi Kena aboard four MC-130s at dusk the second day to start the extraction phase. (See Figure 6, page 206.)

- The C-130s are refueled over Saudi Arabia by KC-135s.

- Four AC-130 gunships (one spare) depart Wadi Kena shortly after the MC-130s and three continue on to Iran

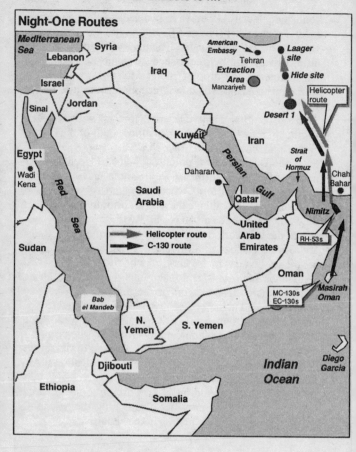

Night-One Routes

after refueling—one to provide close air support for Beck-with's forces at the embassy, one to suppress any fighter ground activity at Mehrabad Airport on the outskirts of town, and the third to provide air support for either Delta or the Rangers at Manzariyeh.

- Two C-141s depart Daharan, Saudi Arabia, so as to land at Manzariyeh ten minutes after the airfield is secured. One is basically a "flying hospital" to tend to any wounded or injured personnel. The other is configured with airline-style passenger seats. These "snort 'n' zoomer" transports will await the arrival of the choppers with Delta and the rescued hostages.

- Meanwhile, Dick Meadows will drive Beckwith into Tehran

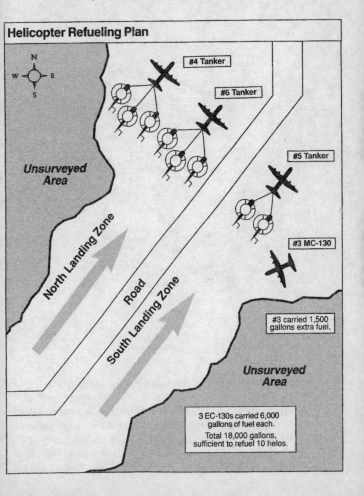

Helicopter Refueling Plan

#4 Tanker

#6 Tanker

#5 Tanker

#3 MC-130

Unsurveyed Area

North Landing Zone

Road

South Landing Zone

Unsurveyed Area

#3 carried 1,500 gallons extra fuel.

3 EC-130s carried 6,000 gallons of fuel each.
Total 18,000 gallons, sufficient to refuel 10 helos.

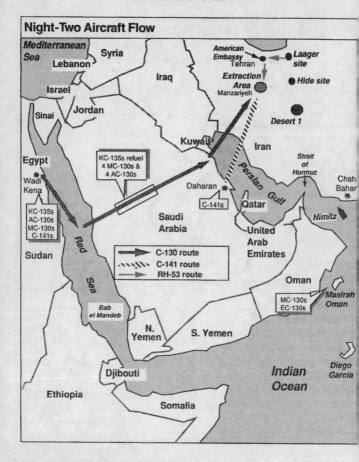

Night-Two Aircraft Flow

Mediterranean Sea

Syria

Lebanon

Israel

Sinai

Jordan

Egypt

Wadi Kena

KC-135s
AC-130s
MC-130s
C-141s

Sudan

Red Sea

Bab el Mandeb

N. Yemen

S. Yemen

Djibouti

Ethiopia

Somalia

Iraq

Kuwait

KC-135s refuel
4 MC-130s &
4 AC-130s

Daharan

C-141s

Saudi Arabia

Qatar

United Arab Emirates

Oman

MC-130s
EC-130s

American Embassy
Tehran

Laager site

Extraction Area
Manzariyeh

Hide site

Desert 1

Iran

Strait of Hormuz

Chah Bahar

Persian Gulf

Nimitz

Masirah Oman

Indian Ocean

Diego Garcia

C-130 route
C-141 route
RH-53 route

from the hide site to reconnoiter the routes Delta will take (Figure 7).

- Another van-type vehicle will then be used to infiltrate the six driver teams, with translators, to the edge of town to pick up six trucks prepositioned in a warehouse by CIA operatives.
- Next, the vehicles will be driven back to the Delta hide site

Night-Two Plan

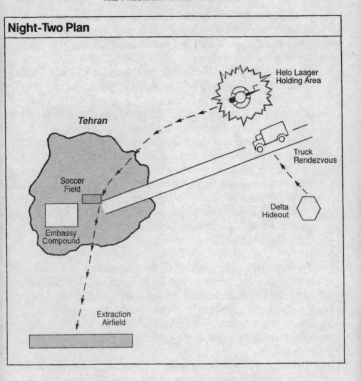

and prepared for movement of the assault force into town, hidden behind false walls in the trucks.

- Based on his reconnaissance of Tehran, if it's a go, Beckwith will start moving the Delta Force into the city. The drivers will have to get past two roadblocks, which it has been determined can be done without too much difficulty.
- A separate vehicle will move a special thirteen-man team into town for the rescue of the hostages at the Ministry of Foreign Affairs. They will use a different route from that of the main force.
- Delta will move into position for the assault, scheduled for 11:00 P.M. Beckwith will have a plus-or-minus-forty-minute leeway on when to breach the wall, based on his

best judgment of what he sees and is confronted with. The assault on Manzariyeh and the appearance of the gunship over the embassy will not occur until Beckwith gives the code word on his radio.

- Once Delta enters the compound, Charlie will call for the helos. Four choppers will proceed to the Amjadieh soccer stadium, and two will fly to a location near the Ministry of Foreign Affairs and pick up the special assault team, which will have Bruce Laingen and two of his staff in tow.

- It is estimated that the hostage release will take forty-five minutes (with most freed within thirty minutes). Once liberated, the hostages will be moved across Roosevelt Avenue into the soccer stadium, where part of Beckwith's force will have set up a helicopter extraction zone.[5] The stadium is a natural fortress from which Delta can hold off a sizable attacking force, if need be, especially with support from the AC-130's cannon.

"We hope five helicopters will be operational so we can get everybody out in one trip. However, one MC-130 will have 1,500 gallons of bladder fuel available at Manzariyeh if one or more of the helicopters has to shuttle back to the soccer stadium to pick up more people. We fervently hope we won't have to do this. The risks are obvious," the general said.

- Upon arrival at Manzariyeh, the freed hostages and rescue team personnel will be sorted out according to any medical care required and then loaded on the waiting C-141s and taken out of Iran.

- The MC-130s with the Rangers aboard will return to Wadi Kena, followed by the AC-130s. The helicopters will be left behind, because there won't be sufficient fuel to get them to friendly territory. (I had heard that they would be destroyed where they sat . . . still a troublesome thought.)

- The hostages, Delta, and the helo crews will be moved out of the Middle East expeditiously, so as to preserve the secrecy of Delta.

[5]There was also a plan for one or two RH-53s to land inside the embassy compound on the athletic field and load hostages. Beckwith would determine if this was possible once inside the embassy grounds.

- The remainder of the JTF assets involved will be redeployed home over a two-or-three-day period.

This was a complex plan. The hostage situation itself was complex. It would require equal portions of skill, teamwork, and luck. But nobody had said it was going to be easy. Pulling this rescue off called for ingenious tactics with bold men to carry them out.

It had taken over five months to finally put together a concept that we believed was feasible and had the best chance possible of succeeding.

Late in coming as it was, removing the geographical shackles on the use of Masirah and Desert-I made a great difference. We now needed to rehearse the Desert-I landing scenario to be sure that nothing had been overlooked.

We would be going to Yuma the next day to conduct that exercise (two C-130s had already been positioned with the helicopters to participate in that event). This would not be a full-blown exercise, but we would accomplish all that was necessary to examine our tactics and test their effectiveness in a desert environment.

We felt that after that, we would be ready for come what may.

24

LAST REHEARSAL

April 11—Hostage Day 160
<u>Associated Press</u>

NEW YORK—One of the Iranian militants in the U.S. Embassy in Tehran said Thursday that the American hostages would be "destroyed" if Iraq invaded Iran.

"Iraq is a puppet of the American government. Iraq does nothing without orders from America," a militant named Habib said in a live interview on the NBC *Today Show*.

The Iranian militants also said Wednesday that the hostages would be killed if there was American military intervention to free the hostages.

After General Vaught had laid out the plan and a myriad of details were hashed over, we were all back in the conference room after a brief lunch break. Standing at the front were Bob Dutton and Jim Keating—the "murder board" hatchet men.

They were here to put us on the grill and hang our plan up and throw darts at it. We had already shed blood at the hands of these two over the Fez option. Now we were going to bleed for our Desert-I plan. They would dissect our plan, and before it was all over we would feel as if we had been dissected, too.

The questions were probing, like:

"What will you do if the lead MC-130 with Delta aboard aborts at Masirah?"

"What will you do if an EC-130 tanker aborts en route to Desert-I?"

"What do you do if the remotely activated lights don't come on at Desert-I?"

"What if a C-130 crashes on landing or breaks through the crust and becomes stuck?"

"How long can you wait at Desert-I for the helos if they are delayed?"

"How many helos must you have operational to proceed on to Tehran?"

"What do you do if one of the C-130s' refueling systems doesn't work?"

"If we have to abort the mission at Desert-I or in Tehran, how do we get everybody out of there?"

The list was endless, the debates heated. Late in the evening it was still going on. Everyone was bushed, totally drained. The nonstop bombardment of questions was relentless.

When all was said and done, the whole bloody session brought home to us the tenuous nature of our rescue plan. There were potential break points all along the way. In some cases, we came up with ways to continue. Others left us no choice but to abort. Some plans were altered on the spot to compensate for obvious weaknesses.

We had thought through all of the possible glitches the murder board could conjure up and were glad in the end that we had gone through the bloodletting. General Vaught's murder-board session had impressed upon us all the importance of performing open-heart surgery on our plan now. Far better to consider right here and now what could go wrong and fix it than to be trying to do it in the middle of the Iranian desert.

True, there might be something we had missed, but now the game plan was structured to contend with all of the vulnerabilities a roomful of experts could come up with. General Vaught and his staff at the Wadi Kena command center would have to follow the mission closely and help sort out any unexpected problems.

The mission commanders on the scene would have to be the JTF commander's eyes and ears, tied in to the center by a satellite communications net. If any called for help, the JTF commander and his staff would have to figure it out and provide guidance.

As far as I was concerned, the satellite communications system was an unknown factor. Most field commanders had little or no exposure to this system. However, Delta's communications experts were highly confident in it, which alleviated a good bit of our concerns.

Pete Dieck and his communications staff had assured us that adequate radios would be in the hands of each element of the force when it came time to execute the mission—and they would "function as advertised." I sure as hell hoped so, because we were putting all of our trust in a bunch of black boxes that had been unavailable for most of our training.

Dieck told us we would have special operators to man the radios and wouldn't need any training in communications for this mission. To me, this had the ring of the old cliché "Not to worry—the check's in the mail."

C'est la vie. The logistics of the satellite radios were beyond the JTF's ability to influence much. This was new equipment and still in extremely short supply.

It was just after dark on Saturday when Chuck Pitman's Huey took off from Yuma, headed for a drop zone in the Arizona desert where we would land and watch C-141Bs perform a blivet drop. These massive MAC jet transports were the latest in the C-141 fleet (in-flight-refuelable and with some twenty feet more of cargo space than the C-141A) and could each carry eleven 500-gallon blivets.

As we watched, thirty-three blivets, hoses and pumps for them, and six tractors landed right on the money in an area the size of three football fields . . . flawlessly. What a beautiful airdrop!

When our chopper was airborne and heading on for Edwards Air Force Base, I remarked to the general that the C-141 people had done a beautiful job of putting their loads right on target with everything blacked out.

He agreed and voiced his concern that if something went wrong once Delta had been inserted into Tehran, the helicopters wouldn't have sufficient fuel to extract them from the country. Using C-141Bs to airdrop blivets to the helos in a remote desert area would allow the helos to refuel and make it back to the carrier or friendly territory. The airdrop of fuel made more sense than an airfield seizure if an emergency extraction had to be made.

During this flight, Chuck leaned over to me and said, "You might be interested in the fact that we now have an Air Force captain named Rakip flying with us and he's doing a bang-up job."

Apparently Rakip, who was chief of standardization in Colonel Bill Takacs's CH-53 squadron at Bergstrom AFB, Texas, had been brought into the JTF to provide some Air Force participation in the helo component. This brought the pilot lineup to eleven Marine, five Navy, and one Air Force.

Chuck got us on the ground at Edwards about an hour before the desert rehearsal was to occur. John Carney and his people were there, laying out the runway and setting up the lights and TACAN.

I was surprised at how close we were to the main airfield at Edwards—only about three or four miles away. The outline of the control tower was clearly visible on the night horizon. I hunted up Carney. "John, are you sure our traffic pattern won't conflict with theirs? I'd hate for our blacked-out birds to get tangled up with some fighter jockey up there in the murk."

"No sweat. The entire area is ours for the night. Edwards is closed to all air traffic." He had visited the base commander and set it all up.

The plan was to land one MC-130 with a few Delta troopers on board, then follow with an EC-130 Bladder Bird carrying 6,000 gallons of jet fuel. Four H-53s would arrive fifteen minutes later, land, and refuel from the tanker.

We had determined that this would give us a test of everything we needed to look at for the Desert-I operation. Delta certainly needed no more practice getting off a C-130 and onto helicopters, and, of course, the Ranger Rat Patrol had no airport to seize in this scenario.

We also felt that if we could land one Combat Talon and one Bladder Bird in the desert we could discover any unforeseen problems in accomplishing this tactic.[1]

Although it would have been desirable to land six at once and run through the complete marshaling plan with the helicopters, we just didn't have enough C-130s available for this exercise. Timing had worked against us. The PACAF crews and

---

[1]Because the Desert-I option came so late, we did not rehearse with the road-block team during any of our CONUS training. The roadblock team did not get organized, trained, and rehearsed until they were at Wadi Kena. Then General Vaught, Charlie Beckwith, and Sherm Williford put them together and ran them through their drills.

aircraft had returned to Okinawa and there simply wasn't enough time to get them back for this rehearsal. We would train the flight leaders and their wingmen would follow their lead—that's how the flying game works.

As midnight approached, Carney and his crew activated the small portable runway lights and got the TACAN operating as a homing beacon. The desert surface was surprisingly solid, with very little loose sand.

Then we heard the faint drone of engines and spotted the MC-130 on final approach. Bob Meller was at the controls. The EC-130 tanker, piloted by Captain Russ Tharp, was close behind, being led over the landing zone by the Talon. Russ then took it around and waited for his turn to land. Since the Bladder Bird was not equipped with the same radar and precise navigation systems as the Talon, we were using follow-the-leader tactics to help Russ get lined up for landing—just as we'd do it in Iran.

Bob set his Talon down perfectly on the desert floor and taxied into the Delta off-load position set up by the combat controllers. Five minutes later, Russ brought his EC-130 along the path Meller had shown him and set it down smoothly. It worked exactly as planned. The Bladder Bird was marshaled up beside the MC-130; the pumps were cranked up and the hoses reeled out.

In the distance, I could see the helicopters now approaching, right on schedule. Within minutes they were on the ground and being marshaled up behind the Bladder Bird.

While the refueling was in progress, General Vaught, Chuck Pitman, and I talked to the pilots of the C-130s and choppers to see if they had experienced any difficulties in landing and maneuvering their birds on the desert. For the most part, they had no problems to report and viewed the additional space in the desert as a substantial plus in safety for the refueling operations. Russ Tharp said that he'd had trouble spotting the portable runway lights but that the follow-the-leader tactic had worked well. With these pathfinder formations in the plans, he foresaw no problems for the three EC-130s on the actual mission.

The refueling crews complained of the stinging sand being blown about by the props and rotors, but this was more just a nuisance than anything else. It had little effect on performance. There wasn't as much dust as I had expected, but I had also experienced the sandblasting. Since we were wearing night-vision goggles the sand didn't hamper our vision, but we did have to shield our faces. We all got pretty well caked up with the gritty stuff.

Within thirty minutes, the choppers were gassed up and ready to go. General Vaught was satisfied that everything had gone well and directed all components to return to their launch bases.[2]

There was one interesting, and somewhat amusing, sidelight to this exercise that really served to underline how effective our blacked-out procedures were.

It was standard practice to have a fire truck standing by about a mile from our operating area, just in case. Well, the truck was there and still standing by long after we had all left the area. John Carney had forgotten to tell the fire crew that we no longer needed their services. Late that night, they finally returned to their station and reported that the aircraft hadn't shown up.

The next day, John had an angry Edwards base commander chewing on him for "not telling the fire department that the mission had been canceled." The fire crew accepted John's apology, but he was certain that they didn't believe his story that we had really been there.

During the short Huey flight back to Yuma AAF, I was thinking of the three options we had developed to conduct the refueling rendezvous: the airdrop of fuel, the Fez assault, and finally, Desert-I. Although Desert-I was the primary option, we had the others to fall back on if something went wrong or the intelligence situation changed at the last minute, dictating a change in plans. All our eggs weren't in one basket.

There's no doubt that we would have been better off concentrating our Night-One rehearsals on the Masirah/Desert-I scenario, but the late approval of these options precluded that. Fortunately, most of the Fez tactics also applied to the desert option—we'd go with that and incorporate our past experience in the dust. The die was cast.

---

[2]One of the RH-53s returning to Yuma was forced to make a precautionary landing for a BIM indication, and it subsequently aborted. It was the second experience with a BIM problem during training. However, no specific guidance was given on how to handle this type of problem should it occur in Iran. It was left up to each crew to decide, based on experience.

PART THREE

THE MISSION

25

MOVE 'EM OUT!

April 13—Hostage Day 162
<u>Associated Press</u>

. . . Hassan Habibi, a spokesman for the ruling Revolutionary Council, said in an interview broadcast by Tehran radio today that Iran is "ready for a world war" if the United States starts one over the hostages.

Hints of American military action do not appear serious, he said. He dismissed the possibility of an economic blockade at the mouth of the Persian Gulf because, he reasoned, it would cut off oil from Saudi Arabia and other Arab countries as well as Iran. . . .

We were flying back to Washington from the Edwards soirée when General Vaught told Chuck Pitman and me that we would be getting deployment orders in the next few days to move JTF forces to our intermediate staging bases.

Now we were on the fast track for sure!

We would hold off any movement to our forward staging base at Masirah until we knew preliminary action had gone undetected.

The general told us that our intelligence people had been studying the Soviet satellite pattern over the Middle East and would schedule the JTF aircraft movements for when we would be least vulnerable to detection. That information would be given to us at a deployment meeting later today—Jerry King was collecting all the necessary information.

The boss wanted the fact that we were deploying confined to his field commanders. The troops and aircrews were only to be told to be ready to move to a new training location, as yet unspecified. For now, the general wanted to minimize the chance of a security leak.

On the other hand, he wanted the field commanders to make sure their forces were carrying all the support gear they needed to conduct the rescue mission.

I reminded him that the Okinawa-based MC-130s would be routed to Masirah via Diego Garcia, their staging base before movement to Masirah. Their flights to that Indian Ocean air base were to coincide with the movement of the CONUS forces to Egypt.

He agreed that they should move at the same time as the others, but only Ray Turczynski was to know the true destination was Masirah. The aircrews and support personnel would be told they were deploying to Diego Garcia to conduct sea surveillance training with the Navy for a week. They were not to know about the rescue deployment until reaching Masirah.

Practically, I didn't think we could fool our aircrews for long once the deployment was under way. They would have to file flight plans for overseas destinations that they knew were jumping-off points for the rescue mission. We would go along with this charade for now.

I moved over to the seat next to Pitman. "Chuck, I think this is it, don't you?"

"Agreed. This is exactly how we figured it would happen— a rehearsal, then orders to relocate to a new training location. I'm preparing my guys to deploy to the *Nimitz*." We both appreciated the general's position on security, but agreed that we had to avoid "shooting ourselves in the foot" with too much secrecy. Anyway, I would tell the Air Force mission commanders to prepare for movement to the staging bases. We'd keep any further action secret until General Vaught released the information.

Arriving at the Pentagon, we found that Jerry King had already gathered the key members of the Joint Task Force staff for the deployment meeting. He reviewed the list of actions from Bob Horton's deployment chart that he had already initiated. These preplanned events had been constantly updated just so they would be ready for now.

I was concerned over whether steps had been taken to direct movement of three ABCCC EC-130s from Keesler AFB to Hurlburt and whether these birds were being painted and configured for the mission. Jerry assured me that this had been done.

All field commanders had been alerted to prepare for deployment and were readying their forces for the "training event." Only one notification remained. I was to call Ray Turczynski on Okinawa and fill him in.

Once the general was satisfied that nothing had been overlooked and that the deployment actions were well under way, he sent us to get cracking on our individual action items with these final words: "We will move the forces on the dates depicted on the deployment charts unless otherwise notified. That means the first elements will start positioning at Wadi Kena on April 14, tomorrow. Keep on top of this thing. We can't afford any screwups now."

I immediately dispatched Lee Hess to the Operations Planning Group to coordinate the movements of the KC-135s and C-141s with Dave Forgan. Dave's people would play important roles in the deployments to Egypt and Diego Garcia. If things were going to run smoothly, we would have to keep them completely informed.

It was late Sunday afternoon when I finally got Ray Turczynski on the secure phone.

"Ray, be in place at Diego Garcia by April 17 and ready to move forward to Masirah on April 19 and 20. Plan on nothing more than fuel and water being available at Masirah. In other words, carry along your own tents, sleeping bags, rations, and whatever minimal maintenance support gear you think you'll need."

I left it up to Ray to determine what they would need at Masirah, reminding him that there would be no special airlift for his gear so he'd only have what he could get aboard his three MC-130s. We'd only be at Masirah, under these austere conditions, for five days—the troops could hack that.

We spent the next few days going over our deployment actions to make sure we hadn't overlooked anything that could later rise up and bite us in the butt. Then we received a hurry-up call to prepare a "special briefing" for the Joint Chiefs of Staff. They were to be updated on the changes to our rescue plan involving Desert-I and Masirah. General Jones set this meeting up to provide the service chiefs an opportunity to get answers to any questions they might have concerning the rescue mission.

General Vaught did most of the talking while we lower-echelon JTF staff members sat in the back of the room and listened. Occasionally, the Chairman would amplify a point, and General Gast added a few supporting comments.

Having sat through one of General Vaught's previous presentations to this roomful of stars, I thought he outdid himself on this one. It was an articulate, convincing, and captivating dissection of a complex subject.

I have no idea what the service chiefs were thinking, but there was no dissent on the surface. After listening to the presentation and a smattering of discussion from all quarters, I left that briefing convinced that there was unanimous support for the Joint Task Force's plan. There were no signs of disagreement. The stage was now set for the main event—briefing the President of the United States.

Later, I saw Charlie Beckwith go behind closed doors with Generals Jones, Meyer, Vaught, and Gast, but I didn't think too much about it at the time. I had gotten used to seeing these huddles over the past few months.

A couple of hours later, I was going over charts in the Back Room when Jerry King suddenly showed up and told me that the "heavyweights have gone over to brief the President and his closest advisers."

My heart skipped a couple of beats. "C'mon, Jerry, you wouldn't be jerking my chain, would you?"

But I could see he was serious as he shook his head and said, "We'll know later this evening if we have a go."

My first reaction was to get to the checklist and go over the events of the deployment, for the hundredth time, to be sure I hadn't forgotten anything. I called Lee Hess in and we began going over the long list of "to-dos" while all the time wondering what was going on over in the White House.

Of course, we were reacting this way because we didn't know

that the President had approved the mission days ago. The President was just now being briefed on the final details of the mission, and this also gave him a chance to meet the key commanders he was sending out to do this job. I'm sure Mr. Carter must have felt better after meeting and talking with General Vaught, General Gast, and Charlie Beckwith.

We later learned from notes taken at that meeting by Dr. Zbigniew Brzezinski and from Charlie Beckwith's book *Delta Force* that the President went over every aspect of the mission as briefed by General Vaught. These records report that the President stated he would not interfere in operational decisions and gave General Jones final authority. He knew that six helicopters were necessary at Desert-I to insert the rescue force into Tehran. He also knew we had eight RH-53Ds aboard the *Nimitz* and were striving to have all eight ready for the mission.

The one proviso the President continued to emphasize was his edict against "wanton killings."

Beckwith responded, "If Delta gets in a firefight, it has to be able to use whatever force is necessary to protect American lives." The President understood this and accepted that provision as the basis for the "rules of engagement."[1]

The President also discussed the chances of success and failure and weighed the chances against expected casualties (estimated to be between three and eight, including hostages and rescue personnel).[2] General Gast said that with eight helicopters operational, he felt we had a 96 percent probability that

[1]"Rules of engagement" is a term I first encountered during the Vietnam War which sometimes translates into protecting the enemy while hindering U.S. forces. I didn't like most rules of engagement then and still don't. One has to question the morality of sending troops out to fight and die while at the same time placing political constraints on their actions. The objective of combat must be victory. On the other hand, unnecessary killings and atrocities have no place in the American fighting man's code and "necessary action" should never be confused with wanton killing.

[2]Author Richard Gabriel strikes again! He wrote that the CIA estimated 60 percent (thirty-two) of the hostages would be killed. Gabriel further reported that he learned from Pentagon planners that they believed the casualties among hostages and rescuers might run as high as one hundred. It is asinine to place any credence to these figures. A rescue mission with predictions of heavy casualties to the hostages would not have been approved by the President, nor would the Joint Task Force have recommended an attempt with such poor odds of success.

six helos would depart Desert-I. This was one of those decisions that makes being the President of the United States a lonely job.[3]

When General Vaught returned to the Special Operations Division, he did not specifically say the mission was a "Go." The White House discussions were not revealed, but the general made it abundantly clear to me that plans to carry out the mission were to proceed. All Presidents of this great nation have had to have the courage to make difficult decisions—sometimes unpopular, sometimes risky—but I believe this was President Carter's toughest, and I admired him for it.

Even though it was after 10:00 P.M. when we heard from General Vaught, we worked on into the night rechecking our plans, making sure that all the correct wheels were in motion to get the forces deployed. We were told to continue the ploy that we were preparing for another full-scale rehearsal, knowing that we would have to tell our people soon that this was for real.

I told General Vaught that I felt compelled to get down to Hurlburt the following morning to look things over and make sure all was in order. I especially wanted to check on the three Keesler EC-130s.

The general agreed with this but told me to be back by 11:00 P.M. on April 18, for that night the staff was to be driven out to Andrews AFB, Maryland, to board a C-141 . . . destination Wadi Kena, Egypt. "This is one flight you won't want to miss," he said with a smile. "It will be a memorable trip."

While I was trying to get to sleep that night, my mind was running back over the past five and a half months.

During that time, the Joint Task Force components had trained continuously—as individual units and jointly—in numerous

---

[3] I was surprised to read in Paul B. Ryan's book that Admiral James L. Holloway, head of the commission to investigate the aborted rescue attempt, stated that the mission had had only a 60–70 percent chance of success. I'd never heard these numbers before and wonder how he arrived at that figure, since he was not an expert in Special Operations. The author suggests that the figure was based on testimony taken from the Joint Chiefs of Staff. If this was truly the case (and not just another example of creative reporting), I can't help wondering why none of them registered these concerns before the mission. They certainly had plenty of opportunities.

events, exercises, and rehearsals. Hundreds of small-scale training events had been capped with five major rehearsals.

The helicopter crews had flown nearly 1,000 hours of night blacked-out missions.

The C-130s, KC-135s, and C-141s had logged well over 1,500 hours of night flying in training with Delta, the Rangers, and the helicopters—not counting the numerous hours spent hauling special cargo and personnel to support the mission.

Collectively, over 2,500 hours of flying time had been accumulated without an accident.

The C-130 crews had adapted to using the night-vision goggles with exceptional skill and could land adeptly on runways with no lighting while completely blacked-out. They could land on dirt and desert runways with equal skill.

The C-141 crews, in a short time, had learned to land with minimum lighting and could perform modified low-level navigation techniques.

Our helicopter crews had flown hundreds of hours using night-vision goggles in cross-country navigation under conditions ranging from full moon to total darkness. Their refueling procedures with the C-130s had become almost routine. The techniques of landing and taking off in the dust had been mastered with great difficulty through hours of concentrated training.

Delta and the Rangers had gone over their responsibilities until each man was intimate with his job. They were highly skilled with their weapons and tactics and moved, thought, and existed as a single entity. They ranked among the best forces ever assembled for this type of mission.

Communications had reached a new high in technical achievement with the satellite radio systems. We would have the minimum number of SATCOM radios required to conduct the mission.

The ability to rescue our people being held hostage, which did not exist on November 4, 1979, was now a reality. Our plans had been reviewed by the highest military leaders and key government officials and been stamped APPROVED, with high probability of success.

Through five and a half months, we had done all of this and still maintained operational security. Quite an accomplishment!

Now we must sustain this secrecy right up to and over the embassy walls.[4]

Thinking about how soon I would be heading toward a date with destiny, I was feeling a pride that words can't describe. I was part of a special organization that was about to undertake one of the more important military operations in our history. There were many uncertainties we had yet to face, but they were clearly understood and accepted as part of the realities that confront commanders with the "guts to try" such daring missions.

[4]Author Paul B. Ryan raises the question "Why did the JCS deny themselves the benefit of an outsider's objective evaluation of the rescue plan?" He suggests that the fear of breaching security was the reason and therefore some of the JCS members who lacked experience in Special Operations had only a limited understanding of the complexities involved in this mission. It is hard for me to accept the idea that the most powerful men in the U.S. military establishment were denied access to whatever counsel was necessary to evaluate the plan. This theory just doesn't wash with me. If any of the chiefs did not understand the complexities of the plan, why did they approve it? There was too much riding on this one to approve it without understanding it. I can't buy Mr. Ryan's conjecture. If we can't trust the Joint Chiefs of Staff to protect against a breach in security, we're in damn sad shape.

26

SMOKE AND MIRRORS

April 14—Hostage Day 163
<u>Associated Press</u>
Two representatives of the International Red Cross and a group of Iranians visited the 50 American hostages in the U.S. Embassy today to check on their condition and report their findings to the families of the captives.

. . . A spokeswoman at the Geneva headquarters of the Red Cross said the Iranian government agreed to three conditions set by the organization—that its representatives meet with all the hostages, that they be allowed to make a list of their identities, and that they be allowed to notify the captives' families of the state of their health.

It is no small undertaking to move thirty-four special-mission aircraft and twenty support aircraft 8,000 miles to a remote corner of the world and set up clandestine operations without slipping up and attracting unwanted attention somewhere along the way—but that's what we did.

When the President approved the deployment of the Joint Task Force we were immediately faced with the tricky job of slipping our forces from the United States and Japan into positions in the Middle East, Indian Ocean, and Arabian Gulf areas.

This would require skillful use of cover and deception tactics—smoke and mirrors. Every move had to be made with an awareness of orbiting Soviet spy satellites, signal intelligence sites, and the natural curiosity of our allies, as well as the prying eyes of our adversaries.

Since early January, Colonel Dave Forgan's gang in the Operation Planning Group (OPG) had been manipulating airlift, tanker, and fighter operations into and out of Wadi Kena, our main operating base. By directing numerous KC-135s, F-15s, F-16s, AWACS aircraft, C-141s, C-130s, and C-5s through Wadi Kena, the OPG had created an operational "footprint" that would serve to mask deployment of the Joint Task Force's aircraft into the area.

No doubt these activities attracted scrutiny from numerous intelligence analysts at first, but after several months of diverse operations involving nearly every type of aircraft in the Air Force inventory it most likely became tedious to the observers.[1]

Eventually, even Combat Talon MC-130s (from the European Command) were introduced into the area to get people used to seeing these unique black aircraft. They conducted air intercept training with American and Egyptian fighter units, thus promoting a credible reason for this type of aircraft to show up at Wadi Kena. Even though the Talons are normally associated with unconventional warfare missions, these routine training events served to dispel any conjecture that they (and later, our birds) were associated with any clandestine operations.

Unknowingly, one Europe-based MC-130 crew did participate more directly with our mission during the first two days of April. A crew from the 7th SOS at Rhein Main Air Base, Germany, was directed to fly a Talon, equipped with a Fulton Recovery System, to Wadi Kena and await special orders from the Pentagon. The man from Washington was Major Rod Toth, JTF C-130 intelligence officer. The orders Toth carried directed that the Rhein Main MC-130 crew fly to an airport in Oman and be prepared to perform a Fulton Recovery System extraction of some people deep in Iranian territory, if called upon. This, of course, was the CIA survey mission to Desert-I.

Although not knowing the actual purpose of their mission, the crew performed a valuable service for the Joint Task Force by being ready to assist if help was needed . . . and by having their black MC-130 seen in the Oman area.

*   *   *

---

[1]One Egyptian general was quoted by the news media as stating that the United States was testing the feasibility of using Egyptian air bases as way stations for flights into Iran. This potentially damaging observation faded into obscurity as time passed and nothing materialized to substantiate such a claim.

The problem of moving our aircraft and supporting elements into position required Lee Hess and me to spend many hours coordinating with our overseas unconventional warfare experts. The agents we had in Germany and Hawaii were the best ones to help us blend the Joint Task Force movements in with activity in their theaters of operation. The guidance they provided was a key factor in our ability to protect our cover.

In our endeavors to come up with the best cover for deployment, we kicked around some extremely innovative "bait-and-switch" tactics that on diagrams looked like neolithic cave paintings. We finally settled on a philosophy of making the obvious seem so innocuous that nobody would pay any attention. We kept it simple so as not to confuse ourselves (more than our adversaries) with some complicated deception scheme.

D-Day was to be April 25.

We used Jerry King's flow charts to check when each aircraft should move to be in place by D-Day minus one, the first day of what was now being called Operation Eagle Claw.[2]

This was another of those management tools (like our unique mission equipment chart) that you work backward to determine decision points at which the aircraft have to start moving to be in place at the appointed time. It was the overview for a master shell game to funnel all types of aircraft into and out of Wadi Kena, Masirah, Daharan, and Diego Garcia. Among other things, the chart showed us when to obtain diplomatic clearances for overflights, departure dates for each aircraft, routings, and where flights would be linking up with KC-135 tankers for refueling.

When the "go" was given, we had to back up twelve days from D-Day and start things moving to maintain a flow and keep any elements from bunching up. We could see at a glance where aircraft should be at any time, and this was the backbone of our deployment schedule.

From the outset, our plan was for our forces to approach the Persian Gulf in stages from two directions. The Okinawa-based MC-130 unit would fly southwest down the South China Sea and

---

[2]Eagle Claw was the operational name for the rescue mission. It replaced Rice Bowl, the cover name.

cross that portion of Thailand that lies along the Malay Peninsula, then cross the Indian Ocean to Diego Garcia. The MC-130 units in the United States would cross the Atlantic, either via Lajes Field in the Azores or nonstop to Germany. From there they would cross the Mediterranean Sea and proceed into Egypt.

27

THE SHELL GAME

APRIL 13, 1980—D-DAY MINUS TWELVE

When Ray Turczynski received my "heads-up" call that Sunday, he went right into action. His first move was to go to the home of Colonel Hugh Milton, wing director of operations, and brief him on the deployment order.

Milton told Ray that the fighter wing was undergoing an operational readiness exercise starting the next day and that it would provide a perfect cover for getting the MC-130s out of Kadena.

He said that all of his units would be scrambling to position cargo and process their troops for airlift movement. Fighters, transports, and tankers would be winding up to peak readiness to jump off to diverse Pacific bases. With Milton covering for them, Ray and his crews could slip out with these birds and nobody would be the wiser.

APRIL 14, 1980—D-DAY MINUS ELEVEN

At Kadena, the three MC-130s were loaded as part of the wing's operational readiness drill and the Talon crews were mobilized and completed their predeployment tasks, then rested for the long mission ahead.

Meanwhile, three Joint Task Force KC-135s were landing at Wadi Kena (the first mission aircraft to move into place) after a flight from the SAC base at Mildenhall, England. Nobody gave these now-familiar aircraft a second look.

APRIL 15, 1980—D-DAY MINUS TEN

Tuesday night, three black Combat Talons took off from Kadena at one-hour intervals. The Kadena exercise controllers believed their destination was Clark Air Base in the Philippines, and Hugh Milton made sure that's where the log books located them.

While the MC-130s were flying toward Diego Garcia, the first of fifteen Military Airlift Command (MAC) C-141s was on its way from Charleston AFB, South Carolina, to Wadi Kena via Ramstein, Germany. This was the beginning of an operation that would be spread over nine days.

MAC had an advance team, called the Airlift Control Element (ALCE), aboard the first C-141. This eighteen-man team from Charleston would set up at Wadi Kena to receive the follow-on transports with Joint Task Force elements aboard.

Also aboard this first C-141 was Colonel Bill Kornitzer, the Charleston wing director of operations, who was to work for General Vaught, managing the MAC airlift assets. John Carney and his six-man combat control team were aboard this bird, accompanying the unique equipment that would be used to set up the twin landing strips at Desert-I.

APRIL 16, 1980—D-DAY MINUS NINE

After sixteen hours and two in-flight refuelings, the black birds from Kadena touched down early in the morning at Diego Garcia, having overflown Clark. The first refueling was provided by Kadena tankers, but the second came from SAC tankers out of Diego Garcia that had been prepositioned to support the JTF mission.

Unfortunately, the welcome mat was not out for these Combat Talon crews and the commander of the naval base there refused to provide quarters or maintenance workspace unless they would reveal the purpose of their presence—an unacceptable demand.

At the same time, one of Pete Dieck's SATCOM crews was trying to set up a command and control station at Diego Garcia and was running into the same trouble Ray was encountering.

Having been told "no way," the crew sent word back to the Pentagon. It wasn't long before that base commander was talking to a flag officer in Washington, and after that he just couldn't seem to do enough for the JTF visitors to his base.

APRIL 17, 1980—D-DAY MINUS EIGHT

While that first C-141 with the Joint Task Force's advance elements aboard was landing at Wadi Kena, halfway across the globe, at Andrews AFB, Chuck Pitman was boarding another C-141 for the long trip to Diego Garcia. Aboard this flight was Jim Keating from the PACOM planning staff, who would be liaison aboard the *Nimitz* for both General Vaught and Admiral Long (CINCPAC). Chuck Gilbert was going along to supervise the installation of the Palletized Inertial Navigation System (PINS) equipment in the RH-53D helicopters. Finally, two Sikorsky technical representatives were going to assist Navy maintenance personnel in preparing the choppers.

This C-141 stopped en route at Yuma to pick up the helo crews and their equipment, then proceeded on to Honolulu, where Keating and Pitman briefed Admiral Long on the rescue plan.

Continuing on, the C-141 made a refueling stop at the tightly controlled SAC installation on Guam, Andersen AFB, where they ran into trouble. Stubborn security personnel, demanding to be allowed to board to search for contraband (plants, drugs, weapons), were rebuffed by Colonel Pitman. After a prolonged standoff, Chuck relented and the security types entered the aircraft with sniffer dogs. As one of the dogs nosed around a grungy-looking mail sack (which just happened to be stuffed with a million bucks in Iranian rials and U.S. currency), Pitman and Keating were sweating blood. Chuck was wracking his brains to come up with a plausible explanation for having all that cash aboard when the dog moved on . . . a close call.

After that, they would pass through the Philippines, Diego Garcia, and Oman, then be shuttled aboard the aircraft carrier *Nimitz* by Navy helicopters. This would put them in position four days before mission launch.

APRIL 18, 1980—D-DAY MINUS SEVEN

By Friday we were moving through the deployment checklist like a hot knife through butter—everything was on schedule and going according to plan.

On Diego Garcia, Ray Turczynski received a prearranged secure phone call from the Pentagon directing him to move his unit to Masirah and commence setting up the forward staging base. Ray was given the names of two Pentagon staff officers, Lieutenant Colonel Bob Lawrence and Lieutenant Colonel Sam Hall, who were already in place and would serve as his contacts for bedding down at the airfield there.

Ray's crews had been flying sea surveillance training missions for the past two days with naval surface vessels operating in the Indian Ocean. This established their cover.

While Turczynski was getting his phone call on Diego Garcia, the lead elements of the Hurlburt MC-130, EC-130, and AC-130 maintenance teams were arriving at Wadi Kena aboard a C-141. Each maintenance team chief was responsible for arranging to receive his particular mission aircraft and having the mission kit, spare parts, and support gear in position and ready to service these birds when they arrived in five days.

Over the next nine hours, four more planeloads of maintenance people arrived and all 124 of these wrench jockeys were soon in place and ready to receive the C-130s.

APRIL 19, 1980—D-DAY MINUS SIX

Saturday was a busy day for JTF personnel.

It was shortly after midnight at Andrews AFB when our staff car approached the waiting C-141. We had a long, boring flight to Egypt ahead of us and were thankful for a couple of hours' stopover at Ramstein Air Base, Germany, where I accompanied General Vaught to the office of the senior MAC theater airlift commander for a brief chat. Our purpose was to inform this general officer who we were and what support we would need during Operation Eagle Claw. A "To whom it may concern" letter from General Jones left no doubt as to our operating authority and the top-priority status of our mission.

*   *   *

That same morning, Turczynski loaded up the first of his MC-130s and embarked on the seven-hour flight from Diego Garcia to Masirah.

I had told Ray that on arriving at Masirah he should get his airplanes back into the air on the fake surveillance mission as soon as possible for cover purposes. It was with this order in mind that he immediately set his people to off-loading and setting up camp. We had a C-130 airlift shuttle—"Klong," as we Nam vets called it—that ran from Wadi Kena once a day to keep the forward base supplied.[1]

Ray picked a campsite for his tent city near the dirt runway which was to be used for parking our aircraft. Our liaison officers got permission to block off the south end of the seldom-used dirt runway for the Joint Task Force to use.

The Klong airlift had also brought in the JTF ground satellite communications terminal, so Masirah would have a command network link to the task force's communications stations at Wadi Kena and Diego Garcia. However, for security reasons, voice communications over this network were to be kept to an absolute minimum until April 23 (D-Day minus two). This terminal would be used for backup command and control for the mission.

Back in Florida, the first two of four MC-130s departed Hurlburt with the other two to follow over the next two days. Three of these Talons would fly the northern Atlantic route, passing near the coast of Newfoundland (where they would refuel in-flight) and proceeding south of Iceland, over Great Britain and France, and on to Rhein Main. These Talons were hidden among the many aircraft participating in a Special Operations exercise called Flintlock (this European Command exercise served us well as a cover).

The other MC-130 was heading for Lajes Field in the Azores. Not far behind were three EC-130 tankers. These would refuel en route and also RON (remain overnight) at Lajes, a less

---

[1]This mini-airline, named after the brackish river waters that flow through Thailand, really saved our bacon in many ways. We continually had people, equipment, and supplies that we had to move back and forth to the various staging bases.

conspicuous destination. They would move on to Wadi Kena the following day, stopping en route for fuel at Sigonella, Sicily.

APRIL 20, 1980—D-DAY MINUS FIVE

Shortly after midnight on Sunday, just four days before we were due to launch into Night-One, the big gray-and-white C-141 carrying General Vaught's entourage (myself included) touched down at Wadi Kena. We assembled at first light inside the large arch-roofed hangar building being set up as the JTF command center.

General Vaught's quarters and the command center were a flurry of activity as Ron Michaels, our advance party liaison officer, directed the communications and intelligence units on where best to set up their equipment. What was a mass of cables, wires, black boxes, and operator panels would soon become the eyes and ears General Vaught would use to direct the mission.

Ron had originally coordinated the planned bed-down of the task force at Wadi Kena, so he was the logical man to send ahead to get things set up.

Ron's reception committee had done an outstanding job, but now it was time for our chief of staff, Jerry King, to complete the task of preparing the command bunker and managing the administrative functions of the team.

After arriving at Wadi Kena, John Carney and his combat controllers had been venturing out into the desert in the cool of night and rehearsing the blacked-out procedures he and his team had devised for setting up the runways at Desert-I. We'd had only a partial rehearsal of this concept, and John's team needed practice. One look at John's "Honda rash" (skinned elbows, nose, and butt) and it was easy to see that he and his cohorts had taken a few too many spills out there racing across the desert.

Far across the Indian Ocean, Turczynski's two remaining MC-130s at Diego Garcia moved forward to Masirah, completing the Kadena part of the task force positioning. The tents and shelter equipment they brought along provided sleeping quarters for the entire group. The Spartan conditions became more acceptable when Turczynski finally told his men the true reason for their being there.

We believed their mission as advance party for the Night-One JTF forces had been accomplished without generating any more than mild curiosity among members of the Sultan of Oman's Air Force.[2] We would continue our sea surveillance charade right up to the time for the rescue mission.

By day's end, the Kadena aircraft were all in position, along with sixty-six support personnel. There were four flight crews (one in reserve in case anyone became ill and had to be replaced), a three-man intelligence team, an Air Force flight surgeon, and a medical technician. A second doctor, from Hurlburt, would be joining the group soon. (The flight surgeons—Lieutenant Colonel Postles from Hurlburt and Captain Contiguglia from Kadena—had by chance been classmates and had graduated from the same medical school.)

APRIL 21, 1980—D-DAY MINUS FOUR

Another eventful day in the flow-chart scheme of things dawned with important events scheduled to take place in several parts of the world, including Tehran.

Four AC-130 gunships departed Hurlburt for a nonstop flight to Wadi Kena that would include four in-flight refuelings and take about twenty-four hours. It is impossible to disguise these distinctive birds, with gun barrels sticking out one side and weird-looking bumps and bulges that contain their sensor systems, so we had timed their arrival to limit their stay in Egypt to one day. This would give the crews time to rest before launching on their fire-support mission for Delta. We routed their flight path along international traffic control boundaries, so no diplomatic clearances were required.

Now it was Delta's turn. These commandos, honed to a razor's edge, were picked up at Pope Air Force Base by three C-141s and were soon on their way to Germany, then Wadi Kena.

---

[2]We didn't find out until later that one of the sultan's generals reported the presence of our aircraft at Masirah to London. He speculated that we were going to attempt a rescue of our hostages in Iran. A State Department official was rushed to brief Mrs. Thatcher and head off any reaction to the report.

*   *   *

While Delta Force was on its way across the Atlantic, Dick Meadows and Fred were arriving in Tehran. They got into the city without incident and met up with American agents already in place, including two Special Forces operatives from Europe.

April 22, 1980—D-Day Minus Three

One MC-130 and three EC-130s moved forward to Masirah. Tom Wicker led this contingent to join up with Ray Turczynski's squadron.

It was going to be necessary to operate these birds at extremely heavy gross weights, in excess of 175,000 pounds, their war emergency limit.

The MC-130 would be hauling maintenance support people and the equipment, tents, rations, and support gear needed at Masirah for the Night-One insertion.

The EC-130s would have the burden of hauling jet fuel in the two 3,000-gallon bladders that each carried. This was to gas up the choppers at Desert-I. For security reasons, we didn't want anyone seeing us filling these bladders at Masirah, so we were carrying the gas there in the EC-130s. Also, a few of the maintenance people would be spread through the tankers to reduce the congestion aboard Wicker's plane. When they were loaded, the tankers grossed out at 185,000 pounds.

I was moving forward in this contingent along with John Carney, his six-man combat control team, their two Kawasaki dirt bikes, and the portable TACAN system.

We taxied at a snail's pace, since our pilots had experienced these heavy weights before and knew how to baby the big birds along so as to minimize the stress and strain on the airframe.

Still, as experienced as everybody was, the heavy gross weight and the 120-degree desert heat teamed up to make this one hairy takeoff for all aboard the MC-130. The extreme heat caused a drop in air density, which reduced engine efficiency, and consequently resulted in less power available for takeoff. In order to reach takeoff airspeed the aircraft would have to use more runway than would be necessary at normal temperatures. Those in the EC-130s would have similar tales to tell.

When we were in position, the pilots shoved the throttles to the wall and the aircraft barely moved. Then we finally started to roll, and we rolled . . . and rolled . . . and rolled. It was damn near two miles before we reached lift-off speed. Even after we were airborne and the gear was up, we struggled along so low that we almost clipped the tops off of the date palm trees. It seemed we were just hanging on the props, the airspeed building ever so slowly. Those of us watching the airspeed indicator were letting out a cheer with each knot of speed gained.

We zoomed along the desert for about an hour before we had burned off enough fuel to lighten the aircraft to the point that we could gain sufficient speed to climb up to 20,000 feet, our cruising altitude. You've got to love the C-130—it can flat do the unbelievable!

We flew for nine hours in radio silence down the Red Sea and over the Gulf of Aden just far enough off the coast not to be seen. We were using the cover set up by the Kadena operation, ostensibly joining the sea surveillance exercise.

After we landed and got settled in, that was it—the Night-One airlift forces were in position at Masirah and ready to go. Seven aircraft were lined up on the dirt strip: four MC-130s (one a spare) and three EC-130 tankers (no spares, but the spare MC could be used in a pinch). The tent city housed 160 JTF personnel.

Meanwhile, at Wadi Kena the three MC-130s bringing up the rear arrived from Germany and were being taxied into the ramp space that had been vacated earlier in the day by the birds moving forward to Masirah. The idea was to make it look as if the aircraft that had taken off earlier had returned after a local flight.

Throughout all of this, the KC-135 crews continued their shell game, coming and going almost every day. Although some fifteen of these flying gas stations had been operating from this location, only eleven of them were in position to support the JTF. It was easy for them to move around Europe and North Africa without attracting any attention, as their worldwide refueling missions make them a pretty common sight everywhere.

* * *

Stateside, three C-141s had picked up the Rangers and were now on their way to Wadi Kena. One of these transports had also stopped at Pope AFB to pick up Delta's surgeons and medical team. This was the last of the JTF movements from the United States.

That evening, Delta Force arrived at Wadi Kena and all 132 of them were immediately isolated from the rest of the base in a remote hangar.

APRIL 23, 1980—D-DAY MINUS TWO

The AC-130 gunships arrived after their marathon nonstop flight from Hurlburt. This tedious flight had, for the most part, gone without incident. However, one crew did receive a full dosage of excitement, liberally sprinkled with terror, during one of their refuelings. It seems the KC-135 that their aircraft was hooked up to was struck by lightning. Needless to say, this momentarily scared the hell out of them. Happily, the outcome amounted to no more than a few scorched rivets and some dirty shorts.

With the arrival at Wadi Kena of the three C-141s carrying the Rangers, the deployment was almost completed. Delta and the roadblock team had yet to move forward to Masirah, but this would come at the last minute. Two C-141s remained at Wadi Kena to handle that move.

At this juncture, seven C-130s were at Masirah and six KC-135s were at Diego Garcia. Nineteen mission aircraft were now on the ramp at Wadi Kena. Although this may sound like an exorbitant number of aircraft sitting around that could attract heightened interest from intelligence observers, the scene actually fit right in with the normal flow that Dave Forgan's Operations Planning Group had established months before. Also, our Joint Task Force intelligence people told us that this was a period of low vulnerability to Soviet spy satellites.

Three JTF C-141s were to be in position at Daharan, Saudi Arabia, by April 24. Two of these were to fly into Manzariyeh as the primary and secondary extraction aircraft. The third would be on standby as a spare.

Two had already taken off from Charleston AFB and were flying toward Ramstein, Germany, with the medical equipment aboard. A third aircraft would move from Wadi Kena on the 24th to join the others.

28

READY AND WAITING

After their easy entrance into the city on Monday, Dick Meadows and Fred joined up with other DOD agents and set right to work.

In the following days, Dick spent considerable time checking out the hiding places for the assault forces and reconnoitering the embassy compound and the routes Delta would take into the city. The others checked out the Ministry of Foreign Affairs.

He drove out to the Delta hide site south of Garmsar and, after looking things over, decided on a better location in a more remote area near there. The first site was too near a railroad line, and he saw that workers were roaming around the area tending tracks.[1]

Dick strolled around the embassy walls and checked out the guard posts. He noted that the guards seemed bored and careless—easy prey. When he saw how young the guards were, he felt a twinge of regret that they would have to be eliminated . . . but then he thought of what they were doing. *C'est la guerre.*

One day, Dick went to the soccer stadium posing as an agent for a European team hoping to set up a match. Incredibly, he was able to make a thorough examination of the facilities while the stadium authorities took him on a tour. During this walk-through, he spotted some tall metal light poles that would interfere with the helicopter operation. Forewarned, Delta's commandos would have the explosives with them to do a job on the poles.

---

[1] The area chosen for the helicopter laager was surveyed by the CIA agent (Bob). He found it uninhabited and acceptable for use.

Dick spent considerable time at the warehouse, tending to the two-and-a-half-ton trucks and two vans stored there. Gas, water, oil, and tire pressures were checked, and he built false panel walls in the trucks' trailer compartments to conceal Delta's shooters.

He then gathered supplies for the night he would spend at the Delta drop-off and hide sites waiting for the force to be inserted.

The team of American agents had a close shave one day when their car was stopped for a traffic violation. Dick had to open the trunk to get a briefcase containing his passport and the car registration paperwork. Dick quickly took care of this while the two agents with him distracted the guards. Had these militiamen looked in the trunk they would have seen weapons and Dick's satellite radio. Talk about cool heads!

Then, a day or so before launch, Iranian laborers suddenly showed up and dug a trench across the warehouse's driveway, which had them a little tensed up. Had their cover been blown? But after the agents lay low for a day, they decided it was just a coincidence. With some fast talking and a small bribe, Fred conned the workers into filling in the ditch enough for the trucks to pass.

By Thursday, the situation in Tehran looked good and everything was neatly tied up, just waiting for Delta. The mission was a "go" on Meadows' end.

WADI KENA, APRIL 19–23, 1980

Egypt's desert heat was overwhelming at first, but Ron Michaels and Jerry King managed to get air conditioners installed in the command center and make it habitable.

Thirst was a continual problem, as the potable-water system was severely taxed. Popping down salt tablets only aggravated the situation, but we certainly couldn't afford to lose anyone to dehydration.

The maintenance people also ran into difficulty finding some of their support equipment that had been shipped ahead. It took them about forty-eight hours to round it all up.

But, other than the persistent flies linked to the foul odor that clung to the bunkers (the Egyptians had used them for commodes), Wadi Kena proved ideal for our main operating base.

After the Rangers arrived, Charlie Beckwith and Sherm

Williford began working with Major Jesse Johnson and Captain Wade Ishimoto from Delta, the two chosen to head up the road-block teams. They began selecting personnel, gathering equipment and working on procedures for security at Desert-I.

Using a mobile-command jeep and motorcycles, the rapidly assembled team rehearsed their tactics on the desert. They would go in on the lead MC-130, rapidly exit the aircraft on the motorcycles, and secure the east and west blocking points on the road that passed through Desert-I. They would communicate through hand-held short-range radios, and Major Johnson would shuttle between the two checkpoints in his jeep to command the operation. Farsi-speaking interpreters were made available to the teams to help calm down and control any Iranians we might detain.

As the sun set on Wadi Kena on April 23, all was ready. The command center was operating smoothly, the intelligence team was updating the situation, and Delta Force and the roadblock team were ready to move forward to Masirah for Thursday's launch.

Later that night, the intelligence team received an incredible piece of information, almost too good to be true.

It seems that a CIA agent had been aboard an airliner heading for Europe from Tehran and, either by accident or design, was sitting next to a Pakistani who had been a cook at the embassy throughout most of the hostage situation. He and his wife had recently been released from those duties.

The cook, called Luigi, told the CIA agent that all of the hostages were being held in the Chancery building. At the first stop, the agent relayed this information to his contacts, who sent it on to Nick Kilgore in JCS/SOD, and Nick passed it to Wadi Kena.

General Vaught was concerned that the cook might be a plant and this might be a setup to deceive any rescuing force. It was decided that Beckwith should use the information but have a backup plan if it proved to be untrue.[2]

---

[2]Steven Emerson, in his book *Secret Warriors*, says Army officials have now revealed that the story about this information coming from Luigi was a complete fabrication. Although there was a cook named Luigi who was released from his job at the embassy at that time, the true source for this key information was a deep-cover Iranian CIA source who had gained access to the hostages. Apparently the Agency cooked up the Luigi story so as not to jeopardize the lives of this man and his contacts. It wasn't until five years after the aborted mission that a senior official of the Joint Task Force learned the real story, if it can be believed.

When Charlie was informed of this, he immediately called his squadron leaders together to work the new information into their plans. They would assault the Chancery first, but be ready to shift to three other buildings they considered most likely to contain hostages (if they didn't find everybody). The total force would still be required, since the information could be unreliable. To reduce the size of the assault force on the basis of Luigi's unsubstantiated information would be unwise. Nevertheless, everyone felt the cook's disclosure was a windfall. If it was true, Delta would only have to be inside the embassy for about twenty minutes.

ABOARD THE NIMITZ, April 20–23, 1980

Like the other components, the helicopter team wasted no time once aboard the big aircraft carrier in the Indian Ocean.

The aircrews (with the help of Sikorsky tech reps) began to check their aircraft thoroughly.

The Marines had brought along several key parts needed to get the two "hangar queens" operational. The eighth bird, which had not flown since it had arrived aboard the *Nimitz* some one hundred days earlier, was still undergoing replacement of the rotor transmission assembly. Also, a leaking seal on the rotor head was irreparable, but this problem was fixed with a heavy greaselike lubricant, which stopped the seepage. There wasn't time to replace the faulty part.

Four days before mission launch our JTF pilots were given two-hour orientation rides with the Sea Stallions flown by Navy crews. This was to familiarize them with procedures used to operate aboard the carrier.

The next day, the Task Force crews flew their assigned birds on a four-hour shakedown flight. The aircraft were then taken below to the cavernous hangar bay so the wrench jockeys could tend to any problems discovered. The paint shop took over and sprayed the exteriors desert brown and tan to mimic the Iranian RH-53s.

A full launch rehearsal was held the third night, and, as before, the maintenance crews took care of the write-ups. The crews reported that these choppers were in as good a condition as any they had flown.

A more significant event took place about this time. The old subject of secure radios was resurrected. Chuck Pitman advised General Vaught that some of the systems didn't work and there were no parts to fix them, and so General Vaught granted permission to remove the black-box components of the secure UHF and FM radios.

With all of these components removed, regardless of whether or not some were working, the crews would rely on light and hand signals to communicate between aircraft. If they did have an urgent need to talk between aircraft or to the C-130s, they had only nonsecure means available.[3]

Perhaps the first harbinger of helicopter bad luck occurred shortly thereafter. Schaefer's maintenance crew was performing a check of the radios in one of the choppers and needed electrical power for the test. When the power cable was plugged into the helicopter, nothing happened.

Then one of the ship's crew, a petty officer, was asked what had to be done to get power. The Navy man pointed to a button mounted on the wall and said, "Just hit the switch." The maintenance man hit the switch, but instead of getting power to the test gear he activated an overhead fire-suppression system. This showered the helos with a fire-retardant foam that was highly corrosive. Before the system could be deactivated, five of the RH-53s had been blanketed with the snowy-looking stuff.

Fortunately, maintenance crews leaped into action and within thirty minutes all aircraft had been washed down with purified water and were being inspected for corrosion. No such damage was found, but it was decided to take the helos on deck earlier than planned on mission day in order to have more "run-up" time in which to check them over.

MASIRAH, APRIL 20–23, 1980

Masirah was a remote, desolate location perfect for a launch base for a clandestine mission into Iran.

---

[3]This was foolish. Better to have limited secure communications than none. In the first place, all radio systems should have been maintained and kept operational. Had I known about this decision to remove all of these components I would have argued vehemently against it.

Personnel of the Sultan of Oman's Air Force (SOAF) ignored us—except for the fighter pilots who gave us a daily near-sonic buzz job as they brought their jets screaming down our flight line, just a few feet above the tails of our parked aircraft. I thought it was too bad there was none of the usual fraternization that occurs when the British and Americans get together. I would have liked to have met those stovepipe jockeys.

Much of our time after arriving at Masirah was spent in attending to the mission aircraft, ensuring that they were in peak operating condition. We went over the insertion and refueling mission at Desert-I in detail to make sure that each man knew his role and to resolve any last-minute questions.

Although the chow consisted of C-rations or I-F (in-flight) rations, some of our maintenance sergeants had the culinary touch of the great chefs of the world. With a skillful blending of various components from the ration kits, they would come up with gourmet delights. These dinners became the highlight of each day.

Also, these ingenious troops had constructed a first-class privy out of packing cases, complete with a half-moon on the door. They had a neat little trick of waiting until one of their compatriots was seated comfortably on this makeshift throne and then sneaking up and shaking the daylights out of the structure, forcing the startled occupant to flee for his life.

That wasn't the only shaking up at Masirah. John Carney and his combat controllers had resumed practicing their night runway preparation drills, only this time John was tooling across the desert with me on the back of his Kawasaki. We would go screaming along at high speed carrying the special gear, then stop and go through a series of covert radio signals, align lights, set up the TACAN, and walk through the landing and marshaling schedules for the mission aircraft. Then we would backtrack and pick up everything, completely sterilizing the area. The idea was to leave no clues that we'd ever been to Desert-I. I was impressed. These guys were good—especially Carney, who kept his dirt bike upright and my butt off the desert.

When the sun went down on April 23, D-Day minus two, with the Day-One launch just twenty-four hours hence, we were ready.

As we sat in the operations tent that night, unsettling thoughts weighed heavily on our minds. Had we really pulled this off undetected, or were the Soviets (or others) just waiting to tip the Iranians we were coming? As far as our intelligence team and that of the National Security Agency (NSA) knew, we had made it undetected (the JTF was still not aware of the report to London by the Omani general who had noticed our aircraft at Masirah).

We well knew that all we had accomplished was nothing more than a giant logistics exercise, as difficult and impressive as it was. The real cutting edge of the sword would not be unsheathed until the next day—the Night-One insertion.

The question was asked, "Do you think we will really go? Will President Carter have the courage to see it through?"

Others expressed apprehension that this was just a test, to see if we could position the forces undetected.

"Baloney," I said. "That doesn't make sense. We're on the ayatollah's doorstep—now is the time to kick their butts! We'll get the launch order tomorrow!"

My deepest concern now was that the eight helicopters and seven C-130s be in top operating condition for the mission. Given that, along with good flying weather and a generous dose of good luck, and we might just pull this thing off.

I felt a need to be close to the airplanes and the maintenance crews, so I headed for the row of C-130s parked near the campsite. I wanted to talk to each crew chief and be reassured that every rivet, nut, and bolt had been thoroughly checked and that all systems were operating properly.

I found Ken Oliver and his technicians, Buie Kindle and Sergeant John Gerke, assisting the maintenance crews by working over the sophisticated avionics systems and peaking them up to maximum performance. Radar systems, inertial navigation computers, and satellite radios were receiving special attention. The aircraft situation at Masirah looked incredibly good—barring unforeseen problems, our aircraft were as ready as they would ever be.

My thoughts turned to Chuck Pitman. I hoped he was having the same good fortune with his birds and aircrews as I was with mine.[4] If we could get eight helicopters in the air, I was con-

---

[4]We later learned that one of the Navy pilots had reported to Ed Seiffert that he was no longer a volunteer and asked to be used as a spare crew member. The backup pilot, another Navy man, was pressed into service and launch preparations continued. However, this required some reshuffling of crews.

fident that at least six would make it through Desert-I and on to Tehran.

As I headed back to my tent, I felt the same anticipation for the challenge of the unknown that I had experienced in Southeast Asia. The intense motivation and dedication of our military people when facing a combat mission had always impressed me, and I had seen it again that night. Each man, in his own way, was giving it all he had. It was an inspiring feeling—spirited emotions and self-confidence were everywhere.

I hope the good Lord is looking down at us with a smile on his face at what he sees and will give his blessing to our efforts to safely rescue these hostages.

It would take a few crucial breaks in this game to make it all come together.

As I settled in on my cot, I couldn't help but wonder what our fate would be at this same time the next night.

29

COUNTDOWN!

April 24—Hostage Day 173

<u>Knight-Ridder News Service</u>
WASHINGTON—The Carter administration Wednesday appeared to be pushing back a date for deciding whether to use military force in Iran.

In the wake of an agreement by European Common Market nations to impose economic sanctions on Iran by May 17, White House press secretary Jody Powell publicly forecast "weeks of waiting" to see what may happen. A top White House official said privately that the administration now hopes "completely to avoid unilateral action" against Iran.

MASIRAH, 0700 HOURS APRIL 24, 1980—D-DAY MINUS ONE

Excitement was running high. Maintenance people were already moving about the aircraft, going over the birds to ensure that all seven were in tip-top shape.

The aircrews had been told to sleep in and be rested up for the long night ahead. But this wasn't possible for a number of them who were already up and out at the aircraft doing "busy work."

The loadmasters were especially active this morning—they were making sure "their" aircraft were prepared to receive the loads and that allowance had been made for all items to be carried. We would be flying these birds very heavy, at the feather edge of safe operating limits, and weights had to be precisely recorded to enable the pilots and flight engineers to compute critical takeoff and landing data.

It had been a quiet but somewhat tense night, until the early morning hours when "Doc" Postles got tangled up with an intruder and created something of a commotion. The Doc had been sawing logs in a sleeping bag under the wing of a C-130 when an inquisitive camel nudged him out of his dreams with a cold nose and foul breath. The Doc's thrashing and yelling created quite a stir. It also gave us all a good laugh and took some of the edge off the tension.

Wadi Kena, Egypt, 0710 Hours

Delta Force was holding an impromptu religious service. The seriousness of purpose hung in the air like a thick fog. Tensions were high. The faces of these combat-hardened veterans were grim.

JTF headquarters buzzed with activity as last-minute details were rechecked. The day had begun with a sense of anticipation and urgency. The Joint Task Force staff had been organized into two shifts, overlapped to ensure continuity of operations expertise throughout the mission.

Lee Hess was in the midst of finishing up a series of complex plans for tanker sequencing, air cover, and possible close air support from Navy tactical aircraft (despite extensive preparation, some timing coordination was still being smoothed out).

Delta moved out to the flight line to begin boarding the first C-141. No one was allowed aboard until his name was checked against a loading manifest. As the troopers went through this processing, General Vaught moved among them shaking hands and telling his usual anecdotes, attempting to calm tightening nerves. The general had slept little during the night and had been up early, trying to speak with every man who would deploy that day.

The processing didn't take long, and the first C-141 lifted off not long after 0745. The second followed a half hour later. Both were to fly down the Red Sea, around the Arabian Peninsula, and then eastward to Masirah, where we were waiting for them.

The Pentagon, 0800 Hours (Wadi Kena Time)

The inner sanctum of the Special Operations Division was a beehive of activity. It was just after midnight in Washington when Nick Kilgore and the remaining staff members were setting up a miniature command center to enable the Chairman and Defense Secretary Harold Brown to monitor the mission and report developments to the President. The Chairman had a separate satellite communications circuit linked to Wadi Kena that would allow private discussions between him and General Vaught.

The primary command and control network for the mission was a separate circuit from General Vaught's Washington link. A pledge from the President not to interfere with the rescue operation served to squelch any temptations others might have had to interrupt our command lines.

ABOARD THE NIMITZ, 0915 HOURS

The level of intensity was also high aboard the aircraft carrier. The helicopter crew members were busily engaged in final systems checks and installing .50-caliber machine guns on the mission aircraft. The helos were clustered in the *Nimitz*'s aft hangar bay below-deck maintenance area.

Grim-looking Marines were patrolling the area, allowing access only to those with a need to be there. No amount of gold braid would have gotten anyone who didn't belong in the area past these sentinels.

WADI KENA, 0930 HOURS

After Delta departed, activity continued at a feverish pace. Even those who were supposed to be off duty were reluctant to leave the command center and were sticking around to make sure nothing had been overlooked.

The Joint Communications Support people and the National Security Agency troops were rechecking their equipment. Pete Dieck was continually talking to Washington in an effort to increase power to the satellite system so that we could more clearly understand voice transmissions.

Each of the Joint Task Force's element commanders had a satellite radio for direct communication with the command post, called "Red Barn," or the alternate command link, General Gast at Masirah, labeled "Gravel Pit." General Vaught, running the show, had the apt personal radio call sign "Foreman." All key players had radio call signs to permit communications without using proper names. General Vaught assigned me the ignominious identifier "Woodpecker," which brought me a little good-natured kidding. Charlie Beckwith's was appropriately "Eagle."

My concerns with the radio net (as they had been all along) were that we hadn't rehearsed with the system. I was hoping like hell that this network and the SATCOM operators would function as advertised, because there wasn't much any of the rest of us could do if they didn't.

We had an elaborate table of code words specially formatted so that we could use a matrix to construct phrases and convey information on both the SATCOM and high frequency radios. It was extremely slow, but that's all we had.

Our primary ground satellite command and control stations were at Wadi Kena, Masirah, Diego Garcia, and the *Nimitz*, but the on-board aircraft arrangement left much to be desired. We were set up so that the lead MC-130 (Kyle) had a SATCOM radio, as did the last EC-130 (No. 6). The lead helicopter (Seiffert) had the system, and Pitman in No. 5 helo had a SATCOM, but both of these were designed to be used during ground operations.[1] The lead AC-130 and the Daharan medevac C-141 also had satellite linkups, and Beckwith was to have his portable ground SATCOM terminal stowed in the lead C-130 so it could be used at Desert-I and carried forward to Tehran. Dick Meadows also had one of these sets to be used by the reception committee in Tehran.

Meanwhile, Stormy Buchanan was trying to mold every little bit of weather information into a precise forecast. The final execution decision would hinge on a clear-weather prediction.

The Rangers who would seize Manzariyeh on Night-Two were continuing to review and rehearse their assault plans.

Others were hard at work putting together the plan we had rehearsed for a C-141 emergency airdrop of fuel bladders if ordered by General Vaught. The C-141Bs had been requested from the Pentagon and were on alert at Pope AFB. Bill Foley's riggers

---

[1]After the mission, Seiffert told me his SATCOM system was not wired into his aircraft like those on the C-130s. He and Pitman both had portable ground SATCOM sets that required that the antenna be manually held outside the aircraft and aligned with the satellite in order to work in flight. None of us really understood enough about the working of these systems, and not having the equipment available for training was a severe handicap.

had been ordered to Pope from Fort Lee, Virginia, to support this effort. If, for any reason, additional fuel was needed while the force was in Iran, the general wanted a backup.

Also in the mill was the long-range post-mission search and rescue (SAR) plan Wayne Purser had put together months earlier. This mission, if needed, would utilize new USAF HH-53H Pave Low helicopters from Kirtland AFB. These helos were being partly disassembled and rolled aboard behemoth C-5A transports to be flown to Daharan, Saudi Arabia. They would be ready to launch a SAR mission approximately thirty hours after D-Day. The search and rescue forces were not being positioned before the rescue attempt to avoid any chance of detection.

MASIRAH, 1000 HOURS

I rounded up some maintenance and support people to help me set up a couple of tents to house Delta, due in the afternoon. We had only a few spare cots, so we covered the ground with tarps to provide some semblance of comfort. We also put Cokes and drinking water in the tents. Now they would at least have some relief from the blast-furnace heat of the afternoon.

I made arrangements with Sam Hall and Bob Lawrence to borrow two trucks from the Brits that we could use to haul Delta's troops from the C-141s to the tents we had set up.

Then, a MAC C-130 Klong arrived with six Rangers, led by Sergeant David R. Littlejohn. This was the advance element of the twelve-man roadblock team that would be providing security at Desert-I. One command jeep and three Kawasaki dirt bikes, to be used by the roadblock team, were also off-loaded.

Since I didn't know how this team was to function, I had Littlejohn brief me. He gave me a rundown on how they would deploy and handle security at Desert-I and told me that Navy Captain John A. Butterfield plus other Farsi linguists would interpret should we have to detain any Iranians. Butterfield's group would tell the Iranians what to do and assure them that they wouldn't be harmed if they followed orders. This is the same bunch that would later serve as Delta's driver monitors during movement of the force into Tehran.

I was taken aback when Littlejohn told me that I was to be in charge of the roadblock team at Desert-I. What? I didn't know enough about their tactics—it wasn't my bailiwick. I made up my mind right then to turn this function over to Beckwith, since I would be busy setting up the airfield and overseeing the marshaling and fueling of the aircraft. Charlie didn't have that much to do during that time and, as he had been in on their planning, would be in a much better position to control the roadblockers.

ABOARD THE NIMITZ, *1200 HOURS*

Chuck Gilbert was keeping busy readying the Palletized Inertial Navigation System (PINS) equipment, no easy task, since these Air Force systems were not designed to be aligned aboard a ship steaming along at sea.[2]

Bill Hoff led the crews through a review of flight plans and recomputed the helicopter performance data from more accurate temperature and density altitude readings projected for Desert-I.

Meanwhile, helicopter engine air particle separators had been removed from jet air intakes to reduce weight and enable the power plants to operate at maximum efficiency (a 200-pound weight reduction and a 2 percent increase in power, but a calculated risk, since without the separators, engines could foul from intake of foreign particles).

The Marines wanted to reconfirm their earlier calculations that six helicopters would be the minimum required to lift off from Desert-I. Each helicopter would have to operate at a weight of around 48,000 pounds. This would include about 14,000 pounds of jet fuel and a cabin load of 5,400 pounds. This meant nineteen to twenty Delta operatives with their individual assault gear.

Optimistically, all eight helos would make it to Desert-I and on to Tehran, increasing the odds of having at least five operational for the extractions at the embassy and the Ministry of Foreign Affairs. We would need one helicopter for the MFA mission and four at the embassy. At worst, we could make do with three (internal fuel tanks would be removed at the laager, which would greatly increase passenger-carrying capability).

---

[2]These navigational systems had to be flown to land (stationary position), where electrical power was applied and the alignment process begun. Once stabilized, the PINS devices were returned to the carrier while still connected to a power source, and remained so until just prior to the mission.

In the remaining time, the helo crews went over their insertion, refueling, and assault plans and made final preparations for launching all eight helicopters, hoping that number would be mission-ready by launch time. We needed some luck to make that happen, but the Navy and Marine maintenance troops were busting their butts to give us all the airframes they could muster.

MASIRAH, 1230 HOURS

We had finished lunch when the SOAF trucks were delivered. Wooden frames were constructed on the truck beds and canvas covers stretched over them to conceal what we would soon be hauling.

I then assembled all of the C-130 pilots and loaded them into one of the trucks for a drive along the taxi route they would be following that night—right to the end of the runway. Then we all got out and walked through each aircraft's taxi routine. I wanted each pilot thoroughly familiar with his aircraft's position in relation to the others. The run-up to check engines—normally done at the end of the runway—would be performed in the parking area that night. This would facilitate repair of any malfunctions that might show up during engine run-up and avoid any delays at the end of the runway.

Having walked through this routine, we returned to the tent area to await Delta's arrival. The aircrews returned to studying their charts, flight plans, and formation tactics.

WADI KENA, 1400 HOURS

COMJTF received the final mission aircraft status report—seven C-130s and eight RH-53s ready to launch. The command bunker filled with cheers as soon as this was announced. Helo No. 8, the hangar queen, had made it! General Vaught went right to his SATCOM booth and reported this directly to General Jones.

Meanwhile, the launch schedule had been moved forward fifty minutes. This decision was made on the basis of a reconnaissance report from Chuck Pitman, who had flown from the *Nimitz* on April 21 to survey the surrounding waters and grab a long-range gander at the Iranian coast. On that flight, Chuck determined that it was dark enough by 1800 hours (6:00 P.M.) to mask a penetration of the coast inbound to Desert-I. By advancing the departure, we would take advantage of the extended period of darkness and get Delta to the hide site earlier.

MASIRAH, 1445 HOURS

The first of two MAC C-141s from Wadi Kena arrived with General Gast and half of Delta Force aboard. The big aircraft pulled to the south end of the runway out of view of the main base complex and its passengers climbed off and immediately boarded the covered trucks. They were then driven to the tents we had set up and settled in to wait for the night's mission.

Members of the assault force team were outfitted in black Army field jackets concealing armored vests, weapons, ammunition, and explosives carried in harnesses. Each man wore a black Navy watch cap, faded blue jeans, and combat boots. Some were carrying what I assumed to be sniper weapons or machine guns rolled up in blankets. There was a Velcro tape patch on the right shoulder of each man's jacket. These patches covered small American flags that would be displayed once the force was inside the embassy to help the hostages recognize them as rescuers.

This was a grim bunch. The faces were deadly serious. Their eyes gleamed as each man contemplated his role. On the outside was total composure, but the charge that was building up inside was like a harnessed bolt of lightning, ready to strike. We all kept our distance—this was no social call.

The C-141, now devoid of its cargo, taxied to the main ramp for refueling. It would wait for the second C-141 to land, offload, and refuel. Then both would return to Wadi Kena.

General Gast proceeded to the communications tent and began preparations to provide backup command and control duties. After that, the general and I reviewed alternative plans for the Night-Two scenario in case anything went wrong at Manzariyeh. These alternatives would involve the residual C-130 assets at Masirah (three EC-130s, two MC-130s). They would be available for an extraction at Fez or Desert-I, if it became necessary. These were truly last-resort concepts, but still worth considering.

WADI KENA, 1500 HOURS

A message came from the *Nimitz* describing a carrier task force plan to divert attention from the helicopter launch. This would involve a number of aerial refueling exercises between Navy tactical aircraft and Air Force KC-135s. Such an operational signature had already been established in the area and it was suspected that the Soviets and Yemenis were monitoring these activities.

Fortunately, the bulk of the Soviet navy's Indian Ocean squadron was involved in an anticarrier exercise some 600 miles to the south of the *Nimitz* near the island of Socotra.

At 1530, Bob Mattingly, the Marine helo intelligence officer, reported that the closest Russian intelligence-gathering ship was 200 miles south of the *Nimitz* trailing the Coral Sea Battle Group. Following a concerted intelligence collection effort near Masirah, it was determined that a Soviet tanker which had been loitering near the island was in the Persian Gulf en route to Basra, Iraq. This was welcome news, as we had been concerned that the Soviets might have detected our helos and C-130s transiting the Strait of Hormuz.

In the meantime, medical and base support personnel were setting up an emergency treatment facility. Base engineers installed sinks with hot and cold running water, constructed shelving, and built operating tables. Plans were made for converting General Vaught's air-conditioned trailer into a postoperative recovery room.

Also, the Rangers responsible for securing any Iranians picked up at Desert-I were being briefed and were preparing a secure holding area. Procedures for handling any detainees were rechecked.

MASIRAH, 1530 HOURS

The second C-141 from Wadi Kena had just landed with Beckwith and the rest of Delta's troops, who boarded the borrowed trucks and were spirited to the tents. We now had 132 members of the assault force waiting at Masirah. Of these, 120 were Delta personnel to be moved forward to Tehran for the rescue mission while the roadblock crew would return to Masirah aboard the C-130s once the refueling mission was completed at Desert-I.

After we secured the Delta contingent, Charlie told us about the bonanza of new intelligence information gleaned from Luigi (a strange name for a Pakistani—Italian, perhaps). Charlie was cautiously optimistic about this information that, if accurate, could mean the rescue itself would only take about twenty minutes. This was the break he had been looking for, but he was also wary of this last-minute intelligence source. It was too much of a coincidence to suit him. The Chancery and the ambassador's residence were his prime search areas.

The lead MC-130, scheduled to depart at 1805 (6:05 P.M.), was being loaded. The roadblock team's jeep, five motorcycles (three for the Rangers, two for the combat controllers), and the portable TACAN unit were put aboard. In addition, two sheets of aluminum planking were loaded. These would be used under the main gear tires should the MC-130 break through the desert crust and become stuck (a trick learned from operation on dirt strips).

While the loading was taking place, Tom Wicker came out with an offhand remark that really sent Charlie Beckwith ballistic. Tom mused, "With all this added weight, I hope we can get off the ground."

Charlie flared, "What the hell is that supposed to mean?"

I jumped in fast, trying to smooth Charlie's feathers. "Look, Tom, these weights have been checked out by the loadmasters. The airplanes will fly just fine."

Later, I told Beckwith not to worry about the C-130 operations, that I'd let him know immediately if we had any problems he should be aware of.

In the meantime, the second and third MC-130s were being loaded with camouflage nets, support systems, riot-control agent, and Red Eye missiles (heat-seekers) for transfer to the helos at Desert-I.[3]

---

[3]Somewhere along the line, President Carter's advisers directed that Delta was to use riot gas during the assault on the embassy to help avoid civilian casualties. Beckwith insisted on having a letter authorizing him to carry out this directive. Charlie didn't want to use gas, feeling it more of a detriment to Delta than any mob. However, Bucky Burruss carried one tear gas grenade in his jacket to keep everybody happy. The Red Eye missiles were to be used to shoot down any Iranian aircraft that might spot the choppers during the extraction. I disliked that idea—a potential danger to our own aircraft.

WADI KENA, 1600 HOURS

Stormy Buchanan had completed his mission weather forecast.[4] The short-range outlook was for a weak frontal system to move eastward out of Iran. This would be followed by high pressure. Isolated thunderstorms were predicted along the Iran-Iraq border, but the eastern two-thirds of Iran was forecast to be clear. No weather patterns were noted which might adversely affect the rescue operation. This general forecast was in addition to a detailed route summary transmitted to the forces around noon which specifically addressed the various aircraft flight paths.

MASIRAH, 1615 HOURS

The fuel trucks made one last circuit of the flight line to top off all wing tanks and fuel bladders (this deterred loss of fuel due to heat expansion). Any fears we had about the Omani truck drivers finding out anything about what we were doing were unfounded. It was obvious they had no idea what we were doing and couldn't have cared less.

ABOARD THE NIMITZ, 1630 HOURS

Formal mission briefings for the pilots began. Major Jim Schaefer, the operations officer, went over the basic plan to ensure that all questions had been fully answered and nothing was left hanging.

At the same time, the other crew members were below deck checking the helicopter maintenance situation and the location of all mission-essential equipment.

While Schaefer was conducting his briefing, intelligence officer Bob Mattingly was finishing his presentation notes. Of particular concern was an updated weather forecast. The daily weather message was not scheduled to be transmitted from the JTF command center until around 1700, so Mattingly had

---

[4] The Air Weather Service had positioned a Defense Meteorological Satellite Program mobile van, communications satellite terminal, and tactical forecast trailer at Wadi Kena to support the JTF forecaster. This equipment permitted receipt of real-time weather satellite imagery of Iran from orbiting satellites. Coupled with Air Force Global Weather Central surface observations from Iran (which were sparse), there were acceptable data on which to base what was considered an accurate forecast.

arranged for the *Nimitz*'s weather section to provide a general weather summary. When the weather report from Wadi Kena arrived, Bob would use both reports, plus an earlier route profile forecast, for his briefing.

MASIRAH, 1630 HOURS

Bob Brenci's lead crew was being briefed. Of particular interest was the latest intelligence data indicating the nearest Soviet ship was well clear of the C-130 flight path to the Iranian coast. There was no change in Iranian radar status. The forty-eight-hour weather forecast was ideal—no significant factors that would affect C-130 operations (some clouds in the mountains and high haze near the desert landing zone).[5]

The navigators and electronics warfare operators went over their charts one more time to ensure that the selected routing and altitudes would avoid radar detection, minimize noise near populated areas, and afford fuel conservation.

The radio operators were reviewing the communications operating instructions with two SATCOM experts that Pete Dieck had assigned to make sure there was a clear understanding of procedures. Attention was focused on aircraft and ground station call signs and code words that would signal the command center when key events had been accomplished (for example, "cue tip" for reporting that the lead C-130 was safely on the ground at Desert-I).

This was the first time we had seen the SATCOM radios and met the operators who would be manning them. We went through sort of a cram course on how the command and control network functioned. I was not overjoyed to learn that one of these men was a "greenhorn"—he had never been on a mission (all were primarily ground radio operators).

With the briefings completed and aircraft loaded and fueled, there was nothing left to do but wait and sweat out General Vaught's launch order. Some skeptics still believed it wouldn't come. Most doubts were laid to rest when Delta arrived—I knew we were going to Iran.

I stayed with General Gast in the communications tent. We sat there waiting and reflecting on the five and a half months of

---

[5]Before General Vaught would give the launch order he had to be assured that the weather would be ideal for both days of the mission.

hard work and frustration that had gone into putting this mission together.

We were confident about everything but the helicopters. The general summed up the prevailing feeling: "Damn, I hope the helicopters don't get screwed up."

My answer was more of a hope than a certainty. "They'll be okay. Time will tell."

At this point, I was more concerned about the first C-130 getting into Desert-I. I was thinking, *God, I hope John Carney's lights come on and we get that MC-130 down in one piece.* I knew that once we did that, setting up Desert-I for the rest of the force would be a piece of cake.

I was confident that once the Marines had our TACAN to home in on, they would easily find the place and we'd have them gassed and ready to continue in nothing flat.

ABOARD THE NIMITZ, *1700 Hours*

When the weather report arrived from Wadi Kena, Mattingly put it together with the one prepared on ship. The gist of these two separately prepared reports was almost identical. The only area of difference was that the ship's summary included mention of a "possibility of blowing sand" (not suspended dust) in some desert regions. However, this was from a general forecast for all of Iran and did not specifically state where the blowing sand might occur. The report from Wadi Kena was much more detailed and highlighted the actual mission areas and route to be flown.

The weather was described as favorable, with no significant headwinds or visibility problems. High clouds were forecast at altitudes above 10,000 feet, and the possibility of thunderstorms in mountain areas was raised. A weather map and the morning satellite photo were used to show frontal systems and cloud patterns. As the weather appeared nearly perfect, no penetration or abort procedures were briefed.[6]

---

[6]Weather penetration procedures are used for aircraft flying in formation to enable safe separation in passing through unavoidable bad conditions. They rejoin, once in the clear. It is not designed for prolonged situations. The JTF purposely avoided establishing preset weather abort criteria, leaving that to the judgment of each mission commander, based on his knowledge and experience of what his aircrews could handle. I would hate to see that flexibility overridden for a fixed set to weather conditions requiring an automatic abort decision.

The topic of principal concern for the pilots involved temperatures and density altitudes on which the helicopter weight-lifting capability was computed for Desert-I. The best available information, collected inside Iran, was provided. The report indicated that they could expect temperatures on the order of 85 degrees Fahrenheit at Desert-I, with somewhat cooler trends farther north at the drop-off point and the laager. Mattingly's intelligence briefing was concise—no significant changes from the previous night. The pilots were told that there were no known Soviet or Iranian ships or aircraft in the area.

Current status of Iranian radars, gendarmerie posts, and air order of battle remained unchanged. The Chah Bahar search and height-finder radars—critical factors in choosing the coastal penetration point—were determined inoperative. Other radars were operational, and their coverage was depicted on a large map graphic that had been posted in the ready room; they were well away from our route of flight.

From the helicopter standpoint, the mission could go as scheduled.

Throughout mission planning, it had been recognized that there was a need to balance the requirement to stay low for navigational purposes against the possibility the choppers' noise might be detected from the ground. Radar was considered a threat only for the early portion of the flight (coastal penetration). Known Iranian radars wouldn't have been able to detect the mission aircraft beyond where they crossed the first mountain range after entering Iran. The requirement to maintain visual contact with the ground was governed by navigational rather than security constraints.

While they were going over these radar capabilities, Chuck Gilbert reminded Bob Mattingly that during the recon mission to Desert-I, radar signals from an unknown location had been detected at 3,000 feet during the exit flight. This discussion allegedly influenced Mattingly to advise the helo leaders to remain at 100 to 200 feet above the ground throughout the trip to Desert-I or they "might blow the mission."

Our electronic warfare people, as well as the rest of us, had heard of these spurious signals and determined that there was a high probability that they had come from U.S. Navy ships and were not associated with the Iranian coastal network. Since the

CIA flight had not been detected on this mission and there had been no Iranian reaction to the airspace penetration, no further intelligence significance was placed on this report.

Insidiously, a seed had been planted, and the chopper leaders decided that the Iranian radar capabilities could be better than anticipated. Therefore, they committed to remain between 100 and 200 feet.

Finally, Bob went over the escape and evasion tactics and challenged each aircraft commander to ensure that every crew member had the required materials—military ID card, dog tags, and survival gear. Earlier in the day, individual money packets were issued. Each of the forty-one mission members was provided Iranian rials and U.S. dollars for escape and evasion purposes. Individual weapons and ammunition were the last items obtained.

Aircraft commanders were responsible for checking each member of their crews before they left the ready room to ensure that all was in order.

This completed the formal briefing in the ready room, and the crews then assembled by their aircraft for final instructions from their pilots. Approximately three hours before scheduled takeoff, crews began final aircraft preflight checks in the hangar bays. They too found it helped to calm the nerves of a man going into combat to keep busy going over his air machine.

As the launch time approached, the situation aboard the *Nimitz* had never been better. All eight RH-53s were operational and ready to launch.[7] Spirits were high among the crews as they awaited the order to go.

WADI KENA, 1700 HOURS

General Vaught, who was supposed to be resting in his quarters, was to be given the complete weather briefing at this time, but he couldn't be located. He was found out on the flight line

---

[7]By the time the mission was launched, the helicopters aboard the *Nimitz* had been flown over 200 hours, most of it in the final two months. Only one helicopter had aborted for a maintenance problem, and that was No. 8, for low hydraulic fluid in the primary supply system. It is ironic that in the final analysis this "hangar queen" would end up flying the entire distance to Desert-I without experiencing any major problems.

talking to the maintenance crews—he was a bundle of energy. Jerry King finally corralled him and they drove to the trailer, where, along with Sherm Williford and a former general in the shah's air force, he received Buchanan's weather briefing. The Iranian, who had had two decades of flying experience in his homeland, said that it was unlikely the weather there could be any better.

There was silence while General Vaught pondered the forecast and studied the satellite photos.

Then he announced his decision: GO.

The execute order was transmitted at 1720 (5:20 P.M.).

30

NEXT STOP, DESERT-I

Message from COMJTF, "Foreman":

EXECUTE MISSION AS PLANNED. GOD SPEED.

Word spread quickly. There was cheering, and fists were jammed into the air with thumbs up. "We're really going to go!" Everyone had fire in his eyes. This was an emotional high for all of us.

The lead MC-130 would take off at dusk (1405 Zulu/1805 Local).[1]

Captain Jim Kelley, the intelligence officer, was going over last-minute escape and evasion instructions and making sure that all flight suits were sanitized (pockets cleaned out). Dog tags and ID cards and some green dollars for escape and evasion were all the C-130 crew members would carry into Iran.

Bob Brenci's crew had been warming up avionics equipment in the lead MC-130 and making final adjustments to their inertial navigation system in anticipation of the launch order.

With takeoff now less than an hour away, the eager human cargo was boarding Brenci's Combat Talon with assistant loadmaster Sergeant Taco Sanchez checking off the name of each man.

First to go aboard were fifty-six members of the assault force, led by Charlie Beckwith, who was escorting the two former Ira-

---

[1] Zulu is Greenwich Mean Time.

nian generals (advisers). Among this group were the twelve men for the roadblock team, six Iranian truck drivers, and the seven Farsi-speaking American driver-monitors. Charlie was also taking Delta's field surgeon.

Finally came John Carney's combat control team, along with Colonel Tom Wicker and myself, as additions to Brenci's eleven-man aircrew. This really was a "sardine-can" load and required the "old-head" ingenuity of our chief loadmaster, Duke Wiley. This arrangement allowed Delta's operators to stretch out on the padded floor and get some rest on the way to Desert-I.

While Brenci and his crew were making final preparations to launch, the pilots of the remaining C-130s were huddled around the briefing tent, reviewing takeoff and en route join-up procedures.

The plan was for a flight of two and a flight of three with the wingmen taxiing out behind their flight leaders for takeoff. Since we had walked through this drill earlier that day, I felt sure there wouldn't be any problems in accomplishing this relatively easy maneuver.

MASIRAH, 1350 ZULU/1750 LOCAL

Bob Brenci had all four engines running and was taxiing out to takeoff position. A second C-130 was following and was going through the same procedures as the lead. If anything came up that meant Brenci's bird couldn't fly, the passengers, load, and crew would be transferred to the backup. This would delay us no more than fifteen minutes, and we could make that up en route.

At Masirah, all takeoffs were on the 8,200-foot north runway. There would be no communication with the control tower, but Lieutenant Colonel Bob Lawrence and Lieutenant Colonel Sam Hall were up there to expedite our operations.

We reached the departure end of the runway, and Brenci lined the aircraft up and advanced the throttles to takeoff power. The brakes were released and we started down the runway—all systems were go!

The big Hercules lifted off at precisely 1405Z/1805L and rose into the calm, smooth sunset sky of Oman—next stop, Desert-I. On the ground, Gravel Pit transmitted to Red Barn: "Dragon-1 airborne."

Meanwhile, support personnel and the remaining crews were busily tending to their aircraft and load plans; they were to depart one hour after Brenci.

The second MC-130 would be carrying fifty Delta troopers, and No. 3 would have thirty-two of the rescue force aboard. MC-130 No. 3 would also be carrying Marine Warrant Officer Bill Lang and two other Marine Corps personnel to operate the doughnut bladder system that contained the backup fuel for use, if needed, at Desert-I. Lang would also be assisting if there were any problems refueling the helos.

Only the basic crews and four fuel specialists would be aboard the Bladder Birds. The only ones going to Desert-I were those essential to the mission.[2]

Aboard the Nimitz, 1405 Zulu (1805 Local)

The eight RH-53 Sea Stallions were being brought on deck via the aft elevators—it was about an hour before takeoff. Visibility was three to four miles in light haze. No other ships were in sight.

As soon as the helos were positioned on deck with rotor blades and tail assemblies unfolded, Chuck Gilbert began installing the Palletized Inertial Navigation System equipment in each aircraft.

Lead Talon, 1420 Zulu

Brenci was now flying our bird on a northeasterly course at between 500 and 1,000 feet over the Gulf of Oman. We were proceeding toward the point where we would intercept the heading that would be used to penetrate the Iranian coast between two radar sites located along the southeast shoreline.

I was sitting on the stairs that led to the cockpit, which put me near the navigators so I could monitor the progress of the flight. Beckwith's radio operator sat near the SATCOM position in the rear so he could keep both Charlie and me advised on what was going on.

---

[2]Dr. Postles pestered me to allow him to go along on one of the C-130s, but my orders specifically prohibited strap-hangers. I would later regret that decision—having a couple of doctors at Desert-I would have been a very wise move.

Aboard the Nimitz, 1430 Zulu

The aircrews started the helos' engines and commenced run-ups and systems checks. Ed Seiffert, the flight leader, discovered that the pilot's spotlight aboard Helo No. 1 was inoperative. Since this was a mission-essential item, necessary for in-flight signaling, it had to be replaced; this took ten minutes. All other systems checked out normally, and the eight choppers were fully operational as the *Nimitz* turned to a course roughly parallel to the Iranian coast.

There were no apparent problems caused by the fire-suppressant dousing the helos had taken. Still, it had been a wise move to get the birds on deck early to make absolutely certain that no critical mission components had been affected.

Lead Talon, 1435 Zulu

Roland Guidry, who was performing safety pilot duties for Brenci, yelled back at me, "Hey, Colonel, there are ships all over out here."

We were about 100 nautical miles northeast of Masirah.[3] I moved forward to Guidry's position behind Brenci and looked out the front of the aircraft. Jumpin' Jehoshaphat! There were five or six commercial ships below us.

"Bob, get this thing up into the haze layer"—3,000 feet— "and vary your course as much as you can to avoid flying near those ships." It was still dusk, and about all we could do now was to press on and try to conceal who we were and hope we would be mistaken for an Iranian C-130 if anyone reported an aircraft flying in that direction.

I could have kicked myself for going along with advancing the launch time because of Pitman's recon mission. I had assumed the Marine planners considered the lead C-130 would need the cover of darkness while crossing the Strait of Hormuz.[4] That obviously was not the case, and I was more than glad the other five aircraft were an hour behind us. At least it would be dark when they passed over this area.

[3] All distances are in nautical miles. A nautical mile is equivalent to 1.15 statute miles.
[4] Nautical twilight charts had been carefully screened to determine the proper darkness for the mission, and we should not have deviated from the original departure time. To assume something as critical as this could have been disastrous.

Now it was up to General Vaught's black-box guys to determine if we had been detected. He would have to call the shots if he wanted us to abort. This was one last-minute change that we could have done without.

MASIRAH, 1440 ZULU

The five remaining mission crews were in the process of starting up the engines of their C-130s. They would soon be taxiing out to make good their assigned takeoff times.

There were two difficulties which would make this departure tricky—the limited taxi area in which to maneuver, further complicated by the heavy gross weights of the aircraft. The MC-130s weighed about 180,000 pounds and the tankers grossed out around 190,000.

The old birds creaked and groaned under the strain of the ponderous weight. The pilots really had to take it easy.

LEAD TALON, 1445 ZULU

Brenci had the aircraft on a northerly heading. We were approximately 140 miles from Masirah, half the distance to the Iranian coast, tracking directly toward the point at which we would penetrate land.

We were also starting our gradual descent that would take us over the coast at an altitude of 250 feet, below any potential radar detection. We were now clear of any surface shipping and enveloped in darkness.

We were scheduled to make landfall at 1525 Zulu (1955 Local) and would have to keep a sharp lookout for the helos, since our flight paths would almost coincide at this point. We had coordinated our altitude separation, routes, and timing into the coast so as to avoid any conflicts between the lead Talon and the helo formation. I was hoping that all eight would make it off the carrier in good shape.

ABOARD THE NIMITZ, 1505 ZULU (1905 LOCAL)

Running about fifty-eight miles from the coast, the carrier had been brought up to 30 knots. The helicopters commenced liftoff.

Within two minutes, all eight were airborne and on their way in near total darkness. The *Nimitz* was about ten miles south of the planned launch position.

As the flight joined up in a wide-sweeping left turn and disappeared from view, Seiffert's radio operator reported to Red Barn via SATCOM radio, "This is Bluebeard-1 . . . eight helicopters airborne!"

The formation was proceeding toward Iran at about one hundred feet above the sea. Visibility was about three miles with light haze. Ed Seiffert was leading the formation in Helo No. 1, and Chuck Pitman was riding in No. 5.[5]

MASIRAH, 1505 ZULU

Flight leader Marty Jubelt had taxied his MC-130, Dragon-2, into takeoff position and was holding. His wingman, Republic-4 (EC-130 tanker), didn't follow as planned because the aircraft became sandwiched in the middle of the other tankers and the group was out of sequence.

There wasn't space or time to resequence the flight in the darkness, so Jubelt shoved the cobs to Dragon-2, and the others followed to make good the 1510Z (1910 Local) planned departure. They would sort out the formation en route. Not only was the departure sloppy, but two aircraft very nearly tangled wingtips in the process.

Soon after takeoff, the pilots started working their aircraft into formation, although it would end up different from the planned lineup. Dragon-2 was out front with no wingman, and Dragon-3 (MC-130) would become the lead aircraft for all three EC-130s in a diamond formation (Figure 8).

Captain Steve Fleming's crew in Dragon-3 was using their FLIR system to monitor the progress of the wingmen joining up.

---

[5]There seem to have been doubts by some authors as to what Colonel Pitman's role was. He was involved in the mission planning and execution early on, and was in charge of the helicopter force when it became a Marine operation. He may not have had the official title of helicopter mission commander, but as the senior Marine, he filled this job and we regarded him as such. He was riding in the back of No. 5 because that aircraft was to make the pickup of Bruce Laingen at the Ministry of Foreign Affairs and Pitman was to ensure that that part of the mission went according to plan.

The flight leaders would hold their airspeed back until they could see the wingmen closing the distance. The C-130 formation as now patterned would not affect the landing sequence at Desert-I, and radio silence had been preserved.

Flying at 1,000 feet, some of the pilots took a while to sort out the lead aircraft from ships on their radars. In fact, Jerry Uttaro, in Republic-6, tried to latch onto a ship until he realized the rate of closure on the radar target was far too fast and broke off to resume chasing the leader. No sweat—still a lot of water to cross before reaching the Iranian coast.

LEAD TALON, 1515 ZULU

We had already heard the Bluebeard leader radio report that the helos had launched.

The SATCOM report from Gravel Pit to Red Barn, saying that the C-130 formation was airborne, was news that brought a smile to my face. Fourteen aircraft, carrying the entire rescue force, were now en route to Desert-I. However, my elation was tempered by the knowledge that we had gotten past only the first of many hurdles.

HELICOPTER FORMATION, 1525 ZULU

Several of the helicopter crews saw a single black MC-130 pass low overhead at about twice their speed, headed toward the coastline into Iran.

All PINS equipment was working well, but the aircraft position readings from the Omega were unreliable. Ed Seiffert lined his formation up on the MC-130's path (both helo and fixed-wing elements had approximately the same flight plans across the coast).

LEAD TALON, 1525 ZULU

We were crossing the Iranian coast at 250 feet. There was no sign of the helos (although they had spotted us); however, we knew they were below us somewhere.

Now that we were over land, the cockpit temperature was rising—it was getting hot. The engineer had the air conditioning

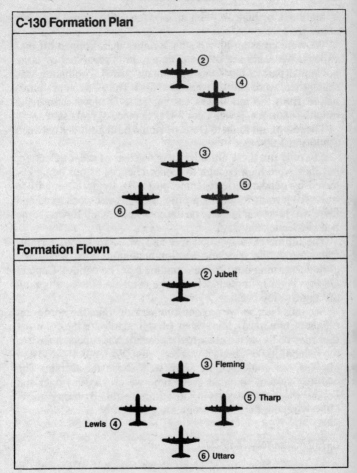

C-130 Formation Plan

Formation Flown

② Jubelt

③ Fleming

⑤ Tharp

Lewis ④

⑥ Uttaro

going full-blast, but it wasn't doing much good. The crew members were unzipping their flight suits, trying to cool off a bit.

Brenci kept us on the deck until we climbed up to cross the first plateau, which looked like the sheer face of a cliff, about 4,000 feet high. From that point, we flew over rugged terrain, staying about 2,000 feet above the ground. Practically all of Iran is highland, or plateau, with an average altitude of 3,000 feet above sea level.

We were crossing long hogback ridges that dropped off into valleys. We could see desolate, craggy hills separated by large badlands (part of the Zagros mountain chain). Population was scant; there were only a few ground fires. The 70 percent illumination from the moon was casting eerie shadows across the moonlike surface. It was a godforsaken piece of real estate.

The rest of our flight to Desert-I would be at altitudes between 1,000 and 3,000 feet.[6]

Not only did these altitudes keep us clear of radar detection, but they were high enough to reduce chances of our being detected by gendarmerie listening posts. By flying the modified (relaxed) terrain-following profile, fuel was also conserved and there was less wear and tear on the crew and assault forces (some became airsick anyway).

The altimeter read 5,000 feet and we were in our terrain-following mode over the semi-mountainous area when the altitude-warning horn began sounding off. The copilot, Captain George Ferkes, immediately hit the override button, stopping the aggravating beeping.

Seconds later, as we crossed another ridgeline, the horn went off again. Obviously, this system (designed to warn the crew that they may be flying too close to the ground) was supersensitive to the radar altitude signals it was receiving. With our night-vision goggles, we could see we were well above the terrain. The warning system sounded every time we crossed a ridge, and Ferkes was kept busy trying to minimize this irritating noise. Otherwise, our flight was progressing smoothly.

C-130 FORMATION, 1530 ZULU

As the C-130s droned along above the Gulf of Oman, the electronic warfare officer in No. 2 picked up several radar warning signals on his threat detection equipment. These signals were assessed to be emanating from a friendly source, probably

[6]MC-130 electronic warfare officers had done in-depth studies of Iranian radar capabilities along the planned route and determined that an altitude of 5,000 feet above ground level was absolutely safe from detection.

the *Nimitz*, since intelligence had determined that there were no Iranian or Soviet ships operating along our flight path. As the flight progressed northward, the warnings ceased.

The last four C-130s were still struggling to get joined up. Even though the lead aircraft had slowed down, it was a drawn-out process.

While this was going on, the navigation radar sets of the wingmen's aircraft were causing false signals on the threat detection equipment aboard Fleming's No. 3 MC-130. This was only a minor concern—getting Jerry Uttaro's No. 6 tanker caught up was his chief worry. Uttaro finally had to break radio silence, making a cryptic secure call, to advise Fleming he was closing in on a flight of three and would take the slot position. Radio silence had been broken briefly—but only for safety reasons.

HELICOPTER FORMATION, 1540 ZULU

The helo formation was crossing the Iranian coast about four miles west of the intended penetration point, speed was building from 100 to 110 knots, and they were about five minutes behind schedule (because of the *Nimitz* launch position and slower speeds resulting from the heavy takeoff weight of 48,000 pounds).

As the flight progressed inland at 200 feet, visibility improved considerably and the helos realigned their formation into a staggered trail, which was to be their normal pattern on to Desert-I. However, when they passed near populated areas they would shift to echelon pattern to place the maximum number of aircraft away from the area of potential detection (Figure 9, page 276).

Although they would have been safe from radar detection at a much higher altitude, the pilots stayed at around one hundred feet, because of the unsubstantiated conclusions they had made after the conversation with Chuck Gilbert.

As they passed the first mountain range, Ed Seiffert was still getting conflicting readings from the PINS and Omega systems—neither could be properly updated. Other helicopters in the formation were experiencing similar problems.

The TACAN in Helo 5 had gone out shortly after launch, and this bird was also experiencing a minor yaw input from the automatic flight control system.

As long as the helos had good visibility, they could map-read and use formation tactics to assist each other in navigation. These malfunctions were not a major concern.

At this point, the choppers had been in the air for about an hour and a half and everything was going as planned. Ed Seiffert

Helicopter Formation

Echelon Right

Formation Over Land (Staggered)

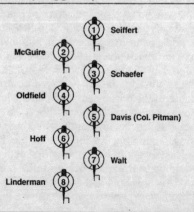

was feeling so comfortable with the situation that he was ready to kick back, open his flight lunch, and enjoy the ride. From his standpoint, everything was picture-perfect. The helicopter formation was tooling along on the deck and heading for Desert-I.

C-130 FORMATION, 1630 ZULU

The five aircraft descended to 250 feet and crossed the south coast of Iran on schedule. They were about 90 miles behind the helicopters and 210 miles back of Dragon-1, the lead Talon. The C-130 formation would overtake the helos approximately 200 miles inland from the coast (coincidence, not a planning factor). Then the two flights would take approximately the same course to Desert-I.

After crossing the first mountain range, the C-130 flight commenced modified terrain-following tactics at 500 to 1,000 feet above the ground (similar to the lead aircraft's procedures). At this point, it was duck soup—things were looking good.

31

HABOOB!

We were sailing along, porpoising above the contours of the barren Zagros Mountains, when Roland Guidry sent word that we were picking up high clouds that were screening out the moonlight. Since moonlight enhances the performance of night-vision goggles, this could have hampered visibility.

I went forward and took a look. I could see the ridges and desert surface clearly. Our weather briefing had indicated that we might encounter a high layer of clouds midway along our route, so I was not surprised. I went back and sat down.

About five minutes later, Roland called me forward again. "Look out there, Colonel." He was pointing at a ridgeline directly ahead. "See that? Something's screwing up our slant-range visibility. At first I thought it was because of the lack of moonlight, but now I'm not so sure."

When we crossed the next ridgeline I could see what he was talking about. Something was definitely restricting visibility. The contours were ill-defined until we got within about a mile of them.

Under the best of conditions, trying to judge distance at night is a wild-ass guessing game. Now I could see that there was indeed a milky condition ahead, but we couldn't tell what it was, nor could we determine what the forward visibility was.

I moved to the navigator's station and asked Captain Sam Galloway to extend the FLIR turret and scan the surface below. I wanted to know what this garbage was. His TV-like screen illuminated almost instantly, and I could clearly see the ground in all quadrants (forward, side, and aft), but hadn't a clue as to what was impairing visibility.

Some ten to fifteen minutes later, we were back in the clear. I figured we had passed through haze lying along the ridgelines. There was certainly nothing alarming about anything we had encountered so far.[1]

As we flew through this haze, the temperature in the aircraft rose considerably. The crew members had slipped out of their flight suit tops and had the long sleeves tied around their waists. Their undershirts were drenched with sweat—it was downright uncomfortable.

I turned to Tom Wicker. "What about that stuff we just passed, Tom? Do you think it's worth breaking radio silence to report it to Red Barn?"

"No, Jim, I don't. It wasn't that bad. Besides, the helos will pass about thirty miles to the east and might not even run into it. What do you think?"

"I agree. I believe the C-130 formation can hack it okay, and the choppers should, too. Based on what I've seen so far, I think it's best to maintain radio silence."

As I settled back down, I was thinking that if the Marines hit that stuff and couldn't use ground references they might have to rely a little more on their PINS equipment. In theory, each helicopter was equipped with the navigation systems to proceed alone, if need be. However, they wanted to stay in formation to the greatest extent possible so they could assist each other en route.

Our rule for an unexpected weather encounter was for the flight leader to determine if he could get his formation through intact. If not, he would devise an alternate plan, or failing that, call the command post for assistance. We were not in a position to determine if the haze constituted a problem for the choppers, nor would I suggest aborting the mission unless we encountered a wall of severe weather.

RED BARN, 1655 ZULU

The command bunker had been boiling with activity since the mission had gotten under way. Although each man was busily

---

[1]Since we were about an hour ahead of everyone else, we would report any weather that, in our opinion, might affect the choppers and C-130s that were following. The problem was in determining the severity of the visibility restriction in the darkness. We would not break radio silence for minor weather encounters.

working on his own specialty, everyone's heart and mind were with the rescue force that was now penetrating deeper and deeper into Iran.

Lee Hess was flight-following the C-130 part of the mission, monitoring time schedule and fuel status, and Maynard Weyers was doing the same with the helicopter force. Colonel Jerry Barton (the tanker task force commander) was monitoring the KC-135 schedule.

Earlier, General Vaught's black-box operators advised him that a gendarmerie post had reported seeing two C-130 aircraft flying toward the port city of Chah Bahar without lights on. Unsettling news at first.

However, it soon became apparent that this report couldn't be related to our C-130s, since none of our aircraft were near the reported location and they were not flying in an easterly direction.

Soon after that, the black-boxers heard the Iranians speculating that it was two of their own C-130s that had been flying in the Chah Bahar area earlier that day (which was probably the case). This information brought a collective sigh of relief from everyone at Red Barn.

It was definitely to our advantage that Iran had C-130s and H-53s, since from the ground no one could tell theirs from ours. It now appeared that the Joint Task Force rescue team had penetrated Iran undetected.

LEAD TALON, 1700 ZULU

We were about 230 nautical miles into Iran when Roland once again called me forward. "Look, Colonel. There it is again!"

As I peered out into the darkness, I could see that same milky haze.

What the hell is it?

Through the night-vision goggles, crew members estimated visibility was restricted to about a mile.

The FLIR continued to show ground definition clearly, with just a hint of restricted visibility. Although the FLIR was primarily looking straight down through the haze in its range of view, this was still a good indication that visibility was not that badly degraded. This was not an impassable wall of clouds. I was remembering the training experience when the helos had been forced to abort because of the weather—this was nothing like that. But I was concerned that the helo crews might have navigation problems in this stuff.

Tom Wicker was just telling me that he still felt this wasn't serious enough to break radio silence to notify Red Barn when John Carney came forward to help the pilots in locating the lights at Desert-I.

"What do you make of that stuff out there, John?"

He looked out the copilot's side window, then said, "We're flying through suspended dust. The Iranians call it a haboob."

This rang a bell. I vaguely remembered Stormy Buchanan's talking about these unusual occurrences of suspended dust in Iran, but I had never flown through anything like this anywhere in the world, especially at night.

John Carney had been briefed on haboobs by his CIA pilots on the recon mission to Desert-I. The condition is caused by the downrush of air associated with distant thunderstorms (usually several hours earlier). The air pressure forces the fine powdery sand up into the air (usually up to one hundred miles from the storm's center), and it hangs there for hours. Haboobs are difficult to predict and had not been mentioned in our premission forecast.

We all recalled the weather briefing—widely scattered thunderstorms over the Iran-Iraq border, well west of our course, that were supposed to be dissipated by the time we got to Iran. That much of it was right—there were no storms—but here we were in suspended dust.

Now I was much more concerned. I told Tom Wicker to work up a SATCOM message and advise Red Barn and the choppers of the condition. This second encounter was worse than the first, and I wanted Seiffert and Pitman to know about it.

I had no intention of telling Ed or Chuck to abort. I simply wanted to give them a "heads-up." It would be up to the flight leader to determine if they could make it through the dust, and from what I had seen, I certainly felt they should try.

I reasoned they had trained in weather penetrations and could employ those tactics to get through the dust. If that didn't work, I assumed they would do what I would—break formation and climb to a safe altitude above the terrain and proceed single-ship. With their PINS and Omega for navigation, I figured that in the worst case they could come within ten miles of Desert-I. From there they could home in on the TACAN Carney would have set up by then. From an altitude of around 5,000 feet, they would be able to receive the TACAN signal out to fifty miles.

I anticipated that the navigation problem for the helicopters would require major adjustment because of the restricted visibility, but that it was well within their capabilities to manage this.

HELICOPTER FORMATION, 1700 ZULU

The helicopter formation was north of a large dry lake approximately 140–145 miles inside Iran when the Blade Inspection Method (BIM) warning lights flashed on in Bluebeard-6.

Major Bill Hoff, the pilot, immediately decreased the speed, as prescribed in the emergency procedures for a BIM warning, and eased his bird down to a precautionary landing to check things out (as noted earlier, the BIM warns of a loss of nitrogen pressure inside the aluminum rotor blade). The crew of Helo 6, now on the ground, was inspecting the blade and its external BIM indicator when Helo 8, flown by Captain Jimmy Linderman, came in to land as en route rescue.

Hoff confirmed the mechanical blade fault indication and determined that Helo 6 was no longer airworthy, so the crew abandoned their chopper, collected all classified material, and transferred to Helo 8.

Within fifteen minutes, No. 8 was airborne again . . . but now Bill Hoff's crew was aboard as passengers.

Meanwhile, Ed Seiffert had seen Hoff's light signals and passed a note to his radio operator to report via SATCOM that two helicopters were landing, but no location was given, nor was any reason for the landing (Seiffert didn't know).

Aboard the *Nimitz*, the general area of the setdown was plotted and confirmed as just north of a dry lake bed. This position was within the range of a Marine CH-53 search and rescue aircraft which had been prepositioned aboard the *Nimitz*. There was concern aboard the *Nimitz* and at Joint Task Force headquarters in Wadi Kena as to why the helo had gone down and where the crew was, but radio silence was not to be broken just to find out.

Everyone in the command and control network interpreted the continued radio silence as meaning Seiffert considered the situation manageable and no assistance was required.

RED BARN, 1710 ZULU

When the first report on the helicopter problems came in over the command net radio, everyone in the command bunker clustered around the radio operators to listen in on what was happening. The earlier excitement was replaced by tense waiting.

Foreman was advised of Seiffert's bad news. Jerry King reviewed the situation with the general, recalling that a similar emergency had occurred during rehearsals and that one helo was designated to land with the ailing bird and retrieve the crew, if necessary, and continue on. This was part of the helicopter contingency plan—seven helos should still be on course for Desert-I.

King radioed the *Nimitz* to find out what those there knew about the incident, but they were also in the dark. They decided to wait until everyone arrived at Desert-I before asking questions about the crew of Helo 6.

In the meantime, the operations section received a report that six KC-135s had launched from Diego Garcia to be in position to refuel the C-130s when they exited Iran. The tankers had to fly over 2,000 miles (about five hours) to reach the refueling orbit. Some of these tankers had a secondary mission of refueling Navy fighters that could become involved if directed by the Chairman or General Vaught.

Also about this time, Red Barn received a launch report from the last C-141 departing Wadi Kena, bound for Daharan, Saudi Arabia. The transport had the Military Airlift Command Special Operations low-level crews aboard that were to fly the medevac extraction aircraft into Manzariyeh on Night-Two. These crews would link up at Daharan with the crews of two other C-141s already there.

HELICOPTER FORMATION, 1715 ZULU

Still flying near 200 feet above the desert, the helicopters had now progressed about 180 miles inland with about 345 miles to go. Seiffert was in visual contact with Helos 2, 3, 4, 5, and 7. He hoped Jimmy Linderman in Bluebeard-8 was no more than twenty minutes back, after stopping to assist the crew of Bluebeard-6. Because of the radio silence, however, this was not a certainty. Ed wouldn't be able to find out what had happened until everyone reached Desert-I.

The mission was proceeding with seven choppers, more than enough for the job. They were about fifteen minutes behind what the master plan called for, but this was not a major concern— their speed was picking up as they burned off fuel.

LEAD TALON, 1730 ZULU

We were about thirty minutes from the landing zone, almost 420 miles into Iran. We had passed the dust and I could see for miles. The last patch of dust had been about twice as long as the first, and I estimated that to be about one hundred miles, since it had taken about thirty minutes to pass through it. My attention was now directed toward preparing for the landing at Desert-I.

Tom Wicker came back up onto the flight deck about ten minutes later lamenting to me, "I wasn't able to send the message about the dust. It was too dark back there and I couldn't make out the code-word message using a flashlight—and the matrix was worthless."[2]

My heart sank. The helicopter leader hadn't been warned about the dust, and it was too late now. According to my rough estimate, they were already in it.[3]

Well, we hadn't heard from Seiffert. Maybe they had missed the dust somehow . . . or had climbed to a safe altitude above the terrain and were plowing ahead, navigating with their PINS. From our experience, the visibility was never less than a half mile at worst. I thought they could hack that.

---

[2]We had been given to understand that we were to use the code-word instructions to construct messages and our SATCOM operator made no suggestions on how to handle the matter, so we stuck with radio silence rather than talk openly over the command net. Not having the SATCOM radios to train with was coming back to haunt us.

[3]I didn't realize at the time that the two systems were incompatible and I couldn't talk to Seiffert over the encoded SATCOM system, but the JTF command center would have heard the report and passed it on to him.

When they get within fifty miles of Desert-I, they can pick up the TACAN and drive right in, I thought.

Maintaining strict radio silence was still a nagging factor in my mind. The only transmissions we had heard over the satellite network were that the helos launched, all C-130s were airborne, and two helos had landed in the desert. Nothing about a dust encounter.

Wicker reiterated his belief that the helos could get through the dust okay, and I agreed.

But the more I thought about it, the more my conscience told me differently! That message should have been sent. To hell with radio silence and flimsy excuses—it was a lick on me!

Too late to agonize over it—we had a landing to get through.

At this time, one of those strange little twists of coincidence was taking place. A report was sent out over the command and control (SATCOM) network that was interpreted as "The lead MC-130 will land in thirty minutes." It was darn near right on the money, but it didn't come from our aircraft—a thirty-minute-out report was not in the communications plan.

Red Barn, Gravel Pit, and Ed Seiffert all believed the lead Talon was right on schedule—and they were right, but the source of this "information" was erroneous.

HELICOPTER FORMATION, 1745 ZULU

Helos 2, 3, and 7 had spotted aircraft to the west about fifteen minutes earlier (200 miles). They identified them as four C-130s flying parallel to their track at about twice their speed and looked to be 2,000 feet above them. The C-130s were visible for about three minutes.

This sighting raised the helo pilots' confidence in their own navigation, and they held to the same course the C-130s were flying. It made the pilots wonder what they were doing on the deck when the C-130s were well above them. This was the first instance that they had reason to question the decision to fly at 200 feet.

The choppers were now completing one of their transitions from echelon back to staggered trail formation when directly ahead the pilots spotted what one likened to "a wall of talcum

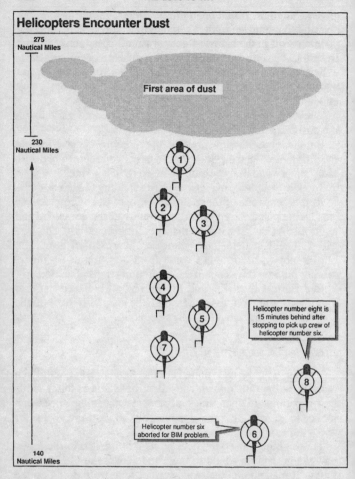

Helicopters Encounter Dust

275 Nautical Miles

230 Nautical Miles

First area of dust

1

2

3

4

5

7

Helicopter number eight is 15 minutes behind after stopping to pick up crew of helicopter number six.

8

Helicopter number six aborted for BIM problem.

6

140 Nautical Miles

powder" and another described as "looking like the inside of a bottle of milk." (See Figure 10.)

Seiffert and his wingman, B. J. McGuire, were flying tight formation with rotor tips about 100 feet apart. The rest of the helicopters were closing on the lead element from 250 feet behind. Speed was about 120 knots, altitude still 200 feet, with negligible headwinds. It had been pretty easy going up to now, but that was changing, and fast. These crews would soon be working their butts off in the haboob that was directly between them and Desert-I.

Seiffert led the formation into the chalky mass, not certain what it was. He was hoping to punch through the murk and break into the clear in short order with the formation intact.

Once inside the haboob, Seiffert realized they were flying through dust—there was a sandy grit entering the cockpit and he could feel it collecting on his teeth. The temperature had risen about 20 degrees to nearly 100.

Initially, the visibility was varying between half a mile and a quarter of a mile and the six choppers were able to maintain formation without too much difficulty. They had spread out a little for safe rotor spacing.

Visibility improved considerably as they passed through this first area of dust, but that wouldn't last long as they soon would enter the second shroudlike cloud.

32

CUE TIP/DESERT LANDING

HELICOPTER FORMATION, 1800 ZULU

The choppers were well into the dust area and, down at their altitude, having one hell of a time. Visibility was becoming progressively worse, and Seiffert was having a hard time seeing the ground.

Finally, Ed completely lost sight of the ground and could only catch glimpses of the other helos. He wrote out a note and passed it to the SATCOM operator for transmission to Red Barn.[1] The note read, "Visibility markedly reduced . . . unable to see the ground."

By now, the only other chopper Ed could see was his wingman. He decided the best thing to do would be to turn the formation around and get out of the dust, then plan the next move.

He made a U-turn and exited the dust curtain with B. J. McGuire in No. 2 right behind him. They then sat their Sea Stallions down on the desert at a point somewhere around 300 miles from Desert-I.

About twenty minutes later, Seiffert sent another message: "Red Barn from Bluebeard-1, two helicopters have landed in the desert . . . zero visibility." (See Figure 11, page 289.)

Ed could see that he was between the proverbial rock and a hard place. His wingman was the only one who had seen him

---

[1] The portable setup of the SATCOM system in the helicopter precluded interphone contact with the radio operator, and therefore Seiffert had to write out cryptic notes and pass them back to be read over the command net. This arrangement for passing information left much to be desired. Also, the ground-oriented radio operator was not conversant with pilots' lingo and just read what was written in the note, which contained limited information.

turn, so the others must still be heading for Desert-I, the lead MC-130 should be just about landing, there were fourteen JTF aircraft in Iranian airspace, and if he didn't proceed, it was doubtful we would get another chance to rescue the hostages. He hoped the dust ended soon so they could pick up speed. They obviously were falling further behind schedule.

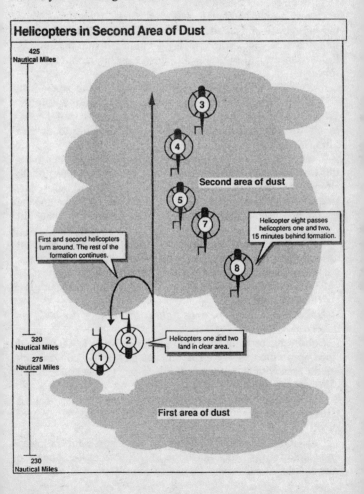

Helicopters in Second Area of Dust

425 Nautical Miles

Second area of dust

Helicopter eight passes helicopters one and two, 15 minutes behind formation.

First and second helicopters turn around. The rest of the formation continues.

Helicopters one and two land in clear area.

320 Nautical Miles

275 Nautical Miles

First area of dust

230 Nautical Miles

LEAD TALON, 1800 ZULU

We were closing in on Desert-I. Outside, it was clear as a bell—perfect weather conditions for our landing.

John Carney had moved forward to help the pilots locate the desert track and get lined up for landing. John positioned himself beside copilot George Ferkes.

Carney's right-hand man, Sergeant Mitch Bryan, came up on the flight deck and stood next to me. He was setting up the remote control panel with which he would activate the runway lights Carney had buried in the desert on his reconnaissance mission.

We were now five miles from the desert landing zone (LZ), and Mitch flipped the switches that would activate the lights. Would they work? They'd been out there at the mercy of the elements for almost a month. All eyes were straining to catch a glimpse of them.

If they hadn't turned on, it was going to be a lot tougher to get this bird on the ground in one piece. Carney would have to talk Brenci and Ferkes down, and make sure we stopped before hitting anything. Meanwhile, the FLIR turret was extended and the navigators were scanning ahead, looking for the road that split the LZ.

"There they are! Off to the right!" It was Carney. A cheer went up and John was on the receiving end of some good-natured back-slapping and kidding about his "Flash Gordon" device.

"Turn right about thirty degrees," Carney directed the pilots.

Now I saw them.

Hot damn! Chuck Gilbert's lights are working perfectly, as advertised.

Bob Brenci brought the Combat Talon down to 1,000 feet and lined up on the road for a surveillance pass so we could check out the area with the infrared system, looking for vehicles or any other obstructions.

"There's the bend in the road, where it turns north," Roland Guidry yelled out. "There're the runway lights! All five of them!"

I was looking over the shoulders of navigators Sam Galloway and Captain Clay Chapman at the FLIR presentation. The road was clearly visible on the TV-like screen. We were all watching intently as the sensors probed for signs of life. I checked my watch—we were right on schedule, it was 1805Z (10:35 P.M. Iran time).

"Dammit! There's a truck," Galloway shouted. Sure enough, there it was, big as life, a truck bumping along the road about half a mile in front of us, headed east toward the distant city of Tabas.

The navigators called for a turn to the north, and Brenci immediately pulled the nose around. We passed well behind the truck and believed that no one saw or heard us.

Bob circled the Talon back so we could take another look at the landing zone and the road. Those with night-vision goggles could now easily see the road and the adjacent landing areas, illuminated by moonlight and marked by Carney's lights.

A funny thought struck me: *That truck driver must have seen Carney's lights out in the desert—wonder what he thought.* He sure hadn't stopped to find out. He was nowhere in sight. He must have put the pedal to the metal and highballed it out of there as fast as he could.

On the second pass along the road, John Carney noticed a problem with the alignment of the lights on the ground. I could hear him explaining it to Brenci: "The lights at the touchdown point are too close to the shoulder of the road.

"Land to the right of the lights at the west end and then aim toward the light at the far end. We sure don't want to hit that soft shoulder and tear up this airplane."

Brenci rogered that and, determining that the road and the LZ were now clear, executed a go-around and turned on the downwind leg for final approach. The pucker factor was really starting to tighten up now!

I felt the flaps and gear being lowered and turned my attention back to the FLIR screen—it was as cold as yesterday's toast. *Dammit, that's right . . . we can't have that turret extended when the landing gear is lowered or the nose-wheel door will jam.* The night-vision goggles were all we had now, and that was like flying into a tunnel—very limited peripheral capability.

If anything shows up out to the side, we'll be lucky to see it.

Brenci had completed his box traffic pattern and we were rolling out on final approach. Then the engines roared back to full power—we were going around. We were in too close for Bob to get the airplane lined up properly.

After another box pattern with Roland Guidry helping to direct the alignment, we again turned on final. This time we were lined up perfectly.

As we descended, the engineer was monotonously calling out airspeed readings.

"Add power—you're too slow," Roland yelled out. He had barely gotten the words out when we made firm—very, very firm—contact with the desert.

That one had to wipe out the nose gear.

But the old bird just shuddered and rolled about 3,000 feet to a stop. It sure wasn't one of the patented landings that Brenci was known for.

In the cargo compartment, the jolt of the landing had bounced Charlie Beckwith up underneath the roadblock team's jeep. As Charlie crawled out of this predicament, he announced, "Great landing! That wasn't bad at all!" (Charlie believed that any landing you walked away from was a good one.)

On impact, I had heard some stowed equipment banging around, but everything seemed to be intact. We had made it!

I told Guidry to send the code word "cue tip" to Red Barn to let them know we had landed (it was 1815Z/10:45 P.M. Iran time).

I hurried down the stairs from the cockpit and was going to follow Beckwith's people out the back ramp. My first task was to get my ground command position set up on the road, then Charlie could crank up the SATCOM so we could contact Foreman and monitor what was going on.

The roadblock team, Carney's combat controllers, and Charlie and his Delta troops were already off the aircraft and proceeding with their tasks.

I was just starting down the ramp when flashing lights from the road caught my eye. As I looked down the road, I couldn't believe what I was seeing. Here came a bus, lights flashing from high beam to low beam and back, boring right into the middle of our operation . . . and the roadblock team and Delta troops were charging into a blocking position, firing warning shots over the bus. A 40mm grenade round sizzling past the windshield convinced the driver of the bus that we meant business. He brought that sucker to a grinding halt.

I headed toward the bus. The heat and dust being kicked up by the aircraft engines were making it tough going—I was forced to shield my eyes against the stinging sand. The aircrew were setting the engine controls to idle, which would help. We had experienced this during rehearsal, but it was worse at Desert-I . . . a bloody nuisance.

When I got clear of the blowing sand, I could see the bus, which had stopped about fifty yards from the Talon. It was a fairly new Mercedes. The interior lights were on and I could see it had a full load of very frightened passengers—they didn't know who we were or what was going on.

As I rounded the back of the bus, I encountered Delta White Element commander Major Logan Fitch, who had a terrified Iranian in his grasp. Logan also had a fat lip. He had gotten it when the rear door of the bus hit him in the face as he was capturing the driver, who was trying to escape out the back and hide in the wheel well.

Delta's White Element took charge of the forty-four captives so the roadblock team members could head out to their positions some three miles to the east and west. Jesse Johnson got his motorbike riders moving in short order. I noticed each bike had two light antitank weapons strapped to the handlebars, which would be used to stop any vehicles that tried to break through the roadblock.

I turned back to the bus occupants, who were being taken off the vehicle and instructed to sit along the shoulder of the road. They had been searched and appeared to be harmless. The Farsi-speaking linguists were trying to calm the captives, telling them they wouldn't be harmed if they followed instructions.

Making an absurd situation bizarre, one of the linguists, Army Major Tyrone Tisdale, was reciting poetry from Omar Khayyam to help calm the passengers. Somebody told me that earlier one of the passengers in the back of the bus had called out in perfect English, "It's about time you came, Yanks."

RED BARN, 1815 ZULU

The Delta radio operators manning the SATCOM at the command post were having trouble receiving the helicopter transmissions because of weak reception on the satellite circuit.

Fortunately, General Gast at Gravel Pit (Masirah) was able to copy most of the transmissions clearly and was relaying them to Foreman.

When Seiffert's report on reduced visibility came in, Jerry King nearly flipped. He cornered Don Buchanan, the forecaster: "What the hell are they talking about, Stormy?"

Stormy turned white as a sheet and was scrambling to review his forecast data. "I just don't know. There's nothing here to indicate restricted visibility as a possibility. They shouldn't be having any weather problems."

Then fifteen minutes later, Seiffert's second report, that two choppers had landed on the desert, had arrived and General Vaught was climbing the walls. He wanted to know what Ed was going to do. Time was starting to get critical and the problems were mounting up.

33

STRUGGLE IN THE DUST

C-130 FORMATION, 1815 ZULU

The C-130s, with No. 2 out front by itself, and Dragon-3 (MC-130) dragging three tankers in a loose four-ship diamond formation, were about 160 miles from Desert-I—they were in the dust. Steve Fleming, the flight leader, had been concerned his wingmen might not be able to maintain formation with the limited visibility, but the tanker pilots could see each other reasonably well. In fact, some of the crews on the wing were unaware there was a visibility problem.

Fleming's crew had little reference to the ground or horizon, but were having no problems with navigation, since they were relying on their terrain-following radar and the inertial navigation system. Wingmen stayed on the leader and let him do the work for them.

DESERT-I, 1820 ZULU

I found Charlie Beckwith and we moved up the road to where Carney's men were setting up the portable TACAN. This was also the predesignated position from which I would direct activities at Desert-I.

Charlie and I discussed the bus captives and agreed that we would advise Foreman that we would haul them and their baggage back to Egypt, then return them to Manzariyeh on Night-Two. We had expected that we might have to take some captives at Desert-I—but forty-four? What incredibly bad luck.

Having to retract the FLIR turret to lower the landing gear had really botched things up. Had we been able to leave it extended,

I'm sure we would have seen the bus in time to hold off landing until it had passed through. As it was, the roadblock team didn't have a chance to get set up before the bus came barreling right into the middle of our operation. I was very impressed with how Beckwith's men had leaped into disciplined action as if they had rehearsed it and had brought the situation under control within minutes.

I was now scanning the landing zone through my NVGs. I could see Carney's combat controllers, unperturbed by the action swirling around them, matter-of-factly setting up the lights for the northside landing strip. Swinging my goggles south, I could see another CCT group realigning the lights on that side of the road.

W-H-U-M-P-H!

Holy shit! What blew up?

I swung the goggles toward the sound. There was a ball of fire rising up from the west perimeter approach. The intense light made the goggles useless.

"What do you make of that, Charlie?"

"That's a damned gasoline fire. Wade Ishimoto's team must have run into more trouble out there."

"Dammit! Is this Desert-I or the Hollywood Freeway? We just got here and already we've encountered two vehicles! The whole world must know we're here by now."

Jesse Johnson came charging up in his jeep to report. "A small gasoline truck came wheeling in from the west and Captain Wade Ishimoto fired his M-16 into the engine but couldn't get the driver to stop, so the roadblock team fired a light antitank weapon at it. The round went under the cab and ricocheted up into the fuel tank. Instant Fourth of July."

"What happened to the driver?" Beckwith asked.

"Just as the truck went up, he made it out and legged it back to a small pickup that had been following. This truck took off fast to the north. Our motorbiker gave chase, but the pickup was going too fast for him in the dark."

I turned to Beckwith. "What do you think, Charlie? Have we got World War III started?"

In a fight, Charlie has a finely honed "streetwise" sense of what's going on around him. While I was thinking everything had gone to hell in a handbasket, he correctly assessed that the situation was under control.

"Those Iranians that got away had to be running some type of contraband. That's the way moonshiners in the States operate—with a backup vehicle following the one with the contraband, just in case there's trouble. I'd make book that they won't be heading to the nearest gendarmerie post bitchin' that their truck was ambushed. Besides, they didn't see what was going on down here. I think we're still okay."

He could be right. I sure hope so. That getaway truck wasn't just coincidence.

"Well, I hope you're right, Charlie. The black-box guys at Red Barn will let us know if the Iranian police start chattering about strange goings-on out in the desert. There's nothing we can do about it now but figure how to cover our tracks so the looks of the place won't raise too many questions come sunrise."

Charlie had an answer for that, too.

"We'll drive the bus into the fuel truck and make it look like a head-on collision. The C-130s can haul all the bus passengers out. You can use the jeep to drag the runways like dragging a ball diamond and nobody will know we've been here."

That'll work! In spite of everything, by God, we've still got control!

A more immediate concern was that the burning fuel truck would make it hairy for the pilots landing on the northside sand strip to see the runway. Any bright light hinders use of night-vision goggles—it essentially magnifies to blinding proportions, an effect similar to going from darkness into a brightly lit room. I was hoping the fire would burn itself out in the some thirty minutes remaining before the other aircraft were due to arrive.

I looked at my watch. My God! We'd been on the ground only a little over ten minutes. With all these fun and games it seemed more like an hour. Anyhow, we'd done all right so far. What else could go wrong?

I didn't have to wait long for the answer to that. Bad news was heading my way at that moment. Roland Guidry was walking over from the aircraft, which was parked off to one side of the south landing strip with the engines still running.

"Colonel, the SATCOM radio won't work. The power amp

busted loose on that strut bender. I had the 'cue tip' message sent out on the HF radio."[1]

I turned to Beckwith. "Let's send the arrival message out on your SATCOM radio, Charlie."

He looked at me with a pained expression. "It's coming on No. 3 Talon."

"Dammit, Charlie. That radio was supposed to come in with us so we could use it as a command radio to stay in touch with Vaught. Why the change of plans?"

"No good reason. It just seemed like a good idea at the time."

Charlie had his radioman break out a small portable HF radio and set it up in the road.

That thing's as useless as tits on a boar hog.

My worst fears about this communications setup had been realized. The high frequency radios were now our primary communications systems, something I'd been trying to avoid since the training for this mission began.

The whole idea had been to have a portable SATCOM set up in the road so we wouldn't have to crawl on the aircraft every time we needed to send or receive a message. Now we were incommunicado except for the HF radios, and we could send only short, coded messages on those. There was no way to apprise Foreman of our problems and discuss options.

When the aircraft SATCOM set broke, that was bad luck. But we screwed ourselves by not having Delta's portable unit along for backup.

We couldn't tell anybody about the bus passengers or the burning fuel truck. We hadn't been able to advise the chopper crews about the dust.

We did receive confirmation over the high frequency net that a remote ground station had received our arrival report. I was hoping the helicopter jockeys had also heard it.

With all the problems we were having, we needed good communications to sort things out.

I wonder how Seiffert and his flight are doing in that dust? We don't need any more trouble.

---

[1]This was the procedure to be followed in case the SATCOM couldn't be used. Although not secure, the code word was so short it would have been extremely difficult, if not impossible, to trace (if some hostile agency was monitoring the frequency).

In the meantime, John Carney's people had successfully set up the two landing strips and had the lights operating, and we were ready for the rest of the force to arrive. At least when the C-130s got in, we would have a SATCOM and could maybe straighten a few things out.

For now, all we could do was wait . . . and hope everyone was hanging tough.

C-130 FORMATION, 1835 ZULU

The two Combat Talons and their three tanker wingmen had broken clear of the dust about one hundred miles south of Desert-I, and from that point it had been a routine flight.

For some time now, the navigators had been picking up signals from the directional beacon located near the small airport at Darband. It confirmed they were dead on course and right on time. It was kind of the Iranians to keep the station operating for us. This might also be of help to the helicopter crews, although no one was sure their equipment was compatible with the beacon (I later learned that most of the helo crews did receive the signal, which helped them confirm their positions).

As the formation bored on in toward its objective, excitement was building among the fliers.

Long before they could see the landing zone, they spotted the big blaze leaping up off the desert floor. At first they thought an aircraft had crashed.

"What the hell is that?"

They knew the lead Talon had landed safely, so it couldn't be that, and they could see No. 2. But what could be burning so furiously right where they were due to land within minutes?

HELICOPTERS 1 AND 2, 1845 ZULU

Ed Seiffert had the word (or thought he did) that the lead Talon had landed. Abort was no longer an option. He would have to plow ahead, no matter what.

After collecting his thoughts, Ed relaunched his bird toward the ominous cloud. B. J. McGuire was right behind in Helo No. 2.

Jimmy Linderman, in Helo 8, was now ahead of the flight leader, but still trailing the four choppers led by Jim Schaefer in

Helo 3. The twenty minutes Helos 1 and 2 sat on the desert floor had given Linderman time to catch up with and pass them. The leader and his wingman were now at the tail end of the flight.

Seiffert directed his radio operator to contact Red Barn and report their situation.

"Numbers 1 and 2 airborne—proceeding to Desert-I."

They were now flying at 500 to 1,000 feet above the desert, and airspeed was averaging a hundred knots because of the visibility.

Red Barn, 1850 Zulu

General Vaught had become extremely concerned about the helicopters after receiving Seiffert's first report that Helos 1 and 2 had set down in the desert. He was pacing the floor, waiting for Ed to announce his intentions.

Although relieved after receiving the follow-up message that Helos 1 and 2 had relaunched for Desert-I, the general was still anxious about the status of the helicopter force. His staff members believed, but were not certain, that there were still seven birds.

He wanted clarification from Seiffert.

"Bluebeard Leader, this is Foreman. How many helos en route to Desert-I?"

"Six helos for sure," came the answer.

Seiffert was reluctant to include No. 8 in his assessment—he was not sure of Linderman's status.

Although he was still uneasy, General Vaught got some relief from this news. We were okay with six still in the game, and the possibility of a seventh just sweetened the pot. There was no means to tie this number down to a certainty without breaking radio silence. He was fervently hoping the Marine crews would be up to handling the visibility problem. He knew these crews were being put to the test but fully supported Seiffert's decision to press on.

Foreman was also uneasy knowing that the helo leader was at least thirty minutes behind schedule. He directed his staff to think of ways to speed up fueling and loading at Desert-I.

The task force was now committed to going forward. The time

for helicopter abort would have had to come thirty minutes ago—before the lead Talon landed at Desert-I.

Trying to assess the extent of the visibility problem was difficult, if not impossible, in the dark. An unexpected situation such as this was not something that could be accurately assessed in minutes. By the time Seiffert was sure the visibility was becoming progressively worse and decided to reorganize his flight, the lead C-130 was landing at Desert-I. We all had been suckered into thinking the situation was manageable, when in reality it had a devastating effect on the low-flying helicopters.

HELICOPTER FORMATION, 1850 ZULU

The lead choppers were 175 miles from the desert rendezvous and in a world of hurt. This was nothing like the mission for which they had planned and trained. They were battling a long unrehearsed instrument flight and had no secure radios to help them hold it all together—it had turned into a blood-curdling experience.

Jim Schaefer, in Helo 3, was now in the second area of dust and had been flying in low-visibility conditions off and on for over an hour.

The dust seemed to hang in layers, but the pilots did not vary their altitude. They stayed in the dust at 200 feet above ground level for fear of losing contact with terrain features depicted on their enlarged navigation charts, specially printed for ease of map reading. The crews still thought that Iranian radar detection ability ruled out climbing to a higher altitude.[2]

The crew members were sweating in the 100-degree heat in the dust cloud, frequently sipping water from their canteens. There was no wind or buffeting but most of them were having trouble with vertigo, or disorientation.

Schaefer, in Helo 3, was still leading with Oldfield in Helo 4 as his wingman. As the flight progressed, Captain L. C. Walt,

---

[2]Arthur T. Hadley wrote that the helicopters should have climbed to 400 feet, "where the air was more clear of dust." In the lead Talon, we encountered the dust at 3,000 feet, and it probably extended upward to 10,000 feet or more. Climbing to 400 feet might have helped, but at 1,000 feet the C-130 formation never had less than one mile of visibility.

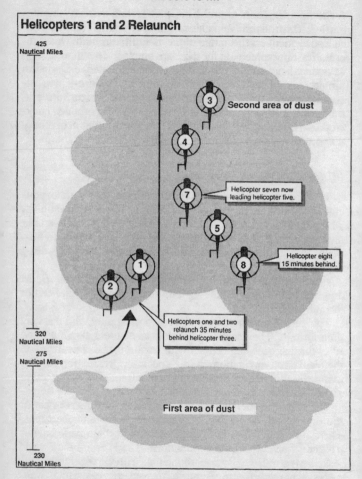

Helicopters 1 and 2 Relaunch

425 Nautical Miles

③ Second area of dust

④

⑦ Helicopter seven now leading helicopter five.

⑤

① Helicopter eight 15 minutes behind.

② ⑧

Helicopters one and two relaunch 35 minutes behind helicopter three.

320 Nautical Miles

275 Nautical Miles

First area of dust

230 Nautical Miles

piloting Helo 7, noticed that Helo 5 was falling too far behind the leader and was in danger of losing sight of the formation. Walt accelerated past Helo 5 (with Navy Lieutenant Commander Rodney Davis at the controls) and joined up on the flight leader so that he could lead Helo 5 and close the gap on the lead. (See Figure 12.)

The flight instrument problems with Helo 5 were beginning to affect controllability of the bird. Also, visual contact with the lead element was becoming more difficult, especially with the formation now spread out for safe separation.

As they headed north over the western edge of the Dasht-e-Lut, a large desert area that adjoins the Dasht-e-Kavir, at approximately 100 miles southeast of Desert-I, there were extended periods during which they couldn't see the ground. They knew that at 130 miles from Desert-I they would be near some 9,800-foot peaks. They hoped to be in the clear so they could see these hazards as they neared the city of Darband.

All crews had adopted similar flight procedures in the dust—they had slowed from 130 to 80–90 knots, and the pilots, wearing the night-vision goggles, attempted to maintain visual reference on the other aircraft (focusing on the miniature lights in the rotor blade tips) while cross-checking on the terrain. Meanwhile, the copilots were riveted on the cockpit instruments, concentrating particularly on the radar altimeters (depicting true altitude above the ground).

As Helos No. 1 and No. 2 reentered the dust cloud, B. J. McGuire's helicopter suddenly lost its second-stage hydraulic system, which powers the No. 1 Automatic Flight Control System and the backup portion of the primary flight controls. Under peacetime flying rules, the loss of the backup hydraulic system is a "land as soon as possible" situation. The aircraft must be cautiously flown with only the first-stage hydraulic system, because any sustained rapid flight control manipulations may cause a complete control lockup. McGuire decided to continue, hoping the leak could be repaired at Desert-I. (No light or hand signal had been devised to indicate this problem to the flight leader.)

Meanwhile, a few miles to the north, Davis and the crew of Helo 5 were having worse problems. The copilot, wearing NVGs, was experiencing vertigo, the severity of which was reaching the point that Chuck Pitman, who was riding in the cargo compartment, was considering taking over for him. (Pitman decided against this because he was not fully qualified in the RH-53.)

Again in near-zero visibility, Davis saw that one of his primary flight instruments, which displays pitch and roll of the aircraft, had failed. The copilot's backup indicator was still reliable but sticking during turns. The electrically powered compass system was also inoperative. He still had the magnetic compass, turn indicator, and PINS working (although it appeared to be about five miles off course). The severe heat affected the PINS on all of the choppers, and the Omega systems had not been reliable since takeoff.

Then to top everything off, Davis lost visual contact with his leader, Helo 7. Knowing that L. C. Walt was off to his left, Davis put No. 5 in a slow descending spiral to the right for safe spacing. At about fifty feet above the ground, the crew began looking for identifiable terrain features, but still couldn't see the desert floor.

Not wanting to chance going any lower in the blind, and unsure of his location, Davis faced a difficult decision. He knew he was about 145 miles from Desert-I and still had to navigate past two 9,800-foot mountains near Darband, some sixty miles apart. Although Chuck Pitman, the senior Marine, was aboard, they had no contact with the rest of the flight or the command net. Pitman assumed that seven helicopters were still en route but had no way of knowing, nor was he aware of the Helo 2 hydraulic problem.

The crew had been trying to tune in the Darband VOR to help guide them past the mountains, but without success. At this point, Davis consulted with Chuck Pitman and concluded they had two choices. They could climb as high as the aircraft would go, in hopes of clearing the dust cloud and perhaps getting some kind of a visual fix on a distant terrain feature, or they could turn back and rely on PINS to steer them in the general direction of the *Nimitz* until they could break out of the dust.

However, there were problems with both choices.

If they elected to climb they had no assurance that they could clear the dust or, if they did, that they would be able to spot anything to assist in navigation. They also were concerned that they might be seen on radar if they chose this option. With their TACAN and the radio-magnetic heading indicator both inoperable, Davis doubted that he could navigate through the mountainous terrain in poor visibility and find Desert-I.

On the other hand, if they turned back it would be cutting the helicopter force down and decreasing the chances for a successful rescue mission.

Davis computed the fuel needed to return to the *Nimitz* and determined they might not have enough. However, they knew that the CH-53 search and rescue helicopter was standing by on the *Nimitz* and would come to their assistance if they went down in or near the water.

After talking it over, Davis favored returning to the *Nimitz*, and Pitman agreed. So, after battling the dust for more than an

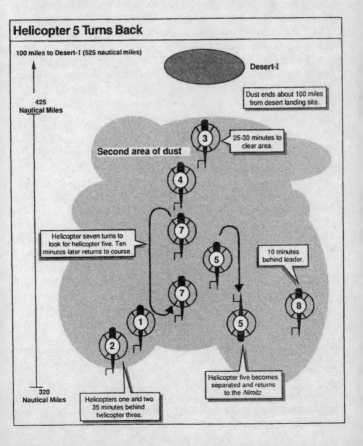

Helicopter 5 Turns Back

100 miles to Desert-I (525 nautical miles)

Desert-I

425 Nautical Miles

Dust ends about 100 miles from desert landing site.

3 — 25-30 minutes to clear area.

Second area of dust

4

Helicopter seven turns to look for helicopter five. Ten minutes later returns to course.

7

5

10 minutes behind leader.

7

1

2

8

5

Helicopters one and two 35 minutes behind helicopter three.

Helicopter five becomes separated and returns to the *Nimitz*.

320 Nautical Miles

hour and fifteen minutes to reach a point 145 miles (one hour and twenty minutes) from Desert-I and not knowing they could have been in the clear in twenty-five or thirty minutes, Davis turned back.[3] The radio operator began trying to raise Red Barn at 1900 Zulu to advise Foreman of their situation, but to no avail.[4] So Helo 5 was out of the ball game, and the crew members of Helo 7 were the only ones that might have even suspected there was a problem.

Jim Schaefer, in Helo 3, didn't see Helo 5 leave the formation, nor did the crew of Helo 7. Moments later, when they broke out of the zero-visibility area, the gunner on No. 7 reported that Helo 5 was missing. Walt immediately turned back down course to see if he could locate the missing chopper. He searched along a ridgeline for signs of a crash and scanned the surrounding terrain to see if Davis might have landed. After a ten-minute search, Walt abandoned this effort and turned north to resume the flight to Desert-I. He had no idea what had happened to No. 5. (See Figure 13.)

---

[3]I was told the copilot vehemently opposed the decision to turn back and voiced his feelings with words to the effect "We must go on . . . this is the Super Bowl." He was told the aircraft commander was in charge and to "sit on your hands."

[4]One story has it that radio contact was attempted with SATCOM, which was futile. The HF radio did not have a secure mode, and therefore any message had to be transmitted in the clear. In any case, nobody in the command net heard a word of it.

34

RENDEZVOUS IN THE DESERT

DESERT-I, 1900 ZULU

My watch said 2330 Local (11:30 P.M.) as we waited on the desert floor. I was checking last-minute details and going over the remainder of the schedule. The last C-130 was due on the ground shortly after midnight, and the helos were to begin arriving twenty minutes after that.

The refueling and loading of Delta Force would take about forty minutes, and then the choppers would head on toward Tehran and the rest of us would be winging back toward Masirah after one hour in the desert. Of course, without radio contact none of us knew how strung out the helicopter force was.

Fifteen to twenty minutes later, droning engine sounds brought me out of my thoughts.

There they are! Right on time! The dust couldn't have caused 'em too much trouble. I hope the helicopters fare as well.

Marty Jubelt began his approach in No. 2, and the other four birds were about five minutes behind, waiting their turns to sequence for landing.

I was anxious for them to get on the ground, especially No. 3, so we could get Beckwith's SATCOM radio set up and tie in with the command net. We needed to check in with Red Barn to find out what was happening and how the mission was progressing.

I was standing on the road with John Carney. We had positioned ourselves where we could observe the C-130s coming in to land and oversee marshaling them into parking position. John's traffic control radio was tuned to the aircraft mission frequency so that he could intervene in the landing operation if safety dictated.

We were both intently watching Jubelt's approach. He was not

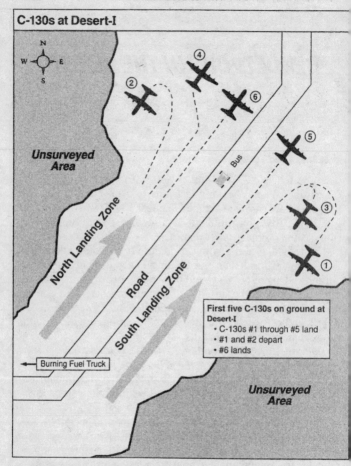

C-130s at Desert-I

N
W—E
S

② ④ ⑥ ⑤

Bus

③

①

Unsurveyed Area

North Landing Zone

Road

South Landing Zone

First five C-130s on ground at Desert-I
- C-130s #1 through #5 land
- #1 and #2 depart
- #6 lands

← Burning Fuel Truck

Unsurveyed Area

tracking right for landing—he passed over the flaming fuel truck at about a 45-degree angle to the northside landing strip.

"Tell Dragon-2 to take it around!" I told Carney.

But Marty had realized the error and was already executing a go-around before John had a chance to tell him to.

Jubelt flew a tight box pattern for the go-around and was on the ground within minutes and off-loading his passengers at the 4,000-foot mark. The CCT then marshaled him in a left turn to the north side of the runway, facing oncoming traffic. The burning truck had obviously affected the night-vision goggles, giving the crew of No. 2 some trouble on landing approach.

Three minutes later, Steve Fleming brought his MC-130, Dragon-3, in on the south LZ without difficulty and disgorged his Delta passengers and their support equipment. Almost simultaneously, Hal Lewis was landing Republic-4 on the north strip, and the controllers immediately marshaled the tanker into position for helicopter refueling.

Meanwhile, Beckwith's people were hustling to get the SATCOM radio set up while I worked with Carney controlling the remaining C-130s. Delta soldiers were moving their equipment up onto the roadbed to get out of the way of the landing aircraft.

Now I heard Beckwith's radio operator advising Red Barn that we were on schedule at Desert-I. Then he reported the encounters with the fuel truck and bus and told them we had forty-four captives and that the driver of the truck had escaped.[1]

As I stood there, I could feel my face turning red as I realized what was going on. The Delta operator wasn't fumbling around with code-word instructions, he was plain, flat-out *communicating*, in short, crisp sentences.

I thought about our fumbling around trying to encode a weather report for the helos.

Why in the world had we made something this simple so difficult?

Why we C-130 types were fooling around trying to encode messages to send out over this secure satellite network can only be attributed to a monumental disconnect when we were being briefed on the system back at Masirah.

While the communications with Red Barn were taking place, No. 5 and No. 6 were in sequence for landing.

Because of some delays in off-loading Delta troops, No. 3 was just being moved off the south LZ when Russ Tharp was

---

[1]In *The Straw Giant*, author Hadley states that we were contemplating telling the others headed to the rendezvous site to turn back. We hadn't even thought of it—from our standpoint, the situation was still under control.

bringing No. 5 in to land. Through the NVGs, it looked to me as if it was going to be close . . .

Too damn close!

Then Sergeant Mitch Bryan of the combat controllers' team broke radio silence and told Fleming to get No. 3 moving. It looked close to him, too. But this took care of it.

The heavy tanker touched down and Russ threw the props in reverse. It slowed rapidly and was well clear of the other three aircraft on the ground. I heaved a sigh of relief.

No. 3 was marshaled to the right side of the south landing zone, and the blivet refueling system aboard was being set up in case it was needed as a backup to the EC-130 tankers.

We now had five C-130s on the ground, and things were getting crowded (Figure 14)—we needed to reduce the congestion. I was now ready to get MC-130s 1 and 2 out of Desert-I and on their way back to Oman. I had held this off till now because I wanted to be sure we had enough C-130s to haul everyone out of Desert-I if anything went wrong.

I had planned at first to fly the captive Iranians out on the first departure and had directed that they be loaded on No. 1, along with their baggage. However, Beckwith learned that when the Delta troops were getting off No. 1, one of the Iranian generals had either lost or discarded a loaded pistol. Roland Guidry searched high and low in No. 1's cargo compartment, but didn't find it. Rather than risk having one of the bus passengers find the gun, we decided to delay their departure and haul them aboard the last C-130 to leave. So this bewildered bunch were put back aboard the bus.

I directed John Carney to launch No. 1 and No. 2 as soon as the dust had settled from No. 5's landing. This would give us more room to operate and we could then bring in the last tanker, which was still circling.

Not long afterward, No. 1 and No. 2 took off and set course for the refueling rendezvous with the KC-135s. Then Jerry Uttaro in Republic-6 set up to land on the north strip. However, the burning truck blinded him and it took him three tries before he finally got his bird on the ground.

The combat controllers marshaled him into position north of the road, to the right of Hal Lewis in No. 4.

Bill Jerome of the mobile fuels detachment had been

checking with his crews, and when he was satisfied that everything was working okay, he put out the word that all systems were go. "Bring on the choppers," he said.

THE HELICOPTERS, 1920 ZULU

Helicopters 3 and 4 were about 125 miles from Desert-I and had cleared the high ground near Darband. (Nobody, not even the helo pilots themselves, knew just how strung-out the helicopter force was.)

Schaefer and Oldfield were running fifty minutes behind schedule, with Walt ten minutes in trail. Linderman was an hour and twenty minutes behind after stopping to pick up Bill Hoff's crew. Ed Seiffert, leading B. J. McGuire, was about ten minutes behind Helo 8 (ninety minutes behind the command post's timetable). Davis was still heading toward the *Nimitz* and unable to tell anybody.

DESERT-I, 1940 ZULU

Charlie was on the SATCOM radio, questioning Red Barn.

"Have you heard anything from the choppers? They were supposed to be here about now!"

"Be advised, Bluebeard leader has been calling for weather at Desert-I." (I recognized General Gast's voice.)

I took the mike. "This is Woodpecker. High, thin, broken clouds. Visibility five miles with negligible surface winds."

Then we heard Seiffert's radio operator. "Bluebeard lead is fifty minutes"—a hundred miles—"from Desert-I and low on fuel."[2]

It was now apparent that the EC-130s would have to remain at Desert-I longer than planned. I told Tom Wicker to stay in touch with each pilot, monitor fuel status, and let me know when their reserves were running low. No way would we leave before the helos got there, out of gas with no place to go. We had to stay as long as possible and, if necessary, would use some of the extra helicopter fuel for the 130s.

---

[2]Beckwith's portable satellite radio was similar to the system carried by Seiffert, so we now had direct two-way communications with the lead chopper.

Meanwhile, Charlie (Eagle) had made contact with Dick
Meadows (code name Esquire) near Tehran to alert him that the
helos were behind schedule and that he would be kept advised.
Dick reported that the weather was good and everything was set
for Delta at the drop-off site. It looked like clear sailing if we
could just get them out of Desert-I. The commandos were getting more restless with each passing minute. It was like being on
a treadmill—we were running in place.

The hours of remaining darkness were becoming a critical
concern—every minute we delayed was cutting into our margin
of safety.

RED BARN, 1955 ZULU

The JTF staffers manning the command post had been busy
for most of the night with the helicopters' problems. Now, with
the report from Desert-I, they had other challenges.

The staff was not overly concerned at the number of Iranian
detainees. That situation appeared to be under control, and the
captives could be evacuated as planned. The Rangers were already preparing a holding area in one of the large bunkertype
hangars.

However, the escape of the truck driver was a horse of a different color. He had them worried at Red Barn, and the black-
box guys were alerted to be listening for any report that might
involve this encounter. But General Vaught had come to the
same conclusion as Charlie—that this involved smugglers and
wouldn't be reported. We'd just have to be alert . . . and wait
and see.

They'd overheard Beckwith's conversation with Esquire, and
the general was heartened by Meadows' weather report. Now if
we could just get the helicopters fueled and on their way. But
that was still a big if.

Lee Hess, with an assist from Maynard Weyers, was continually computing the time/distance factors involving the choppers'
chances of getting to the hide site and laager before daylight.
They figured the helos could still make it if they arrived at
Desert-I within the next thirty to forty minutes.

Their jaws were starting to tighten a little concerning the
status of the C-130s' fuel, so Doug Ulery and Jerry Barton had

their computers spinning on this one and would advise Jerry King when the C-130s had to get off the ground in order to make it back to the KC-135 tanker rendezvous south of the Iranian coast.

Meanwhile, a report came in that the medevac C-141s had arrived at Daharan and were standing by.

Now General Vaught was pacing the floor. With Helo 6 down north of the desert lake bed, and the uncertain location of Bluebeard-8, the en-route SAR, the status of the chopper force was shaky at best. They were obviously behind schedule. The general believed that four helos should arrive in one group, with three others about twenty or thirty minutes behind. He now began to consider the possibility of having the first arriving choppers gassed, loaded with Delta, and immediately launched toward Tehran to take advantage of the remaining darkness.

THE HELICOPTERS, 2000 ZULU

Helos 3 and 4 were now some fifty nautical miles south of Desert-I, with Bluebeard-7 about twenty miles behind. At 200 feet, they hadn't been out of the dust long and still were running into patches of it. Because of the low altitude, the pilots didn't obtain a positive lock on the Desert-I TACAN until a little less than thirty miles out. In fact, they first saw the fire from the burning fuel truck and flew toward it until finally picking up the TACAN signal (some thought that we had set the fire to guide them in).

Meanwhile, Jimmy Linderman in Bluebeard-8 was about eighty miles from Desert-I. Ed Seiffert and his wingman had been separated three or four times in the dust as they neared Darband. At one point, Ed got too close to the mountains and radioed McGuire to execute an emergency climb to 10,000 feet. When they rejoined, McGuire was in the lead. They locked on to the Darband VOR and were soon in the clear, headed for the LZ.

RED BARN, 2020 ZULU

Hess and Ulery were really getting worked up about the C-130 fuel status. They knew that any delay of over one hour at Desert-I, for any reason, would require in-flight refueling from the KC-135s orbiting off the south coast. The C-130s had already been on the ground for one hour and the helos had not shown up yet. Hess was betting it would be another hour before this fire drill got sorted out. By then, the C-130s would be cutting into the fuel needed to get out to the coast to link up.

Lee had twice reminded Jerry King that this situation was getting critical when he decided something had to be done right away. He grabbed Jerry's arm. "Colonel, those birds will never make it back to Masirah unless we launch KC-135s now."

The first group of Diego Garcia tankers lacked the fuel to remain in the tanker orbit, waiting for the C-130s from Desert-I. The standby tankers would have to be launched from Wadi Kena.

King got the message. He turned to Jerry Barton, the tanker task force commander. "Scramble the backups."

"Do we go into Iran to meet them?" Barton asked.

"Go as far as the planned in-flight-refueling point and I'll let you know then," King replied.

With that, Barton was out the door. Five minutes later, two KC-135 tankers, Oil Bath 1 and 2, roared off the runway at Wadi Kena and headed south to get into position for the C-130s.[3]

DESERT-I, 2025 ZULU

Jim Schaefer and Captain Barney Oldfield had just crested the last low ridgeline to the southeast and were still headed toward the fire when they spotted the CCT's pop-on lights.

The whop-whop-whopping sounds from Helo 3 were music to our ears. Since we weren't sure how many choppers were inbound, we were going with the original positioning plans. This called for three helos behind Hal Lewis in No. 4, the northernmost tanker, and three more behind Republic-6, about 300 feet to the right. The remaining two helos were to refuel from No. 5 on the south side of the road.

So, as Schaefer brought Helo 3 in over Desert-I and sat it down, the combat controllers began marshaling this first chopper arrival toward its position.

---

[3]Words are not adequate to express my admiration for the "gas passers." They have never received the credit they deserve for flying some very tough missions at considerable personal risk.

The helo crews were surprised by the amount of sand on the landing strip. They had been briefed that the surface was like a parking lot—no loose sand.[4] While this had little effect on the C-130s, it posed problems for the helos, with their smaller tires.

The nose tires on Helo 3 were damaged and deflated on landing. Schaefer performed what he called a "wounded frog" technique, a combination of air and ground taxiing, to follow CCT directions.[5]

To add to the difficulty, this technique was kicking up quite a sandstorm, which made the going even slower.

Barney Oldfield, in Helo 4, landed right after Schaefer and taxied into position adjacent to Bluebeard-3 by holding his nose wheels off the ground.

In the meantime, L. C. Walt wheeled in with Helo 7 and after landing was directed in behind the southernmost tanker, Republic-5. Walt had less trouble than Schaefer but used a modified version of the hop, skip, and jump.

I checked the time—it was 2035Z (01:05 A.M. Local, April 25). The chopper mission was about one hour behind schedule, and we should have had six birds starting on toward Tehran at that time. We thought four more were still about twenty or twenty-five minutes away.

Timing was becoming critical. I estimated we'd be two hours behind by the time Seiffert landed, refueled, and reorganized his flight.

I picked up the mike and called Foreman:

"We now have three helos at Desert-I and they are being refueled."

"Roger, Woodpecker. Be thinking about going on with less than six fully refueled helos, but take no action at this time."[6]

---

[4]Disseminating accurate information to some field units seemed a constant problem. Some units never got the word.

[5]Schaefer would air-taxi a short distance, then set down and let the dust clear, then leap again, all the time following the lighted wands of the combat controller.

[6]Contrary to what many authors have written, at no time did General Vaught delegate or release command of the rescue operation to any of his field commanders. We each had responsibilities to accomplish certain actions and follow orders received from him over the command net. The fact that we had four mission commanders at Desert-I did not alter the command lines. This follows one of the key principles of employing Special Operations forces—decentralized execution authority that relies on the experience and judgment of each field commander on the scene to perform his phase of the mission.

I'd better talk this over with Charlie, I thought.

I looked around for Beckwith and saw him headed for Jim Schaefer's chopper.

Where in the hell are the rest of the helos? What did the boss mean—"Be thinking about going with less than six fully refueled helos"?

I grabbed the mike again:

"This is Woodpecker. How many helos are still inbound to Desert-I?"

An unfamiliar voice came on: "No. 5 helo is on the way back to the carrier but has not landed yet."

We're down to six. That must have been the Nimitz. *Pitman's on No. 5, so that means Ed Seiffert's now in charge of the helo mission . . . if he ever gets here.*

The *Nimitz* had received an HF radio message earlier that Bluebeard-5 was returning to the carrier. We weren't monitoring the *Nimitz* frequencies and so did not hear the report; Seiffert didn't receive it either.

I made a beeline for the No. 3 helicopter. I wanted to talk with Beckwith and Schaefer. I caught up with Charlie just as he was reaching Helo 3. We yelled for Jim to come down from his bird so we could talk to him and sort out what was going on.

The three of us made our way to a spot away from the whirling CH-53 rotors and churning C-130 engines so we could hear each other talk. As we reached a spot where it was a little quieter, I turned to Schaefer.

He looked whipped. Flying through that dust must have been a terrifying experience.

"Jim, where are the rest of the choppers?"

He shook his head, "I don't know. We got separated in the dust. For all I know, they may be splattered on a mountain someplace."

Charlie looked astonished. "What the hell are you talking about? Dust?" He looked at me. "What's he talking about?" (Charlie hadn't been aware of the dust problems, since the C-130s hadn't had any trouble. But I knew all too well.)

Before I could say anything, Schaefer continued, "I lost sight of everyone but No. 4."

I told him that I had just gotten word from the *Nimitz* that Pitman in No. 5 was on his way back to the carrier.

"Where's Seiffert?" he asked.

"About twenty minutes out, based on his last report to Red Barn, which means three more are coming our way."

Then he surprised—no, shocked—me: "These are the hairiest conditions I have ever flown in, and I think we should abort—I mean get on the C-130s and get out of here."

I had always regarded Schaefer as one of the stronger Marine pilots. If he was that clanked up by what he had just been through, I could imagine what kind of shape the other helo pilots were in.

Beckwith and I both tried to reassure him.

"The worst is over, Jim. Dick Meadows is in position waiting at the drop-off point, and he tells us that the weather is good on that end." This seemed to calm him, and he pulled himself together. I then told Beckwith of General Vaught's message about going with less than six fully refueled choppers.

He said, "I damn sure can't leave anybody behind. I wonder what Seiffert can do to haul more people."

"I don't know, Charlie. We'll have to wait until he gets here to ask him."

When we returned to the road, I said, "Charlie, let's not load up until we get six choppers in position. We just might want to change our plans, and unloading again would be wasted motion."

He agreed and went to pass the word to his element leaders to be ready when the remaining helos arrived.

I was still thinking about Vaught's words: "Go on with less than six fully refueled helos."

I thought that the way Pitman and Seiffert had it calculated they had enough gas to perform the Night-Two mission and land at Manzariyeh with a one-hour reserve.

I knew that they had given hours of thought to this eventuality, and, to my knowledge, the only solution was to have a minimum of six operable helos with the required fuel load in order to go forward. It was now nearing 2050Z/0120L.

Is that what I think it is?

It was . . . the familiar whop-whop-whopping.

Great! Here comes another one. Only two more to go. We'll make it yet.

This one was Helo 8, flown by Jimmy Linderman, and

carrying Bill Hoff and his crew from the disabled Helo 6. Linderman set his bird down and we marshaled it in behind No. 4 tanker and the refueling began. We still didn't know how Seiffert had gotten separated from the flight and why he was behind the rest of them.

I got on the horn and reported Helo 8's arrival to Red Barn and Gravel Pit, adding that the Helo 6 crew was aboard.

The radio crackled, "Bluebeard-1 and -2 are five minutes from landing."

Man! That's Seiffert! We've finally got six!

I told Beckwith and Carney:

"Get ready to load up as soon as we get these two helos parked! We'll make it before daylight yet."

They headed off to get their people squared away. The radio crackled another message out from Red Barn: "Consult with other element leaders and advise on the feasibility of launching with four helos now and the other two catching up later."

Now I understood what they were up to at the command center. They wanted to refuel and load the four helos we had on the ground and send them forward, with the two now arriving to follow. I didn't like it. Separating the helos again after they had finally gotten together seemed like a bad idea to me.

Now I could hear the helo blades slapping the air as Seiffert and McGuire circled their aircraft overhead and lined up to land.

My voice went up a couple of octaves.

"Foreman, this is Woodpecker. We have six helos . . . we'll press on in forty minutes."

35

SO CLOSE, YET SO FAR

DESERT-I, 2100 ZULU

With the arrival of the last two choppers, the command situation shaped up like this:

- I was the on-scene commander, directing landing-zone operations primarily from a location on the road (by the TACAN and SATCOM systems).
- Delta Commander Charlie Beckwith was either with me or moving among his forces.
- Tom Wicker was my go-between with the C-130 crews, who remained in their aircraft.
- Ed Seiffert was the helicopter mission commander and remained in his cockpit; his crews came to him if they wanted to talk.
- John Carney and his combat controllers had radio contact with every pilot on the landing zone through the controller net. The CCT communicated with others face-to-face.
- Jesse Johnson and his roadblock team used hand-held radios to remain in contact with each other and reported to Beckwith and me face-to-face.
- Beckwith, Wicker, Carney, and I communicated eyeball-to-eyeball. When we needed to talk to the chopper pilots, we would go to them. All crew members were to remain in their aircraft. In addition to myself, Beckwith, Wicker, and Carney, only Delta Force and the roadblock teams were to be out on the road.[1]

[1]There has been a multitude of criticism about the command arrangements at Desert-I. The fault-finders focus on there being four commanders at the scene without visible identification, incompatible radios, and no agreed-upon plan, not even a designated location for the commander. I would agree it could have been done better, but in the final analysis it had nothing to do with the failure of the mission.

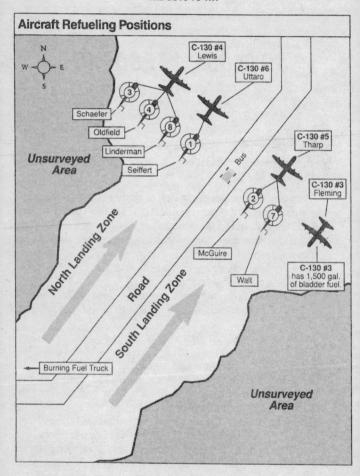

Aircraft Refueling Positions

As the last two helicopters were landing and being marshaled into position, Beckwith and I got ready to leave the command position and head to where Helo 1 was being lined up behind No. 6 tanker (Figure 15). We needed to talk to Seiffert immediately.

Ed had encountered the same problems in the sand as Schaefer and had deflated nose tires. He was now using the "wounded frog" method to move into refueling position. On the south side of the road, McGuire taxied with the nose wheels off the ground and slipped into position behind Republic-5 tanker.

John Carney and I were slapping each other's backs and then did a high five—we had six choppers at Desert-I and it looked as if we were going to make it. We knew we were cutting it close, but according to my figures we would have the helos on their way shortly after 0200 Local. This should put them at the Delta drop-off point by 0420 Local, and at the laager site forty-five minutes before sunrise. Anyway, now there was no doubt in my mind—we should go for it!

I was just starting out to follow Beckwith when Tom Wicker came up to me. "The C-130 fuel situation is getting critical. We're really going to be hurting by the time we get out of here. We'll definitely need the KC-135s."

The tankers had been sitting there for two and a half hours, an hour and a half longer than planned. After talking it over, we decided to tell each pilot to take 1,000 gallons of the extra helo fuel from the bladders and pump it into his airplane's tanks.

I was now certain that six helos were all that would make it to Desert-I, so we could use the fuel programmed for the other two, plus the extra we carried, to keep the C-130s there for more than the additional hour we needed. However, Hal Lewis's No. 4 tanker had no spare fuel in its bladder. He had refueled three helos under the original plan before we found out eight weren't coming. His would be the first C-130 to depart.

As I resumed my trek to talk to Seiffert, I came upon two helo crew members. One, a tall lanky pilot, said to me, "That was the worst sandstorm I've ever flown through. We ought to call this off. Leave the helicopters and get out of here."[2]

I was astounded. "We've got to go on. Dick Meadows says the weather's good on his end, and he's in position to receive Delta at the drop-off point. We've got to get going."

---

[2]Several authors have stated that the Marines were not adequately trained to fly through the suspended dust. This conclusion doesn't hold up in face of the facts. The Marines were obviously trained adequately or six would never have made it to the rendezvous. The seventh became lost due to equipment malfunctions and even then was able to make it back to the carrier. They had to be better-than-average instrument pilots to have survived.

I had to see Seiffert. He was the key. Could he pull his fliers together and keep us on track?

As I approached Seiffert's helo, Beckwith was heading my way. He yelled over the roar of the engines, "The skipper [Seiffert] says we're going on just as soon as refueling is completed. I'm loading up my troops."

I gave him a thumbs-up and jumped up into Ed's helo. "How're you doing?"

He replied, "It's nice to talk to somebody who's still in control of his faculties and can calmly discuss the situation."

Apparently his encounter with Beckwith had been stormy. As I learned, Charlie had arrived while Ed was busy operating his refueling panel and collecting his thoughts. Charlie thought Ed was ignoring his questions about continuing and, I was told, was getting a little physical about it. Seiffert's copilot was out of his seat and about to confront Beckwith when Ed calmed everybody down and told Charlie, "We'll go on just as soon as we get gassed." He did voice concern about the amount of darkness remaining, but Charlie was satisfied with what he had heard and headed off to load up.

Ed told me that flying through the suspended dust had really drained the helo crews physically and mentally but they would be ready to go on. "Where is Colonel Pitman?"

I told him that we had gotten word over the SATCOM net that Commander Davis was returning to the *Nimitz*, but no reason was given. "You're the flight leader and mission commander now."

Ed then asked about the crew of Helo 6.

"They're here at the LZ," I told him. "I've seen Bill Hoff and his crew."

He didn't tell me if he had any plans for this crew, but they'd go back with us if he didn't need them.

"Ed, it's going to be close on the remaining hours of darkness. You'll probably make the Delta drop-off point in darkness, but it may be dawn by the time you reach the laager. General Vaught wants us to continue . . . and Beckwith is loading his troops. So we've got to get moving."

"We'll get going as soon as we gas up."

Beckwith's men were starting to board the helo.

"I'll see you tomorrow at Manzariyeh" were my parting

words as I jumped to the ground and headed back toward my command position.

When I got there, the SATCOM radio was gone—Beckwith's radio operator had packed it up and was now boarding the lead chopper.

Dammit! Now I'll have to use the SATCOM on No. 6 tanker to talk to the command center. Having to share Delta's has been a problem all along.

We now had ten aircraft at Desert-I, all with their engines running. Although this was according to plan, the blowing sand and grit was worse than we had experienced or expected. Even though we'd trained and rehearsed with engines running, you never really get used to the noise, wind blast, and blowing grit. Still, it was more of a nuisance than a hazard.

Tom Wicker reported that the fuel situation was becoming extremely critical for Hal Lewis in No. 4 tanker. He needed to get going now or the bird could become a permanent gas station in the desert. Jerry Barton's gas passers would probably have to pick him up near the south coast. I sure didn't want to force Barton to enter Iran for the hookup while we were still trying to get this mission headed north.

I told John Carney that No. 4 had to leave first, and he set off to coordinate this with his controllers. We had about twenty more minutes of refueling to accomplish at this point. Then we could relaunch the helos and get Lewis headed back.

I wanted to be certain that we wouldn't have any last-minute helicopter arrivals. "Red Barn, this is Woodpecker. Confirm status of the two missing helicopters."

The reply came from Gravel Pit. "They are not inbound to Desert-I."

"Rog. Keep those KC-135 tankers on station as long as possible. We're hurting for fuel."

When I said that there were ten aircraft at Desert-I with engines running, I was not aware that B. J. McGuire in Bluebeard-2 had shut down. Two of his crewmen had climbed up on top of the aircraft to remove the inspection panels and check the hydraulic leak to determine the cause, and check the pump to see if it needed to be replaced. They found the accessory section saturated with fluid that had come from a cracked nut on a servo which leads to the backup pump for the flight controls. On looking closer, they found the pump was burned out because of a lack of fluid. There was no spare pump available (it was aboard No. 5), and besides, we didn't have the forty-five minutes it would have taken to replace it.[3]

When McGuire reported the problem to Ed Seiffert, he was directed to abort. Seiffert told McGuire to inform Charlie Beckwith, who went ballistic when he heard the news. He had twenty Delta troopers and their gear on board that chopper, waiting to launch.

I was just getting off Uttaro's SATCOM-equipped C-130 to see if the refueling was completed when Charlie Beckwith came charging up to me with fire in his eyes.

"That goddam No. 2 helo has been shut down! We only have five good choppers—you've got to talk to Seiffert and see what he says. You talk their language—I don't." (I think he muttered something like "They finally found an excuse to quit." I don't recall his exact words.)

This hit me like a fist in the gut.

I don't believe it. It landed okay after flying over five hours! What the hell could have happened after it arrived here?

I hurried over to Helo 2. Its rotor blades were motionless, sagging limply under their own weight.

Jumping aboard, I yelled at the copilot, "What's wrong with this thing?"

"The second-stage hydraulic system failed." He pointed to a warning light on the instrument panel and to the quantity gauge.

"Can you fly it on just the one system?"

"Captain McGuire is over discussing that with Colonel Seiffert now."

I ran to Seiffert's helicopter. When I fired my question at him, he had obviously already talked it over with B. J. McGuire.

"Ed, can that No. 2 helicopter be safely flown with one hydraulic pump?"

"No! It's unsafe! If the controls lock up, it becomes uncontrollable. It's grounded!"

---

[3] In recalling the events surrounding this key event, B. J. McGuire told me that he speculated two hours from Desert-I that his problem might be a faulty hydraulic pump and that there might not be sufficient time to repair it at the LZ. His plan was to obtain the spare pump that he believed would be at Desert-I and proceed on the mission, repairing the malfunction at the laager. Helos 1, 3, 5, and 7 carried limited spare parts.

Hell's fire! I wasn't an RH-53D expert. If he had decided it was unsafe to fly, then I'd have to accept his decision. Ed knew that all aircrews on this mission were operating under wartime standards (they were expected to fly an aircraft in degraded mechanical condition, if need be, in order to complete the mission).

Since I didn't take part in the discussion between the helo flight leader and his wingman, I didn't know if McGuire told Seiffert he would be willing to continue on to Tehran with the malfunction. It just seemed to me that if Helo 2 had been considered safe enough to fly to Desert-I in this condition, then why couldn't it continue?[4]

Dammit! There has to be a way! I DO NOT WANT TO ABORT THIS MISSION!

I hit him with the $64,000 question: "Is there any way you can continue on with only five helos and still haul Delta and their gear?"

His response was unwavering. "No—we are at the max. We can't carry any more weight."

I was desperate. "Can you dump gas and hack it?"

On Night-Two we'd have extra gas at Manzariyeh for the choppers—could that work?

"No—I need every gallon I have to make it through Night-Two." I could feel the adrenaline draining from me as I wearily climbed down from the chopper to where Charlie Beckwith was waiting impatiently.

I looked him in the eye. "Ed confirmed that Helicopter No. 2 is unsafe to fly. We now have five choppers and they can't take on the added weight of Helo 2's load.[5]

---

[4]Colonel Seiffert later testified that the RH-53D can be flown with only one hydraulic system. However, his concern was that upon departing Desert-I all helicopters would be operating at extremely heavy gross weights—with twenty Delta Force personnel aboard. He said that under those conditions, the pilot must be able to move the flight controls through full cycle rapidly to maintain control of the aircraft. He said there was a danger of overtaxing the remaining system in this situation, causing a hydraulic lock that could have resulted in an accident.

[5]Gabriel's *Military Incompetence* contains computations that he claims are proof that five helicopters were sufficient to execute the mission. However, Gabriel's figures fail to take into account the temperature at Desert-I (in excess of 90 degrees), and his weight factors for the helicopters would have required them to lift off 20,000 pounds over weight, an impossibility. Also, the fuel load for Gabriel's computations failed to provide sufficient gas for the helicopters to reach Tehran.

"Charlie, this is as tough a decision as you probably will ever have to make . . . and history will be our judge. Can you cut down on your force by about twenty men?"

He didn't hesitate. "No way—I need every man I've got and every piece of gear. There's no fat that I can cut. Who do I leave behind?"

No . . . I've got to stick with the game plan—we can't go on. God! I don't want to tell General Vaught that!

"Charlie, if you're absolutely sure there is no other way, get your troops off the helos and back onto the C-130s. I'll radio General Vaught that we have reached an abort situation."

He was already heading for the choppers. I headed for the radio.

Some of us had been out in that damn desert for over three hours, desperately trying to hold the mission together despite a series of monumental problems. Then, just when we thought we had it made, a third helicopter had crapped out, leaving us one short. Never in my wildest nightmares would I have believed that of the eight helicopters launched on the mission, three would abort.

After the pilots had arrived aboard the *Nimitz* they had test-flown the choppers and reported to General Vaught that these particular H-53s were in the best condition of any they had ever flown.

Boy, what a misperception!

The problems on the mission certainly raised questions as to whether the Navy pilots that had been baby-sitting the helos on the carrier had really been putting them through their paces so they would be ready for the rescue mission.

I simply couldn't label it as bad luck.

Those pilots who decided to abort had better be prepared to defend those decisions, because this failure is going to raise a storm of criticism, I thought.

(In the flying game, questioning an abort decision is treading on sacrosanct territory, but I was certain that in this case there would be some investigation of the details of each abort—some head-hunting.)

As I walked to the No. 6 C-130 to put out that dreaded message on the SATCOM, Delta's soldiers were piling out of the helicopters and trudging along beside me.

From what I could hear, it was obvious that the thought of riding back to Masirah on empty fuel bladders only intensified their hostile state of mind. I heard some strong talk about the helicopters' performance mixed with hopes for a second chance if we could get out undetected. I guess this made the abort more bearable. I didn't share their optimism, but kept my thoughts to myself.

My mood was weighed down by what I had to do next—tell General Vaught the bad news. More depressing was the thought that he would then be passing this word on to Washington and within minutes the President would know—*we had aborted!*

This was it! I held little hope that we could reconstitute the helicopter force in the next few days, and the bus passengers only added to the problem. There would be no second chance.

I was devastated, physically and mentally.

36

CATASTROPHE!

"Red Barn, this is Woodpecker. Helo No. 2 determined to be unflyable due to hydraulic failure."

C'mon, guys. Give me a miracle solution. An abort's staring us in the face. Put your heads together and pull something out of the hat.

Minutes later. "Woodpecker, this is Foreman. Consult with the other unit leaders to determine if you can go on with only five helos."

Both Seiffert and Beckwith had insisted they couldn't give up anything . . . so that was that.[1]

"Foreman, I've done that. My recommendation is to abort. Request guidance as to the bus passengers." Our captives were still hunkered down along the shoulder of the road, totally confused by what was going on around them.

"Woodpecker, stand by for final instructions."

By this time, Beckwith's people were all aboard the C-130s. Only the roadblock team and the combat controllers were still out on the landing zone.

We had been waiting about twenty minutes when the word came from Red Barn. "Proceed with the withdrawal. All operational helicopters are to be returned to the *Nimitz*. Have the road-

---

[1]To this day, Beckwith and Seiffert are sticking by their decisions that nothing could have been given up to go on with five helicopters. Years later, I did hear of a contingency plan to remove items like the Red Eye missiles and the .50-caliber machine gun, gunner, and ammunition from each chopper. If that all adds up to around 1,500 pounds, then maybe we could have gone forward. Seiffert and Beckwith swear they never heard of such a plan. If this truly was a viable alternative, then we all should have known about it.

block team rig No. 2 helicopter for destruction. Release all bus passengers and sanitize the area."

I climbed down out of No. 6 tanker and passed the word to John Carney. "We're aborting. Police up your gear and pass the word to Jesse Johnson that I want his roadblock team on the last aircraft to depart." I wanted them to protect our flanks till the last minute. We'd tow Helo 2 out of our way with the jeep and torch it just before launching the last C-130.[2]

I went to Seiffert and told him that his crews were to return the five good choppers to the *Nimitz*. He didn't like the idea of flying back through the suspended dust, but knew he had no choice. (The JTF was not about to abandon good helicopters at this juncture.) He set to getting his flight organized.

RED BARN, 2140 ZULU

A pall had fallen over the command center. When they received my report that Bluebeard-2 had aborted, shock and dismay swept through the staff. All hopes were dashed.

We had been seven and a half hours into the mission and it had looked as if the rendezvous was successful. Now this! A bitter disappointment for the team that spent tens of thousands of hours in planning, training, and rehearsing for this attempt to rescue our hostages.

There was a desperate flurry to come up with an answer. What could be done to enable the force to continue on with five helicopters? There was certainly no magic bag of tricks to reach into for the answer. They had been over this possibility hundreds of times in their long planning sessions—six operational helicopters were the bottom line.

The only options were to either dump enough fuel from each RH-53 to allow for the weight of the extra troopers or reduce the number of Delta Force by some twenty shooters.

The first option meant that about 1,500 pounds of JP-4 fuel

---

[2]I was told that the roadblock team had explosives to destroy anything left behind, but we couldn't find the team leader. The helicopters had not been rigged with a timed destruct system because the Marines felt it would be unsafe to do so. Had we continued on with five choppers, we believed we could hide Helo 2 well enough that it wouldn't be found prior to completion of the mission.

would have to be dumped from each helo so it could carry four additional troopers and their gear—a question that Ed Seiffert could best answer. In the second case, Beckwith was the only one to determine if he could assault the embassy with fewer people.

The staff reasoned that the only course for them was to have me consult with Seiffert and Beckwith and see if either one of these possibilities was feasible—the decision should be made by the commanders at Desert-I, in the best position to weigh all the options. General Vaught had confidence his field commanders would make the right decision—he would respect their recommendation. He was acutely aware of the weight he was placing on our shoulders, but before he accepted the idea of aborting the mission he wanted everyone to think it through one more time. The general could have ordered that No. 2 Helo continue, but he respected Seiffert's decision that it was unsafe and a risk to a lot of lives.

When I came back with the reply that I had already consulted with Seiffert and Beckwith and neither could give up anything to reduce the weights, the general dejectedly accepted the abort decision.

Just minutes earlier, he had radioed General Jones, "We have six helos at Desert-I and will move out in forty minutes." Now he was on the SATCOM informing the Chairman about the helicopter failure and the decision to abort.

WASHINGTON, D.C., 2150 ZULU (4:50 EST)

When word reached Zbigniew Brzezinski, the President's National Security Adviser, he asked Defense Secretary Harold Brown to have General Jones "obtain the opinion of Colonel Beckwith as to going on with five helicopters."[3] Unbeknownst to Brzezinski, the opinions of Beckwith and Seiffert were central to the abort decision—we had exhausted all of our options.[4]

---

[3]This account of Brzezinski's actions and observations during this time is taken from his *New York Times Magazine* article "The Failed Mission."

[4]There has always been a question in the back of my mind as to whether the decision at Desert-I might have been different if Chuck Pitman had been there to pull the Marines together.

Brzezinski then went to the Oval Office to inform the President of the abort situation. The President called Defense Secretary Brown and asked for the latest report on the mission's progress. At Brzezinski's urging, Carter asked Brown "for the opinion of the commander in the field. His attitude should be taken into account."

The President said, "Let's go with his recommendation." Brzezinski watched as the President put the phone down, confirmed that the mission had been aborted, and then put his head down on the desk and cradled it in his arms. "I felt extraordinarily sad for him as well as for the country," Brzezinski relates.

HELICOPTER NO. 5, 2150 ZULU

Bluebeard-5 was still en route to the carrier and, by this time, had been airborne for nearly seven and a half hours. Two Marine CH-53s had launched to intercept Davis and help escort him to the *Nimitz*, which was proceeding at flank speed toward the Iranian coast. They hoped to get him aboard before he had to ditch his Sea Stallion. He was still some thirty minutes away and coming in on the fumes (airborne continuously for eight hours must have been some kind of record).

In response to a query, Helo 5 reported that only the basic crew and Colonel Pitman were on board. (Someone was still looking for Bill Hoff's crew from the chopper that had been forced to land on the dry lake bed. Of course, they were at Desert-I.)

General Vaught was busy advising the Chairman of our withdrawal plans. God help us—we had failed the hostages, the President, and our country. Words cannot express the monumental sadness that I felt and that haunts me to this day.

DESERT-I, 2200 ZULU

As I exited the C-130 and started back for the road, Tom Wicker appeared out of the darkness. "Hal Lewis has got to get moving now," he said.

But before we could move him, we had to get Helos 3 and 4 out from behind. If Lewis brought his engines up to the power needed to turn his aircraft around in the sand, it would bury the helos in a blizzard of sand.

I grabbed John Carney and we hustled to Seiffert's chopper. "Ed, we have to get Schaefer and Oldfield to move their helos so Hal Lewis can get turned around and out of here ASAP. He's dangerously low on fuel."

"Okay, but we've got problems, too. Oldfield needs more fuel to make it back to the *Nimitz*—he's short about 3,000 pounds."

"There's no time for that now, Ed. We'll get Helos 3 and 4 out of the way first by having them move to the north. When Lewis is airborne, we can get more fuel for Oldfield from No. 6 tanker."

Ed agreed with this plan, so Carney and I made our way over to Helos 3 and 4 to explain what was needed to Schaefer and Oldfield.

Schaefer was a bit apprehensive. "I don't like the idea of having to move around the C-130s in the sand . . . but I understand the situation."

Since Hal Lewis's C-130 was forward and about 45 degrees to the right of Schaefer's helicopter, we weren't concerned that any tricky maneuvering would be required. All that was needed was for Helo 3 to proceed straight out to the northeast with Helo 4 following, both staying clear of the takeoff area until Lewis had his tanker airborne.

Schaefer had straightened his damaged nose wheels, hoping to ground-taxi his helicopter. If unable to do that, he would lift off and air-taxi. He was well aware that this would cause the same type of dust cloud that he had experienced upon arrival— he would be unable to see anything until the chopper had lifted above the churned-up cloud.

It was about 2225 Zulu (0255 Iran time) when Schaefer started trying to move his helicopter. It was not responding to the taxi mode, so he elected to lift off for air taxiing.[5]

There was a combat controller standing forward and to the right of the helicopter, between it and the EC-130. The controller

---

[5]Some helicopter experts reviewing performance factors at Desert-I, i.e. temperature, pressure and density altitude, gross weight, etc., have suggested that there was insufficient power developed by the engines to lift off into a hover much higher than twenty feet (not high enough to fly over a C-130). A rolling type of lift-off maneuver was required to get the heavy helicopters airborne.

was there as an observer, since this was basically a straight-ahead maneuver and once the dust was churned up he wouldn't be seen anyway.

The helicopter lifted off and was immediately engulfed in dust. I saw the controller moving toward the C-130 to get away from the swirling dust cloud. As I watched, the helicopter lifted about twenty-five feet off the ground, started to drift left, and then disappeared in the dust. I began walking toward No. 6 tanker to tell Jerry Uttaro that Helo 4 needed more fuel.

I hadn't taken more than a few steps when I heard a loud *whack*, then a booming explosion. As I turned, I saw a raging inferno engulfing the left side of Hal Lewis's tanker. The scene was erupting into a bizarre kaleidoscope of fire, dust, and smoke enveloping the aircraft.

God! What happened?

At first, I thought the bladder system aboard the C-130 had exploded. Then through the leaping flames I saw the unearthly silhouette of the helicopter's blades slowly windmilling above the C-130's cockpit. The helicopter had drifted sideways almost 90 degrees to the right and slammed down onto the topside of the tanker's left inner wing section, coming to a rest on top of the cockpit. The rear of the RH-53D was in the fire on the left side of the tanker, with only the twisted shell of the helo cockpit clear of the murderous flames.

How did the helo get so far right and hit the C-130? My God! No one can survive in that inferno.

There were fourteen C-130 crew members on board, as well as part of Delta Force in the back. The two empty fuel bladders on the cargo compartment floor were bombs just waiting to go off.

I ran toward the right rear door to help the Delta troopers, who were now bailing out like parachutists and rolling in the sand, some with their clothing on fire, others scorched and smoldering.

"Keep moving to the road," I yelled to them, pointing toward a safe area.

Logan Fitch, the Delta Force White Element commander, was sitting in the back of the No. 4 C-130 when two thuds shook the plane. He thought they had taxied into a depression in the desert. Suddenly, like fireworks, a spray of sparks lit up the entrance to the cockpit and the bulkhead where most of the avionics racks were located. The electrical fire and one fed by aviation fuel were turning the front of the airplane into an oven.

Fitch grabbed his weapon. He thought the C-130 was under hostile fire and he was looking toward the rear of the aircraft, trying to spot an exit where he could get out and repel attackers.[6]

Sergeant Wesley Witherspoon, the loadmaster, had gotten the right troop door partly open. His assistant, Sergeant James Mc-Clain, struggled the left door open only to be met by a sheet of flames. He slammed it shut in a hurry. Sergeant Bancroft, another assistant loadmaster, was trying to keep the Delta soldiers from piling up on each other. He was shouting, "Keep calm!"

The cargo area reeked of burning wires, melting metal, and aviation fuel. The starboard door was already open and Fitch's men were leaping the four feet to the ground. With the threat that the fuel bladders might explode at any minute, the troopers were near panic. Men shouted, staggering and stumbling over the hot bladders. They were falling over and clawing one another in their efforts to escape. Someone had to take control.

Sergeant Major Don Linkey (pseudonym), Fitch's senior sergeant, bellowed out, "Don't panic! Don't panic!" The men settled down and began exiting in some semblance of order with flames licking at the heels of those at the end of the line, who were forcefully prodding their comrades to keep moving.

Lieutenant Jeff Harrison, the C-130's safety pilot, escaped down the stairs from the flight deck just before the galley bulkhead collapsed, blocking the stairway exit. He raced aft and jumped off the aircraft, with only minor scorching.

Sergeant Joseph Beyers, the aircraft radio operator, was in the area where the fire started on impact from the helicopter and was immediately enveloped in flames as he tried to get out of the aircraft. He saw he wasn't going to make it and yelled out, "Don't leave me! Help! Help!" Sergeant Paul Lawrence, one of Delta's smaller troopers, heard Beyers's cries and ran back into the flames.

Shielding himself with a field jacket draped over his arm, Lawrence got to Beyers and dragged the badly burned radio

[6]The account of what took place inside the stricken aircraft is described in Logan Fitch's article "Death at Desert One," which appeared in *Penthouse* magazine.

operator to the rear door, where he collapsed. Another of Fitch's men, Sergeant Stuart O'Neill, ran back into the fire and helped Lawrence get Beyers out of the aircraft. (Beyers and Lawrence were burned, but both are alive today because of incredible heroism.)

Jerry Uttaro was wasting no time taxiing his aircraft away from the inferno and then turning it around to get into position for takeoff. John Carney was using his lighted wands to direct Uttaro. Jerry's copilot, Major Bill Diggins, was also giving him directions—"Just a little bit more-more-more . . . that's good! Hold it!"

I anchored myself directly in front of his aircraft and was yelling at the survivors, "Watch out for the propellers . . . spread out on all the aircraft . . . don't bunch up!"

Whummph! Another violent explosion aboard the tanker, which was burning furiously. Missiles, bullets, and grenades aboard the C-130 were cooking off. It was getting damned hairy being anywhere near the aft area of the burning hulk. I moved to the front of the aircraft and looked up at the cockpit area for any signs of life, any survivors needing help.

Then I spotted Sergeant Randy Gingrich, Jerry Uttaro's radio operator, helping two injured men get away from the wreckage. They turned out to be Jim Schaefer and his copilot, Captain Leslie Petty. Gingrich had seen Schaefer exit his cockpit window and slide down over the nose of the crippled C-130, struggling to crawl away from the crash area. Gingrich ran to rescue Schaefer and, in the process, found Petty. The rest of Schaefer's crew, three men, were nowhere in sight, and Gingrich told me he feared they were in the twisted wreckage of the helo's aft cargo compartment.

Uttaro's SATCOM operator had transmitted a barely coherent message to Red Barn and Gravel Pit about a crash, but with few details. The command center was unable to determine what had happened and wanted to talk to Woodpecker, but I didn't have time to talk right then.

As ordnance continued exploding from the twisted wreckage, I looked back to see if Ed Seiffert had gotten his helos into the air and out of danger. I was astounded to see three of them still sitting within 200 feet of the inferno, just where they'd been when the accident occurred (Figure 16). The crews were piling out of the choppers and running to the safety of the road.

There were large holes ripped in the helos' fuselages and external fuel tanks. Fuel was dribbling out onto the desert, dangerously close to the fire. Flying shrapnel from the conflagration had peppered Helos 1, 4, and 8—they looked like sieves. The crews had had to scramble to escape the razor-sharp chunks of

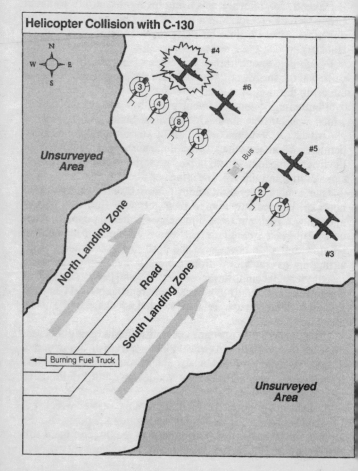

Helicopter Collision with C-130

metal that were slicing through their aircraft. Ed Seiffert reportedly yelled over his radio, "Abandon your choppers and move to safety."[7]

I saw that in their rush to abandon the helicopters, the Marines were getting dangerously close to the churning propellers of No. 6 C-130. I ran to intercept them and guide them to the road and aboard the C-130s.

I then found John Carney and told him to get on his radio and order the C-130 pilots not to move. "Nobody takes off until I say so!"

I instructed Carney to keep the landing zone under control. "Get all the helicopter crews out of their aircraft . . . and try to spread the forces out as best you can, so that no one bird gets them all." I wasn't so much worried about the aircraft being overweight as I was that everyone might bunch up on one aircraft, leaving a lot of them with no place to hang on.

I headed back for No. 6 and the SATCOM radio. I was wondering how many we had lost in the fire. No one had seen Hal Lewis or any of his cockpit crew, except for the two that had escaped. Wicker told me that some of the cockpit crew were missing, and he wasn't sure about the helo crew losses or if Delta Force had any casualties.

I radioed Red Barn and Gravel Pit. "I think we have many burn casualties—we'll need emergency medical help at Masirah. I'll call in with a more precise casualty figure once we're out of here."

I was heading out the aircraft's forward door when a couple of the Marine pilots confronted me. One of them said, "We have to get back to our helicopters. Our classified documents are still on board."

"No way, dammit! You can't get back to the helos without getting killed . . . and I'm not going to let that happen." To my mind, it was enough of a blunder to have left the documents, but it was

---

[7]Author Paul B. Ryan states in his book that one of the Marine pilots said that Seiffert told them to "get out of the bird and prepare to destruct!" Ryan concludes that I countermanded the destruct order. Ed Seiffert does not recall making such a statement. Nevertheless, since I could not hear the Marines talking on their radios it would have been impossible for me to countermand such an order.

even more asinine to even think of attempting to retrieve them with all that shrapnel flying around.[8]

I didn't know what documents the Marines had left on the choppers, but assumed they were cipher codes, the same as we were carrying. In less than twenty-four hours, that information would be useless. So, naturally, I wasn't going to risk any more casualties.[9]

Outside, I huddled in the roadway with Tom Wicker and the combat controllers.

"We have to keep cool heads—we don't need things screwed up any more than they already are. We'll scour the area one more time, making sure that nobody is left behind"—that was my chief concern. In that instruction, I included any bodies that could possibly be recovered.

With that, everyone started searching the area surrounding the burning wreckage. We were being as thorough as we could, but had to stay clear of the rear of the flaming mass, where ordnance was still detonating and sending shrapnel ripping into the helicopters. There were no signs of life, and no traces of those we presumed had perished in the fire. There was a sadness gripping all of us . . . sadness and anger at this final catastrophe that was heaped upon our failure.

---

[8]Anyone who takes classified information aboard an aircraft is responsible for keeping it in his possession at all times. I would later learn, to my astonishment, that the documents left on three helicopters included copies of the helo portion of the embassy rescue plan. Had I known this, I would have had to think very seriously about allowing the Marines to retrieve these secrets.

[9]I'm told the reason the Marines left the documents aboard was that they thought the helos would be destroyed by the roadblock team. Ed Seiffert testified that the crews directly behind the burning wreckage hastily abandoned their helicopters for safety reasons and that groping around for gear in the darkness seemed pointless. Ed felt the data left behind applied only to the helicopter part of the mission and did not jeopardize the C-130 or Delta operations. I'm not sure Dick Meadows, who was still in Tehran, would agree.

37

GET THE HELL OUT!

Returning to the road, I located John Carney.

"Make sure you have all your runway lighting and navigation gear collected and that Jesse has the roadblock team in from their point positions and aboard the C-130s.

"When that's done, launch No. 5 on the south strip, followed by No. 3 on the same side. We'll hold the last C-130 until we're absolutely sure that we have everybody."

Then Wicker and I tried to decide if we could destroy the helicopters and still get past them on takeoff. As we stood there talking, I suddenly noticed that the engines were still running on one of the choppers behind the burning C-130. I was dumbfounded. In all the confusion, it had gone unnoticed for the past fifteen minutes or so. I could see the whirling blades. Some of the windows were cracked, either from heat or from the shrapnel. Apparently, in their justifiable haste to escape the slashing metal that was ripping into their aircraft, one of the crews felt there wasn't sufficient time to round up the classified materials or shut the engines down (or maybe the shut-off controls had been damaged). Nonetheless, getting them shut down was certainly not worth risking any lives.

Meanwhile, the question of what to do about the choppers was begging a decision, one that had to be made soon. I was inclined to destroy them, but Wicker favored leaving them as they were. Carney pointed out that we didn't have any explosives, and to do the job right we would need some fuse-delay ordnance that could be timed to go off after the C-130s were airborne. We couldn't find Jesse Johnson to see if he had anything that would

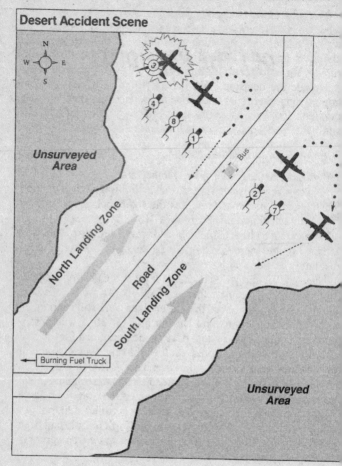

Desert Accident Scene

do the job.[1] We never seemed to know what the roadblock team was doing, especially now that we needed their help.

[1] I have been told that it would have taken about ten to twenty pounds of explosives to destroy the helicopters and about forty-five minutes to rig up the charges. Thermite grenades would also have done the job, but we didn't have any of those either.

Wicker and Carney had convinced me. If we destroyed them where they sat, there was a danger of trapping ourselves behind a wall of flames and exploding helicopters. If we taxied past the choppers and then torched them, there wouldn't be enough runway for us to get off (Figure 17).

I made the decision. "We'll leave them sit. With all that's gone wrong, there's no need to tempt fate any further. The way our luck has been running, we'd probably blow ourselves to smithereens. I'll call the command center and request a Navy air strike for after we've cleared out."

I advised Red Barn of the situation regarding the choppers and the classified documents. I proposed the air strike. "Red Barn, if the fighters drop their ordnance on a north-south heading, fifty meters west of the burning hulks, it will cover the area where the helos are sitting."

The silence was pregnant as I waited for a response. Finally, after what seemed like ages, a voice replied, "Roger, we copied your message—will advise."

In the meantime, General Gast (at Masirah) and Jerry King (at Wadi Kena) were making things happen. Two medevac Starlifter C-141s at Daharan, Saudi Arabia, were ordered to Masirah to receive casualties. The C-141 crews, which had been prepositioned at the Saudi airfield for Night-Two, were on SATCOM standby resting in their aircraft at Daharan. They were advised to declare a medical emergency (screw the diplomatic clearance) and launch immediately.

The C-141s were off about an hour later for the two-and-a-half-hour flight. This would put them on the ground at Masirah shortly after our arrival from Desert-I.

The Military Airlift Command was also directed to scramble a C-9 Nightingale hospital aircraft from Germany to Wadi Kena. This aircraft, specially outfitted and with a medical burn team aboard, would be used to move the injured crew members from Egypt back to Germany.

My request for Navy tactical air strikes to destroy the helicopters was under intensive debate at the command center. Two major concerns were that some of the rescue force might still be at the site and that U.S. aircraft might be forced to engage Iranian aircraft, thus escalating hostilities to an unacceptable level.

Collectively, the staff recommended to General Vaught that the tactical mission not be approved for those reasons.

General Vaught discussed the matter with General Jones in Washington, where higher authority was also weighing the pros and cons of an air strike. Washington agreed that it would not be in the best interest of the hostages to conduct such a bombing mission. The air strike was disapproved.

Throughout all of this decision-making, the serious nature of the classified documents left behind was unknown—the Marines had not disclosed the contents of the material they had carried in to Desert-I.

Also during this time, Pancho Gonzales, Delta's communications officer, got on the SATCOM net and advised Esquire (Dick Meadows) in Tehran that the mission had been aborted. General Vaught wanted to confirm that Dick had gotten the word, and Pancho was using a code-word system to make sure Meadows' reception committee understood the situation and was taking cover. Beckwith had apparently tried to advise Meadows of the situation over his portable SATCOM at Desert-I but was unable to confirm that the message had been received.

The plan had Meadows and his team leaving Tehran aboard the helicopters with Delta and the hostages. Now these men were left to their own devices. Leaving Tehran the same way they entered—commercial airlines—appeared the best alternative.

Because it was the Iranian weekend, the airline ticket office would be closed for two days, so Dick and his team would have to hole up. By then, the secret documents left on the choppers would be in the hands of the Iranians and they would be in a mighty tight spot. It would be just a matter of time before the Islamic revolutionary forces began seeking out strangers who had been seen around the embassy and the warehouse where the trucks were hidden.

For the remainder of the rescue force, waiting at Wadi Kena for the Night-Two part of the mission, word of the abort was a source of deep disappointment mixed with despair at the loss of their comrades. "We've failed before ever getting a chance to try" were the words of a veteran gunship pilot.

Back at Desert-I, I had gone back to the road and was talking to Tom Wicker. He pressed me to commence the withdrawal, but

I wanted to give Carney at least five more minutes to finish up his chores.

At that moment, three more members of the rescue team emerged from the darkness—roadblock people, I guessed. We hustled them aboard a C-130. I was glad we hadn't been in a big rush to leave.

John Carney joined us as we again were discussing putting the torch to the choppers. "I'm launching Russ Tharp in Republic-5 now. My team has replaced the battery-powered lights with Chemlites to mark the runway." I gave him a thumbs-up.

As Tharp's aircraft accelerated down the runway, we were watching through night-vision goggles. The blown fuel truck at the far end had pretty well burned itself out—there were only stars and moonlight.

Then, as the C-130 reached the 3,000-foot point, my heart leaped into my throat. The aircraft hit the sand piled up along the shoulder of the road. There was a giant shower of dust and sand.

My God! We've lost 'em!

Then, out the other side of the billowing mass, the struggling Hercules appeared, straining to recapture its lost airspeed. Another 1,000 feet and the big bird staggered into the air.

They made it! Thank God! They made it!

Just as my heart was calming down, Steve Fleming poured the power to Dragon-3 and the props churned up a huge dust cloud as the aircraft began moving down the makeshift runway. When we caught a glimpse of the shadowy form, damned if it wasn't plowing through the same sand pile Tharp's bird had just cut a swath through. Again, luck prevailed and the C-130 was through the roadbed and Steve was coaxing it into the air.

When my palpitations stopped, I turned to Carney. "I can't say that I think too much of your frapping Chemlites, John. We're lucky somebody didn't bust his ass on that shoulder. You get up in the cockpit, right by Uttaro, and make sure we don't hit that roadbed on takeoff."

John and I were the last ones. We were scanning the area with our night-vision goggles, making certain that nobody was out there . . . no living soul would be left behind.

Finally, I yelled to John, "Climb aboard. We've gotta get the hell out of here!"

We left a lot of hopes and dreams back there at Desert-I, but the nightmares and despair were coming with us, back to Masirah, and would continue to haunt us for years, maybe forever.

As the C-130's four engines droned along above the Iranian desert, I sat deep in thought. I was riding next to the SATCOM operator in the cockpit so I could be in close contact with the command center. I had the radio operator send the message that we were all airborne and heading to Masirah. Each aircraft was on its own and staying fairly low.

Tom Wicker brought me out of my musing with the news that Russ Tharp's aircraft, No. 5, was now on three engines, having shut one down due to a loss of oil. Fate was continuing to take potshots at us.

On three engines, Tharp was slowed considerably, and the rest of us soon passed him. I didn't want to slow down and escort Russ because of the burn victims we had aboard. Besides, we had good radio contact and would be able to monitor his progress until he was on the ground.

I got Wicker busy on the interaircraft radio network seeking an accurate count of the number of personnel on board each aircraft and the number of casualties.

The SATCOM net was coming alive as the shock of failure was wearing off. I thought I recognized Colonel Jim Keating's voice reporting that Helo 5 with Colonel Pitman aboard had just landed on the *Nimitz* along with two rescue choppers that had been sent out as escorts.

Wicker handed me a note with the count of personnel and casualties. The other two C-130s each had one injured aboard; we had two with major burns with us on No. 6. I was amazed to learn that Delta had so few casualties after what they had been through. I guess what I had seen had been clothing burning. The major burn victims were from C-130 and helicopter crews. I passed this information along to Red Barn and Gravel Pit.

About twenty minutes later, Gravel Pit came back with a request for a recount—our figures didn't jibe with what they thought we should have. I discovered that we hadn't included one of the refueling crews in our tally, so I radioed a revised total, adding, "If that doesn't compute, let's sort it out on the ground."

One more thing: we needed to verify the fuel status of the

C-130s to determine if a refueling would be needed. Wicker checked with his pilots and confirmed that all aircraft could make it to Masirah without having to use the tankers. I relayed this to Red Barn.

The tanker crews had busted their butts to make sure we would have enough fuel and now, after all that orbiting, they weren't needed. But they sure would have been if the rendezvous at Desert-I had been successful. Using the extra helicopter fuel had been a good move, enabling us to stay at the rendezvous for over three hours.

One bit of irony crossed my mind concerning the bus and gas-truck encounters.

As it turned out, if we had landed ten minutes later we would have had the place to ourselves for the rest of the refueling operation—no other vehicles entered the landing zone. If it hadn't been for the bad luck, we wouldn't have had any luck at all.

The sun was rising as I completed this last detail and sank back into my seat with my eyelids drooping. Captain Tom Beres, our navigator, tapped me on the shoulder. "Colonel, we're now clear of Iranian airspace."

I looked at my watch: 5:00 A.M., another hour to go. Sitting there numbly, I drifted back into thought. I was thinking about "Murphy's Law" (if there's a possibility for something to go wrong, it will). That certainly applied to this mission, and in grand proportions.

38

TAPS FOR EAGLE CLAW

MASIRAH, 0200 ZULU (0600 LOCAL), APRIL 25, 1980

The sun was coming up Friday morning as the first two C-130s returning from Desert-I touched down, just minutes apart, on the same runway they'd departed from ... nearly eleven hours ago, by my watch. Russ Tharp brought his bird limping in on three engines about ten minutes later.

As we taxied in, our Air Force flight surgeons, Bill Postles and Captain "Count" Contiguglia, jumped aboard to help Delta's medical officer tend to the burn victims. They organized aid teams from some of those in the rescue force with medical experience.

General Gast asked each commander to line up the troops to get an accurate head count so we could positively determine who was missing. It was verified that Hal Lewis, four others from his crew, and three Marine helicopter crew members had perished—eight in all.[1]

I had done a lot of flying with Hal Lewis and members of his crew throughout training and rehearsals, which deepened my grief over the loss. For me, this tragic accident and loss of life would never be satisfactorily explained.

Meanwhile, General Gast returned to the communications tent, accompanied by some of the Marines, and reported to Red Barn that considerable classified information had been left aboard the helicopters at Desert-I and questioned the status of

---

[1]In a few days, I would be struck with disbelief at the Iranians' claim to having nine bodies. They desecrated our dead with the same callous disregard for humanitarian decency that had characterized their actions from the beginning of the hostage crisis, only now we had lost eight good men and didn't have a damn thing to show for it.

the request for a Navy tactical air strike on the area. He was told that this had been disapproved by higher authority—another stinging blow to our already battered sense of guilt. The air strike was our last hope of keeping these secrets out of Iranian hands.

Some time later, we heard crew members from Helo 5 (aboard the *Nimitz*) elaborating for Red Barn just what information had been compromised. Among the classified materials were call signs of individuals, secret operating locations, radio frequencies, strip maps of routes to and from Tehran, information about alternate landing zones (eight to ten of them), and location of the truck warehouse. It was more than enough data to reconstruct the Tehran portion of the helicopter mission.[2]

I couldn't believe that the Marine crews would have even considered taking such extremely sensitive information into Tehran with them. If Dick Meadows, Fred, and the other operatives were caught because of those documents, there would be hell to pay.[3]

The silence was shattered thirty minutes later by the screaming jet engines of the two C-141 medevac transports coming in to evacuate the burn victims, along with Delta and the helo pilots. Those MAC Special Ops crews did a super job for us. When they got the word for the emergency evacuation they smoked off and arrived in nothing flat.

It took about forty-five minutes to load the aircraft, because of the special care required to move the injured, some of whom were still in a lot of pain.

The guys at Red Barn and the airlift controllers had done an outstanding job in getting these birds in to us in such a short time. That effort and the emergency treatment administered by our doctors on the scene undoubtedly saved the lives of the more seriously burned victims.

---

[2]From the helicopter pilot debriefing, it was learned that classified information was left aboard helicopters No. 1, No. 4, and No. 8. Most of the information displayed by the Iranians on television came from Helo 8. It should be noted that the three helos containing classified documents were nearest the fire and exploding debris.

[3]We would learn later that Meadows' reception committee and the CIA agents had made it out, but some of them had been forced to devise ingenious methods to do it. Fred had to lie low for a while, but later slicked his way out in good form. He had a lot of moxie for an amateur.

As the C-141 Starlifters lifted off for the five-hour flight to Wadi Kena, only General Gast, the comm crew, the combat control team, and the C-130 personnel were left at Masirah. Slowly, the aircrews emerged from behind the wall of silence that had existed since the return from Desert-I. They started talking about the mission. They had done their best to make the game plan work—and when it fell apart, they had done their best to salvage the situation. The combat controllers had kept the accident scene under control and prevented further loss of life while ensuring that no one alive was left behind.

You can't rehearse for how to deal with a crash of this magnitude. Men react instinctively, based on their training and experience. It might have been organized chaos, but, by God, we kept it together.

They experienced the pain of failure while doing all that was asked of them—and more. I admired their guts.

However, these positive feelings were short-lived as Jim Kelley, our intelligence officer, asked John Carney and me to his tent for debriefing. Kelley was required by regulation to interview all participants in the mission and record the story for official records. I can assure you, being forced to relive the calamitous events of that night was an agonizing invasion of my reverberating brain. But I understood the awkward and difficult position that Kelley was in—he was just doing his job.

After leaving Kelley's tent, I circulated among the maintenance and support troops, giving each of them a pat on the back. They had made sure the C-130s were in top shape to perform this toughest of missions—they had come through with flying colors.

This was when two of the Sultan of Oman's Air Force personnel—British—came driving up and delivered their morale-boosting cargo—two cases of cold beer. The troops made short work of the much-appreciated suds. "Ah, those Brits have real class," one veteran pilot exclaimed as he raised his bottle in a salute toward the Omani side of the airfield.

And the message on the cardboard case—"To you all, from us all, for having the guts to try." Man, that said it all!

It was a very moving experience, especially since tantalizing visions of what might have been—if we had succeeded—had been running through our minds. We had imagined celebrations all across America as everyone rejoiced in the return of the rescue force with the hostages.

It was hard to sustain this upbeat thinking in the reality of what had happened. Now here we were, just a bunch of dust-caked slobs, a long way from home and struggling to hold our heads up high and our pride together. There would be no celebrations—only dreams, and nightmares.

One of the maintenance troops told me that General Gast had a message for me at the communications tent.

The general had been on the radio most of the morning sorting out the previous night's events. When I approached the communications tent I could see he was weary, but was continuing to attend to the multitudinous post-mission tasks.

"Jim, they want you back in Washington on the next flight out of here. There will be investigations by Congress and the military, and your testimony will be needed."

I just nodded and left the tent to find a place where I could be alone and collect my thoughts. One of our C-130s would take me to Wadi Kena later that morning, and from there I would be whisked on connecting flights to Germany, then on to Washington. I found myself wishing that airplanes didn't fly so fast. This was one trip where a slow boat would have suited me just fine.

Testifying before congressional committees would be a new experience for me, as it would for most of the key members of the Joint Task Force. I imagined that we would get a hostile reception. My sixth sense was telling me that Washington was looking for someone to crucify, and I was getting that old familiar knot in my stomach. My role as the on-scene commander at Desert-I made me a likely candidate. That's how it goes.

I could see that most of the crews were settling into their cots for some long-overdue sleep. Only the maintenance crews were still moving around—out checking their aircraft for possible damage picked up on the desert.

A group of officers were tending to the unenviable job of collecting and inventorying the belongings of the five aircrew members lost at Desert-I. I could see the empty cots in the tent where Hal Lewis and his crew had slept the day before the mission. The first few words of "The Aviators' Hymn" popped into my mind: "Lord guard and guide the men that fly/through the great spaces of the sky . . ."

My despair was becoming overwhelming as my tired mind cast about for some reason to explain why such tragedy had been visited upon such a noble effort.

"Oh, Lord. Why did it have to end this way?"

PART FOUR

RETROSPECTIVES

39

THE AFTERMATH

All too soon, I was back in the air and headed for Wadi Kena, the start of a whirlwind trip that would soon deliver me to Washington and into the hands of those who would pick over the bones of this failed rescue mission.

So, as I began the long journey back to where it had all begun, I was filled with uncertainty as to what the future held.

It seemed fitting somehow that I was aboard the same old warhorse (Dragon-1) that had taken me to Desert-I. It was still running great, but was as tired as I was. This sturdy bird was in dire need of major structural repairs after the beatings it had taken over the past six months and was therefore being nursed back to the States by Ken Oliver's crew from Lockheed.

I hit the ground running at Wadi Kena. Time for a quick shower, some grub, and a short chat with Jerry King, Lee Hess, and Stormy Buchanan.

Shortly, I was again airborne and headed for Germany, where another aircraft was waiting to whisk me away to Washington. Under different circumstances, the VIP treatment might have been impressive.

Marine Lieutenant Colonel Bob Neff from the Special Operations Division was waiting for me as I climbed down the ladder and into the damp morning mist at Andrews Air Force Base.

It was 4:00 A.M. when we pulled up to the Pentagon and I was escorted into the familiar surroundings of the Special Operations Division. It was like a morgue, and the clicking of the Teletype machines only served to punctuate the otherwise soundless void. It felt unreal—sort of like a dream.

I grabbed a cup of coffee and headed for the Back Room, where I had spent so many busy, eventful hours. As I sank into a seat, the memories of the past few days—and months—came crowding in on me. I just sat there staring at the wall, reliving the mission.

Where did it go wrong? What could I have done to prevent it?

Despite all the soul-searching, I was painfully aware that I didn't have many of the answers, and wouldn't have until I could talk to others involved, especially the helicopter crews. The problems they had in the dust and the late arrival at Desert-I deeply troubled me. I somehow felt partly to blame.

Next was a hurried call to Eunice to unravel the mystery of where I'd been for the past couple of weeks and let her know that I was okay.

"I'll probably be here for the next month or so—testifying before congressional committees and military investigation boards, and writing my report on the whole affair.

"I promise I'll be back in Hawaii by Christmas . . . either reassigned or retired."

My debriefing session with General Vaught was a long one. I laid out what I knew for the general with as much detail as I could recall. He was as uncertain about what had gone wrong with the helicopters as I was, and, like me, he was anxious to talk with the chopper crews and get their story.

It wasn't long after I broke off with the boss that I was summoned to the office of the Chief of Naval Operations, Admiral Thomas Hayward. He was also anxious to find out what had gone wrong with the helicopter force and wanted my opinions.

My conversation with the admiral centered on the big question of why three of the helos had failed to complete the mission because of mechanical problems, but it was obvious that until we could talk to Ed Seiffert, the helicopter snafu would remain a mystery.

My next command performance was in the Chairman's office. General Jones had summoned General Vaught, Charlie Beckwith, and me while he decided who from the Joint Task Force would make a statement at a press conference later in the day. As the Chairman weighed the pros and cons, I could see that it was either going to be me or Beckwith, with neither of us wanting the publicity that would come from facing this pack of news-hungry wolves.

When it was all over, Charlie had drawn the short straw—mainly, I think, because of his Vietnam reputation and the fact that he had been the commander of the ground portion of the hostage rescue mission. Also, President Carter had met Charlie and personally knew his background, whereas nobody knew me from Adam, and I didn't have the colorful background that makes good news copy. The main negative in this choice was that it would blow Charlie's cover. After being identified as leader of America's elite Delta Force, he would be closely watched as the key to any future Delta operations, an intolerable situation.

I must say, he was very impressive at the press conference. Charlie was especially convincing in conveying his belief that the mission to rescue the hostages would have succeeded, given half a chance. Although he did a damn fine job in front of the press corps, I know it was one of the more bitter experiences of his military career. As he stood there in front of this probing throng, he was bringing to an end his command of Delta Force.

In early May, President Carter flew down to Camp Smokey, where Delta Force and the Marine helicopter crews had been taken immediately after the mission. As the Commander in Chief stepped down from his aircraft, Colonel Beckwith stepped forward and saluted smartly and then apologized for the mission's failure, but the President said that he considered the rescue force heroes and could not accept an apology from men willing to show the world that America would fight for freedom.

One of the men said, "Mr. President, don't write us off because we failed to hit a home run for you the first time at bat—give us another chance."[1] It was a very moving meeting. The President didn't abandon the rescue team, nor did he point the finger of blame at anyone. He was showing the forces that we would face the consequences together. (The President would later meet with the Air Force team members. At the time of the Camp Smokey visit, they were still in the process of straggling back to their home bases.)

[1]From an article in the May 1981 *Armed Forces Journal*, "President Courage," by Benjamin F. Schemmer.

Throughout this period, the various mission commanders slowly drifted back into the Special Operations Division to prepare for the upcoming inquiries. We still had several days before we were scheduled to appear before the armed services committees of the Senate and the House of Representatives—time to collect our thoughts and prepare for our testimony. There were spurious calls for us to meet with general officers (all services) to go over various aspects of the rescue mission.

One of these meetings, with General Lewis Allen, Air Force Chief of Staff, was particularly disappointing to me. He had heard rumors that personal film taken during the mission by Marine aircrews had shown up at a local drugstore for developing, which would constitute a serious breach of orders, and he wanted my assurance that no Air Force personnel had done this same thing. While assuring him that it hadn't happened, I was amazed that this seemed to be his only concern about the mission. I envied Beckwith and Delta Force the strong moral support that General Meyer, the Army Chief of Staff, had been giving them.

During early May, I noticed many new faces showing up in JCS/SOD. They appeared to be planning for another rescue attempt, but I was not privy to what they were doing. Some of us from Eagle Claw were now outsiders.

To keep us busy as we waited for the dreaded encounters with the congressional committees, General Vaught had directed that field commanders each prepare a list of mission constraints that had affected their ability to perform the mission. This information would be used in our final report and in addressing congressional inquiries.

When Ed Seiffert and Bob Mattingly arrived at the Special Operations Division, we had some quiet moments to discuss the mission. That's when I learned about the plethora of problems the helicopter crews had experienced in the dust. This was the first time I'd heard that they had removed the secure function of their radios and planned to remain at 100 to 200 feet. It was mind-boggling. Naturally, Ed wished they hadn't done either. They sure made it tough on themselves.

I told Ed that I felt like hell for not having broken radio silence to pass on a warning about the dust after we had encountered it in the lead C-130. But at our altitude, none of the C-130s had any trouble. The situation was vastly different at their altitude. He said that would probably have helped him get better organized before the dust encounter, but he probably would not have aborted until at least making an attempt to get through it. (Neither of us realized the incompatibility of our respective SATCOM systems—it was years later before this was pointed out to me.)

I also told Ed that I was surprised at their remaining at low level and thought that they would have climbed to a safe altitude above the terrain and pressed on to Desert-I, picking up the TACAN and landing. I got the impression that they never considered this tactic because of the fears of hostile radar detection that were based on erroneous conclusions from the CIA report.

In turn, Ed was surprised to learn that I had been without a satellite radio for the first hour at Desert-I after mine was disabled on landing. And when I told him that we had not made a radio report that the lead Talon would be landing in thirty minutes, he was shocked—that had been a major consideration in his decision to press on through the dust. Later, while listening to tapes of the mission to determine just who had said what, we discovered that the thirty-minute report had come from a C-141 approaching Daharan.

When we looked at all of the problems we had encountered and the crucial times at which they had occurred, we saw that they had all hit at once and it wasn't long before we were overwhelmed. That dust couldn't have been in a worse place.

On the second day of May, I was taken to the Senate's Russell Office Building to meet with Senator John Warner, R-Va., who was surrounded by his staff, Robert McFarlane, and another man named Datson.[2] The senator and his group of interrogators eventually took many of the rescue mission's key players behind closed doors for lengthy questioning in, as they called it, a fact-finding inquiry.

---

[2]Ironically, Bud McFarlane (who later became National Security Adviser in the Reagan administration) would himself spend a considerable amount of time testifying before a congressional committee during the Iran-Contra hearings.

Before any of us went to Capitol Hill to testify, we were told that we could only talk about the rescue operation from its inception up to and including Desert-I; nothing past Desert-I was to require an answer. The congressional committees knew these were the ground rules.

Throughout my session with Senator Warner and his staff, they asked detailed questions and took voluminous notes. They quizzed me about operating in the dust, aircraft maintenance standards, weather forecasting of en route conditions, rehearsal of potential emergencies (such as a crash causing a fire), and overall command of the mission. One question I recall was: "Were you directed to do something you didn't want to do?" To which I answered, "No, sir. We had a good plan and I'm proud of it."

As near as I could tell, the members of this group were talking mainly to the so-called underlings of the mission—few, if any, generals. What we were all too naive to realize was that our answers at the separate sessions with this private fact-finding group would later be used in a joint session of the Senate Armed Services Committee, which commenced on May 7, 1980.

Senator John Stennis, D-Miss., was chairing the hearing, with fourteen other senators arranged on both sides of him. They were sitting at what resembled a large semicircular judges' bench, each awaiting his chance to ask questions.

Senator John Glenn, D-Ohio, although not a member of the committee, circulated among us shaking hands and encouraging us to be proud of the rescue attempt: "America had to try."

Senator Stennis opened the hearing with a statement to the effect that the committee had pride in the military and just wanted to learn the facts behind the failure.

I sat at a table, facing the senators, alongside Major General Vaught, Lieutenant General Gast, Colonel Beckwith, and Lieutenant Colonel Seiffert. Sitting in the wings were Colonel King, Colonel Pitman, Lieutenant Colonel Guidry, Lieutenant Colonel Williford, Major Carney, and Captain Don "Stormy" Buchanan to assist in answering any questions that fell within their areas of involvement. The principals testifying were labeled "the Visible Seven" by our cohorts at JCS/SOD. I soon came to hate this moniker as each day we were loaded into staff cars and driven to Capitol Hill to relive the desert nightmare.

General Vaught spoke first for the Joint Task Force with a prepared statement. During the reading of this statement, the general became emotional when he pointed out the continual battle the task force had faced in maintaining secrecy, especially in eluding speculation from the press. This was a trying time for General Vaught, who was exhausted and who was being labeled in the media a poor commander and criticized for failing to take actions to prevent the rescue mission from aborting. It was the only time during the entire affair that I ever saw him lose control of his emotions.

Senator Barry Goldwater, R-Ariz., said that he did not want to see anyone from the Joint Task Force downgraded because of his involvement in the rescue mission (the Arizona senator had supported the President's decision to attempt the rescue).

There was a sharp exchange between several senators over what some were calling "illegal use" of the War Powers Act. They were insisting that Congress should have been informed of the rescue plan.

Senator Goldwater called that idea "preposterous." He maintained that the Congress could not keep knowledge of a secret mission such as this out of the newspapers for one day. He maintained that it was proper for the military not to divulge the plans. If it had been appropriate, I'm sure the senator would have gotten a standing ovation from our group.

Next up, Senator Strom Thurmond, R-S.C., generally agreed with the need for military secrecy but expressed concerns over the command and control situation. He said that it seemed to him there were too many commanders. I don't think we were able to satisfy the senator on this question, but then few people understand just how joint Special Operations units are organized.

Senator Henry Jackson, D-Wash., wanted to know why it had taken six months to prepare the operation. The fact that the military was not able to mount a rescue attempt for several months went over like a lead balloon with him. But I think that we made it clear that this was beyond the control of the Joint Task Force—that we had inherited the problem.

Next, things got a little hot when the idea was raised that President Carter's decision to launch the mission was politically motivated. You can bet your sweet bippie that none of us uttered a word during the resulting exchange between Republicans on one side and Democrats on the other.

In the time remaining before lunch break, Senator Warner probed at what weather abort criteria the Joint Task Force had used. It appeared that he became frustrated at the vague answers he was receiving and decided to turn that line of questioning over to Bud McFarlane. He continued to press for what specific conditions we might have considered as constituting an abort situation. Holy Toledo, we didn't have such cut-and-dried rules—we were looking for reasons to keep going, not reasons to stop.

Although the afternoon session was much less lively, it was then that Senator Sam Nunn, D-Ga., locked on to the most important question of the whole situation: What could be done to make the system better for the future? What had we learned from this?

Charlie Beckwith fielded this one, and what a job he did. He had obviously given the subject a lot of thought, based on his experience in putting together Delta Force. He said that it is imperative that a permanent joint-service task force be established and made responsible for the counterterrorism mission. He envisioned as the answer to the problem a close-knit organization committed to the effort—one in which all personnel would eat, sleep, live, and work with the mission twenty-four hours a day, seven days a week.

"You cannot take a few people from one unit, throw them in with some from another, give them someone else's equipment, and hope to come up with a top-notch fighting outfit." In essence, a hodgepodge organization is not the way to deal with terrorism.

Man, old Charlie dazzled everybody, and when he was finished, about all anyone could say was "Amen."

As the afternoon dragged on, we were asked why we hadn't destroyed the choppers abandoned at Desert-I, and Senator Warner got in a few licks about the classified documents being left behind. I remember the senator asking me if I had known the

Marines had the secret documents at Desert-I, to which I replied, "No sir."[3]

I'm not sure anyone who hadn't been at Desert-I could have appreciated our answers to these questions.

I thought we missed a golden opportunity late in the afternoon when a question was posed as to whether we felt we had had the necessary equipment for the mission. The answer was something like "We had the best that was available." Since we were not professionals at this business of testifying, we let the chance to expound on the numerous mission-limiting factors slip by.

As the first day of the Senate committee's session ended, we were told to remain available for future questioning. For me, however, that was it—I never returned to the Senate panel's hearing.

My next testimony came before the members of the House Armed Services Committee. I appeared along with Roland Guidry and Jim Linderman, one of the helicopter pilots. The questioning mostly concerned why we had chosen the RH-53D for the mission. By that time, this committee had already heard from most of the other key Joint Task Force witnesses and seemed to be bored with what we could tell them. However, one House committee member came right out and said that he was looking for someone to blame for the mission's failure. It must have been exasperating for them to listen to all that testimony and not be able to point the finger at someone. At the time, I still didn't have the complete story but suggested that, along with plain bad luck, they'd have to blame all of us. He wasn't satisfied with that either.

On May 9 at 9:30 A.M., we were all in place at Arlington National Cemetery for a memorial service for the eight men lost at Desert-I. President Carter presided over the service and

---

[3]Somehow, my reply later got twisted into the idea that operational security was so strict that the commander at Desert-I didn't know about secret documents aboard the chopper—but operational security had nothing to do with it! During a break in the testimony, Seiffert or Pitman (I can't remember which) confessed to me that they took the documents because they felt there was not adequate security to leave them stored on the ship or the necessary trusted agents to leave them with. I didn't buy that. What about Mattingly (helo intelligence officer) or Keating (CINCPAC liaison)? It was a dumb mistake, and all of us knew it.

delivered the eulogy to the dead airmen. It was an extremely moving ceremony—I could not suppress the tears of grief any longer.

We had all seen the television footage of Iranian authorities ripping open the plastic bags and poking at the charred remains with knives (one even spat on the bodies).

President Carter said it best for all Americans: "This indicates quite clearly the kinds of people we've been dealing with. They did not bring shame and dishonor on the fallen Americans. They brought shame and dishonor on themselves."

Now our comrades were laid to rest—their torment was finally over.

Meanwhile, the debate raged on. A barrage of criticism was forthcoming from armchair strategists and so-called experts on terrorism of all ilk. The Joint Task Force plan seemed to be the main bone of contention. It was criticized as being too complex, too sophisticated, and lacking the proper forces and aircraft to achieve success.

After two weeks of inconclusive testimony, Congress decided to drop its investigation. I'm not sure whether this was because of frustration at the lack of answers or the urging of the military that the Joint Chiefs of Staff could better conduct an investigation and provide Congress with the answers. At about that time, the JCS commissioned a Blue Ribbon Special Operations Review Group to conduct a detailed examination of the Iran rescue mission.

Despite these actions, however, Senator Warner and his staff continued to interview Joint Task Force members throughout most of the month. About all that was to come of that testimony was an article sent out by United Press International and datelined June 6. This story, based on a report allegedly written by Bud McFarlane, ostensibly represented the frustrations of a minority element of the Senate Armed Services Committee at not being able to pin the failure on somebody. The article, which was based on *secret* information obtained during the closed-door Senate hearings, castigated the Carter administration for ineptitude and concluded that the ill-fated rescue mission was flawed by a poor commander, inefficient organization, and a failure to anticipate emergencies. Of course, the chairman of the Armed

Services Committee denied that such a report existed, and the Pentagon issued strong denials about the claims as well. But the report did prove one thing—that Senator Goldwater was right about Congress's inability to keep top secret information from the press.

In the latter part of May 1980, the Department of Defense established the Holloway Commission, so named because its chairman was retired Admiral James L. Holloway III, former Chief of Naval Operations. This top-level panel was made up of luminaries from the various services—six flag officers—and chartered to examine the organization, planning, coordination, direction, and control of the Iran hostage rescue mission with an eye toward recommending improvements in these areas for the future.

Almost immediately, this commission began interviewing members of the Joint Task Force, both those directly involved in the rescue mission and those peripherally associated with it.

However, after appearing before the commission, task force members were returning to the Special Operations Division scratching their heads. The general feeling was that some of the committee members were ill chosen for the task at hand, given that they had little or no background in Special Operations.

I had heard criticism of the choice of General Jones and General Gast, both senior-ranking Air Force officers, for roles in the Iran mission "because they wouldn't recognize a Special Operation if one smacked them in the face." At least they had had the good sense to surround themselves with some pretty decent experts in the business. I'm not sure the same can be said for the Holloway Commission. On reviewing the Special Operations experience of each member of that panel, I would say that maybe half had what I would consider the necessary credentials to judge the "rights and wrongs" of the Joint Task Force's performance. Particularly striking was the selection of the group's chairman, a retired Navy admiral with nothing in his background to indicate any experience in this business. One might suspect that the admiral was placed in that position to control criticism of the Navy's maintenance of the helicopter fleet, for which it was being severely taken to task. I really don't have the answer to that, but I know that many of us were sadly disillusioned at the selection of some of the commission members who would be our judges.

In the course of its investigation, the commission reviewed all pertinent written materials, including planning documents, training reports, mission briefs, congressional testimony, press releases, technical analyses, and the Joint Task Force's After-Action Report.

In analyzing the planning, training, and execution of the hostage rescue mission, the review group admitted to applying a great deal of hindsight in identifying twenty-three issues that it "investigated in depth." Of these, eleven were considered of major import, "having an identifiable influence on the outcome of the rescue effort."

The commission's eleven major findings were:

1. Excessive operational security—aircrews lacked information to perform the mission due to an overly restrictive disclosure policy.

2. No independent review of plans by an outside group of experienced Special Operations experts.

3. Joint Task Force not efficiently organized, which hindered command and control . . . and failure to apply an existing Joint Chiefs of Staff plan to facilitate expedient organization of a functioning staff.

4. Lack of a comprehensive readiness evaluation—Desert-I option not fully rehearsed.

5. Size of helicopter force too small—ten to twelve RH-53Ds should have been used.

6. Overall coordination of joint training lacked central management.

7. Confused command and control at Desert-I—flow of information from responsible authorities hindered by lack of recognition and mode of communications.

8. Centralized and integrated intelligence support external to the Joint Task Force was slow in responding, i.e. the CIA.

9. Alternatives to the Desert-I site—the landing zone presented a greater risk than assessed by the Joint Task Force.

10. Handling the dust phenomenon—poor interface between

pilots and weather officer concerning recognition of conditions associated with a haboob.
11. C-130 "pathfinders" should have been used to lead the helicopters.

In my opinion, only two of these (4 and 10) had any bearing on the mission's failure. However, buried among twelve lower-priority points the commission considered contributing causes for the failure were four significant findings that are directly related to it. They were:

- Alternate helicopter pilots (USAF Special Operations or Rescue Service H-53 pilots) should have been selected to team with Marines.
- Helicopter aborts—pilots lacked certain knowledge vital to reaching an informed decision whether to abort or proceed.
- Enemy radar threat—helicopter pilots based low-level tactics on erroneous intelligence report.
- Helicopter communications—pilots lacked secure modes of communication to receive vital mission information.

I just can't see how anybody reviewing the causes for failure of this mission could place these issues on the lower-priority list. *These are the major reasons that the mission failed.*

Finally, when the commission reached the bottom line, it determined that two factors combined to directly cause the mission to abort: an unexpected helicopter failure rate, and low-visibility flight conditions en route to Desert-I.

I was (and still am) deeply troubled by this report—not so much for what it says, but for how it says it. The facts were not arranged in a logical order to support the commission's conclusions.

It was as if someone intentionally disguised the key factors in the failure by burying them in unrelated subject titles.

In studying the report, I was puzzled to read what some commission members decided the Joint Task Force should have done differently, especially in regard to C-130 operations. Some of their proposed tactics are as archaic as those used at Custer's Last Stand. And yet, one member produced clear evidence that indicated the pilot of one of the helicopters that experienced a rotor blade problem (BIM) should not have aborted his aircraft. However, this clear evidence consisted of Sikorsky technical data, which the helo pilots did not have access to. This is a good example of how the report takes wild swings from vagaries to specific facts.

In fact, only two paltry recommendations came out of the review panel's report.

One was to establish a permanent joint task force for counter-terrorism, something already proposed by Charlie Beckwith to the Senate Armed Services Committee.

The other was for the establishment of a Special Operations advisory panel of high-ranking officers that would review and critique JCS planning initiated in response to a crisis or other contingency (an issue our JTF had surfaced earlier, only we called it a "murder board").

Neither of these proposals was original. It seems to me that for all the time and man-hours expended in researching this report, the Special Operations review group could have at least proposed a list of necessary improvements to the various service chiefs to upgrade their respective force capabilities, which were so obviously in a sad state of affairs. The commission seemed to tiptoe around any such issues, apparently not wanting to rock the boat.

As I see it, the commission's report was a whitewashing of the real issues. The panel seemed interested only in condemning the way the Joint Task Force was organized, directed, and controlled. This direction seemed driven by certain generals and admirals within JCS who felt left out of the JTF decision-making process. Thus the report served as a backlash against the Chairman and General Vaught.

From where I sit, Special Operations was not the culprit behind the failure of the Iran rescue mission. A few conservative-minded conventional-force thinkers led the helicopter component of the JTF, and that made for a poor combination. Special Operations should be kept in-house, with people who are properly trained and equipped for the job—aggressive risk-takers who train together and know one another's strengths and weaknesses and, above all, stick together.

Through the years, my JTF compatriots and I have reflected on our experiences with the Holloway Commission, and most agree that if the underlying purpose of the commission was to get the investigation shifted from congressional scrutiny to military channels, then it was a scheme that worked very well indeed—the hounds were held at bay.

On the other hand, if the commission's purpose was as stated—to investigate and report clearly and concisely just what happened and why this mission failed—then its conclusions went far wide of the mark.

ANATOMY OF A FAILED MISSION

Was the Iran rescue mission a disaster from the start and preordained to fail before it got off the ground? That was the question posed to you, the reader, at the start of the story. Before you close the book on *The Guts to Try* and make your decision, stick with me just a little longer. I want to share with you a few of my own perceptions about the mission and the final outcome. You might see things in a different light at the end.

The story doesn't end at Desert-I—I can't leave it there. The factors that led to the mission's failure need to be dissected and examined under the bright lights of truth—call it hindsight, if you will—in a search for answers.

What were the untold reasons behind the failure? How can we make sure that we never fail again? These were questions that were never satisfactorily answered during congressional testimony nor completely investigated by the Holloway Commission. I don't know why the hard questions weren't asked, or if they were, where the answers are buried. If we send military personnel out to attempt another hostage rescue mission, they deserve to have the benefit of the real lessons learned from this operation, not a bunch of vague nickel-and-dime findings that have little or nothing to do with why the mission aborted.

In the aftermath, we were satisfied to believe that mechanical problems and bad luck were responsible. This has always been hard for me to swallow, and over the years I decided to try to find out all the facts I could about what really went wrong. I now believe that there was a lot more to it than that.

As I summarize the major problems that caused the mission to fail, and add my comments, I want to make it clear that my sole purpose has been to look at the facts, examine causes, and search for answers that can be used as lessons learned . . . let the chips fall where they may.

Although the Holloway Commission cited twenty-three issues as contributing to the failure, I have pinpointed four main problems that broke the back of our mission. These are the major areas that should have been the focus of any investigation, for in them are the key factors that led to the mission's falling apart. In addition, one interesting sidelight caught my interest and is worthy of comment.

They are (in order of the severity with which I feel they affected our ability to succeed):

1. Busted weather forecast
2. Poor use of communications equipment and flawed command and control
3. Questionable pilot abort decisions
4. Absurd tactics restrictions
5. Flight planning factors (the sidelight issue)

1. BUSTED WEATHER FORECAST

The C-130 pilots considered the dust a minor annoyance at their altitude, but if you could ask the helicopter pilots what their major problem was at low level, navigating to Desert-I on the night of April 24, 1980, they'd tell you it was suspended dust. In spite of the mechanical problems and associated malfunctions that occurred, the mission was progressing reasonably well until the dust encounter. From that point on, the helicopter mission became totally disorganized—the leader lost control of the flight as crews had difficulty in keeping one another in sight and became separated in the dust.

That we failed to recognize the suspended dust as a haboob demonstrates a void in our training, but the real problem lies in the fact that the Joint Task Force had unwavering confidence in the Air Weather Service team's ability to forecast the en route weather accurately so that we could cancel the launch if inclement conditions were present.

The necessity for our fliers to be experts at recognizing a haboob was not the issue. The weathermen were supposed to be the experts—able to determine if such conditions existed. We had a rude awakening that fateful night in Iran when we ran smack into the suspended dust and realized that our confidence in the weather forecast had been misplaced. Obviously, the Air Weather Service found out what some already knew—it had a problem with its forecasting ability in remote areas of the world.

The Joint Task Force learned during the post-mission investigation that the Air Weather Service lacked the capability to predict or detect this type of phenomenon accurately with satellite data and its other limited prognostication resources for Iran. Some of its top scientists reviewed the satellite weather photography and associated data on which the launch decision was based and concluded that it was beyond the state of the art to forecast (or detect) the area of suspended dust. In other words, given the same set of circumstances and forecasting data, the Air Weather Service would again issue a forty-hour clear-weather forecast, seeing nothing to indicate the possibility that the forces would encounter a haboob.

This baring of the soul comes far too late—the game is over and we'd been slam-dunked! Where were these experts from the Air Weather Service when we began the training and rehearsals for this mission? Their weather personnel gave no indications of this limitation to General Vaught during the five and a half months leading up to the mission. On the contrary, we were all led to believe that there was a high degree of reliability in Air Weather Service predictions of the en route weather conditions for the period required to complete the rescue operation.

I've been around weathermen long enough to know that they can occasionally bust a weather forecast, usually with minor consequences. However, if they did not have the ability to forecast, or detect, this type of dust activity accurately, General Vaught and his aircrews should have known about it long before that night. It was a hell of a poor time to find it out when we were deep in Iranian territory.

In retrospect, the Joint Task Force was naive to believe that the weather forecasters could guarantee clear conditions for forty hours.

The helicopter mission planners should have been compelled to plan for and train the helicopter force to conduct the mission under adverse weather conditions (short of a major storm). They did this to an extent by installing the PINS and Omega equipment, but then they committed to a visual flight scenario. This may have been the fastest approach to getting the Marine and Navy crews trained, but it turned out to be a shortsighted policy.

The RH-53Ds were adequately equipped to perform the rescue mission under instrument conditions, but lacked radar or FLIR to make operating at low level in the vicinity of mountainous terrain a safe proposition. However, there are modified low-level tactics that can be used which reduce the dangers when this equipment is not installed.

The aircrews flying this or any Special Operations mission should be prepared to cope with adverse weather scenarios. Relying on clear weather leaves the force vulnerable to "unpredictable" conditions, and jeopardizes the mission.

2. POOR USE OF COMMUNICATIONS EQUIPMENT AND FLAWED COMMAND AND CONTROL

The communications arrangements necessary to command and control flight operations of the rescue force under instrument flight rules was an area least understood by most people and, in my opinion, was another key factor in the failure on the night of April 24, 1980.

In analyzing our communications problems, it is clear that they fall under two major headings: inherited, and beyond our control; and self-imposed, and manufactured by misguided and unnecessarily restrictive actions.

INHERITED PROBLEMS

- Satellite radio systems were not available for training and rehearsals. Other than Delta Force, none of the units had any experience with these radios.
- The limited number of satellite radios installed in mission aircraft dictated that any vital information would have to be funneled to the formations through their flight leaders.
- The satellite radios were jury-rigged and manned by radio operators trained in ground operations but unfamiliar with aviator jargon. Aircrew members were unable to hear what

was coming over the SATCOM network and were forced to rely on the radio operators to keep them informed of message traffic.

- Helos 1 and 5 had SATCOM radios designed primarily for ground use. A method of hand-holding the antennae outside the aircraft was supposed to enable limited use in flight, but the one in Helo 5 failed to work in this mode.
- The C-130 SATCOM transmitters were equipped with encryption devices which the systems aboard the helicopters were incapable of deciphering—the C-130s with SATCOMs could receive a helicopter transmission but could respond only by relaying through the command center.

SELF-IMPOSED PROBLEMS

- Task force communications procedures were designed for radio silence under visual flight conditions, with the exception of broadcasting select code words to indicate completion of key portions of the mission.
- Radio silence was to be maintained except in an emergency, one that could seriously affect the outcome of the mission. No calls for assistance would mean that the situation was under control.
- The hard landing of the lead Talon at Desert-I disabled the satellite radio, and the Delta Force SATCOM was not available as planned. An uncoordinated last-minute change placed Delta's system aboard a C-130 due to arrive an hour later.
- The Marines removed the secure interaircraft radio components from the helicopters. These components, if they were functioning properly, would have enabled them to communicate with each other by encrypted means. A system of flashing-light codes and hand signals was devised as a replacement (useless in low-visibility conditions). Other flying units involved in the mission were not aware that the Marines were operating without the secure interaircraft radios, nor that the C-130 SATCOM was incompatible with those on Helos 1 and 5.

There are few doubts that the communications equipment and procedures were adequate to command and control the aircraft under visual flying conditions (when the crews could see one another's aircraft). But when mechanical problems occurred and the dust was encountered, it became an entirely different ball game—then the crews needed the means to talk to one another in order to exchange critical mission information, remain organized, and assist one another through the ordeal.

It is axiomatic to the flying business that you cannot lead a formation without some means to control the wingmen, and under low-visibility (instrument) conditions, that means radios and some type of plan to follow.

The Marines should have ensured that their secure radios were properly maintained and shouldn't have been allowed to remove their encryption components for any reason. It was like needing to bail out of a crippled aircraft and suddenly realizing that it was a mistake to leave your parachute behind. Parachutes and secure radios may be dead weight, but not when you need them.

Without enough SATCOM radios to equip all of the mission aircraft (which is essential in future operations), there was no excuse for not having properly functioning secure interaircraft radios to keep the wingmen tied in with the command and control net. The JTF should not have wavered from this requirement!

It is obvious that the flow of information between field commanders and the command center necessary to control the mission adequately never developed. I believe this was due in large part to the inherent nature of mandated radio silence. But at some point, when it becomes obvious that things are coming unraveled, the leaders must step in and assert control.

There were two major points in the mission when strong command and control should have been—and wasn't—exercised to restore order:

The first was when the helicopter flight leader decided to turn around in the dust and the rest of his flight continued on. At that point, in my opinion, the necessity to remain organized to complete the mission outweighed the issue of maintaining radio silence, and radio silence should have been broken to direct the wingmen to rejoin the leader in the clear area to get reorganized and decide how best to attack the dust. It was at this juncture that the flight leader lost his ability to command his flight—it was every man for himself.

The second point was when the command post was first apprised of the helicopters' dust encounter. From the flight leader's SATCOM report, it was obvious the helicopter force was in disarray and that the leader was uncertain as to the status of his wingmen. Everyone in the command net was making assumptions about what was occurring but nobody really knew.

The mission monitors at Wadi Kena should have restored command and control immediately. The fact that the flight leader did not ask for assistance became irrelevant. It was obvious that something was seriously wrong. The leaders needed to start talking and assert command.

The flight leader should have been directed to break radio silence, sort out the situation, and report the status over SATCOM to Wadi Kena. The electronic intelligence experts tell me this could have been done using short, cryptic transmissions with minimal danger of compromising the mission—and it certainly would have been worth taking the chance. The insecure UHF communications link should have remained open between the helicopters and used as necessary to control the flight as it struggled through the dust. It was utterly ridiculous to sit there in radio silence while the mission was falling apart.

Related to this situation was the fact that General Vaught did not have any helicopter expertise available to him at the command center. None of the Marines connected with the rescue mission were stationed at Red Barn to monitor the progress of the RH-53s and provide counsel to the Joint Task Force commander. In retrospect, one of our helicopter mission experts should have been at Wadi Kena with General Vaught.[1]

One other immensely important lesson learned from all of this was that if the communications plan (or any other part of the

[1] Air Force and Marine component commanders each directed their own flying operations and reported directly to General Vaught. In hindsight, this failed to produce the coordination necessary to provide a cohesive, well-orchestrated flying operation. The JTF should have appointed one individual as the single authority for directing flight operations. This could have prevented such errors as the discarding of the secure radio components, last-minute tactics changes, and reliance on erroneous intelligence data.

plan) is changed, all participants must be aware of what those changes are. The discarding of some radios and the changing of time factors when others would be available had a devastating impact.

A prime example of this was when the radio on the lead aircraft was rendered inoperable. Not having Delta's portable SATCOM prevented us from talking to the rest of the Joint Task Force for over an hour. This came at a time when critical mission data could have been exchanged with the helo leader and the command post that might have helped hold the mission together.

Commanders should stick with the plan and resist last-minute changes based on whim, unless changes are justified by receipt of hard intelligence data. Most of the changes we made the night of the mission hurt rather than helped us, creating more problems—someone never gets the word.

3. QUESTIONABLE PILOT ABORT DECISIONS

To my mind, this is by far the most controversial issue and emotionally the most difficult to come to grips with because of the human factors involved. The Holloway Commission called it an unexpected helicopter failure rate, which pretty much danced around the gut issue: the mechanical problems encountered that night by three helicopter crews and whether these problems did or did not constitute genuine abort conditions. Were there other options that could have and should have been pursued?

To start with, we must consider that by the time the helicopter force started encountering problems it was already over 140 miles into Iranian territory and for all practical purposes facing a one-time shot to do this mission. Any second chance was highly unlikely. What's more, the farther the forces penetrated into Iran the more deeply committed they became to go forward come hell or high water.

As recently as late September 1986, President Carter, reminiscing about the aborted rescue attempt, was asked what he would do differently, to which he replied, "Send one more helicopter to Desert-I." This resurrects the idea that the mission failed because the Joint Task Force did not send enough helicopters on the mission. But how many is enough? The Holloway Commission says ten to twelve RH-53Ds should have been used. This is without even considering the obvious problems involved if the force is not kept to manageable size (regarding restrictions of the landing zone and fuel availability).

It is all too easy to blame an abort situation on mechanical failure since, with human factors involved, most commanders hesitate to challenge a pilot's decision. But in this case I think we have to ask the question "Did the machine fail the man or did the man fail the machine?"

What do the facts concerning each of these mechanical problems experienced that night tell us? Were they severe enough to warrant aborting? Was it unsafe to continue flying these helicopters? What risks were involved?

BIM Abort

A former Marine CH-53 pilot, now a Sikorsky engineer, explained the difference between how Navy and Marine aircrews view a confirmed BIM warning. Having been on both sides of the fence on this debate, he summed it up this way:

A Navy pilot regards a BIM warning as a nitrogen-gas leak from the blade and will normally complete a combat mission.

On the other hand, a Marine views a BIM warning as a crack in the blade that may be expanding and may cause a catastrophe if the operation is continued. He will abort the mission.

At the time of the rescue mission, three Marine CH-53s had crashed as a result of continued flight when encountering a BIM warning. Conversely, the Navy RH-53D has not been involved in a crash associated with a BIM warning to date.

Sikorsky had run extensive tests on RH-53D rotor blades removed for BIM warnings and found all still demonstrated structural integrity. Moreover, Sikorsky performed a blade failure fatigue analysis and found that at reduced weights and airspeeds, rotor blades with cracked spars would retain structural integrity for up to seventy-nine hours.

In a nutshell, what all this technical mumbo-jumbo means is that Helo 6 was capable of continuing to Desert-I and on to complete the insertion of Delta Force (seven hours). The helo would probably have been abandoned at the laager. Why didn't the Marine crews know more about the BIM procedures on the Navy RH-53D? The Holloway Commission blames it on the fact that the helicopter crews were not from an established squadron where unit cohesion would have facilitated the flow of this type of information among the pilots. Unfortunately, BIM warnings experienced during training were not discussed with the Sikorsky technical representative to determine what procedures should be followed if the situation occurred in Iran.

The Marine pilots followed the BIM procedure that familiarity and experience told them was the safest, and that was to abort. However, in this case they were operating a different model H-53, and different criteria applied. Responsible leaders must ensure their crews know the operating limitations of their aircraft.

It's a judgment call, but the pilot of Helo 6 was one of the best and bravest in the group. If he had known then what he knows now about the Navy BIM system, I'll bet he would have kept going.[2]

Second Helo Abort

Helo 5 was just 145 nautical miles from Desert-I when the pilot turned it around and headed back to the *Nimitz*. Thus, this was the most controversial of the aborts and there have been conflicting stories about the pilot's actions.

The key here was for Helo 5 to stay in formation with Helo 7 and let it lead the way to Desert-I. The pilot was unable to do that because of the dust and disorientation problems (vertigo), and consequently became separated from the formation.

In trying to sort this convoluted story out, the Holloway Commission asked the pilot of Helo 5 if he would have proceeded on toward Desert-I had he known that in twenty-five minutes he would have broken into the clear and that weather was good at the landing zone. He replied that if he had known that he probably would have continued on. From this, the commission concluded that the lead Talon crew possessed essential information

[2]In hindsight, a spare rotor blade and necessary tools should have been carried aboard one of the C-130s. I am told that a crew can change a blade in about thirty minutes and resume flight. It was shortsighted not to anticipate this eventuality. Titanium rotor blades are now in use on most H-53s which, it's hoped, will alleviate the problem.

on Desert-I weather and the dust cloud that could have altered the abort decision had it been passed on to Helo 5's crew.

The pilot of Helo 5 also told the panel that he was reluctant to climb above the high terrain and continue on because he was uncertain of the capabilities of Iranian radar sites and felt they might be able to detect his aircraft. Consequently, he continued to fly his aircraft at low altitude.

A statement was made by the commission that had the pilot of Helo 5 been informed of the number of mission-capable helicopters at Desert-I or still en route, it might have influenced his abort decision. I'm not certain if the pilot made this statement or if it was an assumption by the commission.

The commission concluded that failure to pass this vital information to the carrier and support bases over secure high frequency radios (which we did not have) was the result of a very restrictive communications doctrine, itself the result of excessive concern for operational security. The commission added that there were means available to pass the information to the helicopters en route that would have had small likelihood of compromising the mission.

This is pure bullshit! It has been my experience that when a pilot gets in trouble and needs help, he will use his radio and let somebody know about it. With a mission force observing radio silence, nobody is going to start blurting out weather reports in the clear unless the need to do so is weighed against possible mission compromise.

The C-130 people at Desert-I did not have psychic powers to anticipate this pilot was in trouble, but there is no doubt in my mind that had he requested a weather report, he would have had the information in short order. Breaking radio silence would have been justified in that case.

Instead, after turning around, the Helo 5 crew broke radio silence (while the rest of the force was still vulnerable at Desert-I) to notify the *Nimitz* that they were returning. If that warranted breaking radio silence, why not do it to obtain information that could prevent the abort? Also, Helo 5 had a SATCOM set aboard. Why not land, set it up, and ask for help?

The aircraft commander of Helo 5 seemed to need some kind of guarantee, or at least reassurance, before he would be willing to risk continuing on to Desert-I. There were three other choppers out in front of him, and those crews did not know the weather conditions at Desert-I either. Yet they had the guts to keep going, and they made it. No. 5 should have too!

These facts leave me no alternative but to question the motivation of this pilot. General Vaught had not ordered the mission to abort, and this pilot's job was to get his helicopter to Desert-I and on to Tehran. Aborting under these circumstances exceeded his authority. I also question why the senior Marine, aboard this aircraft, permitted the pilot to abort. He should have supported the copilot's argument to continue and ordered the pilot to keep going.

Although this mission took place during peacetime, circumstances dictated that it had to be performed with a combat attitude. Combat is no place for the faint-hearted.

It didn't require much skill for the pilot to fly his aircraft back through the dust for some one and a half hours with some of his flight instruments malfunctioning. If he could do that, why didn't he continue on? The answer to that is . . . he could have![3]

THIRD HELO ABORT

Helo 2 made it to Desert-I after flying nearly two hours with a hydraulic malfunction. In a discussion of this event with the pilot some years later, he told me he had every intention of continuing on, even though the malfunction could not be repaired. He only wanted to inform his leader of the problem, which he knew had an element of risk, but he felt the situation warranted pressing on. His desire to go on was overruled by the flight leader, who believed the risk was too great. This decision aborted Eagle Claw and slammed the door on the entire operation.

Had I known the pilot of No. 2 wanted to keep going, I would have informed General Vaught and gotten him involved in that decision. If the pilot felt it was safe to fly, by God, I would have backed him.

[3]Chuck Pitman stated in a September 1989 interview for *Rotor & Wing International* magazine that No. 5 was flying back to the carrier to refuel and return on the mission. This is preposterous! The rest of the force would have been long gone from the desert refueling site.

Numerous H-53 pilots that I have subsequently interviewed have stated that this helicopter could have been flown on just one hydraulic system, observing certain precautions. Despite the flight leader's concern about overtaxing the hydraulic system, given the importance of this one-time shot, I believe Helo 2 should not have been aborted at Desert-I. This was our Super Bowl and we needed to pull out all the stops. It is my contention that the senior ranking Marines charged with the responsibility to lead the helicopter force on this mission did not measure up to the task. They had some damn good pilots under their command, and all that was needed was top caliber leadership to pull it all together.

In summary, while it is apparent that the aborting of these three helicopters was in each case the safest course of action, it must weigh heavily on the minds of those who made decisions not to continue to know that, collectively, their actions caused the mission to be aborted.

It is my firm belief that the Joint Task Force never had less than seven flyable RH-53s that entire night. What's more, some highly experienced helicopter pilots have told me that all eight helicopters should have made it to the laager, with the five in the best shape completing the mission. Therefore, I cannot accept the conclusion that there was an unexpected helicopter failure rate with a contributory factor of poor maintenance aboard the carrier as reasons for the aborted mission. Admittedly, mechanical problems presented the helo pilots with some very tough decisions; and there is no excuse for the lack of coordination between the JTF and commanders aboard the carrier to ensure the choppers could meet mission requirements.

4. ABSURD TACTICS RESTRICTIONS

Six helicopters made it through the dust to Desert-I using night low-level tactics. This had to be the most harrowing of ordeals for the pilots—it showed on their faces and was reflected in their words. That is the toughest way to approach that situation that anyone could come up with: on the deck, in a large area of suspended dust, and among hills and mountains.

In this case, my training tells me that the only way to go is to climb to an altitude above the highest terrain along the flight path and navigate with the PINS and Omega equipment. There was a navigation aid en route, and one at the landing zone; it should not have been difficult. In other words, one should react to the changing conditions by changing tactics to make the operation safer and increase the chances for success.

I find that there were two reasons the helicopter pilots did not do this.

First was the chance conversation through which they were reminded of the spurious radar signals encountered during the April 1 recon mission to Desert-I.[4] These words were interpreted by their intelligence officer and leaders as meaning that they had to fly the mission at 200 feet to avoid radar detection.

Second was their desire to remain low for map reading. The PINS was used as a backup aid; some crews reported that the PINS information didn't agree with that of the Omega system, and others said the equipment overheated in the dust and malfunctioned. One Marine pilot told me the Omega was incorrectly initialized at the ship. If so, it was useless.

Even at that, most of the PINS devices would have taken the helicopters close enough to receive the navigation beacon at Darband, and that could have gotten them close enough to pick up the TACAN at Desert-I. But they stayed at low level because they had more confidence in their ability to map-read—which greatly reduced the range at which they could receive both the navigation station and the TACAN.

Take your pick of reasons, but failing to change tactics in the dust made the mission far more difficult to fly than it should have been.

5. FLIGHT PLANNING FACTORS

Over the years, I had assumed that the dust was the chief cause of the helicopters' late arrival at Desert-I. I'm sure that it contributed, but a troubling fact came to light as I was recapitu-

---

[4]The CIA liaison Chuck Gilbert assured me that he did not suggest the Marines restrict their flight altitude to 200 feet. Later, the Otter pilot told me that the radar altimeter on his aircraft caused the interference because of low altitude feedback.

lating the various flight plans of aircraft involved in the mission that night.

In the course of researching this story, I asked various helicopter mission planners what ground speed they would use as a planning factor for a mission like the Iran operation. Without exception, they replied 110-115 knots for the entire route. This factor allows for unforeseen difficulties that may arise en route—a little cushion.

The route to Desert-I was approximately 525 nautical miles (535 for the RH-53s) from where the helicopters and C-130s crossed the coast of Iran. Add to that the distance the *Nimitz* was offshore, and you get a ballpark figure of around 600 nautical miles.

A helicopter traveling at 110–115 knots would cover this distance in about five hours and twenty minutes, the time taken by the No. 3 helicopter to arrive at Desert-I. The JTF staff members who compiled the master sequence of events had the helo time en route to the desert site listed as four hours and twenty-five minutes—a discrepancy of nearly fifty minutes.

At the heavy weights at which the Marines were operating their aircraft, it is highly unlikely they could have averaged 135 knots over the entire distance, which is what they would have had to do to arrive in four hours and twenty-five minutes. The experts further stated it would be overly optimistic to plan a mission at that speed.

I don't understand why this timing discrepancy has not been challenged by the helicopter planners before, and efforts made to find some answers. I know if I had been criticized for arriving at Desert-I almost fifty minutes late, I would have screamed to high heaven that somebody was working with the wrong numbers.

Even though the helos slowed to eighty or ninety knots in the dust at various points, the first aircrews to arrive at Desert-I were very close to predicted arrival times (five hours and twenty minutes). One would have to conclude that the suspended dust had a minimal effect on the ability of these particular crews to stay on schedule. Had all crews stayed in formation and arrived together, I think they would have argued with the accusation they were fifty minutes late. This fact apparently became lost in the shuffle when the helicopters arrived spread out over a period of thirty-five minutes.

The JTF based the entire rendezvous operation at Desert-I on the helicopter arrival time, which someone either recorded or computed incorrectly. Consequently, it put the C-130s at the landing zone nearly one hour too soon.

It's a good thing we could use the extra bladder fuel from the C-130 Bladder Birds to remain in position until the helos arrived. Otherwise we would have had to depart and leave them to get out of the predicament on their own. I don't even want to think what the outcome of that might have been!

Here is another strong case for designating one individual on the JTF staff to be in charge of all air operations and responsible to keep a tight rein on flying activities. This is no place for the various flying units to be off doing their own thing. Close teamwork is the name of the game.

There is one other very important question that has troubled me for years. Why was the Joint Task Force denied permission to use the airfield at Masirah, Oman, for nearly five months and then given that permission less than twenty-four days before the mission was launched? Early on, the JTF wanted to establish this airfield as a forward operating base, which would have greatly simplified the operation regardless of which option of the plan General Vaught chose to execute. It was a dastardly problem when it shouldn't have been.

The Carter administration has been blamed by many critics for dithering leadership throughout the hostage situation. The rescue attempt has been labeled by some as "Jimmy Carter's Desert Folly" and is believed in some circles to have cost him the presidency. It was a bum rap where the rescue mission was concerned.

The President directed the military to develop a plan to rescue the hostages. Other than to describe it as a rescue mission to be performed by a small, surgical force with limitations on any violence involved, the President left the military to its own devices to accomplish a formidable task with acknowledged risks. Although Mr. Carter was slow to approve the Desert-I reconnaissance mission, that alone did not cause the mission to fail. The military organized, planned, selected, and trained the forces and executed the mission without interference from the President.

Even though he was the Commander in Chief, Jimmy Carter was not to blame for the failure of the rescue mission. That responsibility rests squarely on the shoulders of the U.S. military and more specifically on those of us who were given the responsibility to develop the plan and make it work. I believe that I have shown that the idea that "no one was to blame, it was all bad luck" just won't hold up under the weight of the facts.

Throughout this summary there is one question that I have not dealt with: just how close did we come to succeeding?

It is my considered opinion that we came within a gnat's eyebrow of success. Despite all of the obstacles, frustrations, human failings, and bad luck, despite all of this, we were on the brink. We were there, we had the combat-savvy commandos of Delta Force within spitting distance of our objective. I knew Charlie and his men—their attitudes, their skills, their competence, their leadership—and I have no doubt that if we could have gotten them to Tehran they would have pulled it off. There is also ample evidence from former hostages interviewed that suggests that the rescue attempt would have been successful.

Think about it!

- At least seven helicopters were mechanically capable of reaching Desert-I. Six made it and could have gone on.
- Even with the bus and fuel-truck encounters at Desert-I, the clandestine nature of the mission could have been preserved for forty hours—sufficient time to complete the mission.
- Although the helicopter timing for the refueling rendezvous was two hours behind schedule, we still could have completed the insertion before sunrise.
- Six helicopters should have relaunched for Tehran and flown in clear weather to join Dick Meadows' reception committee and insert Delta for the assault on the embassy.
- All that was lacking was the guts to try!

GLOSSARY

AAF   Army Air Field
ABCCC   Airborne Battlefield Command, Control, and Communications
AC-130/AC-130H   C-130 armed with 20mm, 40mm, and 105mm cannons
    (*see* **gunship** and **Spectre**)
AFB   Air Force Base
ALCE   Airlift Control Element
AR   armed reconnaissance
ASAP   as soon as possible
AWACS   Airborne Warning and Control System
AWS   USAF Air Weather Service

BIM   Blade Inspection Method. Warns pilot there may be a problem with rotor
    blade
bird   Airplane or helicopter
blivet   fuel bladder

C-9   jetliner equipped for medical evacuation (Nightingale)
C-130   four-engine turboprop tactical transport (Hercules)
C-141   Lockheed Starlifter four-engine jet transport
CAS   close air support
CCT   combat control team
CH-47   twin-engine, twin-rotor Army helicopter used for personnel and equip-
    ment (Chinook)
CH-53/H-53   twin-engine, single-rotor Air Force, Navy, and Marine heli-
    copter used to haul personnel and equipment (Sea Stallion)
chopper   helicopter
Chemlite   luminescent chemical light
CINCEUR   Commander in Chief Europe
CINCLANT   Commander in Chief Atlantic
CINCPAC   Commander in Chief Pacific
CNO   Chief of Naval Operations
COMALF   MAC term for Commander of Airlift
Combat Talon   MC-130 specially equipped for SOF missions
COMJTF   Commander Joint Task Force

COMM   communications equipment
COMSEC   communications security
CONUS   Continental United States
CP   command post

DIA   Defense Intelligence Agency
DOD   Department of Defense

Eagle Claw   operational code name of rescue mission
EC-130   equipped with a removable command-and-control capsule (*see* **ABCCC**)

F-4   two-engine, afterburner-equipped jet fighter used extensively in Vietnam (Phantom)
Farsi   Iranian language
FLIR   forward-looking infrared sensor

GSG-9   German counterterrorism unit
gunship   AC-130/AC-130H

haboob   suspended-dust phenomenon in Iran
HC-130   search-and-rescue version of C-130, used to refuel certain types of helicopters in flight
helo   helicopter
Hercules   (*see* **C-130**)
HF   high frequency radio
HH-53   search-and-rescue version of the H-53
HH-53H   search-and-rescue helicopter transferred to Special Operations and redesignated MH-53H (*see* **Pave Low**)
Huey   UH-1N twin-engine jet helicopter
humint   human intelligence reporting

interdiction   disrupt or destroy enemy's military potential

JCS   Joint Chiefs of Staff
JCS/SOD   Joint Chiefs of Staff/Special Operations Division
JCSE   Joint Communications Support Element
JTF   Joint Task Force
JUWTF   Joint Unconventional Warfare Task Force

KC-135   four-engine jet tanker used for in-flight refueling (similar to Boeing 707 airliner)
Klong   nickname for the C-130 airlift shuttle from Vietnam War

laager   helicopter hide site in Iran
LIC   low-intensity conflict

LPH, LHA   ships specially designed to carry Marine helicopters, landing craft, and troops

LZ   landing zone

MAAG   Military Assistance and Advisory Group

MAC   Military Airlift Command

MACV   Military Assistance Command Vietnam

MACV-SOG   Military Assistance Command Vietnam Studies and Observation Group

MC-130   C-130 specially equipped for low-level flying (*see* **Combat Talon**)

medevac   medical evacuation

NVGs   night-vision goggles

OPG   Operations Planning Group

PACAF   Pacific Air Forces

PACOM   Pacific Command

Pasdaran   Iranian Revolutionary Guard

Pathfinder   C-130 that leads helicopters

Pave Low   Air Force HH-53H helicopter equipped with terrain-following radar and forward-looking infrared

PINS   Palletized Inertial Navigation System

PLO   Palestine Liberation Organization

radar altimeter   measures height of aircraft above the ground

RDJTF   Rapid Deployment Joint Task Force

recce   reconnaissance

REDCOM   U.S. Readiness Command

RH-53/RH-53D   Navy version of the H-53, used for mine countermeasures

Rice Bowl   cover name for Iran rescue mission

SAR   search and rescue

SATCOM   satellite communications

SEAL   Sea, Air, and Land team of the U.S. Navy

SFers   Special Forces personnel

snake eaters   nickname for Special Operators

SOAF   Sultan of Oman's Air Force

SOF   Special Operations Forces

SOS   Special Operations Squadron

SOW   Special Operations Wing

Spectre   AC-130 gunship

TAC   Tactical Air Command

TACAN   tactical air navigation aid

TF   terrain-following radar

UHF   ultra-high frequency radio
UW   unconventional warfare tactics used by SOF

VFR   visual flight rules
VHF   very high frequency radio

ACKNOWLEDGMENTS

There are many people to whom I owe gratitude for the evolution and completion of this project.

First, I am deeply indebted to many of my compatriots from the Iran rescue mission for their unwavering support and assistance in making the story as accurate as possible.

Then there are the contributions of those who provided the expertise and skills that transformed this effort from a manuscript that most likely would be collecting dust in the archives of the Library of Congress to a published accounting of a true story that needed to be told:

V. J. Adkins, a close friend of the family, deciphered my initial handwritten drafts and produced the first coherent typewritten copy of the manuscript. Audrey Milton, wife of Colonel Hugh Milton, one of the best USAF fighter jocks ever to strap in, took it from there and became my chief confidante and critic. She introduced me to the world of computer word processing and with enthusiasm and persistence edited reams of copy and brought new meaning and insight to the story. Sadly, Audrey died before the project was completed.

However, it was becoming apparent that a professional editor was needed to make the manuscript marketable. That's when John Eidson entered the picture. John, a lifelong friend from my early days in Kansas, has been a newspaper editor for twenty-plus years and before that was an information officer and a navigator in the Air Force. He threw himself tirelessly into the story, working nights, weekends, and vacations to breathe new life into the story. His reorganization of the chapters and his perceptive writing put the story on track.

Through it all, my wife, Eunice, provided enduring moral support and helpful "reader's insights," and she patiently shared the frustrations that continually arose during the struggle to get the book published. Also, John's wife, Kathy, was a gracious hostess and stalwart supporter during the long writing and rewriting sessions at the Eidsons' home.

Next was the good fortune of being given a hand by Arthur T. Hadley, author of *The Straw Giant*, who helped me get the manuscript to Bob Loomis, executive editor at Random House. Bob provided the guidance that resulted in the streamlined version of the story.

At Orion Books, where the first edition was published, the text was placed in the hands of Carl Apollonio, an aviation buff in his own right, who shepherded it through the necessary wickets to meet the publication schedule. Steve Topping, Jim Wade, Pam Stinson, Nancy Maynes, and Deborah Rowley combined their multiple talents to put just the right touch on the finished product. Special thanks go to Deb for her patience with me through the give-and-take of the final trimming process, preserving as much detail as possible. Her quick wit, sense of humor, and mastery of aviators' jargon and Special Operations terms made it fun work.

This new edition is due to the interest and effort of Bob Fessler, Lt. Colonel, USAF (Ret.) who worked for me at HQ PACAF and now runs Primer Publishers.

This was truly a team effort.

INDEX

ABCCC *see* EC-130 ABCCC aircraft
ABC News, 193
AC-130 Spectre gunship, 72–73, 77
accident, Desert-I, 331–338
   Carney and, 332, 335, 337
   casualties in, 344, 346
   classified documents in, 337–338
   explosions in, 333, 335
   helicopters damaged in, 336–337
   Kyle and, 331–338
   Marine pilots and, 337, 338*n*
   Schaefer and, 332, 335
   Seiffert and, 335, 337*n*, 338*n*
advisory panel, 366
aerial refueling, 90–92
After Action Report, 364
Air America, 195
Air Force Special Operations Command, 27*n*
Airlift Control Element (ALCE), 232
air strike at Desert-1, proposed, 341–342, 347
Air Weather Service, 260*n*, 369–370
Allen, Lewis, 356
Andre, Pete, 98–99, 112
Arab League, 53
Arlington National Cemetery, 316
Armed Forces Journal, 355*n*

Bancroft, Sergeant, 334
Bani-Sadr, Abolhassan, 166, 188, 193
Barkett, John, 118, 136–137
Barton, Jerry, 280, 312, 314, 323
Batson, Bill, 91
Beckwith, Charlie A., 21, 26, 30, 37–38, 54, 69, 74, 83, 85, 100,
101, 103–104, 111, 123, 142, 143, 181, 185, 187, 356, 384
   abort decision, 328–330
   agenda of, 71–73
   attack plan and, 160–161
   barnstorming pilots preferred by, 95, 96
   call sign of, 253
   Carney and, 109–110
   Carter's briefing and, 223
   Carter's views on mission failure and, 355
   Christmas hiatus concern of, 135*n*
   CIA agent's information doubted by, 160
   in congressional hearings, 358, 360, 366
   deployment of, 258–259
   Desert-I arrival of, 292
   Helo No. 2 abort as seen by, 324
   hostage-location intelligence and, 245, 259
   Kyle and, 295–298, 316–322, 324–326
   Kyle met by, 66
   Meadows and, 312, 342
   in Night-Two plan, 205, 207–208
   one-night operation opposed by, 147, 165
   press conference of, 354–355
   in rescue mission, 266–268, 292, 295–298, 311, 312, 319, 321, 322, 324–326
   riot gas directive and, 259*n*
   roadblock teams and, 213, 243–244, 255

SATCOM system of, 253
Schaeffer and, 316–317
Seiffert and, 322
supply system of, 67
Vaught and, 69–70
Wicker and, 259
Beheshti, Ayatollah Mohammed, 149
Beres, Tom, 345
Beyers, Joseph, 4, 334
Blade Inspection Method (BIM), 131, 215n, 282, 366
in mission analysis, 376–377
Blue Ribbon Special Operations Review Group, 362
Bob (CIA agent), 151, 160, 173, 242n
Brazil, Doug, 13–14
Brenci, Bob, 88, 109, 130, 150, 151, 266–268, 270, 273, 290–291
Brown, Harold, 252, 330–331
Bryan, Mitch, 290, 310
Brzezinski, Zbigniew, 39, 189n, 199n, 223, 330–331
Buchanan, Don, 137, 194, 253, 260, 265, 294, 353, 358
"Bumpkin" (liaison officer), 99
Burruss, Bucky, 25, 37, 109, 164, 173, 174, 180, 259n
Butterfield, John A., 254

C-9 Nightingale aircraft, 341
C-130 Hercules aircraft, 46
altimeters of, 151
crew selection of, 88–89
deployment of, 231–234, 236, 238–239
modifications of, 89–90
in Night-One plan, 202–203
in Night-Two plan, 203, 208
in rescue mission, 269–277, 285, 295, 299, 314, 315
restarting situations and, 131n
shortage of, 27
training and, 84, 225
C-141 Starlifter aircraft, 153, 167–168, 225, 347–348
in final rehearsal, 212
in Night-One rehearsal, 185
in Night-Two plan, 204, 208
in Night-Two rehearsal, 186

call signs, 252–253, 261
Carlucci, Frank, 174
Carney, John, 3, 71–72, 105, 107, 109, 163, 181, 193–194, 262, 281
Beckwith and, 109–110
at congressional hearings, 358
debriefing of, 348
deployment of, 232, 236, 238
Desert-I accident and, 332, 335, 337
Desert-I recon mission of, 189, 195–197
Desert-I withdrawal and, 339, 341, 343
in final rehearsal, 213–215
at JTF commander conference, 201
Kyle and, 3, 213, 307, 308, 310, 318, 321, 323, 329, 332, 337, 343, 348
landing problem solved by, 187
at Masirah, 247
in rescue mission, 267, 281, 290, 291, 299, 307, 309, 310, 318, 319, 321, 323, 329
Carrier Task Force 70, 55
Carter, Hodding, 32
Carter, Jimmy, xi, 1, 18, 39, 45, 49, 55n, 63, 65, 70n, 72, 74, 81, 86, 93, 120, 182, 183, 188, 192, 193, 223–224, 248, 259n, 327, 355
abort decision and, 331
Beckwith and, 223, 355
Camp Smokey visit of, 355
Desert-I recon mission approved by, 189n
Desert-I recon mission initially rejected by, 166, 177
Iranian diplomats expelled by, 198
JTF deployment approved by, 227
at memorial service, 361–362
in mission analysis, 383–384
mission approved by, 223, 360
on rescue mission, 375
rescue mission ordered by, 199–200
casualties, 341
in Desert-I accident, 344, 346
expected, 223
Central Intelligence Agency (CIA), 37, 42, 48, 52, 85, 104, 121, 122, 151–152, 164, 170, 173, 174,

183, 189, 197*n*, 206, 264, 347*n*, 357, 381*n*
  agents lacked by, 43
  casualty estimates by, 223*n*
  Desert-I recon mission and, 189, 190, 195, 228
  hostage location and, 244
  infrared paper supplied by, 122
  Teheran agent of, 146*n*, 160
Chapman, Clay, 290
Christmas hiatus, 134–135
classified documents, 347*n*, 360–361
  abandonment of, 337–338
  composition of, 347
  Pitman and, 361*n*
  Seiffert and, 361*n*
Collins, Bill, 19, 24, 75
combat control teams, 71*n*, 292, 296, 310, 319, 328, 332–333, 338
command and control, 371–374
command lines, 315*n*
communications, 6, 225, 253, 297–298, 309
  call signs and, 252–253, 261
  code words and, 261
  in mission analysis, 371–375
Congress, U.S., 27, 182, 349, 359
Contiguglia, Captain, 237, 346
Coral Sea Battle Group, 258
cover and deception (C&D) tactics, 64, 227

Daigenault, Tom, 123
Datson (Senate aide), 357
Davis, Rodney, 302–306, 311, 322, 331
"Death at Desert One" (Fitch), 334*n*
debriefing, 348
Defense Communications Agency, 43
Defense Department, U.S. (DOD), 43, 363
Defense Intelligence Agency (DIA), 42, 57, 114, 175
Defense Mapping Agency, 43
Defense Meteorological Satellite Program, 260*n*
Delta Force, 42, 52, 67, 90, 152, 187, 242
  casualties of, 344

deployment of, 237–238, 240, 251, 252, 257–259
  described, 34
  equipment of, 257
  force increase of, 101–102
  housing of, 254
  Iran intelligence acquired by, 191–192
  Masirah option favored by, 174
  in Night-One plan, 202, 203
  in Night-One rehearsals, 132, 185
  in Night-Two plan, 205–208
  in Night-Two rehearsals, 132–133
  radio operators of, 162
  religious service held by, 251
  in rescue mission, 266–267, 292, 293, 309, 310, 319, 325–327, 333
  training of, 83, 84, 225
  in Yuma exercise, 106, 107, 111, 113
Delta Force (Beckwith), 223
deployment, 219–249
  of Beckwith, 258–259
  of C-130 aircraft, 231–234, 236, 238–239
  of Carney, 232, 236, 238
  Carter briefed on, 223
  Carter's approval of, 227
  cover and deception in, 227, 229
  of Delta Force, 237–238, 240, 251, 252, 257–259
  JCS briefing on, 222
  of Keating, 233
  of maintenance staff, 234
  meeting on, 220–221
  operational "footprint" for, 228
  of Pitman, 233
  of Rangers, 240, 243
  schedule of, 229–230
  sniffer dog incident and, 233
  of Turczynski, 231–234
Desert-I, xi, 1–9, 159, 164
  accident at, *see* accident, Desert-I
  advance team landing at, 290–293
  Beckwith's arrival at, 292
  Carney's recon mission to, 189, 195–197
  command situation at, 319
  final rehearsal for, 212–215
  JTF requirements and, 163–164

location of, 152
Schaefer's landing at, 314–315
withdrawal from, *see* withdrawal,
Desert-I
Desert-II, 159
Dieck, Pete, 66, 80, 114, 153, 162, 212,
232, 252, 261
Diggins, Bill, 335
Doyle, Ray, 5, 110
Dunwoody, Dick, 23–24, 32–34, 61,
75, 76, 91
dust clouds (haboobs), 201*n*, 278, 280,
287, 298, 299–301, 303, 304,
313, 321*n*, 357, 364–365
cause of, 281
in mission analysis, 369–374
Dutton, Bob, 65, 99, 112, 142, 162, 175
"murder board" conducted by,
210–211

Eagle call sign, 253
Eagle Claw, Operation, *see* rescue
mission
EC-130 ABCCC aircraft, 149–150,
170–171, 198, 221
8th Special Operations Squadron, 9*n*
Embassy, U.S.:
CIA agent's information on, 152,
160, 173, 191–192
Special Forces agents at, 191–192
takeover of, 13, 15, 41
see also rescue mission
Emerson, Steven, 244*n*
European Common Market, 250

"Failed Mission, The" (Brzezinski),
189*n*, 200*n*, 330*n*
Farsi linguists, 254, 293
Federal Bureau of Investigation (FBI),
42
Ferkes, George, 274, 290
Fez airfield plan, 141–144
1st Special Operations Squadron, 84,
167
1st Special Operations Wing, 23, 167
inventory of, 24
Fitch, Logan, 293, 334*n*
Fleming, Steve, 271, 275, 295, 309,
310, 343

flight planning, 381–383
Flintlock exercise, 235
Foley, Bill, 90, 108, 110, 123, 253
Foreign Affairs, Iranian Ministry of, 85,
147, 191, 208, 242, 271*n*
Foreman call sign, 252, 266
Forgan, Dave, 148, 221, 227, 240
forward-looking infrared (FLIR), 145,
164, 278, 280, 290, 295, 371
Fred (intelligence agent), 192, 201*n*,
238, 242, 347
Fulton Recovery System, 177–179, 228

Gabriel, Richard A., 36*n*, 83*n*, 102*n*,
131*n*, 197*n*, 223*n*, 325*n*
Gadd, Dick, 62
Gallagher, John, 76–78, 81, 105, 107,
185
Galloway, Sam, 278, 290–291
Gast, Philip C., 5, 7, 65, 85, 96, 102,
105, 112, 113, 121, 140, 151,
167, 223, 261–262, 348, 349
call sign of, 252
Carter's briefing and, 222, 223
at congressional hearings, 358
criticism of, 363
Desert-I withdrawal and, 341
head count by, 346
at JCS special briefing, 222
Kyle's briefing of, 198
Masirah arrival of, 257
on "murder board," 162
rescue mission and, 294, 311
Gerke, John, 248
Ghotbzadeh, Sadegh, 105, 129, 141,
193
Gilbert, Chuck, 50, 102, 105, 121, 122,
164–165, 170, 233, 255, 263,
268, 275, 290, 381*n*
Gingrich, Randy, 335
Glenn, John, 358
Godowski, John, 97–98, 110, 153, 185,
188
Golden BB Option, 75–77
Goldwater, Barry, 359, 363
Gonzales, Bud, 109
Gonzales, Pancho, 342
Goodloe, Van, 67, 87, 93, 94, 96, 121,
151, 156–157

Gorsky, Paul, 51, 58, 147, 194
Graham, Daniel O., 114
Gravel Pit call sign, 252, 267, 272
GSG-9 Border Guards, West German, 40, 50n, 67
Guidry, Roland, 8, 114, 119, 120, 123, 150, 163, 170, 180–181, 269, 278, 280, 290, 292, 297, 310, 358, 361

Habib (Iranian militant), 210
Habibi, Hassan, 219
haboobs, *see* dust clouds
Hadley, Arthur T., 28n, 131n, 301n, 309n
Hall, Sam, 234, 254, 267
Hansen, Thor, 37
Harrison, Jeff, 334
Hatcher, Jerry, 56, 69, 94–96, 102
Hayward, Thomas, 189, 354
helicopters, 70–71, 93, 102, 151, 158, 264
    abandoned, 341
    crew selection for, 69
    damage to, 336–337
    in Desert-I accident, 336–337
    in final rehearsal, 214–215
    fire foam incident and, 246
    maintenance and condition of, 156–157, 176–177, 190, 199, 245, 326
    Marine pilots of, 133, 139–140, 183, 321, 347, 376
    Navy pilots of, 94–96, 112, 376
    Navy responsibility for, 177, 190, 326
    in Night-One plan, 202–203
    in Night-Two plan, 206–208
    preparation of, 255
    in rescue mission, 268, 270–272, 275–277, 282–287, 299–306, 311, 313
    Sikorsky advisors and, 233, 377
    in Yuma exercise, 108–110
Hess, Ginny, 14
Hess, Lee, 13–15, 18–19, 23, 36–37, 51, 58, 62, 76, 82, 89, 100, 136, 137, 142, 147, 166–167, 170–171, 173, 221, 222, 229, 280, 312–314, 353

HH-53H Pave Low helicopter, 254
Hoff, Bill, 255, 282, 311, 318, 322, 331
Holloway, James L., 224n
Holloway Commission, 40n, 131n, 161n, 224n, 369, 375–378
    abort decisions criticized by, 376–378
    establishment of, 363
    findings of, 364–365
    purpose of, 367
    recommendations of, 366
Horton, Bob, 20, 84, 143, 144, 148, 220
hostage rescue, *see* rescue mission
House Armed Services Committee, 361
House of Representatives, U.S., 356
Huyser, "Dutch," 65

in-flight refueling, 36
infrared-lighting techniques, 122, 129
intelligence:
    on hostages' location, 244–245
    Kilgore's estimate of, 201
    lack of, 29, 42–43, 51, 101
    Soviet, 55–56, 219, 227, 240, 258
    Special Forces and, 191–192
International Red Cross, 227
Iran:
    Iraq threatened by, 210
    Red Cross and, 227
    U.S. freeze on assets of, 63–64
    weather data on, 137
Iran-Contra affair, 357n
Iran Rescue Mission, The (Ryan), 40n
Iran Task Force, *see* Joint Task Force
Iraq, 210
Ishimoto, Wade, 244, 296

Jackson, Henry, 359
JCS, *see* Joint Chiefs of Staff
Jerome, Bill, 150, 310–311
Johnson, Jesse, 244, 293, 296, 319, 329, 339
Joint Chiefs of Staff (JCS), 19–22, 28, 75, 94, 224n, 226n, 362, 366
    deployment briefing of, 222
    Vaught's briefing of, 189–190
Joint Communications Support Element, 66, 162, 252
Joint Task Force (JTF), 374n
    After Action Report of, 364

Christmas hiatus and, 134–135
commander conference of, 201–209
communications system of, 153–154,
162–163
criticism of, 161*n*, 362, 364–365
Desert-I and requirements of, 163
diplomatic situation and, 155
finances of, 67*n*
first meeting of, 37–43
Iranian defenses assessed by, 53–54
Kyle's role in, 21
launch platform selected by, 55–56
logistics officer of, 118
organizational structure of, 21–22
premission achievement of, 225–226
satellite communications and,
211–212
training tasks of, 83–85
withdrawal of, 339–345
Joint Unconventional Warfare Task
Force, 22
Jonathan, Operation, 50*n*
Jones, David C., 19, 28, 39–41, 55, 57,
70–72, 75, 77, 78, 87, 139–140,
146*n*, 155, 159, 166, 167, 181,
183, 188, 189, 195, 199, 200,
234, 283, 354, 366
air strike proposal and, 342
Carter's briefing and, 223
criticism of, 363
JCS special briefing and, 222
rehearsal visit of, 187
security emphasized by, 38
Vaught and, 256, 330, 331
JTF, *see* Joint Task Force
Jubelt, Marty, 150, 271, 307–309
Justice Department, U.S., 63

Keating, Jim, 99, 134*n*, 142, 162, 344,
361*n*
deployment of, 233
Long briefed by, 233
"murder board" conducted by,
210–211
Kelley, Jim, 266, 348
Kelly, P. X., 167*n*
Khomeini, Ayatollah Ruhollah, 32, 41,
48, 53, 63, 65, 75, 114, 129,
136, 182, 193, 198

Kilgore, Nick, 20–21, 28–29, 37, 47,
48, 51, 117, 142, 144–146,
159–160, 169, 244, 251
at JTF commander conference, 201
Kimsey, Woody, 138
Kindle, Buie, 124, 248
King, Jerry, 20–22, 28, 29, 35, 37, 39,
40, 49, 66*n*, 84–85, 89, 98, 117,
118, 136, 142, 173, 175,
219–221, 236, 243, 265, 353
at congressional hearings, 358
Desert-I withdrawal and, 341
flow charts of, 229
Kyle and, 190–192, 194, 222
rescue mission and, 283, 294, 313,
314
Kingston, Bob, 35
Kitty Hawk, 71, 74, 93–94, 102, 122*n*,
151
Klong airlift shuttle, 235, 254
Kornitzer, Bill, 232
Kyle, Eunice, 15, 16, 354
Kyle, James H., 102*n*
Air Force pilots recommended by,
137–139
air strike proposed by, 341
background and experience of, 33–34
Beckwith and, 295–298, 316–322,
324–326
Beckwith met by, 66
C-130 pilots and, 256
Carney and, 3, 213, 307, 308, 310,
318, 321, 323, 329, 332, 337,
343, 348
Desert-I accident and, 331–338
Desert-I withdrawal and, 339,
342–345
Gast briefed by, 198
JTF role of, 21
Kelley's debriefing of, 348
King and, 190–192, 194, 222
one-night operation proposed by, 147
pilots reprimanded by, 119
in rescue mission, 278–282,
284–285, 290–293, 295–299,
307–311, 315–327
Taylor and, 30, 75–77, 91, 96, 140
training and, 84
Vaught and, 32–34, 193–194, 224

Vaught's debriefing of, 354
Wadi Kena arrival of, 236

Laingen, Bruce, 48, 85, 147, 208, 271*n*
Lamonica, John, 90
Lang, Bill, 268
Lawrence, Bob, 234, 254, 267
Lawrence, Paul, 334–335
Lewis, Hal, 7, 309, 310, 314, 321, 323,
331–333, 337, 349
confirmed as fatality, 346
Linderman, Jimmy, 282, 284, 299–300,
311, 313, 317, 361
Linkey, Don, 334
Littlejohn, David R., 254
Long, Robert, 71, 134*n*, 233
briefing of, 233
Luigi (CIA source), 244, 245, 259

McClain, James, 334
McFarlane, Robert, 357, 360, 362
McGuire, B. J., 286, 288, 299, 303,
311, 313, 318, 321, 323, 324
Manor, LeRoy J., 82
Marine Amphibious Group, 200
Masirah, 168–169, 180, 183, 246–247
approval of, 193
Masirah suggested by, 168–169
Mattingly, Bob, 175, 258, 260–263,
356, 361
Masirah suggested by, 168–169
Meadows, Dick, 37, 253, 312, 317,
321, 338*n*, 342, 347, 384
Beckwith and, 312, 342
as intelligence agent, 192, 201*n*, 203,
205, 238, 242, 243
Meller, Bob, 130, 150, 214
memorial service, 361–362
Meyer, Edward, 22, 23, 28, 30, 356
Carter's briefing and, 222
initial briefing of, 24–25
Vaught recommended by, 35
Michaels, Ron, 98, 147–148, 188, 236,
243
Midway, 94
Military Airlift Command, 27*n*, 153,
283, 341
Military Incompetence (Gabriel), 36*n*,
83*n*, 325*n*
Milton, Hugh, 231

mission analysis, 368–384
BIM abort in, 376–377
Carter in, 383–384
command and control in, 371,
373–374
communications in, 371–375
dust encounter in, 369–374
flight planning in, 381–383
Helo No. 2 abort in, 379–380
Helo No. 5 abort in, 377–379
Marines in, 379, 380
Omega systems in, 381
pilot abort decisions in, 375–376
PINS equipment in, 381
radio silence in, 372, 373, 378
SATCOM system in, 372
tactical restrictions in, 380–381
Vaught in, 370, 374, 379, 383
weather forecast in, 369–371
Mobile Fuels Detachment, 150
Mohammed Reza Shah Pahlavi, 48, 63,
144, 145, 188
morale, 155
"murder board," 161–162, 210–211, 366

National Command Authority, 87
National Security Agency (NSA),
42–43, 248, 252
NATO, 120
Neff, Bob, 353
New York Times Magazine, 189*n*, 199*n*,
330*n*
Nightengale, Keith, 122
Night-One scenario, 96–97, 100–101,
169
plan of, 202–203
rehearsals of, 129–133, 155, 184–185
Night-Two scenario, 115–116, 168
plan of, 203–209
rehearsals of, 132–133, 155, 185–186
night-vision goggles, 87, 88, 115, 141,
167
Nimitz, 151, 156, 157, 176, 177, 190,
199, 202, 220, 233, 245, 252,
256, 258, 260, 261, 264*n*,
269–271, 275, 282, 304, 311,
316, 322, 326, 328, 329, 332,
344, 347, 377, 382
Nunn, Sam, 360

Oldfield, Barney, 301, 311, 314, 315, 332
Oliver, Ken, 90, 124, 162, 170, 180, 183, 248, 353
Omega navigation system, 151, 275, 281, 304, 371, 381
O'Neill, Stuart, 335
one-night operation concept, 147, 165
Operations Planning Group, 59, 76, 154*n*, 221, 227, 240
Ornament, codeword, 185
Otis, Glenn, 24
Owen, Robert B., 182

Palestine Liberation Organization (PLO), 50*n*, 52
Palletized Inertial Navigation System (PINS), 121–122, 151, 233, 255, 268, 272, 275, 279, 281, 304, 371, 381
Pars news agency, 172
Penthouse, 334n
Perot, Ross, 42
Petty, Leslie, 335
pilots:
  abort decisions of, 375–376
  Beckwith's preference in, 95, 96
  briefing of, 260–264
  Desert-I accident and, 337–338, 338*n*
  Kyle and, 119, 256
  Marine, 133, 139–140, 183, 321, 347, 376
  Navy, 94–96, 112, 376
  Vaught and, 140
Pinard, Bob, 114, 171
Pitman, Chuck, 56, 68, 69, 94, 102, 112, 113, 121, 140*n*, 156–157, 177, 186, 200, 219, 281, 330*n*, 379*n*
  classified documents and, 361*n*
  at congressional hearings, 358
  deployment of, 233
  final rehearsal and, 214
  Kyle and, 212, 220, 248
  launch schedule and, 256–257, 269
  Long briefed by, 233
  radio procedures and, 184
  in rescue mission, 271, 303–305, 316, 322, 331

in return to *Nimitz,* 344
SATCOM system of, 253
secure radios and, 246
PLO, *see* Palestine Liberation Organization
Postles, Lt. Colonel, 237, 250, 268*n*, 346
Powell, Jody, 250
"President Courage" (Schemmer), 355*n*
press conference, 354–355
Purser, Wayne, 154, 170, 254
Pustay, John S., 57

Quinn, Jim, 76

radar, 168, 261, 263, 274*n*, 275, 365
  Desert-1 recon mission and, 196*n*, 263
radio procedures, 184
radio silence, 279, 279*n*, 283, 285, 301, 356–357
  in mission analysis, 372, 373, 378
Rafsanjani, Akbar Hashemi, 159
Rakip, Captain, 212–213
Rangers, U.S., 71, 72, 90, 153, 253, 254
  deployment of, 240, 243
  in Night-One plan, 202
  in Night-One rehearsal, 130
  Night-One training of, 132
  in Night-Two plan, 203, 204, 208
  Night-Two training of, 115–117, 132, 133, 186
  in rescue mission, 312
  training of, 84, 225
Rapid Deployment Joint Task Force (RDJTF), 167, 167*n*, 187
Readiness Command Counterterrorism Task Force, 20
Reagan, Ronald, 357*n*
Reckermer, Dave, 59, 194
reconnaissance mission, Desert-1, 177, 189–190, 194–197, 228, 383
  radar and, 196*n*, 263
  Vaught and, 166, 170–171
Red Barn call sign, 252
Red Eye missile, 259, 328*n*
remote runway lighting device, 183
rescue mission:
  accident in, *see* accident, Desert-1

advance team landing in, 290–293
backup tankers scrambled in, 314
Beckwith in, 266–268, 292, 295–298, 311, 312, 319, 321, 322, 324–326
BIM warning in, 282
bus stopped in, 292–293
C-130 aircraft in, 269–277, 285, 295, 299, 314, 315
call signs in, 252–253
Carney in, 267, 281, 290, 291, 299, 307, 309, 310, 318, 319, 321, 323, 329
Carter on, 375
Carter's approval of, 223, 360
combat control teams in, 292, 296, 310, 319, 328, 332–333, 338
command and control network for, 252
command lines in, 315n
communications in, 6, 225, 253, 297–298, 309
congressional hearings on, 357–361
Delta Force in, 266–267, 292, 293, 309, 310, 319, 325–327, 333
distances problem in, 36
dust clouds in, 278–282, 287, 298, 300, 303, 305, 310, 313, 321n, 329
Farsi linguists in, 254, 293
gasoline truck explosion in, 296–297
Gast and, 294, 311
helicopter pilots briefed for, 260–264
helicopters in, 268, 270–272, 275–277, 282–287, 299–306, 311, 313
Helo No. 2 aborted in, 324–325, 328
Helo No. 5 aborted in, 305–306
Helo No. 6 abandoned in, 282
Iranian coast penetrated in, 272, 277
Iranian listening post during, 280
Iranian radar and, 168, 263, 274n, 365
King and, 283, 294, 313, 314
Kyle in, 278–282, 284–285, 290–293, 295–299, 307–311, 315–327
Night-One plan of, 202–203
Night-Two plan of, 203–209
onset of, 266–268

Pitman in, 271, 303–305, 316, 322, 331
radio silence in, 279, 279n, 283, 285, 301, 356–357
Rangers in, 312
roadblock teams in, 292–293, 296–297, 319, 328–329
route planning in, 58–59
SATCOM in, 284n, 285, 288, 293, 297–299, 306n, 307, 309, 311, 319, 322–324, 326
Schaefer in, 299, 301, 306, 311, 314–317
security and, 38
Seiffert in, 269, 271, 272, 275–277, 282–287, 294, 299–300, 311, 315–322, 324, 325
Son Tay Raiders compared with, 82–83, 86–87
Soviet intelligence and, 55–56, 219, 227, 240, 258
Vaught and, 294, 300, 312, 313, 315n, 317, 322, 326, 327
weather forecasts for, 201, 260–261, 278, 281
see also deployment; Desert-1; Joint Task Force; mission analysis
Revolutionary Council, 149, 172, 193, 219
RH-53D Sea Stallion helicopter:
BIM warning and, 131, 215n, 282
capacity of, 56
Marine and Navy versions of, 67, 131, 377
PINS equipment of, 233, 255, 268, 272, 275, 279, 371, 381
Rice Bowl, Operation, *see* rescue mission
riot gas, 259n
Rivers, Gayle, 70n
roadblock teams, 258, 267, 319
Beckwith and, 213, 243–244, 255
bus stopped by, 292–293
gasoline truck and, 296–297
Roberts, John, 139n
Robertson, Robbie, 171
Rodriguez, Pancho, 173
Rotor & Wing International, 379n

route planning, 58–59
rules of engagement, 223
Ryan, Paul B., 40*n*, 131*n*, 224*n*, 226*n*, 337*n*

Sadat, Anwar, 47
Sanchez, Taco, 108, 110, 133, 266
SATCOM system, 225, 253, 261, 284*n*, 285, 288, 293, 297–299, 306*n*, 307, 309, 311, 319, 322–324, 326, 342, 344, 357
  in mission analysis, 372–373
Schaefer, Jim, 3, 7, 94, 112, 113, 121, 177, 246
  abort favored by, 317
  Beckwith and, 316–317
  briefing by, 260
  Desert-1 accident and, 332, 335
  Desert-1 landing of, 314–315
  Nimitz visited by, 200
  in rescue mission, 299, 301, 306, 311, 314–317
Schemmer, Benjamin F., 355*n*
Schoultz, "Dutch," 37, 41
search-and-rescue plan (SAR), 254
2nd Infantry Division, U.S., 35
Secord, Richard, 167*n*
Secret Warriors (Emerson), 244*n*
security, 69, 199, 226*n*
  ABCCC aircraft and, 150
  breach in, 94
  Christmas hiatus and, 134–135
  criticism of, 364
  Jones's emphasis on, 38
  rescue mission and, 38
  training and, 85, 225–226
Seiffert, Ed, 121, 131–133, 248*n*, 253*n*, 281, 298, 354, 356–357
  abort decision and, 328–330
  Beckwith and, 322
  classified documents and, 361*n*
  in congressional hearings, 358
  Desert-I accident and, 335, 337, 337*n*, 338*n*
  Helo No. 2 ordered aborted by, 324–325
  radio procedures and, 184
  in rescue mission, 269, 271, 272, 275–277, 282–287, 294,

299–300, 311, 315–322, 324, 325
  SATCOM system of, 253
Senate, U.S., 356
Senate Armed Services Committee, 358–359, 362, 366
7th Air Force, 33
7th Special Operations Squadron, 228
Sheppard, Jack, 15–16
Sherwood, Larry, 156, 157, 177
Shutler, Philip, 37, 68, 134, 140*n*
Sikorsky advisors, 233, 377
Simons, Arthur D. "Bull," 42
1606th Air Base Wing, 15
Smith, Les, 51, 58, 61, 88, 107, 114, 147
  transfer of, 167
sniffer dog incident, 233
Soviet intelligence, 55–56, 219, 227, 240, 258
Special Air Services (SAS), British, 40, 67, 70*n*
Special Operations, 26–27, 27*n*, 363
  career opportunities and, 28
  combat controllers of, 71*n*
  command lines in, 315*n*
  cover and deception tactic of, 64
  Flintlock exercise of, 235
  foreign, 40, 50*n*, 67, 70*n*
  Holloway Commission and, 366
  logistics officer and, 118*n*
  Tehran embassy reconnoitered by, 191–192
Special Projects Office, 162, 180
State Department, U.S., 45, 48
  information exchange and, 85*n*
  military option opposed by, 39, 171
  Thatcher briefed by, 237*n*
  warning ignored by, 48
Stennis, John, 358
Stoles, "Pappy," 65
Straw Giant, The (Hadley), 28*n*, 309*n*
Sullivan, William, 65*n*
surprise, advantage of, 29, 77

Tactical Air Command (TAC), 27
tactical restrictions, 380–381
Takacs, Bill, 138, 213
Taylor, Bob, 14, 16, 23, 29, 37, 76, 138
  Kyle and, 30, 75–77, 91, 94, 140

transfer of, 167, 167n

Tehran Radio, 13, 141, 172, 193, 219

Tharp, Russ, 214, 309–310, 343, 344, 346

Thatcher, Margaret, 237n

Thurmond, Strom, 359

Time, 64, 197n

Times (London), 70n

timing discrepancy, 382

Tisdale, Tyrone, 293

Today Show, 210

Toth, Rod, 228

Train, Harry, 70–71

training:
  in aerial refueling, 90–92
  Christmas hiatus in, 134–135
  extent of, 224–225
  in Night-One scenario, 96–97, 132
  in Night-Two scenario, 115–118, 132, 185–186
  in night vision, 87–88
  of Rangers, 84, 225
  scenario for, 80
  security and, 85, 225–226
  Vaught and, 84, 85, 110–112, 118–119, 124, 177–179
  Yuma exercise and, 100–101

Turczynski, Ray, 89, 91, 115, 141, 145, 150, 167, 180, 220, 221
  deployment of, 231–234

Turner, Stansfield, 43, 104

20th Special Operations Squadron (helicopter), 139n

UH-1 (Huey) helicopter, 165

Ulery, Doug, 51, 58, 147, 194, 312

Unconventional Warfare Branch, 19, 21–22, 85

United Nations, 82, 159, 166, 172, 182

United Press International, 362

United States:
  Iranian assets frozen by, 63–64
  Iranian student crackdown by, 63
  public mood in, 182

Uttaro, Jerry, 5, 130, 150, 272, 275, 310, 324, 333, 335, 343

Vance, Cyrus, 120, 198

Vaught, James B., 5, 22, 23, 26, 38, 46, 50, 57, 66, 75, 87, 89, 95–97, 100, 102–104, 116, 117, 120, 122, 134–135, 137, 140, 145, 146n, 151, 153, 155, 156, 159, 163, 167n, 169, 172, 173, 187, 192, 194n, 197, 210, 211, 219, 233, 234, 253, 258, 270, 280, 283, 298, 366, 374n
  abort decision and, 330
  air strike proposal and, 342
  Beckwith and, 69–70
  call sign of, 252
  Carter's briefing and, 223
  commander conference called by, 200
  at congressional hearings, 358
  Delta Force departure and, 251
  at deployment meeting, 221
  execute order of, 265
  Fez airfield plan approved by, 143
  final rehearsal and, 214, 215
  Fulton Recovery System and, 177–179
  hostage-location intelligence disbelieved by, 244
  initial briefing of, 28–30
  JCS briefed by, 189–190
  Jones and, 256, 330, 331
  JTF training and, 84, 85, 110–112, 118–119, 124, 177–179
  Kyle and, 32–34, 193–194, 224
  Kyle debriefed by, 354
  Marine pilot decision and, 140
  Masirah option and, 174–175
  Meyer's recommendation of, 35
  mission aftermath and, 356
  in mission analysis, 370, 374, 379, 383
  "murder board" established by, 161–162
  night landings observed by, 179–180
  Night-Two rehearsal and, 133
  Nimitz visit denied to, 176
  recon mission and, 166, 170, 171
  rescue mission and, 294, 300, 312, 313, 315n, 317, 322, 326, 327
  "Rice Bowl" term created by, 64
  roadblock team and, 213n
  secure radios and, 246
  selected JTF commander, 35

at special briefing, 222
Wadi Kena arrival of, 236
Yuma exercise and, 107
"Visible Seven," 358–359

Wade, "Slick," 25–26, 37, 99–100
Wadi Kena, 54, 148, 189, 203, 211, 213n, 231, 232
Walt, L. C., 304, 306, 311, 315
War Against Terrorists, The (Rivers), 70n
Warner, John, 357, 360, 362
War Powers Act (1973), 359
weather, 201, 260–265, 278, 281, 360
in mission analysis, 369–371
Weyers, Maynard, 20, 84, 280, 312
White, Floren, 76, 78
Wicker, Tom, 62, 167, 180, 259, 267, 279, 281, 284, 311, 319, 321, 323, 331, 337–339, 342, 344, 345

Wiley, Duke, 108, 110, 112, 267
Williford, Sherman, 66, 84, 115, 213n, 243–244, 265, 358
withdrawal, Desert-I:
Gast and, 341
helicopter abandoned in, 341
Iranian airspace cleared in, 345
King and, 341
Witherspoon, Wesley, 334
Wollmann, Rex, 116, 120
Woodpecker call sign, 253
World Court, 182

Yuma training exercise, 105–113
fuel drop in, 109–110
helicopters in, 108, 110, 111
prelude to, 100–104
Spectre gunship in, 111

Zumwalt, Elmo, Jr., 64